Contents

To Louise

Acknowledgments

The authors and publisher are grateful to those who have given permission to reproduce the following extracts and adaptations of copyright material:

p44 'Husky blowout leaves Cardinal blue' by Mark Soltau appeared in *The San Francisco Examiner*, 1 November 1992.

p69 *The Writing Systems of the World* by Florian Coulmas reproduced by permission of Blackwell Publishers.

p88 Johnnie Walker Red Label advertisement text reproduced by permission of Johnnie Walker.

p92 'Functional Approaches to Written Texts: Classroom Application' by Claire Kramsch 1995, published by the United States Information Agency.

p97 'This is just to say' by William Carlos Williams, from Collected Poems: 1909-1939, Volume I. Copyright © 1938 by New Directions Publishing Corp. Reprinted by permission of New Directions Publishing Corp. and Carcanet Press Limited.

p101 *The House on Mango Street* by Sandra Cisneros. Copyright © 1984 by Sandra Cisneros. Published by Bloomsbury Publishing Plc in 1992. Published by Vintage Books, a division of Random House, Inc., and in hardcover by Alfred A. Knopf in 1994. Reproduced by permission of Susan Bergholz Literary Services, New York. All rights reserved.

p108 'Living Language', copyright © 1973 by The Massachusetts Medical Society, from THE LIVES OF A CELL by Lewis Thomas. Used by permission of Viking Penguin, a division of Penguin Putnam Inc.

p154 'next to of course god america i' is reprinted from COMPLETE POEMS 1904–1962, by E. E. Cummings, edited by George J. Firmage, by permission of W. W. Norton & Company. Copyright © 1991 by the Trustees for the E. E. Cummings Trust and George James Firmage.

p155 U.S. President Bill Clinton's acceptance speech at the Democratic National Party Convention, 29 August 1996. Reproduced by permission of The White House, Washington.

p157 'Fruitvale BART Shooting Delays Train Service' from *The San Francisco Chronicle*, 29 May 1997 © *The San Francisco Chronicle*. Reprinted with Permission.

p205 'Situations d'écrit' by Sophie Moirand, 1979. Reproduced by permission of NATHAN publishers, Paris, France.

pp223–260 *New Ways of Learning and Teaching: Focus on Technology and Foreign Language Education, 1st edition* by J. Muyskens. © 1997. Reprinted with permission of Heinle & Heinle, a division of Thomson Learning.

pp235, 236 'A la rencontre de Philippe' by Gilberte Furstenberg et al. Published by Yale University Press and reproduced with their permission.

p240 'Restructuring classroom interaction with networked computers: Effects on quantity and quality of language production,' by R. Kern. Published in *Modern Language Journal* 79/4 457–76 and reproduced with permission of Blackwell Publishers.

Chapter 8 contains excerpts from *Redefining the Boundaries of Language Study, 1st edition*, by C. Kramsch. © 1995. Reprinted with permission of Heinle & Heinle Publishers, a division of International Thomson Publishing.

p291 *Assessing Writers' Knowledge and Processes of Composing* by Fraigley, Lester et al. Published 1985 by Ablex Publishing Corporation, and reprinted with permission.

Preface

This book has developed out of my experience as a language teacher and researcher over the past twenty years—as an EFL teacher in Spain and France, as a bilingual education teacher in a California high school, as a graduate student in applied linguistics, and as a French professor doing language acquisition research at the University of Texas and the University of California. Because I have never viewed my teacher and researcher roles dualistically, my goal in writing this book has been to draw, as explicitly as I can, the relationships I perceive between theoretical and practical dimensions of teaching language and literacy. The book therefore attempts to ground educational theory as well as to theorize pedagogical practice.

Many people have helped me write this book. Claire Kramsch provided the initial impetus by asking me to write a chapter on foreign language literacy for her 1995 AAUSC volume, *Redefining the Boundaries of Language Study*. Our discussions during that project led me to elaborate the main ideas of this book, and Claire's influence is visible throughout. A grant from the Spencer Foundation provided the leave time necessary for me to write the initial chapter drafts, and the UC Berkeley Committee on Research provided additional support. The book has benefited tremendously from the input of many students and colleagues who generously read and responded to chapter drafts, including Heidi Byrnes, Melinda Erickson, Jennifer Gurley, Mira Katz, Celeste Kinginger, Hsien-Chin Liou, Eva Ponte, Dan Shanahan, Jean Schultz, Steve Thorne, Mark Warschauer, Mark Wilson, and Debra Zaller. I am grateful to Robert Ruddell and Rosie Piller for their good advice. I am particularly indebted to Janet Swaffar and Katie Arens, who offered copious critical feedback throughout the project as well as much needed moral support during a critical juncture in the writing. Ann Delehanty deserves a special word of thanks for her keen insights and substantive contributions as she read and responded to successive drafts of the manuscript.

At Oxford University Press, I am grateful to Cristina Whitecross and Belinda Fenn for their generous assistance. It has been a distinct privilege to write under the editorial guidance of Henry Widdowson, whose careful readings and remarkable insight have improved this book immeasurably.

Finally, on a personal note, I would like to thank my wife Louise and my daughters Maria and Olivia for their understanding, patience, and support during the seemingly endless work of writing this book. I would also like to thank my parents for the education they provided me and for their encouragement during this project—they have helped more than they know.

Internet resources
This book includes a brief selection of web site addresses. The Internet is constantly changing and we welcome readers' feedback and suggestions.

Inclusion in our lists does not necessarily mean that the authors or publishers of this book endorse these sites or their content.

Introduction

As we enter the twenty-first century, global demographic and technological changes are leading to unprecedented levels of intercultural contact in both domestic and international arenas. Immigration in Western Europe, Australia, and North America is creating new 'multicultural' societies where rapid linguistic, cultural, and political change is endemic. Satellite television brings news, images, and entertainment from around the world. Computer networks provide new platforms for interpersonal communication, as well as novel means of publishing, linking, and accessing huge amounts of information from every corner of the globe. For those of us who teach languages, these changes present exciting new opportunities as well as significant challenges.

Communicating successfully in another language means shifting frames of reference, shifting norms, shifting assumptions of what can and cannot be said, what has to be explicit and what ought to remain tacit, and so on. In other words, using another language effectively involves more than vocabulary and structures; it involves *thinking* differently about language and communication. The question is, how can we begin to understand another way of thinking, how can we be sensitized to different cultural frames, when we are in a classroom in Nebraska, Nairobi, or New South Wales? One answer, I will argue in this book, is by reading, writing, and discussing texts. By examining the particular ways in which language is used to capture and express experiences, we not only learn a great deal about the conventions of the language, but can also begin to glimpse the beliefs and values that underlie the discourse. In Paulo Freire's terms, our challenge is to teach our students to read not only the word but also the world.

In their recent book, *Brave New Schools*, Jim Cummins and Dennis Sayers make an urgent call for greater emphasis on cross-cultural communication in school programs. Cultural literacy is essential, they argue, not only for economic competitiveness, but also for basic human understanding and social welfare. And yet many existing programs miss the mark:

> . . . cultural literacy curricula orient us inward, averting our eyes from the cultural diversity that characterizes our own countries and our global community. Even more unfortunate, the 'facts' of cultural literacy are to be internalized without discussion, exploration, or critical inquiry . . . .
> (Cummins and Sayers 1995)

What our times demand, argue Cummins and Sayers, is 'a rigorous approach to the teaching of reading and writing, but at the same time one that embraces rather than ignores issues of cultural identity' (p. 80).

The aim of this book is to outline the rationale and components of such an approach to reading and writing in second and foreign language programs. The basic message is a simple one: academic language teaching must foster literacy, not only in terms of basic reading and writing skills, but also in terms of a broader discourse competence that involves the ability to interpret and critically evaluate a wide variety of written and spoken texts.[1] Preparing students to communicate in multiple cultural contexts, both at home and abroad, means sensitizing them to discourse practices in other societies and to the ways those discourse practices both reflect and create cultural norms. The pedagogical focus shifts from 'what texts mean' in some absolute sense, to what people mean *by texts*, and what texts mean *to people* who belong to different discourse communities (i.e. groups sharing common discourse conventions, cultural models, and so forth). I will argue that this kind of literacy is essential to real communicative ability in a language, and is therefore an indispensable goal in our efforts to prepare future generations for the challenges associated with the increased internationalization and 'interculturalization' of many aspects of our society.

Given this general aim, the book should appeal to a number of constituencies: researchers and graduate students interested in issues of language education and literacy; second/foreign language teachers, language program directors, and curriculum specialists; and teacher educators and language teachers in pre-service training. In particular, the book will be of interest to those concerned with developing ways of integrating the teaching of linguistic, cognitive, and sociocultural dimensions of written language use.

Why 'literacy'?

Although literacy is not a word commonly used in the context of foreign language teaching, it felicitously conveys a broader scope than the terms 'reading' and 'writing' and thus permits a more unified discussion of relationships between readers, writers, texts, culture, and language learning. A focus on literacy, by considering reading and writing in their social contexts of use, frames reading and writing as complementary dimensions of written communication, rather than as utterly distinct linguistic and cognitive processes. The benefit of such a perspective is twofold: (1) it offers a broadened understanding of what reading and writing are, how they relate to one another, and how they are connected to other dimensions of language learning and use; and (2) it offers an organizing principle for language teaching that potentially fosters more coherent instruction within and across levels of the language curriculum. This said, however, it is important to recognize that literacy means different things to different people.

Shifting perspectives on literacy

Literacy is commonly defined as the ability to read and write. For some, it also connotes general learnedness and familiarity with literature. Most foreign language programs aim to develop students' competence in both these areas. They focus on basic ability in reading and writing in introductory and intermediate courses, and on literary and cultural knowledge in advanced courses.

At the lower levels of most foreign language curricula, literacy is conceived as being text-centric, rather than reader- or writer-centric.[2] Teaching is typically focused on correctness and convention (knowledge of standard norms of grammar, spelling, usage, and mechanics), and involves instruction in at least one privileged type of writing (usually the essay). Literacy instruction at this level calls for using 'functional' exercises (for example, reading classified ads, weather reports, timetables, signs, and menus, or filling out informational forms, and writing business letters), as well as reading stories and journalistic texts, often with the goal of providing vocabulary and grammar practice, rather than of fulfilling any genuine communicative purpose. Meaning is treated as a property of the text, and therefore unproblematic once the reader has mastered the text's linguistic elements. It is assumed that a solid knowledge of normative textual forms will provide the necessary foundation for students' success in subsequent literary and cultural studies.

At the upper end of the college curriculum, two additional strands of literacy come into play. One, which we could call the 'high cultural' strand, involves the transmission of cultural knowledge and the development of aesthetic appreciation, literary sensibility, and a cultivated spirit. The study of a particular literary canon, for example, is thought to foster this kind of literacy. The other, which we could call the 'cognitive' strand, involves the development of textual analysis skills and critical thought. Thus, while the kind of literacy taught in introductory and intermediate courses is largely concerned with textual description, the kind of literacy taught in advanced courses is more analytical and critical. This shift in emphasis can contribute to the often discussed problems of articulation between introductory/ intermediate and advanced level coursework (Barnett 1991; Schultz 1991b; Jurasek 1996).

The 'text-centric', 'cultural', and 'cognitive skills' views of literacy share a number of limitations in the context of second and foreign language education. First, they reify literacy as an end product of instruction (i.e. a generic measurable outcome in terms of knowledge or skills) instead of as a variable set of processes contingent on textual, cognitive, and social factors. Consequently, educators' efforts are oriented towards defining boundary lines of acceptable normative standards and a search for what might constitute a minimum criterion level. How well must learners read and write (in general) to be considered functional? How many novels must one read, how many cultural 'facts' must one absorb, to be deemed (culturally) literate? Which, and how many, analytical skills are needed for one to become (cognitively) literate? Problems arise when these arbitrary dividing lines, in the context of public demands for accountability, define instructional objectives. Teachers may orient their teaching to the criterion level of learner skills so they can demonstrate achievement of stated program goals, but students may remain at the periphery of literacy if they have not integrated these various skills.

Second, these definitions of literacy tend to exclude contextual factors—how people in different communities produce and use texts in different ways. In viewing literacy primarily as an individual, 'in the head' phenomenon—a private repertoire of abilities and knowledge—educators often disregard significant differences in the purposes, functions, and social value of literacy across cultural contexts. A good deal of research has shown that purposes for reading and writing are neither individually autonomous nor universal in nature, but rather arise from particular social and cultural needs and expectations (Scribner and Cole 1981; Heath 1982; Heath 1983; Street 1984). Such research raises questions about the extent to which teachers can think of literacy as a uniform set of abilities that learners can simply 'transfer' from one language context to another. Because the ways communities use texts can differ across contexts and cultures, learners' native language literacy conventions may not automatically predispose them to communicative success in the new language. The Chinese learner of English who writes an essay that incorporates sentences recalled verbatim from reading done years earlier, may be accused of plagiarism by his teacher (Pennycook 1996), rather than being acknowledged as operating within the framework of a different scholarly tradition. The American learning Arabic in Egypt who is not attuned to the shifts between standard and colloquial forms in newspapers, letters, and political speeches, may miss subtle yet key clues to the writer's point of view about the issue at hand. The Japanese learner of English schooled in the *yakudoku* tradition of reading as translation may encounter difficulties when, in an American classroom, she is asked to give a critical appraisal of a text because that request breaks with familiar classroom reading practices. So, rather than view literacy as a single, generic, or readily-transferable ability, we must consider the question: In what particular contexts, and for what particular purposes, can one be considered literate?

Third, traditional views of literacy are largely incompatible with the goals of communicative language teaching because they emphasize prescriptive norms rather than appropriateness of use. As Kramsch (1995a) puts it, 'Establishing spoken language and conversational competence as central to foreign language study constitutes a direct challenge to the exclusive monopoly of essayist literacy' (p. 7). On the one hand, we want our students to communicate effectively with different groups in a range of social contexts, using a variety of discourse gambits appropriately in different situations. On the other hand, we teach (and most importantly, test) a standard of literacy that requires adherence to usage prescribed by a socially dominant norm. Moreover, this literate standard becomes increasingly reinforced and insisted upon as one progresses through the levels of academic language study. Treating speaking, listening, reading, writing, and culture as separate 'skills' has led to limited, overly-compartmentalized goals described in terms of discrete behaviors or pieces of knowledge, rather than in terms of integrative abilities.

As an example, some educators currently argue that oral communication skills should be the primary goal of foreign language education, given the opportunities created by the global marketplace. However, it would be a mistake to attempt to attain such a goal by teaching only speaking and listening skills. Effective oral communication generally requires 'literate' sensibilities about the particular ways the foreign language can be used in particular settings, not to mention a familiarity with the cultural premises that underlie all communicative interactions within the target culture. In sum, traditional notions of literacy as norms of produced language or factual understanding[3] are too narrow in scope to permit easy reconciliation of our goals and our teaching practices.

One of the basic aims of this book is to attempt to reconcile communicative language teaching approaches, with their emphasis on face-to-face verbal interaction, with the development of learners' ability to read, discuss, think, and write critically about texts. The two sets of goals are not inherently incompatible, as I shall argue in subsequent chapters; the problem lies in finding a conceptual framework that is sufficiently broad to accommodate both of them. The traditional separation of teaching 'language as a means of communication' and teaching 'textual analysis' has been based on the influence of fundamentally different kinds of theories (Kramsch and Nolden 1994). Introductory and intermediate level ('language') teaching has been based on linguistic and psycholinguistic theories, whereas advanced level ('literature') teaching in postsecondary education has been based on literary theories. In this book, I will argue that this bifurcation of approaches and goals is not only unnecessary, but often detrimental to learners' motivation and learning, and that we must work towards a synthesis by enveloping the 'textual' within a larger framework of the 'communicative'—a framework that links rather than divides these levels of language learning.

By extending the notion of literacy beyond the strict traditional limits of reading and writing skills, and even beyond the skills of text-centric literary interpretation, language teachers at all levels can create a more coherent curriculum—one that maintains ongoing attention to communicative skills in spoken language *as well as* in a range of written genres, from the introductory through to the advanced levels of language study. In taking a broader approach to literacy, one more capable of encompassing the full complexity of language, we can draw on recent multidisciplinary research in literacy studies to extend cognitivist paradigms of language acquisition.

Broadening notions of literacy

Scholars in disciplines such as rhetoric, composition, educational psychology, linguistics, sociology, and cultural theory have recently critiqued mainstream notions of literacy and have contributed to new, socially-based, conceptualizations of literacy (Street 1984; Brandt 1990; Gee 1990; Lunsford, Moglen, and Slevin 1990; Baker and Luke 1991; Heath 1991; Barton 1994; Flower 1994; Kress 1994; Baynham 1995; New London Group 1996). These educators challenge skill-based definitions of literacy, which are focused on the ability to read and write in ways commensurate with a prescriptive, normative standard. They question the notion of a monolithic, generalizable concept of literacy, and favor the idea of multiple litera*cies*— roughly defined as dynamic, culturally and historically situated practices of using and interpreting diverse written and spoken texts to fulfill particular social purposes. Drawing on these theories, this book will discuss the implications for second and foreign language teaching of an expanded view of literacy that involves, not only the ability to produce and interpret texts, but also a critical awareness of the relationships between texts, discourse conventions, and social and cultural contexts.

The approach to language teaching advocated in this book is at once conservative and expansive. It acknowledges the traditional emphasis on the study of texts as essential to any serious exploration of another language and culture. Literature, the core of most academic language programs, also remains integral to a literacy-based approach, even in the early stages of language study. Two additional aspects of the expanded literacy-based approach I am proposing here are less traditional. One is the broadening of curricular goals to include not only *language*, but also the *stories* that are told in that language (which serve as exemplars of social interaction within the particular culture). This move ideally involves broadening what is considered suitable for analysis as 'text' beyond the literary canon, to include a wide range of written and spoken texts that more inclusively represent the signifying practices of a society (for example, advertisements, political speeches, letters, films, newspaper and magazine articles, music videos, and so on). As scholars such as Eagleton (1983) and Scholes (1985) have pointed out, such 'non-literary' texts are often less than transparent; they, like literary texts, can be rich in meanings that tell us a great deal about a society. While such texts are commonly used in beginning and intermediate courses for language practice (but generally not for interpretive purposes), they are less frequently included in advanced courses. Because the juxtaposition and comparison of literary and non-literary texts as different mirrors or 'takes' on the same issue or event can sensitize learners to questions about how texts are produced and received across cultural contexts, what I argue for is a greater interpenetration of text types between the various levels of language study: the use of 'big C', high culture, literary texts, together with 'small c' quotidian culture texts *throughout* the curriculum—not just at the advanced level.

The second distinctive feature of the expanded literacy-based approach I am advocating here, has to do with the particular ways in which teachers and learners use reading and writing in language classrooms. Reading and writing are often valued primarily as a means for out-of-class *language practice*, particularly in the early levels. Instead, we will be concerned with uses of reading and writing that count as real reading and writing— meaningful uses that promote thinking, learning, and (consequently) motivation in patterns acknowledged as part of a culture's interactions. At upper levels of the curriculum, our usual practice is to assign a text to be read at home, discuss it in class, and then ask our students to go home and write an essay about it. This instructional sequence leaves students on their own for what many of them find the most challenging tasks: reading and writing. To counter the potentially isolating effects of this practice, we will consider alternative ways of approaching reading and writing that provide students with structured guidance as they reflect and analyze, revise and refine their ideas. In sum, we will be concerned with ways of developing the *thinking* that goes into reading and writing, to unite social and cognitive aspects of language learning.

Literacy and issues in language education: major themes

Literacy is linked to a number of current theoretical and practical issues in the language teaching profession. They form the central themes of this book and include the following:

- Theories of language acquisition: What role might literacy play in learners' acquisition of a language system? How do reading and writing support language acquisition and the development of metalinguistic awareness? Can reading and writing make contributions to oral language ability?
- Form/meaning debates: What is the nature of the relationship between form and meaning? During the 'audiolingual' era, language teaching went through a period of focus on form at the expense of meaning. This was followed by a 'communicative' period of focus on meaning at the expense of form. How might we achieve a balanced perspective on form and meaning and how might we get learners to attend to the *relationship* between the two?
- Respective roles of linguistic, cognitive, and social factors in literacy acquisition: Discussions of literacy have tended to be balkanized into linguistic/cognitive and social camps. A comprehensive discussion of

literacy requires that all three dimensions be addressed together so that their essential interactivity can be brought to light.

- Teaching culture: Should we teach culture as a product? as a process? How should we integrate it with teaching the language? How can a literacy-based approach foster the creation of what Kramsch (1993) calls 'third places' for exploring intercultural relationships?
- Curricular coherence: As mentioned earlier, the curricular separation of language development from the development of content knowledge and analytical/interpretive skills can lead to a kind of instructional culture shock when students pass from language classes to specialized courses in literature, civilization, or linguistics. A literacy-based approach encourages reflective reading and writing from the beginning, avoiding dramatic shifts in curricular goals and the consequent disjunction between courses and students' experience of those courses.
- Schism between 'language' and 'literature' studies: The view that 'language' teaching is nothing more than a remedial (and somewhat dull) stage of preparation for the more rigorous (and interesting) study of literature can affect both students and faculty adversely. A literacy-based approach, I argue, can help to break down lines of division and assure intellectual stimulation even at the beginning stages of language learning.
- Role of technology: Computer technology offers new and exciting ways to engage students with a foreign language, and it also raises many questions about literacy. How does electronic communication affect the way language is used, and what effects might it have on students' learning? How ought materials such as multimedia web sites, and Internet communication tools be used to support language and culture learning?

Overview of the book

In order to address these questions as part of an integrated approach to the foreign language curriculum, the book is divided into three parts. Part One deals with theoretical concerns. The first chapter deals with key aspects of an expanded definition of literacy—one that goes beyond the basic ability to read and write and includes particular ways of thinking, valuing, and behaving that are essential to becoming communicatively competent within a community as well as multiliterate (i.e. literate in multiple linguistic and cultural norms). Chapter 2 considers the relationship between literacy and communicative ability. It examines metaphors of language use, presenting the argument that communication (written as well as spoken) is more a matter of appropriately *designing* meaning rather than a matter of simply *transmitting* meaning. Chapter 3 elaborates on Chapter 2 by taking a closer look at some of the linguistic and schematic resources used to design meaning in communication.

Part Two explores theoretical implications and pedagogical applications of the design metaphor for literacy. Chapter 4 examines reading as both an individual and a social process of designing meaning within a community, and Chapter 5 illustrates concrete classroom practices for teaching reading as a process of designing meaning. Chapters 6 and 7 provide a parallel discussion of theoretical and applied aspects of writing, as viewed through the metaphor of design.

Part Three moves on to the areas of computer technology, evaluation, and curriculum. Chapter 8 explores computer-mediated literacy practices and outlines the advantages and limitations of using technology in teaching language, literacy, and culture. Chapter 9 discusses implications of literacy-focused teaching for evaluating students' language and literacy abilities. Finally, Chapter 10 recaps the goals of a literacy-based curriculum and considers implications for student and teacher roles, teacher education, and research.

Since teaching conditions, resources, needs, and goals vary considerably from one institution to another, the examples of pedagogical activities throughout the book are intended as illustrations of an integrative way of thinking about foreign language teaching and learning as a social and cognitive phenomenon, not as a universal prescription for classroom practice. The ideas put forward in this book are, in principle, applicable to every teaching/learning context, although they will inevitably be realized in different ways in practice. My intent, then, is to present a broad yet coherent framework that can be adapted and applied to language teaching in a wide variety of settings.

Notes

1 A definitional distinction between 'text' and 'discourse' is in order here. By 'texts' I am referring to physical artifacts of language use: the concrete, observable language data available for interpretation. By the more inclusive term 'discourse', I mean text plus the social and cognitive processes involved in negotiating meaning as people produce and interpret these texts. In other words, discourse involves the dynamic realization of texts as expressive or communicative acts.

2 The 'text-centric' view of literacy was clearly reflected, for example, in the 1980s version of the ACTFL Proficiency Guidelines for reading and writing (ACTFL 1986), which dealt largely with text characteristics rather than what learners actually do when they read and write. See Bernhardt (1986) for reading; see Valdés, Haro, and Echevarriarza (1992) for writing. ACTFL is currently revising these guidelines, and the U.S. National Standards in Foreign Language Education Project (1996) emphasizes the development of learners' awareness of how relationships

between speakers and discourse conventions shift, depending on one's position, intent, and cultural context.

3 E. D. Hirsch (1987) for example, has proposed that learners' lack of cultural knowledge could be addressed explicitly by teaching lists of 'essential' cultural facts.

PART ONE

1 Notions of literacy

Reading and writing are forms of life, not just reflections of it.

Geoffrey H. Hartman (1996)

It is ten o'clock Monday morning. The bell rings, and French class begins. The teacher warms up her students by asking questions in French, using the material covered during the previous week: How many brothers and sisters do you have? How old are they? Where does your family live? Do you visit often? Ask George if he has any brothers or sisters. The teacher then begins a series of exercises to practice 'family' vocabulary: Your father's brother is your____; My sister's husband is my____; Hillary Clinton is Bill's ____, and so on. Next comes a conversational activity: students are asked to form small groups and describe and compare their families. Afterwards, a spokesperson from each group summarizes the family descriptions for the class. The teacher and the students then open their textbooks and read aloud a short passage entitled *La famille française*, which presents a variety of demographic facts about families in France, describes commonalities and differences across social classes, and discusses a number of differences and similarities between the typical customs of French families and American families. The teacher provides definitions of the words her students don't know, and then asks a few comprehension questions from the book, to make sure that they have understood the material. She then asks if they agree with the statements made about American families: some students do, others don't, and a brief discussion ensues, in which issues of stereotyping and overgeneralization are raised. Class ends and the teacher assigns the students their homework: two workbook exercises on family vocabulary, and a one page essay describing their family.

Down the hall, another section of the same French course begins. Students have brought in letters and photographs they received from their French pen pals the week before. Working in groups of three, the students present their correspondents' letters (in which they describe their families) to one another and show the accompanying photographs. Sylvie, for example, is seventeen and an only child, with brown hair and hazel eyes. Her mother was born in Algeria of French parents. Her grandparents emigrated to Algeria but they returned to France during the Algerian war of independence. Her father was born in central France, where Sylvie always spends her holidays—at her grandfather's mill, where she enjoys the company of her many cousins, some of whom are farmers. The teacher asks each group to sketch as complete a family tree as possible for each pen pal, and to take written notes on his or her origins, family situation, and living circumstances. They are also to choose and write down what they consider to be the most striking sentence in each letter, as well as any words, phrases, or sentences they are unable to understand. In presenting their reports to the whole class, the students realize that although most of their pen pals were born in France, many of their parents are from elsewhere: Algeria, Morocco, Spain, Portugal, la Réunion, Martinique, Mali, and Poland. Some live with their families; others live by themselves in rooms or apartments. Some live in prestigious neighborhoods; others live in *cités*, or public housing projects.

The teacher and students then open their textbooks and read the passage on *La famille française*. The teacher asks how the information presented in this passage corresponds to the stories told in their pen pals' letters. To what degree does the textbook passage seem to reflect the pen pals' experience as represented in their letters? What kinds of information did the students get from the letters that they didn't get from the textbook passage, and vice versa? In what ways is reading the letters different from reading the textbook passage? How does the language used in the two types of texts compare? How do style differences affect their reactions as readers? The teacher then asks the students to reflect a moment and jot down on paper (1) three things they have learnt from reading the letters and the textbook passage, and (2) three questions their readings and discussions have raised. Their homework assignment is to write a return letter in which they respond to the content of their pen pal's letter, ask at least three questions, and describe their own families and living situations. The teacher collects each group's written notes, quoted sentences, and lists of comprehension difficulties, which will be photocopied, assembled as a packet, and distributed the following day as a resource for subsequent activities.

On one level these two classes are very similar. They both share the same instructional objectives: to have students review family vocabulary, read a textbook passage on the French family, and write about their own families. Furthermore, both classes accomplish these objectives through a variety of communicative activities in small group and whole class formats. Indeed, in both classes, all students are actively engaged in listening, speaking, reading, and writing in French.

On another level, however, the two classes are quite different. The first class places primary emphasis on *practicing* vocabulary and structures. The topic and context of learners' language use is driven mostly by structural concerns ('family vocabulary') and affective goals (getting students to know one another better), rather than by content (families in France), or critical thinking goals. The conversational activities validate students' personal experience and provide language practice, but do little to expand students' understanding of things outside of their own cultural world. The functional use of language is largely limited to personal description. Because of their limited prior knowledge of French families, students can only evaluate what the textbook says about American families. Information about 'the French family' must be taken at face value (a notion that is reinforced by the testing of learners' reading via factual recall questions). The workbook and essay writing is done out of class and serves as language practice, as well as a display of language knowledge to the teacher (who will be the only audience).

The second class takes a more 'content-based' approach, focused not so much on the expression of students' personal experience, but on their personal readings of French texts. Students are not using the language simply to practice vocabulary and structures, but to explore a different world and to relate that world to their own thinking and experience. The students' focus is on what their French pen pals have to say, how they say it, and how they themselves respond to what the French say. Unlike the students in the first class, students in this class have concrete, personal stories with which to compare and evaluate the relatively abstract and general textbook passage. The students acquire this supplementary knowledge in a meaningful way by communicating in French. The writing students do in the second class is not simply for practice, but serves multiple communicative purposes: it organizes their spoken presentations, informs others in the class about the content of the letters they have received, and expresses reactions, questions, and personal experience to a real, native-speaking French audience (from whom they can anticipate a subsequent response). Their writing involves making decisions about what is understandable, what is interesting, and what is worth pursuing in greater detail with their French-speaking peers.

In sum, the two classroom scenarios depict different ways in which teachers and students engage with language and literacy. It is not so much a difference of *authenticity* of communication (after all, describing one's family and comparing it to those of one's classmates is certainly genuine communication). Rather, it is a difference in the ways that teachers and students make use of *texts*—their own and others'—to expand their awareness of a new language and culture. In the second classroom, reading and writing are treated not just as linguistic skills, but also as cognitive and social processes. Oral and written activities are not separate, but tightly interwoven. Critical thinking is not reserved for special lessons, but is integrated into students' regular classroom tasks. Cultural exploration is not restricted to the content of the textbook reading passage, but permeates all aspects of the lesson.

The second classroom scenario is less typical of mainstream foreign language education than the first. But I would like to argue that the approach it exemplifies—what I will call a literacy-based approach—represents a style of teaching educators ought to consider if they wish to prepare learners for full participation in societies that increasingly demand multilingual, multicultural, and multitextual competence. I am not suggesting that the teaching in the first class is somehow 'wrong', but simply that it does not go far enough. That is to say, the ways in which instructional goals are implemented in the first class effectively limit the range of uses to which language is put, and the extent to which students' understanding of the interrelationships between language and culture can be deepened. A literacy-based approach, on the other hand, by focusing not only on language but also on the *effects* and communicative *consequences* that particular texts can have for different audiences, can clear a path to new levels of understanding of language, culture, and communication.

Principles of a sociocognitive view of literacy

To begin our exploration of this approach, I propose as a working definition for an expanded notion of literacy, one that weaves together linguistic, cognitive, and sociocultural strands. This definition is not meant to describe all forms of literacy, but rather to characterize literacy in the specific context of academic second and foreign language education.[1] *Literacy is the use of socially-, historically-, and culturally-situated practices of creating and interpreting meaning through texts. It entails at least a tacit awareness of the relationships between textual conventions and their contexts of use and, ideally, the ability to reflect critically on those relationships. Because it is purpose-sensitive, literacy is dynamic—not static—and variable across and within discourse communities and cultures. It draws on a wide range of cognitive abilities, on knowledge of written and spoken language, on knowledge of genres, and on cultural knowledge.*

Definitions like this one may be useful as a conceptual starting point, but they are often difficult to translate into the concrete realities of classroom teaching and curriculum design. For this reason, we will consider seven principles that arise out of this definition and the foregoing discussion which will be elaborated on and applied to language teaching throughout the rest of the book.

1 Literacy involves *interpretation*. Writers and readers participate in double acts of interpretation—the writer interprets the world (events, experiences, ideas, and so on), and the reader then interprets the writer's interpretation in terms of his or her own conception of the world.
2 Literacy involves *collaboration*. Writers write for an audience, even if they write for themselves. Their decisions about what must be said, and what can go without saying, are based on their understanding of their audience. Readers in turn must contribute their motivation, knowledge, and experience in order to make the writer's text meaningful.

3 Literacy involves *conventions*. How people read and write texts is not universal, but governed by cultural conventions that evolve through use and are modified for individual purposes.
4 Literacy involves *cultural knowledge*. Reading and writing function within particular systems of attitudes, beliefs, customs, ideals, and values. Readers and writers operating from outside a given cultural system risk misunderstanding or being misunderstood by those operating on the inside of the cultural system.
5 Literacy involves *problem solving*. Because words are always embedded in linguistic and situational contexts, reading and writing involve figuring out relationships between words, between larger units of meaning, and between texts and real or imagined worlds.
6 Literacy involves *reflection* and *self-reflection*. Readers and writers think about language and its relations to the world and themselves.
7 Literacy involves *language use*. Literacy is not just about writing systems, nor just about lexical and grammatical knowledge; it requires knowledge of how language is used in spoken and written contexts to create discourse.

These principles, although here framed in terms of reading and writing, are not unique to literacy, but can be applied broadly to human communication in general. In fact, the seven principles can be summarized by the macro-principle: *literacy involves communication*. This seven-point linkage between literacy and communication has important implications for language teaching, as it provides a bridge to span the gap that so often separates introductory 'communicative' language teaching and advanced 'literary' teaching. By practicing literacy in a non-native language (and by that I mean engaging in real literacy events, not just rehearsing reading and writing skills), students learn not only about vocabulary and grammar but also about discourse and the processes by which it is created. They learn to deal with uncertainties and ambiguities, rather than relying on simplistic and rigid form-meaning correspondences. They learn new, alternative ways of organizing their thought and their expression, ways which go beyond the learning of facts about the second culture. Literacy is therefore not only relevant for students with literary aspirations—but essential for *all* language learners, and at all levels of language study.

To return to the example at the beginning of this chapter, what differentiates the teaching in the two French classrooms is the extent to which these seven principles of literacy and communication are put into practice. In the first classroom, students' work involves primarily language use, conventions, and collaboration. In the second classroom, somewhat greater emphasis is placed on interpretation, problem-solving, and reflection about a topic which may contribute to their understanding of French culture. The goal of a literacy-based curriculum is to engage learners in activities that involve as many of these principles as possible, not only at advanced levels of study, but at introductory and intermediate levels as well.

Such an approach is not new. In fact, it draws on the oldest tradition of textual analysis: rhetoric. Within the context of applied linguistics, the approach emerges from a well-established movement of applying principles of *discourse analysis* to the teaching of languages—a trend that has perhaps been most visible in language teaching for adult immigrants, for professionals, or for those studying languages for special purposes. Many materials and techniques designed for ESL (English as a Second Language) and ESP (English for Specific Purposes) over the last thirty years, for example, as well as for *Français langue étrangère* and *Deutsch als Fremdsprache*, reflect this trend. But it is only relatively recently that discourse analysis has made inroads into mainstream foreign language pedagogy in American and European secondary and higher education. In the following section we will take a closer look at shifts in language teaching paradigms that make these principles possible, with particular emphasis on new conceptions of the role of literacy.

Shifting paradigms in language teaching

Foreign language teaching has long relied on written texts as a source of language input. Until relatively recently, however, the *sentence* has been the privileged unit of meaning and analysis. The grammar-translation method of the nineteenth and twentieth centuries, for example, illustrated grammatical principles via exemplary sentences. The pedagogical goal was to recode sentences written in the foreign language into one's mother tongue, with heavy emphasis placed on accuracy and completeness. During the audiolingual era, from the 1940s to the 1960s, the emphasis shifted to spoken language and dialogues were used as language models, but the individual sentence remained the focus of repetition and drills. Again, formal accuracy remained paramount. In the 1960s, with the advent of 'cognitive-code learning' theory (following Chomsky's rejection of behavioristic models of language learning in the late 1950s), teachers' goals gradually shifted from instilling accurate language habits, to fostering learners' mental construction of a second language system. Rule learning was reintroduced, but still only at the level of the individual sentence. Indeed, even today, many introductory level foreign language courses are organized around a planned sequence of grammatical structures that are exemplified in sample sentences for intensive practice.

It has long been recognized, however, that communicative language use involves a good deal more than the ability to understand and produce structurally-correct sentences. In the 1960s, British linguist Michael Halliday and American sociolinguist Dell Hymes argued that the individual sentence was too narrow a lens to look through if one wanted to understand language as it is used in social practice. Because the structure of a given sentence is influenced by the larger textual structures in which it is embedded, Halliday argued that *texts*, not sentences, ought to be the basic unit of linguistic analysis. Halliday and Hasan (1976) define 'text' as 'any passage, spoken or written, of whatever length, that forms a unified whole' (p. 1). Therefore a text can range from a single word (for example, a stop sign) to a lengthy novel or report. Hymes, who coined the term 'communicative competence', shifted attention from grammatical well-formedness to the *appropriateness* of language use in real social contexts. His position is aptly expressed in his well-known remark 'There are rules of use without which the rules of grammar would be useless' (Hymes 1971: 10). Halliday's and Hymes' contributions to a broader, socially-based view of language set the stage for the development of communicative approaches to language teaching.

During the 1970s and 1980s, language educators called for a pedagogy that shifted emphasis away from language *usage* to language *use* (Widdowson 1978); from language as *code* to language as *communication* in social context (Breen and Candlin 1980). Indeed, in the context of teaching literacy, this meant an extension of focus beyond *text* (i.e. stretches of concrete, observable language data) to *discourse* (i.e. text plus the social and cognitive processes involved in its realization as an expressive or communicative act). Table 1.1 below summarizes some changes in instructional focus commonly associated with this shift.

Language as autonomous structural system	→ Language as social phenomenon
Product orientation	→ Process orientation
Focus on isolated sentences	→ Focus on connected stretches of language
Focus on texts as displays of vocabulary and grammar structures	→ Focus on texts realized as communicative acts ('doing things with words')
Teaching of a prescriptive norm	→ Attention to register and style variation
Focus on mastery of discrete skills	→ Focus on self-expression
Emphasis on denotative meanings	→ Emphasis on communicative value in context

Table 1.1:   Shifts in pedagogical focus from structural to communicative frameworks

Although the influential models of communicative competence developed by Canale and Swain (1980), Canale (1983), Savignon (1983), and Bachman (1990) all included written as well as oral discourse abilities in their scope, communicative language teaching has, on the whole, focused predominantly on face-to-face, spoken communication.[2] Communicative teaching programs have largely succeeded in their goal of promoting learners' interactive speaking abilities. They have tended to be somewhat less successful, however, in developing learners' extended discourse competence and written communication skills—areas of language ability that are extraordinarily important in academic settings.

An early and strong proponent of developing language learners' ability to handle written discourse, Widdowson (1978) argued that *interpretation* underlies all communicative language abilities. Because meanings are not inherent in language itself, but need to be worked out, learners should have guided experience in selecting, organizing, and interpreting linguistic clues through the creation and re-creation of discourse. Key to Widdowson's scheme for developing learners' interpretive ability was an integrated approach to reading and writing: 'What the learner needs to know how to do is to compose in the act of writing, comprehend in the act of reading, and to learn techniques of reading by writing and techniques of writing by reading.' (p. 144). Widdowson's integrated approach involved cycles of reading and writing that relied on two primary exercise types: rhetorical transformation (for example, reformulating directions into description and vice versa) and information transfer (for example, using tables, drawings or other non verbal representations to mediate a transition from one form of discourse to another). The aim of these activities was 'getting the learner to write something based on his reading and so to represent these two abilities as aspects of the same underlying interpreting process' (p. 156).

Many of Widdowson's ideas are echoed and extended in two, more recent books, *Reading for Meaning* by Janet Swaffar, Katherine Arens, and Heidi Byrnes, and *Context and Culture in Language Teaching* by Claire Kramsch. Both books articulate a vision of foreign language education that shifts emphasis from sentence-grammar, structure drills, and information retrieval to a more thoughtful mode of learning that involves students' reflection on language and content, and specifically on the connections between the details of texts and students' personal responses to those texts. Both books make the point that many approaches to language teaching have focused on linguistic form, without a simultaneous focus on the semantic and pragmatic consequences of form, leaving the links between discourse and culture insufficiently explored.

Swaffar *et al.* deal extensively with the cognitive dimensions of language learning. They question the teaching profession's assumption that practice in speaking about concrete objects and events will eventually prepare learners to express and evaluate abstract ideas and concepts in the new language. Reading for 'meaning' means going beyond the facts referred to in a text and probing the implications and significance of those facts. Swaffar *et al.* present a structured series of classroom practices to lead students through processes similar to those Widdowson had proposed, designed to foster transformation of knowledge. From the earliest stages of language learning, they argue, students must do more than just talk; they 'must hear and read about verbally created worlds' (p. 2). In order to become articulate speakers, Swaffar *et al.* contend, students must go beyond mastering grammar rules and vocabulary lists and develop *literacy* in the sense of being 'able to use the other language's structure to mediate the comprehension or expression of meanings outside their immediate experience' (p. 2).

But the 'immediate experience' of the classroom need not be dismissed in the process. Kramsch, who emphasizes the social dimensions of language learning, points out that grammatical exercises, communicative activities, and discussions of texts can be seen as important sites of cross-cultural dialogue:

> The language classroom should . . . be viewed as the privileged site of cross-cultural fieldwork, in which the participants are both informants and ethnographers. In the course of this fieldwork, two kinds of dialogue are likely to occur: the first is an instructional conversation in which forms are practiced and the status quo of the school's educational culture is confirmed and validated; the second is an exchange of ideas and emotions through language, which has the potential of putting in question the status quo.
> (1993: 29)

For Kramsch, then, what is most important is a reflective engagement on the part of students as well as teachers: to learn, to use, to enjoy the new language, but at the same time to reflect on that very learning, use, and enjoyment in order to arrive at a deeper understanding, not only of the language, but also of themselves as explorers of the realm that lies between the new language/culture and their own. In order to accomplish this kind of reflective engagement, Kramsch envisions 'a new type of literacy' in foreign language education: one that is 'centered more on the learner, based more on cross-cultural awareness and critical reflection' (Kramsch and Nolden 1994: 28). The goal is a 'pedagogy of interpretive practice' (Kramsch 1995b) in which students and teachers 'use the unique literate environment of the classroom to reflect consciously and explicitly on interaction processes in various social contexts . . . .' (Kramsch 1989: 248).

Swaffar *et al.* and Kramsch are not alone in calling for an emphasis on literacy in foreign language teaching. Mueller (1991), for example, identifies the need to make students aware of how systems of interpretation are historically created and vary over time and place. She recommends the teaching of a 'pluralistic literacy', which introduces students to 'diverse ways of reading that will enable them to recognize the political and moral implications of diverse ways of understanding' (p. 22). Similarly, Berman (1996) calls for 'foreign cultural literacy' as a pedagogical goal that entails 'a student's familiarity with and facility in the language, values, and narratives of a culture not his or her own' (p. 43). According to Berman, such a goal would highlight the interplay between language and culture, and familiarize students not only with the literary canon, but also with the 'stories another culture tells about itself' (p. 43), as reflected in films, songs, status symbols, political discourse, and everyday language. In treating these other manifestations of material culture alongside literary works, Berman suggests language faculty and departments should look not only to literary criticism or linguistics, but also to cultural studies for intellectual grounding. A cultural studies approach, which considers how target language groups structure and represent themselves and their world through a variety of symbolic means, has become increasingly well established in language teaching programs in Europe (Zarate 1986; Byram 1989; Byram and Esarte-Sarries 1991; Byram 1993; Byram, Morgan, and colleagues 1994).

Byrnes (1998) echoes Mueller's and Berman's calls, asserting that:

> Foreign language departments must learn to play a crucial role in enhancing students' literacy, students' ability to interpret and produce texts, orally and in writing, in a fashion that shows a rich awareness of the relation among the sociocultural contexts of use, meaning, and significance (p. 283).

Byrnes argues that such a perspective provides an overarching conceptual framework that allows the teaching of language, literary interpretation, and culture to be more effectively integrated throughout the curriculum.

Like Byrnes, Jurasek (1996) sees literacy as a key concept for curricular integration. Focusing on the often problematic transition from language study to literary study at the second year college level, Jurasek proposes an intermediate-level language curriculum that incorporates literacy-related 'inquiry subsets'. These include topics such as the reading process (including metacognitive strategy training); the conventions of narrative cinema (how films tell their stories in different cultures); literacy (using texts to heighten students' awareness of how we construct meaning); and cultural literacy (exploring cultures as perceptual systems).

Although the details of their proposals differ somewhat, Swaffar *et al.*, Kramsch, Mueller, Berman, Byrnes, and Jurasek all share a common interest in *literacy* as a means to encourage more reflective inquiry, purposefulness— *and* language skill development—at all levels of the curriculum. They see reading and writing not as peripheral support skills, but as an important nexus where language, culture, and thought converge. They believe in the importance of moving from a pedagogy of information-transmission to a pedagogy of meaning construction, in which learners acquire more than a knowledge of linguistic facts and textual conventions. They argue for systematically guiding learners in their efforts to create, interpret, and reflect on discourse and knowledge, in order to promote their awareness of how meanings are made and received in both their own and the other culture.

This rethinking of literacy in foreign language teaching has occurred in the context of a larger discussion about literacy in a number of academic disciplines such as rhetoric and composition (for example, Brandt 1990; Lunsford, *et al.* 1990; Flower 1994), education (for example, Eisner 1992), educational anthropology (for example, Heath 1982; 1983; 1987; 1991; Hull 1991), history (for example, Graff 1979), psychology (for example, Scribner and Cole 1981), educational psychology (for example, Langer 1987a), sociolinguistics (for example, Gee 1986; 1990;

John-Steiner, Panofsky, and Smith 1994; Kress 1994; New London Group 1996), and educational sociology (for example, Street 1984; 1993; 1994), among others. Although it would be misleading to suggest that these various strands of scholarship are fully harmonious, a new general characterization of literacy is nevertheless emerging from this inter-disciplinary discussion. Literacy is construed as a collection of dynamic cultural processes, rather than a static, monolithic set of psychological attributes. It is both public and private, both social and individual. It is about the creation and interpretation of meaning through texts, not just the ability to inscribe and decode written language. And it is 'critical', involving a spirit of reflective skepticism.

This conception of literacy is not, however, one that is widely shared among language teachers, and especially among language students. What is generally more familiar is an understanding of reading and writing as separate *skills* to be exercised alongside the skills of speaking and listening. Reading represents the skills involved in decoding words in order to get meaning, and writing represents the skills involved in putting words on paper in prescribed ways in order to produce meaning. Such a view, while of course partially true, tends to limit reading and writing to straightforward acts of information transfer. For many foreign language students, the *de facto* goal of reading is uncovering *the* meaning, *the* theme, *the* point of a text (i.e. what the teacher reveals in class). Likewise, writing is all too often about capturing in *the* right words, *the* summary or *the* analysis of something one has read.

Because our conceptions of literacy will inevitably influence how we teach reading and writing in the classroom (Farley 1995), it is essential to understand that literacy is more than a set of academic skills, more than inscribing and decoding words, and more than prescribed patterns of thinking. It involves an awareness of how acts of reading, writing, and conversation *mediate* and *transform* meanings, not merely transfer them from one individual or group to another. Literacy is neither natural, nor universal, nor ideologically neutral, but culturally constructed. It is precisely because literacy is variable and intimately tied to the sociocultural practices of language use in a given society that it is of central importance in our teaching of language and culture.

In the remainder of this chapter I will present literacy from a variety of perspectives. I begin with a brief discussion of how definitions of literacy are relative to time, place, and social perspective. I will then elaborate on the linguistic, cognitive, and sociocultural dimensions referred to earlier in my definition of literacy for second/foreign language teaching. I will conclude by considering implications of such a definition of literacy for language teaching.

Multiple perspectives on literacy

Literacy is an elastic concept: its meaning varies according to the disciplinary lens through which one examines it. Ostensibly referring to reading and writing, literacy can be viewed as a technique, as a set of language skills, as a set of cognitive abilities, as a group of social practices, or, as Brandt (1990) puts it, 'a part of the highest human impulse to think and rethink experience in place' (p. 1). Literacy is a moveable target from an historical perspective too: although *litteratus*, its etymological root, referred to learnedness in Latin, literacy has at times simply referred to the ability to write one's name. In addition, the functions, values, and practices associated with literacy vary cross-culturally: what literacy means in African-American communities in rural South Carolina (Heath 1983), for example, is not the same as what it means for the Vai people of Liberia (Scribner and Cole 1981) or for Punjabis in London (Saxena 1994) or for Moroccans in Quranic schools (Wagner, Messick, and Spratt 1986; Baynham 1995).

Even within a single society, getting a handle on literacy is not an easy task. Consider the variety of ways the word 'literacy' is used in the following headlines quoted from major American newspapers. We find that literacy is closely tied to economic and social progress ('Literacy—the third world's beacon of hope'), and is therefore highly political ('The politics of literacy'). It is not easy to obtain ('The long road to literacy'), and there is not enough of it ('Literacy of 90 million is deficient'), but it can be fought for ('Mississippi's fight for literacy') and the fight is worth it ('The empowerment of literacy'). It is subject to deterioration ('Thais combat literacy erosion') and its absence is akin to disease ('Illiteracy resists treatment in Brazil'), but it can be improved by spending money on it ('Literacy drive set by Unesco; U.S. to resume its annual $50 million payments'). Above all, it should be shared, for the common good of society ('Literacy—Pass it on'). The 'distribution' of literacy is accomplished not only in schools, but also in the workplace ('At GM, the three R's are the big three'), in families ('Family literacy, family values'), and in prisons ('Literacy in the lock-up'). Finally, its meaning can be metaphorically extended beyond reading and writing to other areas of knowledge or ability—one frequently encounters phrases such as 'computer literacy', 'science literacy', 'visual literacy', 'economic literacy', 'geographic literacy', 'TV literacy', 'junk food literacy', 'label literacy', 'ecological literacy', 'religious literacy', and, of course, 'cultural literacy'.

Looking at how literacy is represented in the popular media, one is struck by the catch-all nature of the term. Its reference is decidedly wide ranging and vague. However, there is consistency in the metaphorical representation of literacy as a uniform substance—a valuable commodity—that some have and others don't, that confers power and enlightenment, that can be acquired (at a price) and transmitted to others. This notion of 'literacy as substance', what Street (1984) has called the 'autonomous' model of literacy, represents the mainstream conception of literacy in many societies and educational systems.[3] It is also the view that has traditionally informed the teaching of reading and writing in second and foreign language teaching.

We are now ready to examine some of the linguistic, cognitive, and social bases of literacy in order to develop an understanding of literacy that is more adequately suited to the needs of students and teachers in communicatively-oriented language programs.

Linguistic dimensions of literacy

Literacy has to do with people's use of written language. As suggested by its etymological link to the Latin *littera* ('letter'), literacy involves mastery of a writing system and its attendant conventions. But literacy has to do, first and foremost, with language and knowledge of how it is used, and only secondarily with writing systems. That is to say, knowledge of the Roman alphabet does not make one literate in Italian and Dutch if one only knows English. This is an obvious point, but one worth making at the outset, since in the context of language teaching it is sometimes assumed that once literacy is developed in one language, it can be largely transferred to another that shares the same writing system. As we will see in Chapters 4 and 6, this may hold true in certain respects, but not all.

From a linguistic perspective, literacy involves the ability to recognize and produce graphic representations of words and morphemes, and knowledge of the conventions that determine how these elements can be combined and ordered to make sentences. In French, for example, we must know that a final -s on a noun frequently designates the plural in writing (even though it does not in spoken French), that *Dessert le délicieux est* is not a well-formed sentence, but that *Le dessert est délicieux* is, and that *ma propre chemise* and *ma chemise propre* are equally well-formed but do not mean the same thing ['my own shirt' versus 'my clean shirt']. We also need to understand the various types of dependencies among the elements within and between sentences—dependencies that contribute to a text's internal cohesion as well as to its coherence. For example, in reading the sentence 'The cat fell off the roof because it was slanted' we must be able to recognize that 'it' refers to the roof, whereas in 'The cat fell off the roof because it was drugged' we must recognize that 'it' refers to the cat. Similarly, we must be able to follow shifts in pronoun reference in sentences such as:

You won't believe it, but he told *me*, '*I* want *you* to sit next to *me*,' so *I* did.

Finally, we must also understand the various ways in which sentences are combined into paragraphs, and how paragraphs are in turn organized into larger units of writing.

It is important to recognize that written language is not simply speech written down. Although writing ultimately draws on the same lexical and grammatical resources as speech, it has its own distinctive formal tendencies. Halliday (1989) claims, for example, that writing tends to be more 'lexically dense' (i.e. it has a higher proportion of content words) and less 'grammatically intricate' (i.e. it has fewer clauses per stretch of language) than speech. Whereas writing tends to involve a greater degree of syntactic embedding (for example, the clause you are reading right now), speech tends to involve a greater degree of syntactic coordination (i.e. series of clauses linked with conjunctions such as 'and' or 'but'). Whereas speech generally relies on stress and intonation to convey tone or emphasis (for example, *Eric* was supposed to write the letter), writing generally accomplishes this either via typographical modification (as in the preceding example) or via syntax (for example, It was Eric who was supposed to write the letter). Chafe (1985) asserts that writing tends to be more integrated and less fragmented than speech, and tends to include different lexical and syntactic structures (for example, nominalizations, attributive adjectives, participles, prepositional phrases, and various forms of subordination). Furthermore, Chafe claims that whereas conversational speech typically manifests a high degree of speaker involvement (with self, with the hearer, or with the subject matter), writing is characterized by detachment, as reflected by passive constructions and abstract subjects. Becoming literate obviously does not require any explicit awareness of these sorts of things—if it did, only linguists would be literate—but it does require an intuitive *sense* of the ways in which the formal characteristics of verbal expression can vary across spoken and written contexts of language use.[4]

It is commonly observed that writing is 'decontextualized' or 'autonomous', whereas speech is more dependent on contextual features such as prosody (for example, the intonation, stress, rhythm of utterances), paralinguistic phenomena (for example, gestures, facial expressions, 'body language'), and the situation in which a particular act of communication is taking place. This notion that written language is decontextualized can be misleading in two ways. First, it seems to imply that written language does not need a context in order to be interpreted. While it is true that written language is generally less bound to a particular spatial and temporal situation than speech is, it nevertheless requires readers to mentally construct a context of interpretation, based on their existing knowledge of the world, their purpose in reading, and the text itself. Second, although they are not often remarked upon, non-verbal contextual elements play a significant role in written as well as spoken discourse. Visual features that accompany texts (for example, tables, graphs, diagrams, maps, illustrations, and photographs), as well as punctuation and the typography and layout of the text itself, can be extraordinarily potent factors in written communication (Waller 1987; Kress and van Leeuwen 1996), and therefore form an important component of literacy. As Widdowson points out,

> These paralinguistic modes of communicating are intrinsic to the discourse in which they appear and the ability to read such discourse must involve the ability to interpret such devices as well as the verbal material within which they are embedded. Furthermore, the reader has to recognize the

relationship betwen [sic] these two modes of communicating, the manner in which the information to be conveyed is distributed between them, the manner in which they complement each other to form coherent discourse. It is often the case that verbal and non-verbal elements in a discourse only make sense in relation to each other and we cannot be said to be dealing with such discourse if we confine our attention simply to those elements which are available for processing by the comprehending skill.
(1978: 99)

Rather than equating literacy narrowly with competence in written language, then, we might more broadly think of literacy as involving an ability to understand relationships of visual and verbal forms in contexts of written communication.

But if literacy has to do with written language and visual forms, it nevertheless cannot exclude spoken language. In fact, most recent scholarship has emphasized the interdependence of oral and written modes of communication (for example, Tannen 1982; Heath 1983; Gee 1986; Dyson 1990; Reder 1994). In reading a newspaper, for example, one draws on one's familiarity with how people speak in various social contexts and how a wide variety of language events (for example, press conferences, interviews, congressional assemblies, business meetings, and lectures) are handled. Conversely, listening to a news report on the radio or television involves understanding spoken language that is based on a written text. New developments in technology and telecommunications have contributed to the blurring of traditional functions of spoken and written language. Electronic mail exchanges, for example, are based in written language, but share many characteristics of face-to-face oral communication. Television has adopted genres once reserved for print (for example, news reports, editorials), incorporating 'literate' rhetorical devices, while newspapers have enhanced their 'personal' features, such as advice columns, health hints, and lonely hearts advertisements (Langer 1987b: 4).

A helpful distinction in sorting out this mixture and overlap of forms and functions of speech and writing is that between the *medium* and the *mode* of expression (Widdowson 1978; McCarthy and Carter 1994). Medium has to do with the physical manifestation of a stretch of language—i.e. whether the language is presented aurally (in speech) or graphically (in writing). Mode, on the other hand, has to do with the way language is used to convey a spoken or written 'feel'—i.e. whether a stretch of language contains features normally associated with speech, or writing, or both. For example, while a formal lecture is delivered orally (medium), it will likely contain lexical and syntactic structures associated with written academic texts (mode). A personal letter to a friend, on the other hand, is written (medium) but its mode may well be spoken and conversational. The chosen form (i.e. medium and mode) of language is tied to certain communicative functions and contexts: the formal lecture is meant to convey information and abstract ideas to people present in a lecture hall; the personal letter creates a sense of communion between two individuals that are in separate and perhaps distant locations. But as function and context change, so does the form: the mode of a letter written to impart information to unfamiliar individuals is no longer conversational, whereas the mode of a lecture to a small group of familiar students may be decidedly so.

The point as far as literacy is concerned is one that Widdowson made over twenty years ago: there are *communicative abilities* that relate to *mode* that go beyond *linguistic skills* related to *medium* (1978: 66–7). Literacy with respect to medium is not the same as literacy with respect to mode. Whereas the former has to do with language *usage* (i.e. reading and writing correct sentences), the latter has to do with language *use* (i.e. understanding and creating meanings through written texts).

As the reader may have gathered from the above discussion, the complex relationship between spoken and written language has important implications for what can be rightfully considered a text. Although in everyday parlance 'text' generally refers to written (and especially printed) material, many linguists understand texts to include spoken as well as written language (for example, Halliday and Hasan's definition referred to earlier). Furthermore, audiotape and videotape recorders have made it possible for speech and events to be 'objectified' and 'textualized' just as much as written texts.[5] Some scholars extend the notion of text beyond language to other modes of symbolic expression, such as music and art (for example, Bakhtin 1986: 103). But other scholars, such as Kress (1994), argue that applying the notion of literacy to such an inclusive definition of text glosses over important differences in the ways in which we deal with different modes of representation. In this book, our primary concern will be written and verbal texts, although some mention will be made of how nonverbal and multimodal texts (for example, photographs, paintings, advertisements, films, and videos) can be used to develop students' interpretative abilities.

From a linguistic perspective, then, literacy involves more than turning graphic symbols into verbal forms and vice versa. It certainly demands knowledge of morphological, lexical, and syntactic relationships in sentences. But because we read and write connected discourse and not just sentences, literacy also requires understanding of relationships between larger segments of text as well as knowledge of genres and styles. Furthermore, literacy requires us to understand relationships between oral and written discourse. Becoming literate, Hamilton (1994) has pointed out, 'involves complex translations between the many styles of spoken language and the many forms and purposes that written language may take' (p. 2). Finally, literacy involves the realization that graphic symbols can be verbalized in different ways to reflect different 'readings' or interpretations. It is in this realm of interpretation that cognitive dimensions of literacy play a particularly important role.

Cognitive dimensions of literacy

Since the beginning of the twentieth Century and the writings of Huey (1908) and Thorndike (1917), it has been acknowledged that reading requires more than perceptual and sensory-motor skills; it also demands the reader's active participation at a cognitive level. That is to say, reading is a *thinking* process through which readers must relate the written symbols they perceive to their knowledge of language, of texts, of content areas, and of the world, in order to bring meaning to a text. Reading therefore does more than establish links between words and referents; it requires prediction, inference, and synthesis of meaning. It requires elaboration of mental representations, and reconciliation of expectations with features of the text—all influenced by the reader's values, attitudes, and beliefs. Thorndike likened the process to problem solving:

> Understanding a paragraph is like solving a problem in mathematics. It consists in selecting the right elements of the situation and putting them together in the right relations, and also with the right amount of weight or influence or force for each. The mind is assailed as it were by every word in the paragraph. It must select, repress, soften, emphasize, correlate and organize, all under the influence of the right mental set or purpose or demand.
> (Thorndike 1917: 431)

Like reading, writing also requires active thinking and problem solving. In fact, if we were to replace the word 'understanding' with 'writing' in Thorndike's characterization of reading, we would have a reasonable description of what is involved in *composing* a paragraph. In a very broad and general sense, then, both reading and writing can be seen as acts of meaning construction, in which individuals make connections between textual elements and existing knowledge structures to create new knowledge structures. This view takes us beyond a conception of literacy as a process of decoding and encoding information, and leads us to a conception of literacy as a process of creating and transforming knowledge.

To illustrate the role of knowledge and thinking in language processing, let us consider what is involved in reading the following two sentences:

> A cigarette was carelessly discarded. The fire destroyed hundreds of acres of prime timberland.
> (adapted from Cambourne 1981)

Although these two sentences refer to entirely distinct events, we can readily see them as related to one another by inferring a causal relationship between the carelessly discarded cigarette and the forest fire. In order to make this inference, we must elaborate a mental scenario around the text, based on what we know about 'carelessly discarded cigarettes' and fires. Specifically, we must assume that the cigarette was still burning, that it came into contact with dry vegetation, that the dry vegetation caught fire, and that the fire spread and consumed many trees. The text makes no mention of any of these facts, but they are all essential to understanding the two sentences (i.e. perceiving a relationship between them). We are led to connect the sentences partly by their graphic juxtaposition and partly by the familiar cultural association of cigarettes and fires, here reinforced by the use of the definite article 'the' in the second sentence. Although no fire has been previously mentioned, 'the' nevertheless signals shared knowledge between the author and reader, prompting the reader to understand 'fire' as an assumed consequence of the discarded cigarette. Had the second sentence begun with an indefinite article ('*A* fire destroyed . . .') the pair of sentences would have seemed much less coherent. What is interesting about this inference, is that the knowledge it presupposes is not likely to be based on direct experience: few of us have actually watched a carelessly discarded cigarette ignite surrounding grass and then surrounding trees. Rather, the knowledge that allows us to make the inference has been mediated by newspapers, magazines, children's books, television, and warning signs in parks (for example, Smokey the Bear's motto: 'Only YOU can prevent forest fires!'). We have repeatedly heard *stories* about cigarettes causing fires, to the point that we 'know' about their relationship.

As suggested above, one cognitive outcome of literacy is that we are disposed to seeing relationships among words, sentences, or paragraphs that are visually organized to appear as connected discourse. In fact, it is hard to avoid inferring relationships among juxtaposed words, even when they are *not* assembled in normal textual form, such as:

Dog   Man
          Hand   Bit

This predisposition to 'making sense' based on our prior knowledge sometimes leads us to read texts as we want to see them, rather than as they really are, particularly when syntax is complicated. Consider the following sentence for example:

This is the hole that the rat, which our cat, whom the dog bit, made, caught.

Most people interpret this sentence to mean that the dog bit the cat, the cat caught the rat, and the rat made the hole, even though that is not what the sentence says (Schlesinger 1977). Bernhardt (1991) offers numerous examples of how language learners can develop coherent but highly erroneous interpretations of foreign language texts.

Existing knowledge, then, is of central importance in cognitive dimensions of literacy. Cognitive scientists commonly divide knowledge into two basic categories: *declarative* (knowing that) and *procedural* (knowing how).[6] Declarative knowledge consists of the ideas, concepts, facts, and definitions one can draw on to make sense of a text or to write about a particular topic.

It is explicit, conscious knowledge that can be verbally communicated. Procedural knowledge, on the other hand, has to do with one's ability to do things, like drive a car, write a letter, or speak one's native language. It may be explicit or implicit, conscious or unconscious, verbally expressible or not. If I pick up a research report on astrophysics, I will manage to decode it, but I will most likely not understand it without learning something about astrophysics. That is to say, I have sufficient procedural knowledge, but insufficient declarative knowledge. In this sense we can think of literacy as a domain-specific, rather than universally applicable, ability.

A recurrent theme in educational discussions is how individuals' declarative and procedural knowledge can be improved, in order to make them better readers and writers. Hirsch (1987), for example, argues that in order for individuals to read, write, communicate, and function effectively in society, they need to acquire the essential shared cultural knowledge of that society. In a move that has been both commended and condemned, Hirsch and his colleagues have prepared a lengthy list of items they deem essential for 'cultural literacy' in America. Among the first entries, for example, are 'abominable snowman', 'Absence makes the heart grow fonder', 'absolute zero', and 'acrophobia'. As Hirsch puts it, 'Only a few hundred pages of information stand between the literate and the illiterate, between dependence and autonomy' (1987: 143). Hirsch predicts that individuals will improve their reading comprehension and communicative success once they acquire this informational base because they will have a frame of reference with which to contextualize, interpret, and assimilate new information.

The problem with Hirsch's 'shotgun' approach to background knowledge, however, is that it mistakes facts for meanings. It is not knowledge of an assortment of scattered facts that helps people to become culturally literate, but rather understandings of the contexts and relationships that bring coherence to facts. It is knowledge of the stories and ideas that connect facts and make them meaningful, not the facts themselves, that can help learners to contextualize and interpret what they read.

On the procedural knowledge front, many educational psychologists have studied the behavior of expert readers and writers, in order to identify strategies that can be directly taught to less proficient readers and writers. Because researchers have found, for example, that good readers often infer the meanings of unfamiliar words from context, or find logical relationships among text elements, reading teachers often teach their students specific routines for doing this. In our cigarette-fire text above, for example, the teacher might tell students that when they see the definite article 'the' preceding a noun that has not previously been mentioned, they should look for associative connections with what *has* been mentioned. Similarly, because studies have shown that good writers plan their writing and revise often, writing teachers commonly teach strategies for planning and rewriting drafts. The results of research on the effectiveness of strategy training have been largely positive, although it is important to recognize that 'effectiveness' is not an inherent quality of certain strategies. Rather, it is contingent on a variety of contextual factors, including the reader/writer's purpose, language competence, learning style, and literacy background in the native language, as well as the specific features of the particular text being read or written. Context-sensitive strategy instruction that is grounded in specific texts and reading/writing tasks is therefore optimal.

Another principle of cognitive psychology is that knowledge, whether it is declarative or procedural, is organized schematically in the mind. According to *schema theory* (which will be discussed more fully in Chapter 2), we represent our knowledge of things, events, and situations in abstract mental structures called *schemata*. Schemata represent 'typical instances' (i.e. norms) of things and ideas, both concrete and abstract, from the component graphic features of a letter of the alphabet to notions of 'love' and 'democracy'. And they are often embedded within one another in complex hierarchies, such that a 'birthday party' schema might contain a schema for a 'birthday cake', which might in turn contain a schema for 'birthday candles', all of which would contribute to culturally-based stories about what happens at birthday parties (for example, that one's wish will come true if one blows out all of the birthday candles with a single breath). Schemata thus help us to make sense of the world around us by allowing us to organize our perceptions into coherent wholes. They make it possible for us to 'fill in the gaps' in communication through inferences and elaborations, while constraining our interpretations of ambiguous messages.

Perceptual recall experiments clearly demonstrate the importance of schemata. For example, when expert chess players are shown a configuration of chess pieces on a board during an actual game, they are able to recall the exact positions of many of the pieces. But when they are shown a random configuration of chess pieces they are no better than novice players in recalling the positions of the pieces (de Groot 1965).

So when we do not have, or are unable to access, relevant schemata with which to organize our perceptions, we can feel that things don't make sense. The culture-specific nature of schemata can potentially lead to difficulties when we read and write texts in a non-native language. If I read a passage about riding on a city bus in Brazil, for example, I may be confused if my schema for 'getting on a bus' does not include getting on at the back of the bus, paying a cashier at a turnstile in the middle, and exiting through the front (Harris, Lee, Hensley, and Schoen 1988). Similarly, my knowing the conventions of how to write a 'summary' or an 'analysis' in English does not necessarily mean that I will know how to do these things appropriately in another language and culture.

Knowledge by itself, of course, only takes us so far. Our purposes and goals direct our use of knowledge, and influence everything we do as readers and writers.[7] We generally do not read a cookbook the way we read a poem, nor do we write personal notes the way we write formal reports. Learning context-specific *uses* of reading and writing to accomplish particular purposes is what literacy is all about. Goals and purposes are associated with the *metacognitive*, or *executive* component of cognitive processing, involved in processes such as planning, monitoring, and revising in both reading and writing.

What is not always acknowledged is that, just as the purposes of reading and writing are culturally based, so are the goals set by the metacognitive component. In other words, the goals of reading and writing are not universal and based on properties of the human mind, but are a question of socialization. This, of course, has important implications for education. Flower (1990) argues that American students are trained primarily to recall and reproduce factual content, leading to a brand of literacy that emphasizes the consumption of information, what she calls *receptive literacy*. Flower characterizes receptive literacy as the ability to understand information, facts, rules, and instructions that allow individuals to function in society.[8] Her argument is consistent with the results of national writing assessments, which have found that American students perform most adequately at straightforward informative writing tasks (factual reports, descriptions) and least adequately at persuasive and imaginative writing tasks (Applebee, Langer, Mullis, and Jenkins 1990). Not surprisingly, information-based writing tasks are also the most common type of writing done in American foreign language classes at the introductory and intermediate levels.

Flower contrasts receptive literacy with *critical literacy*, which involves the ability to think about and through written texts: to read not only for facts but also for intentions, to question sources, to identify others' and one's own assumptions, and to transform information for new purposes (Flower 1990: 5). Flower distinguishes critical literacy from *critical thinking*, which is not dependent on literacy (Scribner and Cole 1981), by emphasizing the specific contribution of writing.[9] Flower's critical literacy involves more than evaluating other people's arguments—it involves making and supporting one's own. It is therefore rhetorical in nature. Critical literacy is absolutely essential in academic contexts, Flower claims, because '. . . it is the means by which students enter the conversation of their disciplines and learn to talk and think like historians and physicists' (p. 5). In other words, critical literacy is key to full membership in an academic discourse community because it provides access to the particular frames that 'club members' typically use in interpreting and producing texts (Smith 1988a).

Flower's distinction between receptive and critical literacy reaffirms a current call in our profession to rethink our goals and teaching practices. For example, in reading instruction, it suggests the need to guide our students beyond mere recognition and gist (which was unfortunately the real-world outcome of much of the 'strategic' reading pedagogy of the 1980s) toward the careful identification, structuring, restructuring, and evaluation of explicit textual elements in an effort to infer implicit rhetorical and ideational patterns (Widdowson 1978; Swaffar, Arens, and Byrnes 1991; Kramsch 1993). In short, to encourage learners to read with a 'writerly' eye. Similarly, in writing instruction, Flower's model reminds us of the need to guide students toward conscious awareness of how their choices concerning content, style, and rhetorical organization depend on their understanding of their audience and, moreover, the way these decisions can influence how their audience interprets what they have written. That is, to show learners how to write with a 'readerly' sensitivity.[10]

Flower's conception of literacy nevertheless has its own limitations, particularly within the context of foreign language teaching. Because her model was designed in the context of a study of first-year American college students' responses to English (L1) writing assignments, it is not well suited to take into account cross-cultural differences in the functions of written language, or the way literacy is valued in different societies. In light of research showing that purposes for reading and writing are neither autonomous nor universal in nature, but rather *arise from* particular social and cultural needs and expectations (for example, Heath 1980; Scribner and Cole 1981; Street 1984), Flower's model seems to put the cognitive cart before the social horse. Because issues related to sociocultural variation are so basic to foreign language teaching, we now turn to sociocultural perspectives on literacy.

Sociocultural dimensions of literacy

In the second/foreign language teaching profession, the predominance of cognitive research on L2 reading and writing makes it easy to forget that literacy is a socially constructed phenomenon, not a naturally occurring process. As Scribner (1984) reminds us, people whose language is not written do not become literate. From a sociocultural perspective, reading and writing are communicative acts in which readers and writers position one another in particular ways, drawing on conventions and resources provided by the culture. Texts do not arise directly and naturally from thought, but develop out of an interaction between writer and reader (even when writer and reader are one and the same person).

The work of Russian psychologist Lev Vygotsky has helped to illuminate the social basis of language and thought. According to Vygotsky, a child's cultural development is actualized in two stages: first on a social, or interpsychological, level, and later on an individual, or intrapsychological, level (Vygotsky 1978: 57). Furthermore, as individuals come to master tools and signs (created by society) for their own personal uses, two things happen: (1) their behavior is transformed as they become full-fledged members of their culture, and (2) they modify their own environment and thereby collectively effect change in the sign systems of their culture. Thus, there are bidirectional influences linking individuals and society. One implication of Vygotsky's theory is that literacy (and indeed cognition in general) is not the personal, idiosyncratic property of an individual, but rather a phenomenon created by society and shared and changed by the members of that society.

This leads to another implication related to the *acquisition* of literacy. That is, the need for socialization or acculturation into the particular conventions of creating and interacting with texts that characterize a particular discourse community. Educator Frank Smith (1988a) discusses this process as 'joining the literacy club', stressing the importance of apprenticeship and the learner's personal sense of group membership, which leads to a literate identity.

Sociolinguist James Gee argues along similar lines, asserting that the process of becoming literate means more than apprenticeship with texts—it means apprenticeship in particular ways of being:

> One does not learn to read texts of type X in way Y unless one has had experience in settings where texts of type X are read in way Y. These settings are various sorts of social institutions, like churches, banks, schools, government offices, or social groups with certain sorts of interests, like baseball cards, comic books, chess, politics, novels, movies, or what have you. One has to be socialized into a practice to learn to read texts of type X in way Y, a practice other people have already mastered. Since this is so, we can turn literacy on its head, so to speak, and refer crucially to the social institutions or social groups that have these practices, rather than to the practices themselves. When we do this, something odd happens: the practices of such social groups are never just literacy practices. They also involve ways of talking, interacting, thinking, valuing and believing.
> (Gee 1996: 41)

Because literacy practices are always interwoven into larger social practices, Gee urges us to look beyond 'reading and writing skills' and to explore *Discourses*. Drawing on the work of Foucault (1966; 1985) and Bourdieu (1979/1984; 1991), Gee defines Discourses (capital D) as 'ways of behaving, interacting, valuing, thinking, believing, speaking, and often reading and writing that are accepted as instantiations of particular roles (or 'types of people') by specific *groups of people* . . . .' (Gee 1996: viii). Gee argues that an individual cannot be accepted as a full-fledged member of a given group until he or she has mastered the relevant Discourse(s). The problem for those trying to gain access to a particular group, however, is that Discourses are manifested in subtle ways, do not lend themselves to explicit teaching, and can conflict with one's previously mastered Discourses (Gee discusses, for example, the Discourse of sharing time in primary education and the Discourse of law school classrooms, both of which can pose significant learning obstacles to non-mainstream students). Mastering a Discourse is therefore not a matter of conscious rule learning, but rather a process of apprenticeship and enculturation into the practices of a social group (1996, p. 139).

Gee asserts that because all literacy practices are tied to particular Discourses, discussions of reading or writing need to be contextualized in terms of particulars. People do not read and write to engage in abstract processes; rather, they read and write particular texts of particular types, in particular ways, because they hold particular values. Literacy is therefore not monolithic but multiple in nature; it is not just about language or reading and writing *per se*, but about social practices.

If literacy is a form of social practice, it is also a means for critique of social practice. The Brazilian educator Paulo Freire, for example, argued that an important aspect of literacy is critical reflection on how language (cf. Gee's Discourses) shapes our representations of our experience and the world. For Freire, literacy is not simply a process of acquiring and sharing information, but a state of social and political consciousness—one which permits critical examination of the existing social order (Freire 1974; Freire and Macedo 1987). Literacy is therefore a matter not only of reading and writing words, but also of attending to the dynamic, dialectical relationship between words and worlds:

> Reading the world always precedes reading the word, and reading the word implies continually reading the world . . . . In a way, however, we can go further and say that reading the word is not preceded merely by reading the world, but by a certain form of writing it or rewriting it, that is, of transforming it by means of conscious, practical work. For me, this dynamic movement is central to the literacy process.
> (Freire and Macedo 1987: 35)

According to Freire, then, literacy education is not a matter of transmitting 'authorized' knowledge to students (what Freire calls the 'banking' concept of education). Rather, teaching must always begin with students' own lives and culture:

> The command of reading and writing is achieved beginning with words and themes meaningful to the common experience of those becoming literate, and not with words and themes linked only to the experience of the educator. Above all, their reading of what is real cannot be the mechanically memorized repetition of our way of reading what is real.
> (Freire and Macedo 1987: 42)

By viewing literacy as a relationship of learners to the world, as a form of cultural politics, and not merely a process of reproducing knowledge, Freire's approach emphasizes literacy's role in social as well as personal transformation.

The views of Vygotsky, Smith, Gee, and Freire lead to a number of implications for foreign language teaching. First, if literacy is a social construct, both shaped by and shaping of culture, then we and our students can learn a great deal about the languages, cultures, and societies we study by attending to the particular sets of values reflected in the ways texts are constructed and in the ways literacy is used in those societies. Second, if literacy acquisition *requires* socialization into new practices, beliefs, values, attitudes, ways of thinking, it also *fosters* socialization into the foreign society. If literacy in part constitutes learners' 'ways of being,' as Gee would argue, then language learners who read and write with an awareness of the literacy conventions particular to the language and culture will take significant steps toward becoming biliterate, bicultural thinkers. Third, the view that literacy is not a uniform, monolithic entity but a collection of social practices that operate within particular Discourses, suggests that literacy needs to be developed through multiple experiences, in multiple contexts, with multiple text genres (both oral and written), for multiple purposes. Moreover, attention must be paid to the *relationships* among the particular text types, particular purposes, and particular ways of reading and writing in a given literacy practice. Finally, if literacy is not passive acceptance of Discourse conventions but a process involving critical examination of how language can be used for purposes of social control as well as for purposes of social change, we need to encourage learners to take an active, critical stance to the texts and discourse conventions we teach them. By 'critical' I mean two things: (1) 'critical' in the cognitive sense of Flower, involving the analysis, synthesis, and evaluation of information and ideas presented within the textual system; and (2) 'critical' in the social sense of Freire, involving evaluation of the textual system itself in relation to societal ideologies and values: a stance that involves problematizing of both textual and social realities.

Sociocultural approaches to literacy disabuse us of the notion that how and why we read and write is an entirely private and individual affair. A sociocultural perspective is therefore extremely useful in understanding how literacy practices are learnt and how they vary culturally and historically. It is nevertheless important to recognize that sociocultural views of literacy sometimes take linguistic competence and psychological processes as unproblematic and unanalyzed givens—or to subsume and reframe them entirely as social constructs, downplaying the role of individual differences and individual decision making. Taken alone, any one of the perspectives we have considered—linguistic, cognitive, or sociocultural—provides only a partial view of literacy. Taken together, however, the three perspectives complement one another and more adequately illuminate literacy's multiple facets.

We have seen that literacy involves a good deal more than inscribing and decoding words. It is a linguistic process that relies not only on knowledge of vocabulary and grammar, but also on knowledge of textual organization beyond the sentence level, knowledge of genres, and knowledge of conventions of spoken and written language. It is a cognitive process that involves creating links between our knowledge and textual forms and, ideally, an ongoing critical assessment of the quality of those links. It is a social practice, interwoven into larger social practices, that is developed through apprenticeship and shaped by its users to conform with social needs. It is ideally not a passive process of socialization into certain conventions of language use, but rather an active process of critically evaluating those practices into which one is being socialized. These imbricated dimensions of literacy are summarized in Figure 1.1.

Sociocultural
- Collective determination of language uses and literacy practices
- Interweaving of literacy practices with other social practices
- Apprenticeship into ways of being (social acculturation, acquiring Discourses, joining the literary club)
- Social and political consciousness: problematizing textual and social realities
- Awareness of dynamism of culture and of one's own cultural constructedness

Linguistic
- Lexical, morphological, syntactic, semantic, pragmatic knowledge
- Familiarity with writing system and graphic and organizational conventions
- Awareness of interdependencies at all levels (orthography, lexicon, sentence, paragraph, text)
- Awareness of relationships between oral and written language (including awareness of distinction between medium and mode of expression)
- Familiarity with genres and styles

Cognitive/Metacognitive
- Existing knowledge (schemata)–allowing a person to establish relationships among pieces of information and to predict, infer, and synthesize meaning
  - Declarative knowledge–the 'what'–facts, ideas, stories embedded in cultural contexts
  - Procedural knowledge–the 'how'–strategies for reading, writing, and understanding, also embedded in cultural contexts
- Ability to formulate and discern goals and purposes–including planning, monitoring, and revising–in line with cultural norms
- Ability to create and transform knowledge

Figure 1.1:   Summary of linguistic, cognitive, and sociocultural dimensions of literacy

These dimensions of literacy are not only overlapping and interdependent, but are also infused in each of the seven principles of literacy outlined at the beginning of this chapter. *Interpretation* requires declarative and procedural knowledge, an ability to create relationships among symbolic elements (for example, linguistic elements), and transformation of one's knowledge, but it also requires apprenticeship in the particular interpretative practices of a given community, as well as familiarity with relevant genres and styles. *Collaboration* is often thought of primarily as a social construct, but it requires motivation and knowledge (and anticipation of another's knowledge), as well as some common ground in terms of a symbolic system (for example, language). *Conventions* relevant to literacy certainly include linguistic patterns, but they include cognitive patterns and social patterns as well—all culturally constructed. *Cultural knowledge*, although partly cognitive in nature (for example, cultural schemata), is dynamically produced and reproduced through social activity, and is often mediated through language. It is therefore as much a social, 'outside the head' construct as it is a cognitive, 'inside the head' construct. *Problem solving* is sometimes thought of as a purely cognitive affair, but it is only acquired through social activity, is defined in terms of sociocultural norms, and usually depends on language as a tool for thinking. Similarly, *reflection* is indeed cognitive, but it is also a socially-constrained and socially-mediated process that usually draws on language. Finally, *language use* is always embedded in sociocultural contexts, draws on cultural as well as linguistic knowledge, involves apprenticeship, and requires both declarative and procedural knowledge.

Although cognitive and sociocultural views of literacy have sometimes been pitted against one another, it is time not only to acknowledge the involvement of both cognitive and social components, but to recognize the essential interactions and interdependencies among linguistic, cognitive, and sociocultural dimensions of literacy. Bernhardt (1991) has forcefully argued this same point, showing that much of what is dealt with in the cognitive realm of literacy (for example, goals and purposes, uses of procedural and declarative knowledge, rhetorical thinking, and so forth) is shaped by sociocultural forces, and played out in language use. Conversely, certain social aspects of literacy (such as the internalization of a language or a society's sign systems, for example) obviously depend on cognitive processing. Literacy, then, is both private and public, both creative and conventional, both cognitive and social. One draws on resources and practices that have existed long before oneself, but one uses them in unique ways. As members of the New London Group (1996) describe it, one makes use of established, 'available designs' for particular, personal purposes, but in so doing one effectively 'redesigns' them. We will explore this point further in the next chapter.

Conclusion

To contrast the view of literacy developed in this chapter with the more conventional view that has predominated in foreign language education, literacy is not seen as a uniform and universal construct, but rather as a dynamic set of linguistic, social, and cognitive processes that are culturally-motivated. Because this view of literacy includes both spoken and written language in its purview, and considers these to be partially overlapping rather than dichotomous, it acknowledges the holistic, unified nature of what has traditionally been treated separately as 'reading', 'writing', 'speaking', and 'listening' in foreign language pedagogy. Finally, the view of literacy presented here combines a focus on language use in social contexts (essential to communicative approaches) with an additional component of active reflection on how meanings are constructed and negotiated in particular acts of communication. Becoming literate is therefore not so much a matter of achieving a particular criterial level of reading or writing performance, as it is a matter of engaging in the ever-developing process of using reading and writing as tools for thinking and learning, in order to expand one's understanding of oneself and the world.

Definitions are important, for if we think of literacy as merely the ability to decode and encode written messages, then our teaching of reading and writing will likely emphasize the code itself (i.e. vocabulary and grammar) and its relationship to a universal, 'objective' world. If we think of literacy in the broader terms described in this chapter, on the other hand, our emphasis will be on how texts *create* worlds as well as reflect them. Our focus will shift from the *referents* of words and texts to the *illocutionary force, cultural associations*, and *contextual meanings* of words and texts. Our practice will emphasize, not minimize, the importance of linguistic form, but will do so in the context of learners' active, imaginative, and critical involvement with their own and others' texts.

But many questions remain. In the case of foreign and second language learning, students are generally already literate in one language. What is the relationship between native language literacy and literacy in another language? Does literacy simply transfer from one language to another? Can literacy affect learners' ability to communicate orally in the new language? How does one come to learn to 'read' another culture through texts when one is predisposed to see the world from the perspective of one's own culture? Indeed, how can students be expected to reflect critically at all when they often do not understand the basic meanings of the texts they read? How can we integrate the teaching of reading, writing, speaking, and thinking? What are the implications of computer technology for the teaching of language and literacy? In the following chapters we will visit these and other issues as we explore the implications of a literacy-based view of language teaching.

Notes

1 Inevitably, the particular conception of literacy I am presenting here is a product of my own sociocultural conditioning and my experience as a foreign language teacher in an American institution of higher education. Language teaching, like literacy, is socially constructed and varies widely in its assumptions, goals, and methods across diverse communities, institutions, and cultures. I therefore recognize that what I have identified as the 'context of academic second and foreign language education' is far from monolithic and uniform, and that the particular view of literacy I espouse here cannot be applied in universal fashion. I nevertheless hope that most readers will find elements of my argument relevant and applicable to their own settings.

2 Significant exceptions are the traditions of teaching English for Specific Purposes (ESP), teaching English for Academic Purposes (EAP), and discourse-oriented approaches to the teaching of literature in a foreign language, which will be discussed in Chapter 2.

3 Street (1984) contrasts the 'autonomous' model with what he calls the 'ideological' model of literacy. The 'ideological' model treats literacy as a set of culturally embedded and ideological practices, defined in terms of the social institutions that perpetuate such practices.

4 See Tannen (1982), Chafe (1985), and Halliday (1989) for more on relationships between spoken and written language.

5 A passerby's personal video footage of the beating of Rodney King by Los Angeles policemen in 1991, for example, became a 'text' viewed by millions of people throughout the world. Through its repeated viewings during the Rodney King trial, this ostensibly 'objective' videotext was interpreted and reinterpreted to the point that it was used by both defense and prosecution attorneys as evidence to argue both for and against the innocence of the policemen involved in the incident.

6 Anderson (1980) has discussed this distinction at length in the context of cognitive learning theory. The distinction was first made by Ryle (1949).

7 See, for example, Flower (1994); Ruddell, Ruddell, and Singer (1994).

8 In his fascinating historical essay, Ohmann (1986) discusses the 'scientific management' approach begun by Frederick Winslow Taylor, and its impact on American educational institutions. Taylor's manufacturing assembly line was based on three principles: (1) the dissociation of the labor process from the knowledge of workers, (2) the separation of conception from execution, and (3) the guarding of understanding and control within management (p. 15). Clearly, in this model, receptive (and *not* critical) literacy is called for in the training of American workers to insure optimum productivity.

9 McPeck (1981) defines critical thinking as 'the propensity and skill to engage in an activity with reflective skepticism' (p. 8), but points out that one cannot think critically *in general*: one can only think critically *about* something. Moreover, being able to think critically in one domain does not necessarily mean that one is able to think critically in another. McPeck therefore argues that efforts to teach 'critical thinking' in the absence of any particular subject matter are misguided.

10 Foreign language teaching materials adopting this approach are becoming increasingly common. An excellent and early example is the intermediate/advanced Spanish composition textbook *De lector a escritor* (Finneman and Carbón Gorell 1991), in which the authors explain: 'Discussion and activities . . . aid the student as 'reader' to a) identify the audience and its requirements, b) identify the voice, attitude, intent of the writer/author, and c) analyze the reading structurally and linguistically to appreciate how the general structure of the text and the specific language work to guarantee the intent of the author' (p. viii).

2 Communication, literacy, and language learning

[Literacy is] not the narrow ability to deal with texts but the broader ability to deal with other people as a writer or reader.

Deborah Brandt (1990)

François Gouin, a nineteenth century French pedagogue, described in great detail his attempts to learn German via what we might call a 'classical literacy' approach based on grammar books, dictionaries, and textual translation. Gouin's faith in this approach was absolute: 'To learn first words, then the rules for grouping these words, and of these to make up sentences, this seemed to me to include the whole art, the whole secret, the whole philosophy of the teaching of languages' (1894: 10). Armed with a German grammar and a dictionary, Gouin 'devoured' the grammar in one week and set out to a Hamburg academy to put his newfound language knowledge to the test by attending a lecture. 'But alas!,' he wrote, 'Not a word, not a single word would penetrate to my understanding' (p. 11). Turning to reading and translation, Gouin began with Goethe and Schiller:

> . . . when I opened the first page of my author, I found I could recognise hardly any of the words I had acquired, though the page must have contained many of them . . . . When my glance fell upon a word of my native tongue, the idea represented by this word shone or sparkled forth, so to speak, under my eyes. The word became transfigured with a certain mysterious element of life. I beheld no longer mere letters; I saw the idea itself. Strange that this phenomenon would not occur for the German word, even when I had been able to determine its meaning by the aid of the dictionary. The word was always as a dead body stretched upon the paper. Its meaning shone not forth under my gaze; I could draw forth neither the idea nor the life. (pp. 15–16)[1]

Next came a series of attempts to learn from method books that emphasized phrase learning—Ollendorf, Jacotot, Robertson, Plötz—but none proved viable. Gouin moved to Berlin and tried consorting with Germans, but they only wanted to practice their French. He tried taking classes at the university, but understood nothing. Resolute in his desire to learn German, Gouin finally turned to the last method that remained: he devoted one month of all-consuming study to the memorization of all 30,000 words in his German dictionary (going temporarily blind in the process). On the evening of the day he completed this gargantuan task, Gouin went to the university to 'seek his crown', fully confident that he would at last enjoy the fruit of his extraordinary efforts. But Gouin was devastated to find that he was no more capable of understanding the university lecture than he had been before he began his intensive studies. Where did Gouin go wrong?

Like Gouin, many language learners today often 'know all the words' but nevertheless fail to understand much of what they read, sometimes even after several years of language study. And their comprehension difficulties are rarely due simply to laziness: foreign language students commonly report spending hours reading relatively short texts.[2]

Artificial intelligence programmers who try to get computers to process human language know this problem well. A computer program designed to read and summarize reports on the United Press International news wire one day received a story that began 'Rome was shaken this morning to learn of the death of Pope John Paul I . . . .' The computer program summarized the story by reporting that an earthquake in Rome had resulted in one casualty (Bolter 1991: 180).

And of course even native speakers can experience difficulty in understanding some texts, especially when they are extracted from their context, like the following:

HUSKY BLOWOUT LEAVES CARDINAL BLUE[3]

How do we explain this? Gouin and the computer had dictionaries and grammars. And native speakers of English know the meanings of all of the words in the headline. They know what the text says. Why should they have problems knowing what it means? The problem, of course, is that the meanings of words, sentences, and texts are not fixed, but contingent upon one another, upon the contexts in which they are embedded, and upon the knowledge that the reader brings to their interpretation. Contrary to some popular notions of reading, we don't comprehend just by remembering strings of words; we understand by constructing meanings based on our recognition of the particular *relationships* among words in texts, and between the particular text we are reading and other texts we have read before. What we remember from our reading is our constructed meanings, not the exact words used in the text. Ironically, in fact, one of the important tasks in getting computers to preserve meaning accurately is programming them to 'forget' the actual words they have processed (Schank 1984: 96).

Gouin's problem, as well as that of the computer program and many foreign language learners, is rooted in an assumption that successful communication and literacy hinge primarily on a thorough mastery of the linguistic code: that knowing the code allows one to tap into the current of meanings unambiguously encoded in speech or print. This assumption, which I will shortly discuss in terms of the *conduit* metaphor of communication, has traditionally justified the separation of interpretation from communicative ability by emphasizing the importance of the linguistic code and the autonomy of textual meaning, and by de-emphasizing the contextual, intersubjective, and interpretive dimensions of communication.

This separation of teaching 'language as a means of communication' and teaching 'textual analysis and interpretation' is represented diachronically in periodic shifts of emphasis on teaching written versus spoken language (for example, grammar-translation and reading methods versus direct and audiolingual methods). It is also represented synchronically in postsecondary language programs that place interpersonal communication and textual analysis at opposite ends of the curriculum (i.e. introductory and advanced level coursework).

As I hope to show in this chapter, however, even the most basic, ordinary acts of communication require interpretation, involving the use of resources that extend well beyond the grammar and vocabulary of a language. I will contrast the conduit metaphor of communication with an alternative metaphor—that of *design*—which emphasizes the *construction* (not simple transfer) of meaning in communicative acts. From the metaphorical perspective of design, communication occurs at the intersection between language and context and relies on the perception of linguistic, cognitive, and social *relationships*.

The point I will argue is that the aims of teaching face-to-face verbal interaction and developing learners' ability to read, write, and think critically about texts are not incompatible goals but, in fact, mutually interdependent. Unlike children, who can learn a good deal by immersion and interaction in their native language and culture, foreign language learners must rely extensively on second order experience in learning a new language and culture. In a foreign language context, exposure to (and, eventually, learning of) a wide range of genres, styles, and conventions of language use, as well as cultural schemata, comes principally through reading. Without extensive exposure to foreign language texts, the breadth and depth of learners' communicative abilities cannot but be limited. On the other hand, communicative abilities are essential to learners' ability to *learn* from that reading, for without them, they can neither understand nor discuss the texts to which they are exposed. In other words, there is a symbiotic, mutually-reinforcing relationship between literacy and communicative ability—a relationship that must be nurtured in academic foreign language curricula.

A literacy-based orientation to language teaching does not mean abandoning a communicative focus and reverting back to a grammar-translation variety of teaching that emphasizes the analysis and manipulation of language structures. Rather, it means engaging learners in reading and writing as acts of communication. It means sensitizing learners to relationships between language, texts, and social contexts, in order to deepen their understanding of language and culture, and ultimately to enhance their communicative capacity as human beings. As Vivian Cook has argued,

> Teachers should be clear in their minds that they are usually teaching people how to use two languages, not how to use one in isolation. The person who can speak two languages has the special ability to communicate in two ways. The aim is not to produce L2 speakers who can only use the language when speaking to each other . . . . Rather the aim is people who can stand between two viewpoints and between two cultures, a multi-competent speaker who can do far more than any monolingual. (1996: 149–50)

Texts—written, oral, visual, audio-visual—offer more than something to talk about (i.e. content for the sake of practicing language). They offer learners the chance to 'stand between two viewpoints and between two cultures'. They can be the locus of the thoughtful and creative act of making connections between grammar, discourse, and meaning, between language and content, between language and culture, and between another culture and one's own. In short, the reading, writing, and discussion of texts can lead students to become aware of the complex webs, rather than isolated strands, of meaning in human communication.

Before I elaborate this argument, however, we must first explore some of the assumptions, long pervasive in language education, that have contributed to dichotomous thinking about communicative competence and literacy.

Conduits, containers, and communication

According to a common sense view of communication, we use language in a straightforward, literal way in our ordinary everyday transactions, to 'say what we mean' as plainly as possible in order to avoid ambiguity and misunderstandings. Communication happens something like this: a speaker or writer begins with a message (for example, information, ideas, thoughts), which is encoded and sent via a channel or medium (for example, speech or writing) to another person. This person receives the coded message as an auditory or visual stimulus, which must be decoded to reconstitute the original message. Assuming that (a) both the sender and the receiver know the code, (b) the signal has not been degraded en route, and (c) the receiver is attentive, the message can be expected to arrive intact. That is to say, the receiver now 'has' the same information, ideas, or thoughts that the sender originally encoded. The receiver may then formulate a response, which may be kept to himself, encoded and sent back, or relayed to someone else. In this model, human communication is directly analogous to fax transmission, in which graphic images are scanned and encoded into digital strings of zeros and ones, sent as electronic impulses through telephone wires to a distant location, then reconverted to the original images by the receiving fax machine.

Of course, human communication is not as simple as the fax machine model would suggest. When we communicate we do not merely transfer information to one another—we create and interpret meaning, and those acts of creation and interpretation are based on an ever-shifting matrix of cultural, situational, and personal factors that make it difficult to talk about messages or meaning as autonomous, fixed entities that can be simply moved from one person or place to the next.

Nevertheless, the information-transfer model of communication has been extremely influential—not only because it has appeared in numerous textbooks on communication, but also, and much more significantly, because it is encoded in our everyday language. We commonly say things like: 'Try to get your thoughts across better' or 'Let me have some of your ideas on this' or 'The passage conveys a feeling of excitement'. Reddy (1979) has collected numerous similar examples of what he calls the *conduit* metaphor. In this metaphorical system, language is represented as a conduit through which information, thoughts, ideas, and feelings are transferred from one person to another. The underlying assumption is that people will have few problems understanding each other as long as they agree on the conventions used to encode information. Samuel Butler represented this view in his well-known essay 'Thought and Language':

> ... the essence of language lies in the intentional conveyance of ideas from one living being to another through the instrumentality of arbitrary tokens or symbols agreed upon and understood by both as being associated with the particular ideas in question .... . To acquire a foreign language is only to learn and adhere to the covenants in respect of symbols which the nation in question has adopted and adheres to. Till we have done this we neither of us know the rules, so to speak, of the game that the other is playing, and cannot, therefore, play together; but the convention being once known and consented to, it does not matter whether we raise the idea of a stone by the words 'lapis,' or by 'lithos,' 'pietra,' 'pierre,' 'stein,' 'stane,' or 'stone'; we may choose what symbols written or spoken we choose, and one set, unless they are of unwieldy length, will do as well as another, if we can get other people to choose the same and stick to them; it is the accepting and sticking to them that matters, not the symbols.
> (Butler 1962: 20–5)

One important implication of the conduit metaphor for language education, then, is that mastery of the *code* is of central importance—not because of any inherent quality of the code itself, but because it is a shared convention that makes communication possible with particular groups of people.[4] Meaning, because it is 'conveyed' as effectively through one language conduit as through another, is seen to be objective and independent of language. Ideas 'float around' but they can be 'grasped' or 'captured' and 'put into' words. Following this logic, complete knowledge of the code (the clearest possible conduit) allows meaning to be received in its purest state, without distortion or ambiguity. As one language educator put it, students wishing to read a foreign language in its fullest sense

> . . . must become familiar with the essential characteristics that make the language a modern literate construct: its fundamental lexicon, its syntactical and semantic norms, and its common idiomatic, allusive and elliptical expressions, all of which must be sufficiently mastered so that the intended meaning of any utterance, spoken or written, is unambiguously communicated.
> (Sachs 1989: 74–5)

This notion of unambiguous communication introduces a second important implication of the conduit metaphor: that words, sentences, and texts are *containers* of meaning.[5] As David Olson once argued in a widely-cited essay, one important outcome of the transition from oral to literate culture in the Western world was that language was 'increasingly able to stand as an unambiguous or autonomous representation of meaning' (Olson 1977: 258). Written language was not subject to the influence of contextual elements, Olson claimed, for, unlike speech, writing contained all the meaning to be had within itself: 'if the text is formally adequate and the reader fails to understand, that is the reader's problem. The meaning is in the text' (Olson 1977: 277).[6] This assumption of text autonomy was at the heart of the 'New Criticism', which influenced the teaching of literary texts for generations. It has also been influential in certain strands of composition theory (see Dillon 1981).

And if texts are construed as containers in this metaphorical model, so are human heads and minds, as suggested by expressions such as 'He can't seem to get the idea into his head', 'I'll tuck that thought away in my mental file', 'her thoughts spilled out as she spoke', and 'clear your mind of extraneous thoughts'. Needless to say, the head-as-container metaphor has significant implications for education. The teacher's role is understood as filling learners' heads (containers) with information. This metaphor underlies E. D. Hirsch's 'list learning' approach to cultural literacy, alluded to in the previous chapter, and informs many common classroom practices for teaching language and literature (Goodlad 1984; Nystrand and Gamoran 1991; Marshall, Smagorinsky, and Smith 1995).

To summarize, the conduit and container metaphors reflect (and perpetuate) the following assumptions about language and communication:

1 Thoughts and ideas can be encoded, but they are independent of their encoding.
2 We *transfer* thoughts, ideas, feelings, and so on to others through language.

3 Words, sentences, and texts *contain* meaning; language is a neutral, transparent medium for carrying meaning.
4 The transfer of meaning can be unambiguous if we construct our utterances carefully; we use language literally when we want to convey our meaning accurately.
5 Clear, understandable texts are informationally complete and autonomous.

In the context of language teaching, the conduit/container model is encoded in the traditional binary opposition of 'productive' versus 'receptive' skills (i.e. speaking/writing versus listening/reading). It also drives the expectation, common among language students, that they should be able to understand a text if they look up all its words, or that they should be able to write a successful essay in the foreign language by simply translating a native language version word by word. Such beliefs are a legacy of the grammar-translation method (which emphasized decoding and translating), the structuralist reading method of the 1930s (which emphasized the study of word frequency lists), and the audiolingual method (which emphasized accurate mimicry, often at the expense of understanding discourse in other than the most common social contexts). Such beliefs also impede integrative thinking about communication and literacy.

Limitations of the conduit/container model

The story of communication outlined above does capture certain aspects of communication (we do, after all, manage to communicate thoughts, and the encoding/decoding model proposes an explanation for this), but it dangerously oversimplifies the complexity of communication in a number of ways. First, by suggesting that meaning exists *a priori* (on the printed page or in the writer's head), no account is taken of the interactive, collaborative, and intersubjective dimension of communication. When people talk, listen, read, or write, meaning is jointly constructed by the participants involved. In order to know what to say and how to say it, speakers and writers must take their audience into account: one generally does not say something to an adult in the same way that one would say it to a small child (and if one does, that manner of speaking itself conveys its own message). Furthermore, one may start out by saying one thing, then shift direction midstream or even end one's turn entirely in response to some kind of verbal or bodily feedback from one's interlocutor. In conversation and writing, meanings are frequently not determined in advance but conceived at the moment of utterance, and sometimes a speaker (or a writer) realizes alternative possible interpretations only after having spoken or written. This is why people often talk or write in order to discover what they really think about something: the very process of articulation in speech or writing can bring coherence to previously inchoate ideas and thoughts. In this sense, language serves not only to encode but also to generate meaning.

Second, speakers and writers don't *transfer* meaning as much as provide linguistic cues that allow others to predict and reconstruct meaning. Just as we don't wait to make sense of an event until after it happens, we don't wait until the end of a message to form a response to it. Sometimes a fragment of an utterance may be enough: we may see where our interlocutor is going after just a few words and respond either by nodding patiently or by jumping in, completing his or her utterance ourselves. As we read or listen, we may quickly shift interpretive frames in response to a particular word or phrase, rather than waiting until the very end of the text to 'decide' on its meaning. For example, consider your understanding of the sentence 'Ted and Roger looked at the score and felt a sudden wave of panic.' Then read its continuation: 'They would have to tell the conductor that they could not play the arpeggios as written.' For many readers, the words 'conductor' and 'arpeggios' bring about a rapid shift in frame of reference from a sports performance to a musical performance—but the shift comes *during* the act of reading, not in subsequent deliberation. Prediction of meaning is of great importance in all forms of communication, but it cannot be easily accounted for by an information transmission model predicated on the packaging and sending of whole messages. We are not empty vessels waiting passively to have messages poured into us; rather, we understand by actively constructing meanings based partly on what we see and hear, and partly on our expectations derived from our existing knowledge and experience.

Third, contrary to Butler's claim, words are not neutral references to universal notions. Linguistic symbols, once they are adopted and adhered to, become cultural property. Their uses and connotations in particular contexts become indissociable from them. Across languages, 'equivalent' words always have different functional contexts and associations. Eye is *oeil* in French and *ojo* in Spanish, but whereas '¡ojo!' signals caution, '*mon oeil!*' signals skepticism. 'Participation' is a favorite buzzword of American educators, but *participation* in French has such strong political overtones from the DeGaulle era that it has never been successfully adopted in French pedagogical discourse (Galisson 1987). Even within a given language, meaning is not a property, but a *function* of words used in particular ways. Consider the word 'corner'. A child standing alone *in* a corner is not the same as a child standing alone *on* a corner. We envision different physical settings, based on our knowledge of corners: interior versus exterior; walls versus streets; floor versus sidewalk, and so on. We may well 'read in' cultural associations as well: a child who is being punished for naughtiness (but who is safe at home) versus a child who is lost or abandoned (whose safety is potentially threatened). The prepositions ('in' versus 'on') cannot be said to 'contain' the meaning difference, for if we maintain the in/on contrast but substitute 'sand' for 'corner' (for example, 'A child standing alone in the sand' versus 'A child standing alone on the sand'), we no longer perceive a dramatic difference in meaning. The meanings of phrases cannot be derived simply by adding up the literal meanings of their constituent words. Rather, it is the particular *relationship* among the particular words that matters. This is why a Christian cross has no more to do with a cross Christian than a Venetian blind has to do with a blind Venetian (Smith 1988b: 29).

Fourth, communication is rarely just a matter of encoding and decoding literal messages. Meaning depends on interpretation, based on one's understanding of the situational context as well as on one's motives, knowledge, beliefs, and experience. If I say 'My oil pan has a leak' to a car mechanic at a garage, what I really *mean* is that I want him to fix the leak. When I then say the same thing over the phone to my boss, I am really offering an explanation for why I will be late for work. The referential meaning of my words is only part of the story. In some cases, the intended meaning may even be the opposite of the literal meaning (for example, 'That was a *fine* thing to say!'). Much of our language use is not literal.[7] In fact, one of the greatest virtues of language is that it frees us from literalness, allowing us to represent the world as we wish to represent it—indeed, allowing us to create worlds that do not exist on a material plane but can be experienced by others through verbal description, narration, and argument.

Fifth, even clear, understandable texts are always informationally *in*complete, leaving unsaid what readers or listeners can be expected to fill in from their knowledge of the world. If I receive a note saying 'John W. will not be in class due to illness,' I can assume that John W. refers to my student John Woods, that it is my class (and not someone else's), that he will not be attending, that it is today (and not some other day), that he will be absent, and that it is John himself (and not someone else in his family) who is ill. The note does not say these things, but it is presumably meant to make me believe them. It is in fact hard to imagine a 'natural' text that would be informationally complete. Cook (1994) offers this example of an overly-helpful court witness asked to tell 'the whole truth' about his actions on a particular morning:

> I woke up at seven forty. I was in bed. I was wearing pyjamas. After lying still for a few minutes, I threw back the duvet, got out of bed, walked to the door of the bedroom, opened the door, switched on the landing light, walked across the landing, opened the bathroom door, went into the bathroom, put the basin plug into the plughole, turned on the hot tap, ran some hot water into the washbasin, looked in the mirror . . . .
> (Cook 1994: 12)

Such a testimony would, of course, be more irritating than helpful—most of the information is trivial and irrelevant to the needs of the court. But even this text is far from informationally complete: we still don't know which hand was used to throw back the duvet, on which side the witness got out of bed, whether he put on slippers, and so on. Some claim that legal contracts are informationally complete texts, but this does not seem to save lawyers the trouble of interpreting and debating their meanings.

In sum, the conduit/container model of communication does not adequately account for the complexities of human communication. If it did, Gouin might have fared more favorably in his initial attempts to learn German. What is needed is a broader view of communication in which meaning is seen to be contingent, not only upon linguistic knowledge, but also upon multiple cognitive and social factors.

In the following section, I will show how work in discourse-oriented linguistics provides the basis for an alternative metaphor of language use and communication: one that allows us to understand communicative success despite imperfect mastery of a linguistic code—a metaphor that places creativity and social processes at its heart and that can accommodate literacy as a communicative practice.

An alternative metaphor: design of meaning

Language learning, as Halliday (1978) has described it, is learning how to mean—in a sociocultural context in which the culture is itself constituted partly by language, partly by other semiotic (sign) systems. In this view (which Halliday describes by the phrase 'language as social semiotic'), language is seen as a primary symbolic resource among other symbolic resources that people draw on when they communicate.

For Halliday, language is a system of choices, a system of meaning potential. We come to any communicative event with knowledge of the potential sets of choices made available to us by our language. These choices have to do with what we can *do*, can *say*, and can *mean*. Our selection from the potential choices (our 'actualized potential' in Halliday's scheme) is influenced by, among other things, the situational context, the cultural context, and our communicative goals. The choices we make are significant—not only in and of themselves, but also in relation to the backdrop of competing options that were *not* selected.

To illustrate this last point, consider Japan's recent public apology for its acts during World War II. The initial parliamentary resolution, made in June 1995, used the word *hansei* (remorse, reflection) instead of two other potential choices: *kokai* (remorse, regret) and *shazai* (apology). Avoidance of the latter word had the convenient effect of placating two factions in the Japanese government. As one journalist put it,

> . . . those Japanese who feel penitent can interpret the resolution as meaning that Japan feels terrible that it invaded and colonized its neighbors. But those legislators who feel proud of Japan's war record can interpret the resolution differently. They can argue that it means that Japan

feels terrible that Europe and America colonized other countries, forcing
Japan into the war as a matter of self-defense.
(Kristof 1995: A1)

Understandably, Japan's Asian neighbors were not appeased by this
conscious evasiveness, and two months later Prime Minister Tomiichi
Murayama unambiguously apologized for damage and suffering caused by
Japan during the war, using the word *owabi* (apology) (WuDunn 1995). In
this case we can see how a particular lexical choice, considered in the light of
competing alternatives, can have significant communicative consequences.
Indeed, in cases such as this one, choices can not only reflect sociopolitical
realities, but also shape them.[8]

The notions of choice, context, and pragmatic consequences lie at the heart
of communicative approaches to language teaching, and yet, on the whole,
they have tended to inform the teaching of oral communication rather more
than the teaching of literacy in foreign language contexts. Two important
exceptions, as noted in Chapter 1, are the (predominantly British) traditions
of (1) applying discourse analysis and stylistics to the teaching of literature in
a foreign language and (2) the teaching of foreign languages for specific
purposes. Discourse-oriented approaches to teaching literature (Widdowson
1975; Carter and Burton 1982; Brumfit and Carter 1986; Widdowson 1992;
Carter and Simpson 1995) make a point of examining how particular
communicative effects are born of particular language choices in particular
contexts. And not just in literary texts. As Carter (1986) points out,
linguistic-stylistic analysis 'enables us to work on the *literariness* of texts
rather than on texts as literature' (p. 110). This approach will be further
discussed in the section on 'style' in Chapter 3.

The second, and more often overlooked, exception has been the teaching
of languages for specific purposes (LSP), which was developed in the 1970s to
deal with the language needs of people preparing for work in specialized
academic or technical fields. LSP focused attention not only on surface
grammatical features but also on the 'implicit presuppositional rhetorical
information' (Selinker, Trimble, and Trimble 1976) cued by particular
linguistic choices. Swales (1978), reflecting on the writing of his textbook
Writing Scientific English (1971), recalled that one of the things that was new
and important was getting students 'to learn to identify suitable places in a
piece of written English for various kinds of statement' (p. 48). As Candlin
(1978) pointed out, the goal of teaching English for Specific Purposes in
general, and of teaching English for Science and Technology in particular,
was not to look at scientific or technical language 'as merely a collection of
specialist lexis and structure,' but rather to account for 'the ways the
reasoning and conceptual processes of 'doing science' were reflected in
language choice' (p. vii). In the same volume, Allen and Widdowson (1978b)
presented a series of exercise types designed expressly to serve this end—to

sensitize learners to the complex linkages between textual features, rhetorical functions, and reasoning processes represented in English scientific texts. Like Swales, they drew attention to the importance of learning how discourse conventions differed across various kinds of writing, arguing that learners needed not only to analyze others' writing, but also 'to achieve a *synthesis* of many disparate grammatical and lexical elements in the form of a coherent composition of [their] own' (p. 71). Their synthetic approach to teaching reading and writing as communication was put into practice in the influential *English in Focus* series (for example, Allen and Widdowson 1974; 1978a).

The discourse-oriented approach to literacy developed in LSP programs developed in the 1970s and 1980s laid the foundation for current work in teaching literacy as communication. As outlined in Chapter 1, what has now been added to the teaching of literacy is a greater focus on its sociocultural and critical dimensions. Building on Halliday's notion of language as social semiotic, as well as work in sociolinguistics and discourse analysis over the past thirty years, the New London Group (a team of ten scholars from Australia, Great Britain, and the U.S., including Courtney Cazden, Bill Cope, Norman Fairclough, James Gee, Gunther Kress, and Allan Luke among others) has proposed a vision of literacy education, the goal of which is to prepare learners to interpret, express, and negotiate meaning within a variety of contexts. A central concept in the New London Group's vision, which will serve as an organizing metaphor for the rest of this book, is *design of meaning*: As the New London Group describes it,

> The notion of design connects powerfully to the sort of creative intelligence the best practitioners need in order to be able, continually, to redesign their activities in the very act of practice. It connects well to the idea that learning and productivity are the results of the designs (the structures) of complex systems of people, environments, technology, beliefs, and texts.
> (New London Group 1996: 73)

As suggested by the above statement, *design* is conveniently ambiguous, referring either to product or process, so that 'the design of a text' can be interpreted to mean either the text's configuration of structures or the act of its creation. In the process of designing meaning, the New London Group argues, one draws on 'Available Designs': grammars of languages and other semiotic systems as well as conventions associated with their use in various communicative contexts (p. 74). But one does not simply *reproduce* these Available Designs, as the conduit model might suggest.[9] Nor does one bypass them, creatively constructing meaning in an entirely individual and idiosyncratic way, as some 'personal voice' theories of composition might suggest. Rather, according to the New London Group, every act of designing (for example, reading, writing, speaking, listening, seeing) is a productive process of recycling old materials in fresh ways—establishing new relationships among stock elements. Breen and Candlin represented this view from a language teaching perspective fifteen years earlier, saying language users:

> typically exploit a tension between the conventions that are established and the opportunity to modify these conventions for their particular communicative purposes. Communicating is not merely a matter of following conventions but also of negotiating through and about the conventions themselves. It is a convention-creating as well as a convention-following activity.
>
> (Breen and Candlin 1980: 90)

The design metaphor also recalls Flower's conception of critical literacy (see Chapter 1), in that the designing process 'transforms knowledge in producing new constructions and representations of reality'—yielding what the New London Group calls 'the Redesigned' (p. 76). The Redesigned in turn becomes a new Available Design for subsequent acts of meaning-making, and the cycle is complete. We can visualize the relationship among Available Designs, Designing, and the Redesigned as in Figure 2.1.

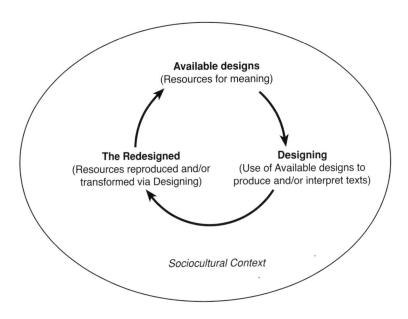

Figure 2.1:   Design of meaning (based on New London Group, 1996)

To illustrate how the design process works, let's begin by considering a very mundane example of a message written on the back panel of a shampoo bottle, below the directions for use:

* NOT TESTED ON ANIMALS

In order to design the meaning of this text, we must of course have some knowledge of English *vocabulary* and *syntax*, as well as its *writing system*, but we must also draw on a variety of other Available Designs. These will be italicized in the discussion below, and further elaborated in the rest of this chapter. Beginning at the level of textual description, we have an asterisk and four words—an elliptical phrase with no explicit subject that nonetheless functions as a complete text. These are the only words on the entire bottle that are written in capital letters and, apart from the product name on the front panel, they are the most visible words on the bottle.

Moving to the level of interpretation, what might be the communicative intent of these words? Based on our familiarity with *typographical conventions*, we might infer that the capitalization is for emphasis. The asterisk also appears to serve this purpose, since there is no indication that this text is a footnote. Drawing on our familiarity with the 'product label' genre, often characterized by a terse, elliptical style, we can fill in what language has not been made explicit in the text, namely the subject and verb: [This product has] NOT [been] TESTED ON ANIMALS. For someone living in the United States or Great Britain in the 1990s, who is familiar with the well-publicized protests of animal rights activists against laboratory testing of new chemical products on animals, the meaning of this statement in this particular context will likely seem quite clear and unambiguous: no animals were put at risk or suffered harm in the development of this product. And the pragmatic value of this message is equally clear: this is a 'politically correct' product—one that you (positioned as a 'politically correct' reader) can use without guilt. In order to arrive at this particular interpretation, however, the reader must have access to certain *background knowledge*. Specifically, he or she must have a *schema* for 'animal testing' (i.e. the knowledge that animals are often used to test products destined for humans) and a schema for 'animal rights protection protests' (i.e. the knowledge that animal testing is a subject of moral debate and is protested by people who wish to protect animals' rights to humane treatment). This kind of knowledge is generally not acquired through direct experience (relatively few people have participated in, or been a first-hand witness to, animal rights protection protests). Rather, it is communicated 'second hand' in the form of *stories*, through newspaper, radio, and television accounts, person-to-person discussions, explanations to children or cultural outsiders, and so forth. Although such stories recount particular circumstances, they also promote schematic background knowledge. The knowledge that would allow one to arrive at the above interpretation of the shampoo bottle text might be narrativized something like this:

> Starting in the 1970s some people demonstrated their concern about the treatment of laboratory animals. One way they showed their concern was by not buying products that required testing on animals before they could

be sold. In order to reassure customers that it was all right to buy their product, companies that didn't test their products on animals said so on their labels.

The person who knows this is in a position to interpret the shampoo bottle as outlined above, which may influence his or her decision to purchase it:

> This product says it was not tested on animals, so I don't need to worry about whether any animals were mistreated while the product was being developed. It's okay for me to buy this product.

This brings us to the ideological component of the discourse derived from the text, in which liberal social activism (protection of animal rights) is placed in opposition to conservative scientific and commercial interests. Even the reader unsympathetic to the cause of animal rights protesters, who resists being positioned as a 'liberal' reader, will nevertheless recognize the intended alignment of this product with a liberal, 'politically correct' value system. Ironically, this intention is ultimately designed to enhance the commercial interests of the shampoo company, which in effect 'cashes in' on consumers' liberal attitudes concerning animal rights.

We have elaborated at length one particular interpretation of the shampoo bottle text. But is that the only interpretation possible? Someone who is unfamiliar with animal rights protests might interpret the message from the standpoint of medical safety. The message might be 'use at your own risk: this product has not yet been tested on animals'. Another interpretation, particularly plausible for someone who is familiar with shampoo but who does not have the 'animal testing' schema, might be: 'This product may not be effective in improving the sheen of your dog's coat: it has not been tested on animals.'

These latter interpretations may seem far-fetched, but they are precisely the kind of interpretations that readers can make when they are reading in a non-native language. The reason is not necessarily that they don't understand the words (although that obviously can and does happen). It may be that they do not have, or are unable to access, the particular background knowledge that the author presumed of his or her audience.

The fact that these ostensibly logical interpretations are likely to be considered 'naïve', 'quirky', or 'silly' by many acculturated speakers of American or British English, attests to the importance of social dimensions of interpretation. How we design meaning from texts is constrained not only by the language of the text but also by our cultural experience, which involves the declarative and procedural knowledge we have acquired and internalized, and that we share in common with other members of discourse communities to which we belong.

One way we know how we are supposed to interpret a given text (i.e. how we know what the 'default' or 'anticipated' interpretation is in our particular culture) is from our exposure to other similar texts in our everyday experience. Just down the street from where I live, this sign is painted on the side of a beauty salon:

```
ORGANIC PERMS
NO ANIMAL TESTING/PRODUCTS
NO PETRO-CHEMICALS
526–9900
```

This advertisement activates the same 'animal testing' and 'animal rights protection' schemata that the shampoo bottle text did, reinforcing the notion that animal testing and beauty products tested on animals are undesirable things. It also introduces new, partially overlapping schemata about protecting one's health and one's environment, triggered by the terms 'organic' (commonly associated with natural, healthful food products) and 'petro-chemicals' (often associated with health risk and damage to the environment). The message is: beautiful hair need not entail either guilt or risk. We therefore modify and transform (i.e. redesign) existing schemata to accommodate their application to new contexts. Seeing similar product claims and advertisements repeatedly in stores, in magazines, and so forth leads us to develop an intertextual web of associations and meanings that allows us to interpret other similar texts 'transparently' as we encounter them—even when they are in quite different contexts. A cartoon in a computer magazine, for example, shows a computer salesman talking to a 1960s-style hippie couple. The salesman points to the computer on display and says 'It's not organic, but I can guarantee that animals were not used in its testing.'[10] The redesigning of the animal rights protection schema to accommodate its application to this ostensibly incompatible high-tech context is precisely what creates the humorous effect. Of course, if the animal rights protection schema is not available, the cartoon makes little sense.

The interpretation of short texts, such as those we have considered here, tends to rely heavily on specific reader knowledge. How might foreign language learners acquire such knowledge? Teachers' explanations are certainly an important source, especially at the early stages of language learning. But ultimately learners will need to derive background knowledge the same way native speakers do—through extensive experience dealing with spoken and written texts. The more we hear or see references to animal testing in contexts such as those above, the more the corresponding schemata become reinforced. Of course at other times when we encounter references to animal testing these particular schemata and stories may be challenged. For example, when we encounter the phrase 'animal testing' while reading a pharmaceutical company memorandum, or a journal of animal behavior, or in a textbook on veterinarian medicine, it may well evoke different associations than it did in the contexts discussed above, simply because the phrase is now embedded in a text intended for an entirely different readership. To return to Gee's notion of Discourses, discussed in Chapter 1, a given act of reading occurs within some Discourse, never outside all of them:

> *Any* way of reading ... involves apprenticeship to *some* social group that reads (acts, talks, values) in certain ways in regard to such texts (there is no neutral, asocial, apolitical reading). So the choice, in any 'literacy' program, will always be 'to what sort of social group do I intend to apprentice the learner?'
> (Gee 1996: 44)

Design and language learning

Seen in the light of the above discussion, learning a language is not so much a matter of learning 'the words of the language', as Gouin tried to do by memorizing the German dictionary, but rather, as Bakhtin (1986) described it, a 'process of *assimilation*—more or less creative—of others' words', which 'carry with them their own expression, their own evaluative tone, which we assimilate, rework, and re-accentuate' (p. 89). By 'words', we must here understand linguistic Available Designs: the phrases, idioms, aphorisms, stories, and so on that make up our language environment. These linguistic Available Designs are in turn used and interpreted in relation to schematic Available Designs that organize our declarative and procedural knowledge. This process, which Bakhtin describes as *assimilation*, goes hand in hand with the process of the learner's socialization into certain ways of using language. It is, in Gee's (1996) terms, an *apprenticeship* into particular Discourses.

At this point it is appropriate to return to the story of François Gouin. He finally did learn German and eventually became professor of German and director of the Ecole Supérieure Arago in Paris. And interestingly, the insight to which he attributes his achievement has to do with the notion of design of meaning. One day, back in his native Normandy, Gouin accompanied his three-year-old nephew on a visit to a local mill. Following their visit, Gouin noticed how the child reconstructed his experience by talking about it and by acting it out with a makeshift mill his father made from scraps of wood. For Gouin, the boy's 'setting in order' of his perceptions, the organization of his memories in a sequential series of events—first this, then that, then this, and so on—was crucial not only in transforming his knowledge of the milling process but also his knowledge of language. The boy was using new words, learnt during his visit to the mill, along with familiar ones, to reorganize a lived experience, to 'mould it into a conception of his own' (p. 37). But in the process he was also using the lived experience to explore and expand the meaning resources—the Available Designs—he possessed. Gouin described his insight as follows:

> I saw that to express each new perception, it was necessary . . . to employ the whole of the vocabulary already acquired. Language appeared to me under the form of an embroidery, where the same thread ran from end to end, always identical in itself, yet nevertheless creating constantly varying designs by combining with its neighbors.
> (p. 47)

Whereas Gouin had 'remembered' one abstract word after another, his nephew had reconstructed and redesigned his experience via utterances and actions. 'To learn a language', Gouin concluded, 'was to translate into this language not Ollendorf, not Goethe, not Virgil, not Homer, but the vast book of our own individuality' (p. 49).

How Gouin applied his insight to language pedagogy is perhaps somewhat less interesting. Based on the mill episode, Gouin developed a system of verbal 'series' for actions such as chopping wood, lighting a fire, pumping water, and so forth, designed to allow learners to relate verb phrases to individual experiential perceptions.[11] By Gouin's claim, it was the exploration of such 'series' with children in a German family that enabled him to speak, understand, dream, and lecture in German within less than three months. While Gouin's method acknowledges the necessity of mastering basic language forms, sometimes in semi-rote fashion, the limitations of reducing experiences to event sequences and verb lists are obvious. Nevertheless, Gouin's original insight about the dynamic interplay between language, experience, and cognition is important.

To summarize the argument, language learning both promotes and depends upon learners' ability to design meaning. Children learning their native language gradually acquire Available Designs (grammar, vocabulary, formal conventions, schemata, and so on) by experiencing and using language in meaningful situations. It is in the very process of creating and transforming meanings via existing resources that new resources can be produced and, in turn, become available for subsequent acts of meaning design.

One might reasonably wonder, however, to what extent the story of Gouin's nephew's acquisition of language as a *child* is applicable to foreign language acquisition. After all, adolescent and adult learners have already acquired a set of Available Designs in their native language. How might one accommodate the notion of Available Designs to foreign language learners?

Awareness of design

Adolescent and adult foreign language learners are not blank slates—they are knowledgeable about 'how to do things with words' and are already familiar with the technical and conceptual aspects of literacy in their native language. What they need to learn, besides vocabulary and grammar, is in what ways conventions and practices of communication and literacy in the new language and culture might differ from those they already know. They may need to learn a new writing system (or at least new rules of spelling and punctuation), new conventions governing written genres (for example, interpersonal correspondence versus academic prose), as well as new social practices (for example, oral recitation of texts, ways of discussing texts). In acquiring these new literacy conventions and practices (or modified forms of familiar ones), it is helpful for learners to be *reminded* of the many Available Designs they already have, and to *develop greater awareness* of what they do as readers and writers in their native language in order to apply those resources to their foreign language reading and writing and to become more cognizant of the specific reasons for their difficulties.

Of course, some of the Available Designs that language learners attempt to employ won't work in the new language. They are 'false friends' that can lead to inappropriate forms of expression or misunderstandings. How can learners determine which Available Designs are functional allies and which need modification or replacement in the context of the new language and culture?

Second language acquisition studies suggest that when learners actively notice morphological and syntactic features of the language around them, *and* compare those features with those they habitually use themselves (called 'noticing the gap'), they tend to incorporate those structures into their own language use (Schmidt and Frota 1986; Schmidt 1990; Ellis 1993; Ellis 1994). I would offer as a hypothesis that the principle of *noticing* applies to learners' acquisition of literacy as well. By noticing the gaps between their own and others' interpretations of texts, by noticing the gaps between their own and others' writing on a given topic, language students learn to become more aware of the linguistic, rhetorical, and cognitive options available to them as readers and writers. If this is true, then an important goal for language programs with a focus on literacy is to systematically encourage students to notice relationships between particular language uses and meaning. Written language, because of its graphic form and its permanence, lends itself particularly well to the facilitation of noticing and subsequent reflection.

And, of course, conscious encounters with new Available Designs in the second language that are incorporated into the learner's repertoire can lead to a greater range of options in one's native language as well. As one intermediate-level French student remarked,

> We learnt how to do *explication de texte* in my French class, and at first I didn't really get why we were doing that . . . but I tried using it as a way of organizing an essay in my history class and it worked out really well. My professor loved it and I got the highest grade in the class on that essay.

An important difference between academic and naturalistic language learning is that Available Designs are generally made explicit in the classroom in order to expedite students' learning. While relatively simple elements such as verb conjugations can be effectively handled by systematic presentation followed by practice, more complex text level structures often lend themselves better to a comparative approach, in which the teacher encourages students to notice similarities and differences in how the two languages work.

Available Designs: resources for making meaning

So far the argument has been that communication involves the creative use of a stock of socially-shared linguistic and cultural resources. It is precisely because these resources are shared, however, that their use is not totally free but governed by conventions valued by the members of any given social group. Communication is thus, as Harold Rosen puts it, a matter of 'playing the game of free choice according to the rules' (1985: 14). How might we visualize the relationship among these resources and constraints in the process of reading and writing?

Figure 2.2 offers one way of conceptualizing literacy as design. At the center is the text and a constellation of Available Designs drawn upon in its production or reception. The circular arrows around the text are meant to represent one's cyclical back-and-forth movement between Available Designs and text during reading or writing. That is, Available Designs provide the initial knowledge, know-how, and patterns that allow reading or writing to begin. But once reading or writing has begun, the text itself will influence many of the reader/writer's subsequent decisions and choices. Furthermore,

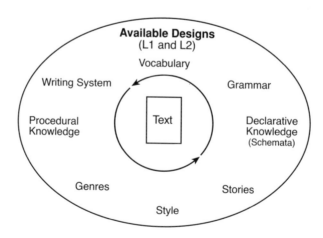

Figure 2.2:   Available Designs in literacy

acts of reading and writing commonly lead to modification or transformation of certain Available Designs, adding a developmental dimension to the model. For example, one's procedural know-how of the 'reading process' or the 'writing process' is formed in the act of reading and writing. Vocabulary, grammar, organizational schemata, and spelling knowledge may also be enhanced. Of particular importance is the modification and transformation of one's existing declarative knowledge through reading and writing.

What is not represented in Figure 2.2, however, is the fact that reading and writing are not singular, unitary constructs, but rather culture-, context-, and task-dependent constructs. We can account for such factors by adding two surrounding layers of 'communicative' and 'sociocultural' context, as shown in Figure 2.3. Both of these additional layers play an important role in shaping the interaction between Available Designs and text in any given act of reading or writing. Within the 'immediate and eventual communicative contexts' layer, for example, the topic will influence the extent to which the reader or writer can draw on existing knowledge. The kind of literacy task will influence the relative emphasis put on content as opposed to form, and the degree to which one's familiarity with genres and styles can be put to use. The physical situation of the reader/writer determines the availability of time, reference materials, and other resources and may influence the degree to

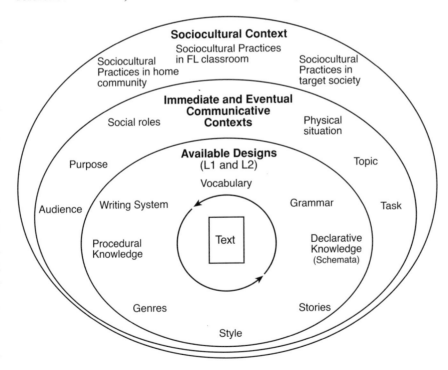

Figure 2.3:   Available Designs and contextual layers in literacy

which concentration and care can be applied to the task. The purpose of one's reading or writing and for whom one is doing it are also key to decisions concerning how one will proceed.

These dimensions of communicative context are in turn influenced by the larger social context, represented by the outermost layer of Figure 2.3. In the case of learning a foreign language, the social context of literacy involves at least three influences: the student's home language community, the target language community (which the learner may or may not wish to join), and the foreign language classroom community, which is usually a subset of the home culture educational community. The purposes and practices of literacy that one is familiar with in the context of one's home community and culture will be particularly influential when learning to write in a new culture and community. However, because of differences in functions and conventions of writing across cultures and discourse communities (as well as differences across schooling traditions), it cannot be assumed that because students can read and write in their native language, they can necessarily do so effectively in a second language when they have simply learnt a set of words and structures, or even a set of process skills. What must also be taken into account are epistemological considerations that not only underlie rhetorical conventions, but even more importantly frame what writing, reading, and learning are all about in a given community and culture. All these dimensions of the meaning design model will be elaborated in greater detail in subsequent chapters.

Conclusion

In this chapter I have presented communicative ability and literacy as the essential bases of foreign language study in academic contexts. Moreover, I have argued that literacy and communicative ability are not divergent goals but are in fact intrinsically intertwined as dimensions of meaning design. Both involve new learning but also a considerable degree of restructuring and redesigning of existing knowledge structures and meaning resources (Available Designs). One implication of this point for classroom teaching is that language learners' reading and writing difficulties may not be due so much to a lack of vocabulary and syntax knowledge *per se* (although these certainly play a crucial role), but rather to different understandings of the world, of communication, and of literacy.

In Chapter 3, we will explore the nature of Available Designs in greater depth, focusing attention on the 'inner circle' represented in Figure 2.2. Then in Part Two of the book we will examine how reading and writing can be modeled as meaning design processes, taking into account the larger contextual and sociocultural layers represented in Figure 2.3.

Notes

1 Consider the striking similarity between Gouin's experience and the following passage from Eva Hoffman's *Lost in Translation*; 'The words I learn now don't stand for things in the same unquestioned way they did in my native tongue. "River" in Polish was a vital sound, energized with the essence of riverhood, of my rivers, of my being immersed in rivers. 'River' in English is cold—a word without an aura. It has no accumulated associations for me, and it does not give off the radiating haze of connotations. It does not evoke' (Hoffman 1989: 106).

2 Cohen *et al.* (1979), for example, found that their English for Specific Purposes students spent from three to six times more time reading passages than did native English speakers.

3 This is a headline from the Sports section of the *San Francisco Examiner*, describing a resounding defeat of the Stanford Cardinals by the Washington Huskies in a crucial football game.

4 The American linguist Leonard Bloomfield (1933) elaborated the groundwork for structural methods of language instruction culminating in the audiolingual method of the 1940s and 1950s. Strongly influenced by the work of behavioral psychologists such as John Watson and B. F. Skinner, structural methodologists emphasized the mastery of a language by means of dialogues and pattern drills designed to condition learners to produce automatic, correct responses to linguistic stimuli. Contrastive analyses of the structural differences between the native and target languages (see Lado 1957) provided the basis for the careful selection, gradation, and presentation of structures which were to be memorized for language mastery.

5 The text-as-container metaphor is exemplified by utterances such as 'This story is full of meaning'. 'Don't load a sentence with more ideas than it can hold'. 'We'll try to unpack the meaning of this text'. 'His words were empty/hollow'. 'This essay lacks content'.

6 David Olson has, in his most recent book (Olson 1994), changed his perspective on the autonomy of textual meaning.

7 It is important to distinguish the claim that much of our language use is not literal from a claim that language use is ambiguous and that meaning is therefore in some sort of essential flux. The point is that people generally have little difficulty interpreting nonliteral uses of language. If I say 'It's getting late' to my wife at a party, it is unlikely that she will interpret my utterance as nothing more than an observation of the hour. We are all well socialized in interpretive conventions of language use that prevent us from interpreting utterances in all possible ways—including literal ones. These conventions have been explored in Speech Act theory (Searle 1969; Grice 1975).

8 Sometimes it is conscious avoidance of a particular word that shapes sociopolitical realities. In June 1994, for example, the Clinton adminstration instructed its spokespeople not to describe the killing of up to 400,000 Tutsis by Hutus in Rwanda as 'genocide' even though the secretary-general of the United Nations had described the killings as a deliberate attempt to exterminate an ethnic group. Because use of the word genocide would entail moral responsibility to take action, the U.S. government's avoidance of the term was in effect a decision to avoid military intervention and a potentially long-term entanglement in Rwanda.

9 Bakhtin's distinction between sentences and utterances is useful in understanding this point. *Sentences* can be identical in form and repeated, but *utterances*, because of their contextualized nature, can never be repeated—attempts at repetition always produce new utterances, even in cases of direct quotation (Bakhtin 1986: 108). As the New London Group points out, some uses of language involve closer reproduction of Available Designs than others (for example, writing a form letter versus a personal letter; composing a classified advertisement versus creating a magazine advertisement for a new product).

10 *MacWeek* vol. 10, no. 28, July 22, 1996, p. 21.

11 The exercise 'The maid chops a log of wood', for example, begins as follows:

—The maid goes and seeks her hatchet,   seeks
the maid takes a log of wood,   takes
the maid draws near to the chopping block,   draws
the maid kneels down near this block,   kneels
the maid places the log of wood upright upon this block   places . . .
(Gouin 1894: 69)

3 Available Designs in literacy

... there is always room for creativity in any discursive order, but it is attained by mastering the practice of the discourse to a degree that enables new utterances to be formed, which in turn become a part of the body of discursive models and finally effect changes in the code itself.

Robert Scholes (1985)

We can think of meaning resources, or Available Designs, as roughly organized along a continuum, with linguistic resources such as writing systems, vocabulary, grammar, and cohesion conventions at one end, and schematic resources such as rhetorical organization patterns, genres, styles, schemata, and stories at the other (see Figure 3.1). These Available Designs are all put to use in accordance with one's procedural knowledge (itself a kind of Available Design). A continuum, rather than a dichotomy, allows us to acknowledge that linguistic resources have schematic aspects, just as schematic resources have linguistic aspects. It is, furthermore, important to note that each of these Available Designs involves both a cognitive and a social component—no element is fixed and independent of the humans who determine it. In this chapter we will explore these Available Designs in greater detail and show how they can be brought to bear in the teaching of a foreign language.

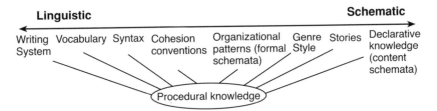

Figure 3.1: *Continuum of Available Designs on a linguistic-schematic axis*

Although it is not possible to comprehensively list here all of the many resources and conventions that constitute the Available Designs of a given social group we will focus in this chapter on the 'core' Available Designs lying within the innermost circle of Figure 2.3 presented at the end of

Chapter 2. Because procedural knowledge is a major focus of Chapters 4 to 7, I will defer its discussion to those chapters. Although I will discuss these Available Designs individually in turn, I hope to make clear that they are functionally inseparable in acts of reading and writing. It is the *interaction* of all these Available Designs, drawn upon by writers and readers operating in a given sociocultural context, that allows readers/writers to produce and interpret meaning through texts.

Linguistic resources

The most fundamental of Available Designs is language itself. The most obvious and essential difference between reading and writing in one's native language versus a foreign language is that one is operating with a new set of linguistic resources. The writing system, phonological system, lexicon, syntax, semantic relations, and pragmatic conventions of the new language may differ considerably from those of the native language, and, even in the case of closely related languages, it takes years of study for learners to develop anything near the same level of linguistic comfort that they enjoy when using their native language. In this section we will briefly and selectively discuss linguistic resources, and consider some of the ways in which learners' existing linguistic Available Designs can promote (or hinder) the development of literacy and communicative ability in a new language.

Writing systems and media

The first thing that strikes beginning language students is the way the new language sounds and the way it looks on paper. In academic language study, the writing system is often an immediate point of focus, as it serves as the entry point for vocabulary and grammar study.

Coulmas (1989) makes a useful distinction between writing systems, scripts, and orthographies. Writing systems are not language-specific but are differentiated by the particular ways they segment and represent language (for example, ideographic versus alphabetic writing). Scripts are particular manifestations of a given writing system (for example, Roman, Greek, Arabic, Cyrillic alphabets) and may or may not be language-specific. Orthographies are language-specific conventions (for example, accents and other marks, spelling rules) that may differentiate among varieties within the language (for example, American versus British English, Chinese versus Taiwanese, or Standard German versus Swiss-German orthographies).

From a language learning perspective, some writing systems are simpler to process and learn than others. Alphabetic and syllabary systems, for example, have small symbol inventories. Even when one must learn an entirely new script (for example, an English speaker learning Cyrillic, Greek, Persian, Arabic, or Hebrew alphabets), the task is infinitely easier than learning an ideographic system that has thousands of distinct characters. Layout and directional processing conventions can also influence the difficulty of learning. Hebrew and Arabic, for example, are written and read from right to left. Chinese and Japanese are generally written and read in columns from top to bottom, proceeding from right to left. While reading and writing tend to be slower in a second language than in the first language because of increased attentional demands, the slowing effect is likely to be most pronounced in cases where one is learning a new writing system or script—and particularly troublesome in tasks that emphasize speed, such as skimming, scanning, dictation, and note-taking.

Another potentially problematic aspect of acquiring a new writing system or script is learning the parameters of variability in written forms. In all languages, written symbols often assume multiple forms depending on their position in a text or whether they are printed or handwritten. The printed letter 'a' for example, appears as 'A' at the beginning of a sentence or a name, and usually appears as something resembling 'a' in handwriting. In Arabic, some letters can assume up to four different shapes depending on their position in a word (Thompson-Panos and Thomas-Ruzic 1983). As shown in Figure 3.2, Chinese characters can be written in five styles of increasing degrees of cursivity: 'small seal', 'scribal', 'regular', 'running', and 'cursive'. To the uninitiated reader, the differences across these styles are much more striking than the resemblances, especially when one compares the endpoints of the stylistic continuum (i.e. 'small seal' and 'cursive').

Figure 3.2:   The sentence 'Gold can be found in Lishui' written in five styles (from left to right): small seal, scribal, regular, running, and cursive (Coulmas 1989: 96)

As suggested in Chapter 1, familiarity with a language's writing system is essential for literacy, but that familiarity is useful only to the extent that one knows the *language* which the writing system represents. This is because any given writing system encodes only selected features of a language and leaves others unspecified. For example, Semitic alphabets, such as Arabic and

Hebrew, consist only of consonants. While vowels are indicated by marks above or below the line of writing in pedagogical materials, these vowel markers are usually omitted, forcing the reader to rely extensively on the linguistic context to disambiguate word meanings (Pei 1965: 99). The Chinese writing system, on the other hand, makes no reference to the sound system at all and thus provides no clues for oral pronunciation. In sum, writing 'works' only when readers can compensate for what is *not* represented. As Coulmas puts it,

> The abstractness of writing is possible and functional because the typical reader—that is, the reader for whom the script is made—knows the language in which the written message is coded, and can thus rely on the redundancies of the language as an aid for deciphering (reading) written expressions which represent speech only incompletely or vaguely. (1989: 47)

Use of a writing system, then, requires familiarity not only with the script, but also with appropriate strategies that allow one to fill in unexpressed information, based on one's knowledge of the language.

The problem of compensating for what is not represented in a writing system extends beyond surface language structures. In his historical analysis of literacy, Olson (1994) concludes that, although different writing systems bring different dimensions of language into focus, they all succeed quite well in expressing what Austin (1962) called *locutionary acts* (i.e. what was said). However, one thing that no writing system does adequately, Olson argues, is specify the *illocutionary force* of such acts (i.e. how what was said was intended). Whereas speech generally provides multiple overt clues to the illocutionary force of an utterance (for example, through stress, intonation, tone of voice, as well as gestures, facial expressions, body language, and other features of the situational context), writing is much more limited in this capacity. Should we, for example, interpret 'Riders will mount their horses' as a prediction, as part of a future narrative, or as a command? Knowledge of the written code alone does not suffice—we must rely on a situational context, either real or imagined, in order to interpret this sentence. An essential problem of reading, then, is compensating for the absence of an immediate, shared context of communication which might clarify communicative intentions.

Olson's point meshes well with many teachers' observations that their students are generally quite good at identifying 'what the text says' but they often have a good deal of trouble understanding what it means—precisely because this is often not explicitly encoded in the text. While the point is well taken, it is nevertheless extremely important to bring to students' attention the various linguistic and graphic devices that writing *does* offer to express illocutionary force, however limited these may be. To convey emphasis in written English, for example, one can use typographical devices such as capitalization, italic and bold font styles, underlining, centering, or punctuation (for example, exclamation marks and asterisks). One can also use syntactic devices such as cleft constructions to simulate the effects of spoken stress (for example, 'It was a mushroom that Alice ate' compared with 'Alice ate a *mushroom*'). Verbs such as 'command', 'whisper', 'ask', 'bark', 'yell' and adverbs like 'sharply', 'soothingly', 'jokingly', and 'gravely' provide lexical means to suggest the tone of voice intended for stretches of written direct speech.

Punctuation, such as question marks and exclamation points, performs a similar function to intonation and stress in spoken language. Commas provide important clues about how the elements of a sentence are segmented. The phrase 'However you need to do it' means something very different from 'However, you need to do it'. The choice of dashes, commas, or parentheses can either accentuate or attenuate the importance of an embedded phrase:

> Linguistic communication—both oral and written—is multimodal in nature.
> Linguistic communication (both oral and written) is multimodal in nature.

And of course, we could further attenuate the embedded phrase by removing it from the sentence altogether and putting it in a footnote. It is important to recognize that punctuation conventions vary somewhat across languages. For example, Berman (1975: 249) points out that commas are normally required before 'that' clauses in Hebrew (for example, 'Some of them claimed, that the idea was impossible'), but that Hebrew does not observe the English convention of distinguishing restrictive and non-restrictive clauses by commas ('All the children, who do well in school, love to read' versus 'All the children who do well in school love to read'). Such differences in punctuation conventions are important to teach, since they can lead to confusion if learners are not aware of them.

The recent explosion in the use of computer-mediated communication has given rise to the use of typographical 'smileys' or 'emoticons' to simulate some of the paralinguistic features of face-to-face communication. For example, in the following e-mail message a committee chair is trying to persuade a colleague to accept a duty that no one else wants:

> Several people on the board have mentioned your name in regard to this. I agree that you'd be the ideal person to handle it. :-)

The appended :-) suggests that this is a 'friendly' act of persuasion: 'I know I'm twisting your arm, but won't you please consider doing this?' Emoticons sometimes differ across cultures, however. Consider the differences between emoticons used in Europe and the U.S. and those used in Japan, shown in Table 3.1.

	Japan		U.S. and Europe	
		Smiles		
Regular smile	(^_^)		Regular smile	:-)
Very happy	(^o^)		Very happy	:-))
Banzai smiley	\(^_^)/		Wink	;-)
Girl's smile	(^.^)			
		Other emotions or states		
Cold sweat	(^^;)		Angry	:-II
Excuse me	(^o^;>)		Sad	:-(
Exciting	(*^o^*)		Wow!	:-o

Table 3.1:   Differences between Japanese and Western emoticons
(Based on Pollack 1996)

The Japanese 'smiley' is more immediately recognizable as a face than the Western version because it is right side up rather than rotated to the left. But because the 'mouth' line does not curve up at the ends, it is less obviously a 'smile'. Particularly interesting is the 'girl's smile', in which the mouth is represented by a dot, reflecting the politeness norm of women not baring their teeth in a grin. The 'banzai' smiley represents arms raised in an ebullient cheer. 'Cold sweat' and 'excuse me' (the most popular Japanese emoticons) use the semi-colon for dripping sweat and the > symbol to represent the bent arm of an embarrassed or apologetic person scratching the back of his or her head. According to Pollack (1996), the Japanese use emoticons more frequently than Westerners do in their electronic communications, perhaps because of their habitual use of pictograms, or perhaps because of their particular reliance on facial expressions and contextual features to express what is not explicitly expressed verbally. As one official at a Japanese online information service put it, 'If it's only words, it's hard to express your feeling to the other party' (Pollack 1996: C5). Pollack points out, however, that the Japanese tend not to use emoticons that express emotions such as surprise, anger, or sadness, as they might potentially offend one's correspondent. In a Japanese foreign language classroom, such differences in textual/communicative conventions could provide an interesting starting point for exploring underlying differences between the native and target cultures.

Layout of print and typographical features can also provide important clues to meaning. Waller (1987) characterizes features such as headings, paragraphing, formatting, and typeface as 'macropunctuation at the discourse level' (p. 91), which directs readers' strategies and explains the organizational structure of a given text. Consider the difficulty you might have processing the following bit of text:

It is the *interaction* of all these Available Designs, drawn upon by writers and readers operating in a given sociocultural context, that allows readers/writers to produce and interpret meaning through texts. Linguistic resources The most fundamental of Available Designs is language itself.

When it first appeared at the beginning of this section, however, it probably caused no difficulty at all because its particular formatting made the relationships among the elements clear (i.e. ending sentence, new section heading, first sentence of new section). Bernhardt (1991) showed that some of her American students of German had difficulty identifying who was writing to whom in a German letter because of errors in interpreting the formatting conventions of letters. Formatting conventions are clearly elements that teachers should bring to language students' attention, particularly in light of the fact that they sometimes differ across languages (Gremmo 1985; Régent 1985).

Finally, it is important to recognize that the physical location of texts can influence how they are interpreted. One might argue that a word is a word, wherever it might appear. But a moment's reflection leads one to realize that the physical situation of written words—whether on a computer screen, on a printed page, traced in a schoolchild's notebook, or displayed on a billboard—influences how we understand them and the reasons for their being written. The physical situation tells us something about how to read writing by providing clues about the relevant arena of language use (public versus private), the possible communicative intent (whether it is meant to inform us, persuade us, caution us, inspire us, touch us emotionally, and so on), and its relative permanence (for example, skywriting versus an inscription in stone). The physical situation can consequently influence our goals and actions: reading the word 'coffee' on a roadsign versus on a menu versus on a bag makes us do different things in response to our reading.

The point is that both speech and writing provide verbal and nonverbal clues to illocutionary force, but the clues are different—because speech and writing involve different media and are used in different social contexts. Language learners need to learn how speech and writing work differently to support the tacit relationship between speakers/listeners and readers/writers in acts of communication. They also need to learn what devices are appropriate for different contexts of written communication. Using 'smileys' in a formal letter or essay, for example, will not likely impress employers or teachers.

Learning to read and write thus involves a great deal more than mastery of the writing system—it involves a broader ability to understand relationships of visual and verbal forms in contexts of written communication. It involves creating 'discourse worlds' mediated by a variety of linguistic and non-linguistic devices and conventions. Teachers play an important role in promoting students' understanding of these devices and conventions so they can use them appropriately to improve their ability to read and write in a second or foreign language.

Vocabulary

Words loom large in the minds of novice- or intermediate-level language learners. While familiar words inspire confidence, unfamiliar words breed uncertainty and frustration. This is particularly so in the areas of reading and listening, for although learners can *say* quite a lot in a language when they have only 1,000–2,000 words, they must have a considerably larger vocabulary in order to *understand* most unsimplified speech or writing (Saragi, Nation, and Meister 1978).

Among the first words that beginning foreign language learners recognize are those that resemble words they know in their native language, and students of cognate languages can make substantial use of their existing lexicon, especially once they become aware of how the morphological system of the new language relates to that of the native language.[1] English-speaking learners of Spanish, for example, can easily recognize that the suffix -*dad* (for example, *brutalidad, dignidad, prosperidad*) corresponds to -*ty* in English, but they must learn that the correspondence is not perfect (for example, beauty–*belleza*). Learners of French find it helpful to know that the circumflex accent (^) often indicates a deleted *s* (for example, *honnête*, honest; *mât*, mast; *île*, isle) or that an initial *é*- sometimes indicates a similar word in English beginning with *s*- (for example, *étudier*, study; *épouse*, spouse; *épeler*, spell). When learners see relationships such as these they are not learning isolated items, but rather the workings of a lexical *system* that can help them predict meaning.

But recognition can mask differences. A native English speaker might easily understand *un personnage truculent* to mean a cruel or pugnacious person, rather than a lively, colorful individual. 'Coin', 'crayon', 'figure', 'large', and 'sale' are very common words in both English and French, and yet they have entirely different meanings in the two languages. Teachers can play a crucial role by alerting students to specific cases of false cognates as they come up in assigned readings, and by encouraging students to test all 'assumed' meanings against the context established by the text.

A more general problem is that many beginning learners assume a one-to-one correspondence between words in their native language and words in the second language, what Bland, Noblitt, Armington, and Gay (1990) call the 'naive lexical hypothesis'. This assumption is reinforced by textbook glossaries, which generally provide one-word translations. Sometimes, of course, there is no lexical equivalent, as when a student looks up the Spanish word for 'would', only to find a note about the use of imperfect or conditional forms of verbs. Other times, such as when a student asks the French word for 'privacy', paraphrases are required (although most student dictionaries will still offer one-word glosses such as *solitude*). And, of course, some terms (for example, 'fraternities', 'Ivy League') are so specifically tied to a particular culture that they can only be made clear through lengthy explanation. Just as problematic, and more subtle, however, are the many common L1–L2 'equivalencies' such as 'bathroom' and *salle de bain*, whose semantic fields overlap but only partially. Again, the teacher can play a key role in explaining such differences.

A related problem is understanding the affective connotations of words. When we use language we don't just refer to the world; we express and interpret particular *perspectives* on the world. For example, in pointing to a man standing in a hotel lobby I can refer to him as 'that gentleman', 'that person', 'that guy', 'that brother', 'that bozo', 'that nerd', or any of a number of other ways—each expressing a different relationship and a different attitude. It is relatively easy for language students to learn the dictionary definitions of words, but much more difficult to learn their affective connotations.[2] With dictionaries I can translate 'house' as *casa* or *maison* or *Haus* or *nyumba* or *rumah*, or *hale*, but that does not mean that I understand how native speakers interpret or represent the *meanings* in their respective languages. In traditional language classes, there is a tendency to limit vocabulary lessons to making connections between words and their referents, leaving aside their connotational auras. This is understandable, if for no other reason than that the affective and cultural connotations of words are often difficult to explain in a systematic fashion. It is nevertheless important to recognize that sometimes it is only the cultural connotations of words, not their referential meaning, that matters in understanding utterances (for example, 'What a *magpie*!' in reference to a chatterbox).

One of the reasons that words' connotative meanings do not readily lend themselves to systematic explanation is that they are generally contingent on the particular words that surround them. Everybody knows, for example, that 'good' is a general descriptive label for things that are of high quality, positive, approved of, or appreciated. But when we use 'good' to describe things, it takes on subtle additional meanings. In an utterance such as 'She's really a good person', it connotes someone who is generous, kind, thoughtful, honest, and reliable. When we say 'She's a really good student', however, the connotation shifts in the direction of 'bright', 'motivated', 'hard working', 'organized', 'assiduous', 'cooperative', and so on. In the context of describing a story (for example, 'that's a really good story'), 'good' generally means 'interesting' and 'involving'. In other words, what makes a *person* 'good' is not the same set of qualities that makes a *student* 'good', or a *story* 'good'. And of course, when uttered in a sarcastic tone, 'good' does not mean good at all. A good dictionary (i.e. one with multiple examples showing subtle shades of meaning) can be of some help here. What is most helpful, however, is the careful guidance of a teacher, as well as extensive and intensive experience with texts. It is ultimately by seeing and hearing words in actual contexts of use—by 'assimilating others' words,' as Bakhtin put it—that learners will be able to acquire their connotative meanings.

And *hearing* is important. Knowledge of a language's sound system is obviously essential in speech, but it is also important in reading, and especially the reading of poetry. Poems' 'design of meaning' often relies heavily on the associations evoked by particular sounds, rhythms, rhymes, and alliterations. Consider, for example, the first stanza of Guillaume Apollinaire's poem 'Le Pont Mirabeau':

> Sous le pont Mirabeau coule la Seine
>> Et nos amours
>> Faut-il qu'il m'en souvienne
> La joie venait toujours après la peine

Here the repetition of rounded vowels (/u/, /o/, /õ/) and liquid consonants (l, r, m, n) reinforces, at the level of sound, both the lexical reference to the flowing river and the theme of fluidity of time.

In sum, vocabulary involves multidimensional knowledge of words. Although students must certainly learn basic word meanings, they must also learn how those basic meanings are contingent on actual use. They must develop a sense of how words can be put together appropriately, how context may affect their connotational auras, how they may be used metaphorically, and so on.[3] This is obviously a long-term, gradual process—one that is best facilitated in foreign language study by reading, writing, and talking about texts. Seen in this light, the relationship between vocabulary and reading and writing is circular: one needs vocabulary to read and write effectively, but one also learns a good deal of one's vocabulary through the process of reading and writing. In order for this circular process to be productive, however, other Available Designs such as syntax, rhetorical conventions, and cultural knowledge must come into play.

Syntax

In order to use words to produce and understand sentences, students need to know the rules that govern syntactic relations and clause structure. This is particularly important in learning to deal with written language since *syntactic* resources are frequently used to achieve rhetorical effects that are achieved by *paralinguistic* means in speech. In the early stages, language learners tend to focus their attention on content words and to neglect structural clues (for example, Cohen, *et al.* 1979; Bernhardt 1987). Consequently they are often unable to grasp the overall meaning or purpose of a text, even if they know the meanings of the individual words that compose it. Teachers can be of immense help in this regard by bringing learners' attention to key words or phrases that signal relationships between elements in a sentence. For example, in English, 'if . . . then', 'because', and 'by virtue of' can alert the reader to causal relationships; 'although', 'but', 'despite' suggest contrast; 'after', 'before', 'while' indicate temporal relationships; and 'compared to', 'like', 'unlike' suggest relationships of comparison.[4]

But explicit item learning is not enough. A significant problem, of course, is that these kinds of propositional relationships are not always overtly expressed through lexical signaling of this kind. Teachers must therefore help learners to understand how subordinate constructions can also be used to encode certain relations, as in these sentences:

> Certain he would fail the exam, John skipped school   [reason]
> on Friday.
> Her cup of tea finished, Sylvia opened the newspaper.   [sequence]
> Arriving at the top of the stairs, Dagobert saw the corpse.   [simultaneity]

Students' ability to distinguish subordinate and main clauses can also help them to determine the relative importance of pieces of information in the text—what is backgrounded and what is foregrounded. Their sensitivity to such weightings is as important to comprehension as their understanding of the meanings of the individual words making up the text.

Basic word order differences between L1 and L2 are, of course, an important consideration in language learning. Verb-Subject-Object (VSO), Subject-Verb-Object (SVO), and Subject-Object-Verb (SOV) are the most common orders typologically, but Thompson (1978) has shown that some languages follow these general patterns more rigidly than others. English, for example, is a relatively rigid SVO language, whereas Russian and French are more flexible SVO languages. Odlin (1989: 87) cites research showing that adult learners tend to make more errors in production (speaking and writing) when word order in their native language is more flexible than in the second language (for example, a French learner of English who says, 'It think it's very good, the sport.'). Conversely, learners tend to make more errors of comprehension (listening and reading) when their native language word order is more rigid than that of the second language.

When noun-adjective order is variable, meaning differences ensue: in French, an *ancienne maîtresse* (former mistress) should not be confused with a *maîtresse ancienne* (elderly mistress). Conversely, in languages with fixed noun modifier placement, word order can clarify meaning when both words can be used either as a noun or an adjective, allowing a reader of English to distinguish a 'prize academic' from an 'academic prize' or 'discourse research' from 'research discourse'.

Complex noun phrases can be a source of processing difficulty. In English, nominalizations such as 'increased hormone production rate' can be impenetrable to ESL readers until they are broken down into series of simple statements: the human body produces hormones; hormones are produced at a rate; this rate can be increased. Berman (1984) found that heavy noun phrases in English sentences such as 'That the note of fear in his parents' voice is uncontrollable is not understood by the child' were difficult to understand by Hebrew-speaking learners who thought that 'is uncontrollable' was the main verb. The teacher's role in clarifying the kernel structure of such sentences is crucial; in this case, the students' confusion was immediately resolved when the instructor framed the problem as follows: 'Well, there is something that the child does not understand. What doesn't the child understand?' (p. 149).

The transitivity structure of clauses and sentences is another important, if often neglected, consideration. For example, 'He drinks' has different connotations from 'He drinks a glass of wine', just as 'The vase broke' presents a useful alternative to the self-incriminating 'I broke the vase' (Simpson 1993). Identifying who does what to whom, and how it is represented grammatically, with agency highlighted or suppressed, is an important ongoing task for language learners to pursue, as it teaches them that language never refers to the world in a purely neutral, 'objective' way, but rather encodes speakers' and writers' particular perspectives on the world.

Finally, learners need to understand how sentence structure is influenced by the semantic properties of verbs. Who does the 'going' in each of the following sentences?

John told me where to go.
John asked me where to go.

As these various examples suggest, syntax and vocabulary interact with one another. Once one moves beyond the level of individual, isolated words, the question of 'lexical meaning' becomes inextricably intertwined with questions of structure. Research in second language reading (for example, Barnett 1986) largely supports the view that the respective contributions of vocabulary knowledge and syntactic knowledge to learners' text comprehension are interrelated, not separate. Consequently, our teaching of reading must attend not only to both vocabulary and syntax, but also to the complex interactions between the two. The importance of interelationships among elements also extends to the important, but frequently confused, notions of cohesion and coherence.

Cohesion and coherence

In order to discuss cohesion and coherence, it is necessary to return to the terms text and discourse, mentioned in the introduction and in Chapter 1. To use a construction metaphor, if words are the basic materials—the 'nuts', 'bolts', 'beams', and 'mortar'—and clauses and sentences are the 'walls', 'rooms', and 'hallways', then texts are the end-products: the whole structures recognizable as 'houses', 'offices', 'churches', 'hospitals', 'towers', 'sculptures', and so on.[5] We attribute meaning to these whole structures (and their parts) when we relate them to their physical and social contexts, associating them with functions they serve or experiences we have had in or around the same structures or those similar in kind. We can think of discourse as this meaningful linkage between text and context and experience. So when we read or write we are of course concerned with text (i.e. the words and the structural and semantic relationships among them). But we are also vitally concerned with discourse—the functional and pragmatic relationships that we create to dynamically link text, context, and knowledge in order to produce meaning.

Although cohesion and coherence both imply unity and connectedness, the essential difference between the terms is that cohesion operates in texts, and coherence operates in discourse.

To be more precise, *cohesion* has to do with overt syntactic and semantic dependencies within texts. One of the most common cohesive devices is the use of pronouns. For example, in the text 'Don't cheat! It can cost you a grade', the pronoun 'it' provides the cohesive link across sentences by referring to an implied noun 'cheating'. Halliday and Hasan (1976) outline five categories of cohesion, which include: *reference* (for example, John was exhausted. *He* had worked three double-shifts in a row); *substitution* (for example, Are you coming? I guess *so*); *ellipsis* (for example, I read your paper but not *Patrick's*); *conjunctions* ('and', 'but', 'because', 'then', and so on); and *lexical cohesion* (for example, use of reiteration *car . . . car*, synonyms or metonyms *car . . . vehicle*, or collocation *car . . . driver*).

Although such devices in principle facilitate understanding by marking relationships among elements of a text, passages that are dense in co-reference markers can often be difficult to process for non-native readers (Demel 1990). A useful exercise in such cases is to have students circle all the pronouns and other cohesive devices they can find, and then to underline their co-referents, drawing arrows to link the two, as illustrated in Figure 3.3. In this particular passage, the teacher could show how most of the marked items point back, either directly or indirectly, to *l'égalité des conditions*—the pivotal phrase in the passage. This kind of exercise thus helps students to see concretely how identifying pronominalization and co-reference patterns can often clarify the thematic structure of a text.

One point not always well understood by language learners is that the co-referential relations marked by the use of pronouns and other devices are *semantic* as well as syntactic in nature. Consider, for example, how the respective referents of 'they' and 'them' shift from cops/robbers to robbers/cops in the following two sentences:

The cops chased the robbers. They caught them.
The cops chased the robbers. They eluded them.
(Halliday and Hasan 1976: 310)

Excerpt from Alexis de Toqueville, *De la démocratie en Amérique* (Vol. 1, pp. 1–2)

Parmi les objets nouveaux qui, pendant mon séjour aux
Etats-Unis, ont attiré mon attention, aucun n'a plus vivement
frappé mes regards que l'égalité des conditions. Je découvris
sans peine l'influence prodigieuse qu'exerce ce premier fait sur
la marche de la société; il donne à l'esprit public une certaine
direction, un certain tour aux lois; aux gouvernants des maximes
nouvelles, et des habitudes particulières aux gouvernés.

Bientôt je reconnus que ce même fait étend son influence fort
au-delà des mœurs politiques et des lois, et qu'il n'obtient pas
moins d'empire sur la société civile que sur le gouvernement: il
crée des opinions, fait naître des sentiments, suggère des
usages et modifie tout ce qu'il ne produit pas.

Ainsi donc, à mesure que j'étudiais la société américaine, je
voyais de plus en plus, dans l'égalité des conditions, le fait
générateur dont chaque fait particulier semblait descendre, et je
le retrouvais sans cesse devant moi comme un point central où
toutes mes observations venaient aboutir.

Figure 3.3:   Exercise showing cohesive relations in a text

It is therefore important for learners to be made aware that while structure can clarify meaning, meaning can also clarify structure.

Whereas cohesion has to do with dependencies among the surface features of texts, *coherence* has to do with the unity and continuity of the discourse derived from the text—that is, the degree to which the concepts and relations that underlie the surface text are mutually relevant (Beaugrande and Dressler 1981: 4). As Enkvist (1990) has put it, coherence is what makes texts summarizable and interpretable (p. 14). Because 'mutual relevance' and 'interpretability' are ultimately matters of reader judgment, coherence cannot be considered an inherent property of a text, but rather a function of the degree to which a reader can make sense of the text (i.e. the extent to which the reader can relate the text to his or her prior experience and knowledge). It is therefore possible for a text to be tightly cohesive but not conducive to coherent discourse, as in the following example:

Madeline ran all the way to the corner of the street. In the corner she saw an ugly spider. Spiders are arachnids, and are therefore related to scorpions and ticks. Her dog used to get ticks all the time. Time, of course, is man's enemy, whereas dogs are man's best friends.

Conversely, texts can produce coherent discourse without displaying any surface cohesion:

A: That's the telephone.
B: I'm in the bath.
A: O.K.
(Widdowson 1978: 29)

Most readers would probably find it difficult to derive a coherent representation of the 'Madeline' text, despite the text's many cohesive ties, because the various propositions expressed are difficult to reconcile and unify.[6] Although the text does express a *progression* of ideas, there is no *thematization* (Fowler 1986). The 'telephone' text, on the other hand, can be realized as eminently coherent discourse in spite of its lack of cohesion *if* one can envision a mental scene that makes it possible to interpret the communicative functions of A's and B's utterances as a sequence of 'request', 'refusal', and 'acknowledgment of refusal'—in a particular cultural context. The semantic dependencies in this case lie in the implied propositions rather than in the surface text:

A: That's the telephone. (Can you answer it, please?)
B: (No, I can't answer it because) I'm in the bath.
A: O.K. (I'll answer it).
(Widdowson 1978: 29)

Coherence, then, depends on our ability to identify the tacit discursive relations that underlie and connect surface elements of a text. As suggested above, this ability depends not only on linguistic resources but also on the availability of relevant background knowledge. Consider the following three sentences:

The train to Princeton was fifteen or twenty minutes out of Penn Station, and everybody was settling into the dim blue haze of the car and the jouncing and bouncing. The roadbed was in a little better shape than it used to be. They were starting to replace the old wooden ties with concrete. (Wolfe 1987: 313)

From a structural perspective the relation among these sentences is not obvious. Each has a different subject and there is no co-referential link between 'they' in the third sentence and 'everybody' in the first sentence. But if one has knowledge of trains and experience in riding them, one is able to recognize the rich lexical cohesion (train, Penn Station, car, jouncing, bouncing, roadbed, ties, wooden, and concrete) and perceive the relations among these words: trains jounce and bounce depending on the condition of the roadbed on which the track is laid. The condition of this roadbed is improving (and therefore jouncing and bouncing is lessening) because the old, less stable, wooden ties are being replaced by highly stable concrete. It is the activation of this knowledge (i.e. 'train' and 'track maintenance' schemata) that leads the reader to infer that 'they' in the third sentence refers to railroad workers, even though none have been explicitly mentioned in the text. It is this kind of inference that leads to coherent discourse. If, on the other hand, readers do not have or are unable to access, relevant background knowledge, they will have difficulty in developing a coherent semantic representation of the text (and the text will seem to lack cohesion as well).

In the following sections we will further explore the importance of schematic knowledge-based Available Designs in the realization of texts as discourse.

Schematic resources

Formal Schemata

Schema theory, described briefly in Chapter 1, attempts to develop models of how knowledge is organized in the mind, and how it is used in acts of interpretation and understanding. A central tenet of schema theory is that people's existing knowledge is not a random assortment of facts, but rather is organized systematically in networks of knowledge structures called *schemata*. Rumelhart (1981) defined a schema as 'a kind of informal, private, unarticulated theory about the nature of events, objects, or situations which we face' (p. 9).

For our purposes it will be useful to follow Carrell and Eisterhold's (1983) distinction between *formal* and *content* schemata. Formal schemata have to do with knowledge of form-related aspects of language use, whereas content schemata have to do with topical knowledge, familiarity with real world events, and cultural notions. We have already seen a number of examples of formal schemata in the previous section on linguistic Available Designs, such as schemata for letter forms (for example, 'a' versus 'a'), punctuation and formatting conventions, and word order typologies. We will now turn to more formal schemata in the form of rhetorical organization patterns, genres, and style conventions. We will then discuss content schemata, cultural models, and stories.

Rhetorical organization patterns

Here we are concerned with underlying discourse relations that are often only subtly signaled in the surface text, sometimes making them hard to identify, especially for readers who are not yet very experienced in the language. It seems, moreover, that certain patterns of rhetorical organization are more easily processed and remembered than others. Meyer (1975), for example, found that five expository organizational patterns (collection, description, causation, problem/solution, and comparison) had differential effects on native English readers' recall of text information. Carrell (1984) tested Meyer's findings on 80 ESL readers (native speakers of Spanish, Arabic, Korean, Chinese, and Malay), using four versions of a passage about athletic coaches requiring athletes to lose body water in order to meet weight specifications. The rhetorical structure of these four versions is schematically summarized in Figure 3.4, based on Carrell (1984: 445–52):

Collection of descriptions

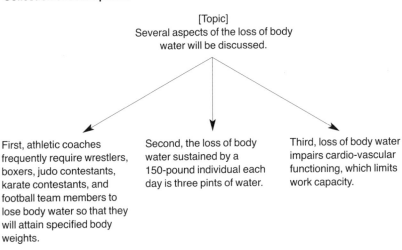

Causation

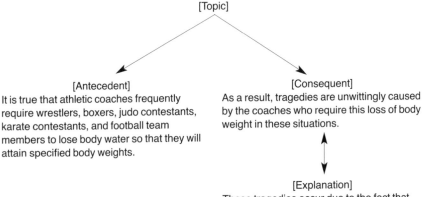

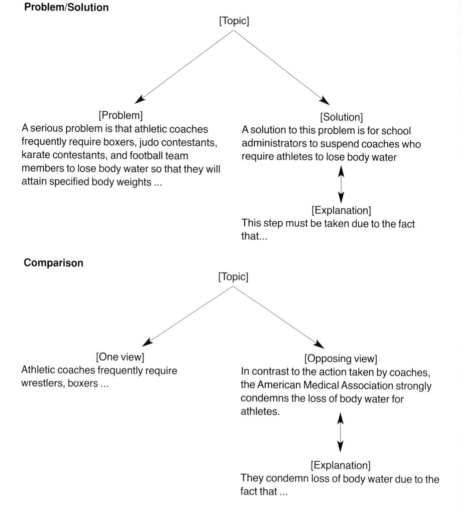

Problem/Solution

[Topic]

[Problem]
A serious problem is that athletic coaches frequently require boxers, judo contestants, karate contestants, and football team members to lose body water so that they will attain specified body weights ...

[Solution]
A solution to this problem is for school administrators to suspend coaches who require athletes to lose body water

[Explanation]
This step must be taken due to the fact that...

Comparison

[Topic]

[One view]
Athletic coaches frequently require wrestlers, boxers ...

[Opposing view]
In contrast to the action taken by coaches, the American Medical Association strongly condemns the loss of body water for athletes.

[Explanation]
They condemn loss of body water due to the fact that ...

Figure 3.4:   Four rhetorical patterns compared in Carrell (1984)

Carrell found that the 'causation', 'problem/solution', and 'comparison' passages tended to be remembered more fully than the more loosely organized 'collection of descriptions' type, but there was evidence that subjects' native language also had some influence on which organizational patterns most facilitated recall (for example, 'collection of descriptions' was facilitative for the Arabic speaking ESL students). One of the most important findings of Carrell's study was that when subjects were *aware* of the particular organizational scheme used, and utilized that same pattern in organizing their own recall protocols, they recalled substantially more information from the texts. In a follow-up study, Carrell (1985) found that explicitly teaching the 'comparison' and 'collections of descriptions' text organization patterns improved both the amount and quality of what ESL readers recalled from their reading of texts that incorporated those patterns.

Cooper (1984) tested non-native English readers' sensitivity to relationships between sentences, both explicitly marked by rhetorical connectors and not explicitly marked. Here are two examples from the test:

1 Contrast, with rhetorical connector:
   In ancient times, when man needed more food, he cleared and planted new land which had never been planted before. Today, *however*, ...

   a. great areas of forest are being cleared to make room for food and other crops.
   b. new land is very scarce and even where large areas of unused land exist, they are very difficult to develop.
   c. countries like Malaysia also have large-scale programmes for clearing the land to make room for food production.

2 Correction, without rhetorical connector:
   It is mistaken to say that heavy industry is an essential basis for economic development.

   a. Most developed nations are heavily industrialized.
   b. The prosperity of New Zealand is based on agriculture, not on heavy industry.
   c. Japan and Germany are advanced countries with complex heavy industries.
   (Cooper 1984: 131–2)

Cooper found a high correlation between learners' awareness of intersentential rhetorical relationships and their general comprehension, as well as a marked performance difference between learners with greater and lesser reading experience in English. The less experienced readers got low scores, even on explicitly marked intersentential relations (Cooper suggests that it is very likely they did not know what the rhetorical connectors meant). The only category of relationship that was relatively unproblematic for unpracticed readers was addition (for example, 'furthermore', 'moreover', 'in addition').

In a study of 100 university ESL students' comprehension of logical relationships, Geva (1992) found that learners' ability to identify intra- and inter-sentential relationships 'is a necessary but not sufficient component' (p. 731) of understanding logical relations in written texts. Learning to recognize logical relationships at the text level, Geva suggests, is a gradual, developmental process, which she models as a pyramid. At the base of the pyramid is learners' understanding of conjunctions within sentences. The midsection of the pyramid is learners' understanding of how conjunctions operate between pairs of sentences. Finally, the top of the pyramid is learners' understanding of logical relationships between and across larger chunks of text. Adult L2 learners will progress toward the top of the pyramid, Geva proposes, as their language proficiency improves and their reading processes become more automatic (Geva 1992: 744).

The research of Carrell, Cooper, and Geva suggests that (1) learners should be provided with frequent opportunities to read whole texts, and (2) teachers should focus their students' attention on how ideas are represented in a text and how the organization of ideas is signaled lexically or structurally in the text. Asking questions about a text is a very important technique in this regard (for example, Does the paragraph have a main idea, or is it really a set of equally important sentences? Which sentence is more important, sentence X or sentence Y? How do you know? What words tell us how X is related to Y? and so on). Students can be explicitly taught the various rhetorical connectors which serve as 'signposts', directing the reader's attention to the most important ideas or information of the text. Phrases such as 'the key point is' or 'of critical importance' fulfill this latter role, while 'on the other hand', 'conversely', 'however', and the like, suggest inter-sentential contrast, 'one example is' indicates exemplification, 'furthermore' signals expansion, and 'as a result', 'thus', 'hence', and others, mark consequence. Mapping (see Chapters 5 and 7) can also be a helpful technique in developing students' awareness of structure.

Genres

Moving to a more global level of rhetorical organization, we will now discuss genres. Although in literary studies genre has traditionally referred to the principal types of literary production (for example, novels, plays, short stories, poems), linguistic definitions extend beyond literary texts to include a broad spectrum of spoken and written discourse forms (for example, 'conversation', 'editorial', 'research article', 'interview', 'campaign speech', 'form letter', 'joke', and 'lecture'). Recent work in sociolinguistics, rhetoric, and communication has contributed to an even broader view, in which genres are seen as dynamic social processes rather than as static textual forms.

This latter view is particularly relevant to our purposes in this book, since it allows us to consider how genres may differ across cultures and how they reveal something of the sociocultural realities in other societies. Work in this social perspective is dominated by two groups: scholars influenced by Bakhtin's (1986) theory of speech genres, such as Berkenkotter and Huckin (1995) and Miller (1984), and those schooled in Hallidayan systemic/functional linguistics such as Kress (1989; 1994) and Martin, Christie, and Rothery (1994). Despite differences in their approaches, both groups see genres as fundamentally social phenomena, and not simply patterns of words. Genres establish norms of interaction by codifying the respective roles of readers/listeners and writers/speakers and the relationships between them, and by setting corresponding parameters of appropriateness for language use. (Compare, for example, the 'generic' participant roles and types of language you might expect to encounter in an interview, a lecture, a debate, and an intimate conversation.) Genres, understood in this light, are closely tied to Gee's notion of capital-D Discourses—particular ways of being in the world, which include particular ways of using language.

Genres operate in very specific cultural interactions. Kress (1994) makes the important point that although genre conventions 'are arbitrary when considered in isolation, they are not arbitrary within the context of any specific society' (p. 125). The 'curriculum vitae' or 'personal résumé' genre is a case in point. Connor (1996) describes a résumé writing exercise at a summer TESOL institute in Czechoslovakia in which two ESL/EFL instructors (one American, one Hungarian) each wrote a résumé for a fictitious Hungarian individual. The two versions differed dramatically—the American version was organized very schematically and emphasized individual achievements, whereas the Hungarian version was written as a stream of personal narrative, including such lines as 'I have pleasant memories of my childhood years, especially of those afternoons when the summer air was filled with the sweet smell of my mum's very special Sunday cookies' (Connor 1996: 144–7). A Polish colleague of mine noted that the personal narrative résumé was common throughout Eastern bloc countries and speculated that this form lent itself well to providing subtle clues about one's background that could be turned to one's social advantage in a communist state.

Familiarity with genres is important in communication, because it allows us to make connections between particular instances of discourse and others we have experienced previously. If we are reasonably competent in a language, we can usually identify jokes, stories, reports, and instructions upon hearing or reading just the first few words.[7] Once we have identified the particular genre, we are better able to anticipate what is coming, and have a sense of what details might be significant. For example, if we know we are reading a fable, we will expect the story to culminate in a moral and we will read characters' actions as contributions to that end. Readers who do not know that the text is a fable (i.e. do not know what to read *for*), however, may fail to see the moral significance of characters' actions and read the text as a simple narrative (Beach and Appleman 1984: 139).

Teachers can take advantage of students' existing knowledge of genres in order to get them to shift perspectives on the words and grammar they are learning. After students have been presented the French verb *être* (to be), for example, elements of the verb paradigm can be extracted and presented as a 'poem':

Je suis	[I am]
Tu es	[You are]
Mais	[But]
Nous ne sommes pas	[We are not]

Seeing these verb forms reframed as a 'poem' can lead students to read them from a different stance, to look for relationships among them (triggered by the conjunction 'mais'). The teacher could ask: Is this logical? In what context? What could this mean? Beginning students can express in gesture and movement what they cannot express in language (for example, by acting out the text as a silent play). This redesigning of a verb paradigm moves the grammar lesson beyond rote memorization of strings of forms to active thinking about relationships between words and genres. As a consequence of this genre frame shift, the verb forms become more memorable because they are meaningful, being tied to an interaction between speaker and hearer in context.

A teacher would be right to object at this point and say, 'Yes, that's fine, but you certainly can't do that kind of thing with all verbs.' No, one can't, and one shouldn't. The point is to get learners to shift perspectives from time to time, to expose them to the poetic side of what seems to be 'just words' and to get them to see how, in context, and examined from particular perspectives, ordinary words can take on new layers of significance.[8] Such moments can make learners aware of the signifying value of genres.

In the realities of the textual world, of course, texts often do not represent 'pure' examples of singular genres (Derrida 1980). Just as texts often contain mixtures of spoken and written modes, so they frequently exemplify multiple and mixed genres. In both cases—mode and genre—the mixture is dictated by particular purposes and communicative intents that can vary within, as well as between, cultural communities.[9]

An important aspect of genres is that, like other social conventions, they can be subverted to create particular effects. Publicity writers, for example, commonly play with genres to achieve a witty appeal. Consider a two-page magazine advertisement for 'Johnny Walker Red Label' whisky.[10] The left-hand page shows a rearview shot of a woman dancing in a night club. The right-hand page presents the following text, centered and written in red letters against a black backdrop:

CAUTION:

DRINKING RED LABEL CAN CAUSE

SERIOUS CONVERSATIONS

AND SOMETIMES EVEN DANCING.

Consumers are very familiar with 'Caution' notices on products such as medicines, cigarettes, and alcoholic beverages. The genre is signaled by the word 'CAUTION:', by the typeface and formatting of the text, and by the collocation of the phrases 'can cause . . .', 'serious', 'and sometimes even . . .'. Here, it is only the insertion of two words—'conversation' and 'dancing'—that subverts this 'consumer warning', replacing negative outcomes with positive ones. The real caveat appears in minuscule print at the bottom of the left page: 'Enjoy Red Label Responsibly'. Thus the literate insider of the cultural community sees a symmetrical mismatch in genre and message: the consumer caution is phrased as an advertising slogan, while the advertisement adopts the form of a consumer caution. The net effect is that the notion of 'caution' is transformed from prohibition to enticement.

This kind of analytical reading is teachable in conjunction with grammar study, even at early levels. For example, ESL learners can be guided in reading such texts by first becoming introduced to the 'consumer label' genre and its importance in American society. They could begin by looking at food labels (which in the U.S. must by law list not only all the product's ingredients but also its protein, fat, and carbohydrate content). They could then look at the warning labels on cigarettes, alcoholic beverages, medicines, and so forth. All these labels (like the 'Not tested on animals' notice discussed in Chapter 2) are designed to allow the individual consumer to make an 'informed decision' about whether or not to buy the product. Individual 'informed decision-making' is at the heart of the democratic process and therefore an important theme for ESL learners in North America to learn about. Once students are familiar with the consumer label genre, then advertisements that manipulate that genre, such as the Johnny Walker advertisement above, can be analyzed and discussed.

Genres, like all other discourse conventions, both enable and constrain communication. If attention to genre is attention to conventions of communication, the question that arises for language teachers is 'can and should we explicitly teach genres?'

Heath (1986) asserts that access to models, as well as direct practice of genres, is essential to academic success and recommends 'repeated and multiple experience' with spoken and written genres to 'ensure that individuals learn their forms and structures—the molds from which they are made' (p. 167). Scholars such as Dixon (1987), however, argue that a focus on formal features of different genres may distract teachers' and students' attention from what is most important—understanding the social contexts (for example, readers' and writers' purposes and goals) in which texts are produced and interpreted. Both views have their merit. In fact, I would contend that what must be taught is not just formal features of genres or just social contexts, but precisely the linkages between the two in particular instances of communication. Genres 'look' different in different discourse contexts, even within a given culture. In academic settings, for example, the genre of 'doctoral thesis proposal' differs widely not only across disciplines, but also within disciplines (for example, quantitative versus qualitative research frameworks). So it is not enough to familiarize learners with genres as ready-made, stock 'molds' or 'containers' for text. Teachers must show learners how particular rhetorical patterns reflect social and communicative needs within particular discourse communities.

This requires a contrastive approach to teaching genre. First, one cannot understand a genre by looking at a single model text; rather, one must look at multiple examples of a given genre in order to allow learners to identify what rhetorical features are common across them (Johns 1997). Second, by extension, one cannot understand a given genre by looking at examples of that genre alone; one must compare with examples of other related genres as well, in order to see what features a given genre does *not* have and to see how genre features vary with communicative purpose (Caudery 1998). A similar principle holds for writing. As Caudery (1998) points out, 'we cannot expect students to be able to write texts of even just one or two genres successfully if they have never attempted to go beyond these to establish precisely where the boundaries lie between one genre and another' (p. 4). In other words, one may not be able to do a genre well if one cannot do its 'other'.

Style

Whereas genre has to do with the global rhetorical functions and global organizational schemes of texts, style has to do with the individual and particular ways in which those global functions and schemes are expressed or manifested toward particular communicative ends. In terms of the construction metaphor introduced in the section on cohesion and coherence, if office buildings, churches, libraries, houses represent different functional *genres*, then now we are concerned with different architectural *styles* of office buildings, churches, and so on. Genre and style are important concepts for the teaching of foreign language literacy because, as Scholes (1985) points out, 'they give us access to the invisible forces that shape textual production, just as the concept of 'language' gives us access to the forces that shape our speech' (p. 3).

It should be recognized, however, that genre and style are not always easy to separate neatly. For example, 'poem' is a genre, but 'poetic' is a style. The distinction is thus one between a kind of whole rhetorical act (for example, poem) and resonances of that kind of act within other (for example, 'non-poem') rhetorical acts.

Stylistics is the use of linguistic analysis to explore the ways writers design meaning by making particular choices. As Halliday puts it, 'We are interested in what a particular writer has written, against the background of what he might have written—including comparatively, against the background of other things he has written, or that other people have written' (1978: 57–8). This kind of analysis can also provide insight into how *readers*, in turn, are led to develop particular interpretations over others.

This kind of literate sensitivity is not 'natural' and must be learnt, even by native speakers. In a native language context, Church and Bereiter (1984) have shown that whereas many students attend to a text's informational content, they much less often attend to its stylistic features, even during repeated readings. Church and Bereiter found that simply asking American twelfth grade English students to 'pay attention to the way the text is written' had little effect, however. Much more effective, they found, was asking students to compare stylistic variations of a text. For example, they asked students (1) to compare two versions of a translated passage from Dante's Inferno (one contemporary, one archaic and ornate), (2) to decide which style they preferred, and (3) to convert a different passage into that style. This is a good illustration of how students' awareness of stylistic Available Designs can be developed and then applied by redesigning a text within particular stylistic parameters.[11]

Stylistic analysis is also relevant to another dimension of literacy: the interface between the spoken and written language. How, for example, does the writer represent speech at various points in a narrative? Second language readers generally have greater difficulty understanding Free Indirect Speech (for example, Surely he would not ask him for his passport) than they do understanding Free Direct Speech (I sure hope he doesn't ask me for my passport) or Direct Speech ('Do you need to see my passport?'). Simpson (1993) provides a framework for analyzing the various ways of representing speech and their communicative effects, useful in making language learners aware of the specific patterns required in different narrative contexts.

Stylistic analysis also helps students see how point of view is encoded in texts. Point of view refers to the psychological or ideological perspective from which a narrative is told or information is presented. Simpson (1993) presents various transposition exercises to get students to rewrite texts from different points of view. Rewriting texts in different spatial, temporal, psychological, or ideological frames forces students to look beyond the plot and can help them see how particular uses of language contribute to the text's 'feel' and predispose readers to certain interpretations over others. Checklists of linguistic markers of point of view, such as those provided by Short (1994), can also be helpful in making students aware of the wide range of stylistic techniques available for expressing point of view. As with all checklists, however, teachers should be careful not to merely teach series of discrete items, but show how the use of a given device may affect the reader's interpretation of the text.

Widdowson, in his (1992) book *Practical Stylistics*, demonstrates the pedagogical value of redesigning poems, rather than explicating them, in order to understand better *how* they mean rather than just *what* they mean. Widdowson goes through a series of verse and prose reformulations of Yeats's poem 'Memory' to expose the contradictions and incoherence of the poem's underlying propositional structure, and to show the futility of reading the poem as *referring* to the nature of memory. Rather, Widdowson argues, the particularities of the poem serve the function of *representing* the very experience of remembering. Widdowson goes on to describe a number of ways in which students can redesign poems in order to become more aware of the multiple ways that poetry signifies. For example, students can reassemble the scrambled (and unpunctuated) lines of a poem, either individually or in small groups, and then compare their respective 'designs' in terms of their literary effect. Or they can complete poetic text containing 'gaps' ranging from individual words to whole lines. Such gap-filling exercises focus students' attention on both propositional content and the patterning of language in the poem. To extend the literacy paradigm further, different versions can be compared for their literary effects. Widdowson also demonstrates how students can profitably derive poems from prose descriptions, how they can use prose paraphrases of poems, and how they can compare different modes of poetic writing—all towards the goal of fostering learners' ability to 'authenticate poetic texts as poems on their own authority' (1992: 150).

Although stylistics is often associated with the analysis of literary texts, it can (and must, I will argue in Chapter 7) also be applied to students' own writing. As Short (1994) points out, students are generally more motivated to discuss the linguistic details of their own writing than they are to analyze the style of a published text. Kramsch (1995b) describes a classroom activity in which students compare their own written summaries of Robert Olen Butler's (1992) story 'Crickets'. In order to illustrate the key importance of the teacher's role in probing students' remarks, reflecting on their choice of words, and drawing connections and contrasts, I have reproduced Kramsch's transcription of a classroom discussion of two student summaries below:

Jeff:	*(born in Burma, 2 years in U.S.) reads his summary on the board)* Mr. Thieu was an immigrant who escaped from Vietnam. He and his wife and American-born child, Bill lived in La., where Mr. Thieu was called Ted as he worked in a refinery. When Ted saw that his son was bored, he tried to introduce the idea of fighting crickets but as he and his son searched for crickets, they only found one type which made the whole game uninteresting and Ted was sorry that he had introduced the idea to his son.
Teacher:	How does your summary compare to the others?
Jeff:	Mine doesn't include attitudes . . . mine is pretty shallow . . . I think . . . You asked us to summarize, so I just summarized, I really didn't think about it.
Teacher:	Anyone else wants to comment on Jeff's summary?
Edmond:	*(reading Jeff's summary)* He ends with Ted being, 'sorry that he had introduced the idea to his son' even though he wanted it . . . I see there the idea of pain. I was just wondering . . . Although he claimed he didn't intend to put any attitudes in there he **did** end

his summary in a pretty sad way . . . sort of open-ended, like the story itself.

Teacher: *(to Jeff)* Your summary says he worked in a refinery. The others didn't mention where he worked. Is that important?

Jeff: The people at work respect him.

Teacher: Is it significant that he works in a refinery?

Jeff: Hm . . . yeah . . . because he is smarter, like the crickets.

Tim: *(reads his summary)* The short story 'Crickets' is about a man's transformation into the United States. Ted (Mr. Thieu) is from Vietnam and fleed to America because of all the problems in his country . . .

Teacher: *(to Tim)* What distinguishes your summary from that of others?

Tim: I'm interested in the transformation of an immigrant to another country =

Teacher: =that you represent in your text by keeping the two names, Ted and Thieu, transformed one into the other?

Tim: *(smiles)* Yeah, it's the transformation that you see playing a symbolic role.

Teacher: Why did you feel it was important to tell in detail the story of the crickets?

Tim: Well . . . I noticed that he was really disappointed that his son couldn't understand, just because his son is an American. I thought his disappointment was the very thing . . . not just the fact that they couldn't play the game . . . it was deeper than that . . . this was a very important part of the story, because the fire crickets were the ones that were better armed, and the fact that he was smarter and smaller, ahead of his people, like the fire crickets . . .

(Kramsch 1995b: 73–5)

By being asked to reflect on and compare their summaries, students are led beyond the level of listing their gut-level reactions to texts. Furthermore, in the process of comparing summaries they come to see the importance of *choice* in language use, and that just as the author of 'Cricket' has made particular choices in writing the story, so have the students themselves in the process of summarizing it. And in talking about *why* they made the particular choices they did, students are often able to make connections they had not seen before.

In summary, one goal of a literacy-based instructional program is to make learners aware of the multiple *relationships* among all levels of text structure—how word choices, syntactic choices, and text-level organization choices all interact and affect meaning. As learners become increasingly aware of the linguistic options available to them, they gain the power to make choices that are appropriate to their communicative goals.

We now turn to the last of our 'core' Available Designs that compose what is commonly called 'background knowledge'. Background knowledge has to do with individuals' and communities' experience, beliefs, conceptualizations, and understandings of themselves and their world. Specifically, we will discuss knowledge as it is organized in content schemata, shared in cultural models, and expressed in stories.

Content schemata and cultural models

Earlier, we made the distinction between formal schemata and content schemata. Content schemata, it will be recalled, have to do with knowledge of the topic of a text, (for example, buses in Brazil, the American Stock Exchange, the French Revolution), event structures ('scripts' of roles and actions involved in activities such as birthday parties, going to restaurants, buying gasoline), and cultural notions (for example, what 'open doors' can mean to Germans versus Americans (see Kramsch, 1993)). It is important to recognize that all schemata, whether of 'formal' or 'content' type, are culturally shaped. This has led some theorists to treat schemata of various types as 'cultural schemata'.

Cognitive anthropologist Roy D'Andrade, for example, states that cultural schemata broadly 'portray not only the world of physical objects and events, but also more abstract worlds of social interaction, discourse, and even word meaning' (D'Andrade 1990, cited in Cole 1996: 126). When a cultural schema is intersubjectively shared (i.e. every member of a social group knows the schema, knows that every other member knows the schema, and furthermore knows that all members know that all members know the schema) it becomes what D'Andrade (1987) calls a *cultural model* (p. 113). Cultural models are taken as 'objective fact', 'the way things are', 'self-evident truths'. Importantly, the intersubjectivity of cultural models means that a great deal of information can be assumed as common ground, and therefore need not be made explicit in communication.

To illustrate how a cultural insider of a particular community uses schemata and cultural models in reading, let us consider a text that begins as follows:

> Mary heard the ice cream man coming down the street. She remembered her birthday money and rushed into the house . . . .
> (Rumelhart 1977: 265)

In order to make sense of these sentences readers fill in non-specified pieces of information by making a number of assumptions based on their conception of the world (content schemata) and their knowledge of texts and their organization (formal schemata). As the culturally 'inside' reader reads the first sentence, he or she may assume that Mary is female because of prior familiarity with the cultural practice of assigning this name only to females.

He or she might furthermore suspect that Mary is a girl, rather than a woman, because of the cultural association between birthday money and children.[12] He or she may assume the 'ice cream man' is human (rather than a frozen confection analogous to a 'gingerbread man'), because Mary can hear him coming. The use of the definite article 'the' suggests that Mary has seen the ice cream man before, or at least has some familiarity with ice cream men. Depending on his or her culture, the reader might envision the ice cream man driving a truck or walking on foot, pushing a cart. In either case the reader might assume that what Mary actually hears is not the ice cream man himself but perhaps bells, or rattling wheels on the pavement, or a simple, repetitive melody played through a loudspeaker. He or she may furthermore assume that the ice cream man actually has some ice cream held in some form of cold storage. The reader makes all these assumptions based on knowledge developed through past experience, which is organized in the form of schemata.

As the reader continues, his or her knowledge of cohesion conventions also comes into play. 'She' in the second sentence may be assumed to refer to Mary because it corresponds in gender and number with Mary, and moreover, because there is no one else mentioned in the text to which 'she' might refer. For the same reason, 'her' birthday money will be understood to refer to Mary's and not, for example, her sister's. By now the reader will likely have activated an 'episode' schema whose slots can begin to be filled in: 'Mary' is the *protagonist*, 'heard the ice cream man' is the initiating *event*, 'buying ice cream' is the *goal*, which can be inferred as a logical connection between hearing the ice cream man and remembering the birthday money. So far, so good. Our reader's 'designed' mental story appears to be consistent with all aspects of the text.

But suppose the second sentence is appended with the phrase '. . . and locked the door.'[13] Suddenly the ice cream man and Mary's rushing into the house are seen in a new light. The schema has shifted. The text is no less coherent, but the reader has had to quickly redesign its meaning. What triggers this redesign is the incompatibility of the previously assumed goal (buying ice cream) and locking oneself in one's house. The reader now has to reassess and reconfigure the schematic building blocks that had led to his or her initial interpretation, and develop a new interpretation (i.e. instantiate a new global schema) that is consistent with *all* of the facts. We can see in this instance how language itself creates contexts of interpretation that constrain the meanings of words, sentences, and texts. Foreign language readers, when cultural outsiders, however, are not always sensitive to such language-generated contexts.

Schema theory has brought to educators' attention the importance of background knowledge not only in reading, but in communication in general. Like linguistic theories of pragmatics (for example, Speech Act theory), schema theory provides an explanation for the fact that misunderstandings arise not just because of one's inability to comprehend the *words* expressed, but also because of differences in what speakers/writers and readers/listeners tacitly assume (which remains *unexpressed* in words). For example, while waiting in line at the supermarket recently I witnessed the following interaction between an Asian customer and the cashier. As the cashier prepared to pack the man's groceries in a bag, he asked, 'Paper or plastic, sir?' In American supermarkets this question refers to the type of grocery bag one prefers. The customer, however, immediately reached for his wallet and presented his plastic bank debit card. The cashier's words had been clearly understood, but the customer had (quite logically) instantiated a 'payment' schema, which, as it so happens, also contains slots for 'paper' and 'plastic' just as the 'grocery bag' schema does.

In the language classroom, when readers are unable to access a schema that is adequate to reconcile their personal experience with what they read in a text, they can feel lost. Kohn (1992), teaching English in China, describes teaching a passage from Jane Austen, in which the expression 'drawing room' appeared:

> The students had dutifully looked up 'draw' and 'drawing' in their dictionaries, but were puzzled about why there should be a room set aside for 'tugging,' or for 'designing.' When I explained that the expression came from *withdrawing* and meant a place to have a private conversation, I next had to explain that many middle-class houses in England had enough rooms that one could be set aside simply for private conversations. This explanation met with much doubt from my students, whose families lived in apartments consisting of only two small bedrooms and a toilet.
> (p. 122)

Research substantiates how crucial knowledge is to effective communication. As mentioned earlier, Bernhardt (1991) offers examples of readers misinterpreting a German business letter, largely because they did not have an appropriate formal schema for the format of such letters. Interestingly, once Bernhardt's subjects established their faulty interpretations, they tended to cling tenaciously to them, ignoring disconfirming textual evidence. This kind of 'schema interference' is particularly well documented in studies of children learning scientific concepts in school (for example, Alvermann and Hague 1989; Hynd and Alverman 1989), which have shown that activating learners' prior knowledge can facilitate comprehension, but only if that prior knowledge is consistent with the new information presented in the text. Given that schemata are not universal but vary across cultures, it is easy to see how language learners' schematic knowledge of their native culture could lead them to misinterpret foreign language texts, even when the general topic is a familiar one (Furry 1990; Hammadou 1991). Consequently, foreign language reading instruction ultimately needs to provide some mechanism for allowing students to recognize mismatches between their own background knowledge and the cultural assumptions made in the text, as well as to foster in learners a stance of *receptiveness* to unfamiliar meanings involving new or modified schemata.

A major goal for the literacy-based classroom, then, is to encourage the sharing and comparison of multiple perspectives on what meanings seem 'natural', in order to illuminate the underlying schemata that have given rise to those particular perspectives. Consider, for example, how Sandra Silberstein's ESL students voice different cultural frames in their classroom discussion of William Carlos Williams's poem 'This Is Just to Say':

> I have eaten
> the plums
> that were in
> the icebox
>
> and which
> you were probably
> saving
> for breakfast
>
> Forgive me
> they were delicious
> so sweet
> and so cold

'I think it is a love letter,' the German student proposes. Other students begin to agree. 'The writer shares a delicious experience,' offers the Kuwaiti student. 'It is a love letter between two sisters who live together,' volunteers a Japanese student. 'Two sisters cannot write a love letter,' the German student responds. 'Yes they can,' chorus the Thai and Japanese students.
(Silberstein 1994: 5–6)

This vignette makes an important point about multicultural perspectives: differences in interpretation are not always stark, but frequently subtle. Among these students there is basic agreement that the poem is expressing something good, and a number of students think that it is a love letter, but there is a discrepancy between the German and Asian students' conceptions of what a love letter is, who can write one, and to whom. This is due to differences in their culture-specific schemata about what love letters are and how siblings relate to one another.

A classic study by Steffensen, Joag-Dev, and Anderson (1979) demonstrates how subtle cross-cultural differences in cultural models can affect readers' interpretations. Two groups of students, Indian and American adults living in the U.S. and fluent in English, were asked to read two personal letters describing a traditional Indian wedding and a traditional American wedding respectively. According to the authors, weddings in India and America differ significantly. In Indian marriages, the groom's family is dominant, and the emphasis is on financial interests and social status. A marriage can be a traumatic occasion for the bride's family. In American weddings, on the other hand, the bride's family is dominant, the emphasis is on pageantry, and it is a stereotypically happy event for all. The researchers reported a number of interesting findings. First, both groups took longer to read the text describing a wedding in the *other* culture, even though the language in the two texts was not difficult for either group. Second, both groups recalled the 'familiar culture' text better than the 'foreign culture' text, suggesting that the more the schemata underlying a text are congruent with those in the reader's existing repertoire the easier it is to remember it accurately. Third, the idea units that each group deemed most important were strikingly different. For example, in the American wedding passage, the Americans thought that what was important was that there was a rehearsal and a rehearsal dinner, and that the attendants all wore dresses that matched the bride's. The Indians, on the other hand, found statements about the marriageability of the daughter, and the cost of the diamond ring to be very significant. Finally, there were five times more elaborations (extensions consistent with the text) in both groups' recall of the native passage, and at least five times more factual distortions in both groups' recall of the non-native text. The findings of this study highlight the importance of cultural values and cultural schemata in reading comprehension.

The above discussion raises an additional point, concerning the two-way relationship between schemata and language use as seen in a communicative model. Schemata help us to make sense of language use, but language use contributes to the ongoing shaping and refinement of our schemata (Cook 1994: 10, 182). This point is important in the context of foreign language learning. Foreign language students often do not possess the relevant cultural knowledge that would allow them to interpret a text as a native speaker might. This fact has led some teachers to assume that their students should only read texts written about topics with which they are already familiar, or, alternatively, that their students need to be 'primed' with lots of detailed background information before they read texts dealing with unfamiliar topics. While it is true that students need to have a certain familiarity with the topic, providing too much background can reduce students' opportunities to *learn* from their reading, and hence diminish their motivation to actually read.[14] After all, we rarely bother to read texts that tell us what we already know. For *foreign* language students, in particular, reading and discussing texts constitute the primary means to explore the intricacies of language use in a wide variety of contexts and thereby to glimpse the workings of another culture. At the same time, however, it is crucial to recognize that foreign language readers are, by definition, not intended readers, and therefore must be taught to handle the difficulties of reading complex texts as cultural outsiders. These difficulties cannot be circumvented but must be dealt with head-on.

One important way that teachers can help learners in this regard is to expose them to the stories that members of the target culture tell to themselves.

Stories

Because the stories we read and hear about events, places, and people can sometimes exert a greater influence on our schemata and interpretations than direct experience itself, examination of the stories told within a culture (as well as those told to outsiders) can help us to learn a considerable amount about that culture, even without direct personal experience. Stories are therefore an essential element in the development of language learners' literacy and communicative capacity.

To extend our 'construction' metaphor, stories are the social histories of structures—tales of who built them and when, who lived there, what memorable events occurred there, and so on, that become indissociable in social memory from the buildings themselves, and that are passed on through generations of families and community members. They provide the background narratives that make new narratives seem 'natural' (i.e. readily interpretable) or not to a cultural insider. Stanley Fish makes the point that 'what we know is not the world but stories about the world' (1980: 243). Stories are the overt expression of schematic knowledge. Like schemata, stories serve to organize our perceptions into meaningful patterns. But whereas schemata are structured as hierarchical webs of knowledge, stories are structured as narratives. Perhaps the most important reason for making the distinction between schemata and stories in the context of this book is that the term 'stories' allows us to see a direct link between abstract mental narratives and the textual narratives that we hear and read and think about. That is to say, it makes clear the socially constructed nature of our knowledge and beliefs. Stories—those we have been told, those we tell to ourselves, and those we tell to others—not only help us to understand and explain the world, but also to control and resist it. Through our stories we tell the world not 'as it is' but rather as we see it, or as we would like to see it, or as we would like others to see it. Rosen (1985) argues that it is a 'predisposition of the human mind' to narratize our experience, not only in moments of explicit storytelling, but also throughout our everyday lives:

> . . . narrative will always be there or thereabouts, surfacing in the daily business of living and less obviously framed as a text than *Alice in Wonderland* or *Three Little Pigs*. So it is that we are always in a high state of readiness to transform into story not only what we experience directly but also what we hear and read—a cross on a mountainside, graffiti, . . . a limp, a scar, a dog howling in the night, a headline, a cryptic note.
> (Rosen 1985: 12)

The stories we hold in common with other members of the groups we belong to (a significant part of culture) allow us to intersubjectively share views of reality, to interpret texts in mutually understandable ways—to plot out and predict meaning in communities. But, as Rosen points out,

> There is no one way of telling stories; we learn the story grammars of our society, our culture. Since there are irreconcilable divisions in our society of sex, class, ethnicity, we should expect very diverse, but not mutually exclusive, ways of telling stories.
> (Rosen 1985: 14)

With this background in mind, let's briefly consider two stories, *The Little Engine That Could* (Piper 1930), a well-known children's story, and *The House on Mango Street*, the first vignette in a collection with the same title by Sandra Cisneros (1989), that offer ESL/EFL learners not only accessible reading for an enjoyable language experience, but also rich source material for gaining insight into American culture.

In *The Little Engine That Could*, a determined little train engine succeeds in pulling a train loaded with toys and food over a mountain top. The train's original engine has broken, leaving the train stranded, unable to deliver its cargo to the children who live on the other side of the mountain. The clown and dolls on the train ask a succession of large, capable engines that pass by if they will please help by pulling them over the mountain. All these engines refuse (they are too self-important or too tired). Finally, a little blue engine, who has never been over the mountain, says that she (the engine is feminine gendered) will try. Repeating 'I think I can, I think I can' over and over as she chugs up the mountain, the little blue engine succeeds and the toys and dolls cheer as they head down the other side of the mountain.

This story poses little linguistic challenge for novice learners of English, and yet it offers an important cultural lesson about the value of positive thinking in the face of adversity. It tells the American story of how motivation, determination, cooperation, and hard work can overcome seemingly insurmountable difficulties. It is a story about underdogs 'rising to the top' despite disadvantage, through goodwill and optimism. A story known to generations of Americans, its refrain 'I think I can. I think I can . . .' is an ideological mantra that resounds in many realms of American life.

The first vignette in Sandra Cisneros's book *The House on Mango Street*, reproduced in Figure 3.5, presents a somewhat different American story. It tells of personal dreams that coexist with, but do not necessarily overcome, a reality of adversity and shame. Lottery tickets, bedtime stories, TV shows, and promises are the stuff of hope and dreams, but the narrator's 'But I know how those things go' exposes them as just that. American individualism and the possibility of self-betterment are alive and well—the family is able to buy a house—but there are limits ('it's not the house we thought we'd get'). This is a text to which we will return repeatedly throughout the rest of the book to illustrate particular teaching techniques. For now, it will suffice to say that when learners of English read, think about, discuss, and compare stories such as these, they enter into a dynamic and ongoing process of cultural exploration.

The House on Mango Street

We didn't always live on Mango Street. Before that we lived on Loomis on the third floor, and before that we lived on Keeler. Before Keeler it was Paulina, and before that I can't remember. But what I remember most is moving a lot. Each time it seemed there'd be one more of us. By the time we got to Mango Street we were six—Mama, Papa, Carlos, Kiki, my sister Nenny and me.

The house on Mango Street is ours, and we don't have to pay rent to anybody, or share the yard with the people downstairs, or be careful not to make too much noise, and there isn't a landlord banging on the ceiling with a broom. But even so, it's not the house we thought we'd get.

We had to leave the flat on Loomis quick. The water pipes broke and the landlord wouldn't fix them because the house was too old. We had to leave fast. We were using the washroom next door and carrying water over in empty milk gallons. That's why Mama and Papa looked for a house, and that's why we moved into the house on Mango Street, far away, on the other side of town.

They always told us that one day we would move into a house, a real house that would be ours for always so we wouldn't have to move each year. And our house would have running water and pipes that worked. And inside it would have real stairs, not hallways stairs, but stairs inside like houses on T.V. And we'd have a basement and at least three washrooms so when we took a bath we wouldn't have to tell everybody. Our house would be white with trees around it, a great big yard and grass growing without a fence. This was the house Papa talked about when he held a lottery ticket and this was the house Mama dreamed up in the stories she told us before we went to bed.

But the house on Mango Street is not the way they told it at all. It's small and red with tight steps in front and windows so small you'd think they were holding their breath. Bricks are crumbling in places, and the front door is so swollen you have to push hard to get in. There is no front yard, only four little elms the city planted by the curb. Out back is a small garage for the car we don't own yet and a small yard that looks smaller between the two buildings on either side. There are stairs in our house, but they're ordinary hallway stairs, and the house has only one washroom. Everybody has to share a bedroom—Mama and Papa, Carlos and Kiki, me and Nenny.

Once when we were living on Loomis, a nun from my school passed by and saw me playing out front. The laundromat downstairs had been boarded up because it had been robbed two days before and the owner had painted on the wood YES WE'RE OPEN so as not to lose business.

Where do you live? she asked.

There, I said, pointing up to the third floor.

You live *there*?

There. I had to look to where she pointed—the third floor, the paint peeling, wooden bars Papa had nailed on the window so we wouldn't fall out. You live *there*? The way she said it made me feel like nothing. *There*. I lived *there*. I nodded.

I knew then I had to have a house. A real house. One I could point to. But this isn't it. The house on Mango Street isn't it. For the time being, Mama says. Temporary, says Papa. But I know how those things go. (Cisneros 1989: 3-5)

Figure 3.5:   The first vignette from The House on Mango Street

Just as reading and discussing published stories is important, so is the opportunity for learners to write and tell their own stories. Family histories are particularly interesting and students can learn a good deal in the process of researching and telling them. When such stories can be exchanged and compared with those of native speaker peers through cross-cultural classroom partnerships, the potential for learning is even greater (Kern 1996).

Conclusion

In this chapter we have examined a number of the diverse but highly interrelated resources we draw on consciously or unconsciously in understanding and creating meanings from texts. These resources, which we are calling Available Designs, provide a heuristic matrix of potentials and constraints that allow us to communicate, despite the inevitable incompleteness and inexplicitness of speech and writing. It is the overlapping and redundancy of functions among Available Designs (and the potential interference patterns they produce together) that provides us with a rich array of expressive choices. We have seen that vocabulary, grammar, sound, and writing systems are necessary but not sufficient resources for communicative language use, and yet these are frequently the only Available Designs explicitly addressed in language teaching. Also essential to learning and using language and literacy are schematic Available Designs, which allow us to generate coherent discourse from texts.

In Part Two we will look in greater detail at the communicative bases of reading and writing, and how learners can be helped to design meaning in a new language by applying the theoretical principles established in Part One.

Notes

1 Learners of non-cognate languages may not be able to apply their native language lexical knowledge directly, but they can certainly use their abstract knowledge of the nature of lexical systems.

2 This may well explain the mixed results of studies of the effects of looking up unfamiliar words on reading comprehension. Although some studies (for example, Knight 1994) suggest a positive relationship between dictionary use and comprehension, other studies (for example, Bensoussan, Sim, and Weiss 1984; Hulstijn 1993; Chun and Plass 1996) have found no such relationship. Even in the case of the Knight study, the relationship was found only among the low-verbal-ability students.

3 I am not suggesting that exhaustive analysis of all words in a text is necessary. It is often enough to demonstrate, with a few vivid examples, that words can take on unexpected meanings. In this way, students are open to that eventuality as they read.

4 Teachers must be careful, however, to show that some expressions can have multiple functions (for example, while, then, since).

5 In order for this metaphor to account for one-word texts (for example, 'Exit'), it must be acknowledged that simple, single-element 'functional structures' exist (for example, an empty signpost, an upright log that will serve as a telephone pole, a wooden railroad tie set in the ground as a step or as a garden border).

6 Of course, considered in the situational context of a word association chain game (in which participants follow a procedure of picking a word from the last sentence and making up a new sentence with this word) this text might seem eminently *appropriate*, but the point of such games is generally to avoid conventional patterns of mutual relevance.

7 Jackendoff (1994) makes a striking analogy to music perception. When we listen to music, we hear it not just as a sequence of notes (analogous to words), but as a representation of a particular genre, which we identify based on a collection of prototypical musical patterns in our head: 'This collection of patterns is general, in that it doesn't depend on knowing any specific tune, and it can be applied to an indefinitely large number of new tunes in the same style' (p. 167). On the other hand, Jackendoff points out, music that does not conform to familiar patterns sounds odd—not because the notes are unrecognizable, but because the patterns of organization are not familiar.

8 In French, Prévert's 'L'accent grave', which plays on the *ou/où* alternation in the phrase *être ou/où ne pas être* can highlight the significance of even orthographic accents.

9 Consider, for example, François Mitterand's 16,000 word *Lettre à tous les Français*, written before the French presidential elections of 1988. The text takes the form of a personal letter, although the language and the content diverge from the 'personal letter' genre and establish a clear hierarchical relation between author and reader (Gaffney 1993).

10 *Wired* Magazine, December 1996, pp. 142–3.

11 See also Gaudiani's (1981) description of the *pastiche* technique in foreign language writing.

12 It is important to point out, however, that there is nothing to rule out the interpretation that Mary is, for example, a middle-aged mother or even a physically-fit elderly woman (i.e. one capable of rushing into the house).

13 From a lecture by Charles Fillmore, cited by Carrell and Eisterhold (1988).

14 Furthermore, it is questionable to what degree providing background information of a factual type contributes to L2 readers' comprehension. Chen and Graves (1995), for example, found that, although previewing the thematic content of a story significantly improved ESL learners' understanding, providing background knowledge alone was much less effective.

PART TWO

4 Reading as design

Texts are lazy machineries that ask someone to do part of their job.

Umberto Eco (1979)

So far in this book, I have argued that reading and writing, as *recursive* acts of communication, lend themselves particularly well to analysis and reflection about the processes of producing and interpreting meaning through language. Although my ultimate point is that reading and writing ought to be viewed as intertwined, integrated processes from both theoretical and pedagogical perspectives (hence my choice of the word literacy), it will now be useful for exposition purposes to discuss them individually. In this second part of the book we will take a closer look at reading and writing as acts of meaning design. The four chapters are organized in pairs, two on reading and two on writing. The first of each pair will consider how the notion of design relates to certain theories of reading (Chapter 4) and writing (Chapter 6). The second chapter of each pair (Chapters 5 and 7) will detail a range of teaching techniques aimed at enhancing learners' ability to design meaning appropriately in reading and writing respectively.

In the present chapter, we will begin by focusing on two central aspects of reading: (1) its interactive nature as a dynamic process of deriving discourse from text, and (2) its determination by both individual and social factors. This leads into a discussion of reader-response theory as it informs the issues of social constraints, individual interpretative freedom, and intended readership. Finally, we will consider reading in terms of the design metaphor presented in Chapter 2, discussing the relationship between first and second language reading, and showing how the conception of reading and its teaching varies across sociocultural contexts. Pedagogical and curricular implications will then be pursued in detail in Chapter 5.

Reading as a dynamic rhetorical process

In Part One, we saw that reading is not simply an act of absorbing information, but a communicative act that involves creating discourse from text. To illustrate, consider the following passage from Lewis Thomas's *The Lives of a Cell*:

'Stigmergy' is a new word, invented recently by Grassé to explain the nest-building behavior of termites, perhaps generalizable to other complex activities of social animals. The word is made of Greek roots meaning 'to incite to work,' and Grassé's intention was to indicate that it is the product of work itself that provides both the stimulus and instructions for further work. He arrived at this after long observation of the construction of termite nests, which excepting perhaps a manmade city are the most formidable edifices in nature. When you consider the size of an individual termite, photographed alongside his nest, he ranks with the New Yorker and shows a better sense of organization than a resident of Los Angeles. Some of the mound nests of *Macrostermes bellicosus* in Africa measure twelve feet high and a hundred feet across; they contain several millions of termites, and around them are clustered other small and younger mounds, like suburbs.
(Thomas 1974: 156)

This information-dense passage is the kind that some ESL learners find difficult to understand. If students see the passage merely as a collection of facts related to termites, they can feel quickly overwhelmed by the informational load, and their comprehension may consequently suffer.[1] The key to understanding passages like this is looking at them as rhetorical acts of communication, not just lists of facts. What this entails is an awareness of the relationships among the various sentences and an ability to follow the tacit 'discourse trail' established by the author. Following Widdowson (1983), this discourse trail might be redesigned in dialogic form as follows, with 'A' representing the writer's contribution, and 'B' representing a potential reader's response:

A: 'Stigmergy' is a new word, invented recently by Grassé to explain the nest-building behavior of termites, perhaps generalizable to other complex activities of social animals.
B: What exactly does 'stigmergy' mean?
A: The word is made of Greek roots meaning 'to incite to work', and Grassé's intention was to indicate that it is the product of work itself that provides both the stimulus and instructions for further work.
B: How did Grassé hit upon the notion of stigmergy?
A: He arrived at this after long observation of the construction of termite nests, which excepting perhaps a manmade city are the most formidable edifices in nature.
B: That's a provocative statement. How can you compare a termite nest with a manmade city?
A: When you consider the size of an individual termite, photographed alongside his nest, he ranks with the New Yorker and shows a better sense of organization than a resident of Los Angeles.
B: I'm not sure I follow. Could you give me an example?

A: Some of the mound nests of *Macrostermes bellicosus* in Africa measure twelve feet high and a hundred feet across; they contain several millions of termites, and around them are clustered other small and younger mounds, like suburbs.

B: That's interesting. Can you tell me more about these nests?

To reiterate a point made in Chapter 3, the coherence of the passage does not result so much from the surface features of the text (i.e. cohesion), but from the patterns of thought that underlie the text's organization. Understanding the rhetorical *functions* of particular facts as comparisons, illustrations, and so forth within the framework of the whole text can go a long way toward making the text more comprehensible. Understanding these rhetorical functions depends, in turn, on the reader's understanding of what the writer has assumed to be shared cultural knowledge (for example, familiarity with New York, Los Angeles, and suburbs).

The dialogic example above suggests that the way we design meaning through written texts (i.e. by reading or writing) may not be so different from the way we design meaning in spoken language use. Tannen (1983) has argued that so-called 'oral' discourse strategies may in fact be crucial to effective writing and reading:

> Successful writing requires not the production of discourse with no sense of audience but, rather, the positing of a hypothetical reader and playing to the needs of that audience . . . the act of reading efficiently is often a matter not so much of decoding . . . but of discerning a familiar text structure, hypothesizing what information will be presented, and being ready for it when it comes. By making maximum use of context, good readers may be using oral strategies. (p. 91)

It is precisely the sense of 'context', however, that makes face-to-face oral interaction quite different from reading and writing. In face-to-face interaction, the situational context is shared experientially and may not be readily inferable from the linguistic text of the exchange. In written interaction, on the other hand, the writer must explicitly provide whatever 'contextual' information he or she deems necessary to allow the reader to make the intended inferences. The reader, in turn, must reconstruct a context of interpretation based not only on the cues provided in the writer's text, but also on the reader's own experience and knowledge. Consequently, as Riley (1985) puts it, 'We may all 'read' the same text, but no two people ever 'read' the same discourse because they never bring exactly the same knowledge, expectations and contexts to bear on the text' (p. 71).

Moreover, reading does not necessarily require us to submit to the writer's discourse world as we would do in an interpersonal communicative encounter. In this sense, Widdowson (1984) argues, the problems of reading are of a different nature from those of conversation:

the difficulties of reading, unlike those of conversation, have to do less with the negotiation of constraints than with the use of freedom. The reader can negotiate meaning on his own terms. His problem is to know what these terms should be on particular reading occasions. If he is too assertive there is a danger that he may distort the writer's intentions and deny access to new knowledge and experience. If he is too submissive, he runs the risk of accumulating information without subjecting it to the critical discrimination necessary to incorporate it into the schematic structure of existing knowledge. In both cases, reading is deprived of its essential purpose since it does not result in the change of state which . . . is a defining feature of the communicative process.
(Widdowson 1984: 226)

And of course the principal problem in the early stages of foreign language learning is that readers sometimes produce no discourse at all, but simply a series of decoded words. The difficulty is clearly not just in understanding words, but also in elaborating an appropriate context in which to interpret the text.

But if readers can negotiate meaning on their own terms, then how do they determine an *appropriate* context of interpretation? To answer this question we have to consider social constraints on individuals' responses as readers.

Reading as a social and individual process

As Tierney and LaZansky (1980) have pointed out, reading relies on a tacit 'contractual agreement' of shared conventions and assumptions between readers and writers. When the writer and reader of a given text operate out of different conventions or assumptions, the contract breaks down and comprehension can suffer. We have already seen how this can happen when one reads foreign language texts, but it can happen in one's own language as well, whenever significant differences exist between writer and reader (i.e. when the reader is not yet familiar with the writer's choice of design conventions).

Consider, for example, my daughter Maria's first written story, composed when she was four:

> GHSTOPRV
> NGSORV
> HLIHGRW
> CWHIGKN
> !ILVPVO! ♥

I didn't know how to proceed when Maria asked me to read it aloud, so I asked her to read it to me. This is how it went:

The G was very happy to see the H. The H was very happy to see the S and the S was very happy to see the T. The T was certainly happy to see the O, and the P was going on a picnic with the R. But the V was not very happy!

The N was happy to see the G, and the S was very happy to see the O, and the O was certainly delighted to see the R, and the R was . . . But the V was not very happy!

And the H was very delighted to see the L, and the L was very delighted to see the I. The H and the G were getting married and the R was surely happy to see the W. But the W was not very happy!

And the C loved the W, and the H was certainly delighted to see the I. The G wanted to go play with the K, but the N wasn't very happy!
I love you, exclamation point!

This is obviously a text whose full meaning is not contained in its graphic representation. Indeed, because of the unconventional nature of the writing, the story is uninterpretable to most readers without its accompanying oral version.[2] On the other hand, *seeing* the writing is essential to an understanding of the story because relationships are represented graphically (for example, the last letter of each line is 'not very happy'—presumably because there are no letters after it to interact with). Consequently, this is a story that could not be told without writing. Once I learnt the design conventions of the writing (which only took one line of the story) I had no trouble interpreting (if loosely) similar subsequent stories—I had learnt *how* to read my daughter's 'alphabet' stories. Admittedly, this is an extreme example, but it makes the point that reading and writing are always *socially-embedded* activities involving relationships, shared assumptions, and conventions as well as *individual*, personal acts involving imagination, creativity, and emotions.

In order to further explore the interplay between social and personal dimensions of reading we will consider how reader-response theory complements both the cognitive and social perspectives referred to in Part One, and contributes to a notion of reading as design.

Reader-response theory

In the 1920s, I. A. Richards conducted a series of classroom experiments with his undergraduate students at Cambridge, a project that Richards characterized as 'field-work in comparative ideology' (1935: 6). During class he would hand out sets of four poems, without indicating their various authors, and invite his students 'to comment freely in writing upon them' during the following week (p. 3). His subsequent lecture would then explicate not only the poems in question, but also the widely-variable responses of his students. By comparing students' responses in the light of the poems themselves, Richards's intention was to explore both the diversity and the internal consistency of the interpretations. Richards's hope was that by examining students' readings and misreadings, insight could be gained into how language works, how opinions and perspectives are formed, and, ultimately, how communication could be improved. Despite his apparent intention to do what is now called ethnography of reading, Richards nevertheless ended up emphasizing his undergraduates' shortcomings as readers, presenting a list of pitfalls one ought to avoid in reading poetry. Nevertheless, Richards' experiments served as an important move in the development of literary theories centered on the role of the reader.

In contrast to later New Critics of the 1950s and 1960s (whose approach might be described as 'conduit'-oriented because it emphasized 'the work itself' as an autonomous container of meaning), scholars in the 'reader-response' and 'reception theory' traditions such as Wolfgang Iser, Hans-Robert Jauss, David Bleich, Norman Holland, and Stanley Fish took a more 'design'-oriented approach. Although their work differed in significant ways, they shared an interest in the dynamic relationship between reader and text, challenging the assumption that meaning exists independently of the reading and interpretation of an audience. They attributed an 'authorly' role to the reader, who, by responding to the words on the page and by bridging the semantic gaps that lie between them, effectively 'realized' the text during the act of reading (thus in a sense making reading a sort of 'writing'). Iser, for example, characterized the reader-text relationship as follows:

> . . . reading [is] a creative process that is far above mere perception of what is written. The literary text activates our own faculties, enabling us to recreate the world it presents . . . . [O]ne text is potentially capable of several different realizations, and no reading can ever exhaust the full potential, for each individual reader will fill in the gaps in his own way, thereby excluding the various other possibilities; as he reads, he will make his own decision as to how the gap is to be filled.
> (1980: 54–5)

From this characterization one might surmise that readers have complete freedom to interpret texts in any way they please, and that reader-response criticism therefore inevitably leads to 'irresponsible subjectivism' and 'interpretive promiscuity'. This would be an exaggeration, say the reader-response critics, for although the meaning of any given text can never be fixed in any absolute sense, arbitrary and irrelevant interpretations can be ruled out by appealing to *interpretive constraints*. Some reader-response theorists emphasize the constraining force exerted by linguistic features of the text (for example, Iser 1974; Holland 1975), while others emphasize the particular framework of expectations, ideas, and knowledge brought to bear during a reading event (for example, Fish 1980). Either way, it is the *justification* of one's personal response that matters.

From the reader-response perspective, then, texts are understood to be not so much *things* as *events*, and consequently the teacher's task becomes one of focusing students' attention not just on what texts *say*, but also on what they *do* (Fish 1980). Of course what texts 'do' to us is ultimately what we 'do' to them by interpreting them in relation to contexts of which we may or may not be consciously aware. Fish has developed this point extensively. Consider his example of the following text displayed on the door of the faculty club at Johns Hopkins University:

PRIVATE MEMBERS ONLY

Fish claims that when he wrote this on the blackboard of his classroom and asked his students what it meant, they invariably made up meanings having to do with genitalia—even though they fully realized what it 'really' meant. Fish argued that it would be a mistake to conclude that a text like PRIVATE MEMBERS ONLY is ambiguous by its essential nature. Rather, in a single given situation (for example, someone approaching the faculty club and seeing the sign on the door) it can have a single, clear, unambiguous meaning—namely, that only individuals who are members of the faculty club are welcome. That is to say, the person approaching the faculty club has knowledge of door signs and what to do with them, and this knowledge stabilizes the meaning of the sign when it is encountered in this particular context. In terms of the design model proposed in Chapter 2, the *physical situation* of the text activates particular *declarative knowledge* related to signs on club doors.

Fish's students, on the other hand, are in a different context. The knowledge organizing their perception has to do with English literature classrooms, with what kinds of questions professors ask, and with what kinds of things get written on blackboards (for example, ironic or problematic texts). The ambiguity of PRIVATE MEMBERS ONLY is therefore not a property of the text itself, but a function of the particular expectations we have when we read it in a particular context. When we are compelled first to imagine one context and meaning and then a second context and meaning we are in what Fish calls a *third* context 'in which the single meaning the sentence has is that it has more than one single meaning' (p. 283).[3] In the context of his students' *classroom* reading then, Fish argues, the plural meanings assigned to PRIVATE MEMBERS ONLY constitute its 'literal' meaning (i.e. that the text has multiple meanings *is* its meaning in that particular interpretive context). Rejecting the notion that 'literal' meaning is singular and objective, Fish concludes that 'there always will be a literal reading, but (1) it will not always be the same one and (2) it can change' (1980: 277).

According to Fish, then, texts are never inherently ambiguous, for that would presuppose the existence of some autonomous, pre-interpretational level of meaning. We don't understand the faculty club door sign in some sort of absolute, acontextual way and then adjust its meaning to the situation. Instead, our being in a particular situation predisposes us to interpret the text in a particular way. That is why, Fish says, a phrase like 'I will go' can be understood at times as a threat, at times as a report, at times as a prediction, but never as an 'unsituated kernel of pure semantic value' (p. 284). In other words, it is the interpretive situation—not language itself—that stabilizes meaning in an interpretive act.

For Fish, interpretation is 'the only game in town'. Meanings we take as 'obvious' or 'literal' may seem to require no interpretation, but this is only because they are entirely consistent with the 'interpretive structure of the situation' which is organizing our perception at that moment. In other words, 'self-evident' meanings result from interpretations based on contexts so 'normal' that we do not even recognize them as contexts at all.

But if all meanings are interpreted, how can people so often agree on the meaning of a given text? Fish argues that writers and readers do not act as fully independent agents, but are socialized into *interpretive communities* that embody particular interpretive rules, ideologies, assumptions, attitudes, beliefs, and values which constrain the ways they produce and interpret texts. From this point of view, a reader does not interpret a given text as an autonomous individual, but rather as a representative of a particular interpretive community (hence a 'feminist' interpretation or a 'Marxist' interpretation of a text). According to Fish, interpretive communities and the interpretive strategies they embody can therefore explain both the variety and the stability of reader response. Divergent responses result from readings produced by different interpretive communities, whereas similar responses result from readings produced within a particular interpretive community.[4]

It is crucial to acknowledge, however, that even within one culture, language communities and interpretive communities do not necessarily overlap in their membership. Furthermore, as Scholes (1985) has argued, it seems unreasonable to think, as Fish sometimes seems to suggest, that our perception and thought are enslaved to a particular interpretive community when virtually everyone belongs to more than one interpretive community. Instead, Scholes adopts a view consonant with the design metaphor, seeing 'individuals with many codes, some more and some less relevant, trying to see which ones will serve best in dealing with structures that have their own necessities' (p. 162). It is this multiplicity of codes and their potential conflicts, Scholes argues, 'that allows humans scope for any freedom or choice in writing or reading' (pp. 162–3).

Texts have intended readers, then, but intended readers are not the only kinds of readers, nor are their interpretations the only interpretations that count (Chatman 1978). Foreign language readers are, by definition, not intended readers. Their interpretations are inevitably influenced by their own particular historical, sociocultural, and personal circumstances. The goal of foreign language reading, then, should not be for language learners somehow to achieve normative 'in-group' interpretations, but rather for them to understand, first, that their interpretations may well be different, even in opposition to certain 'native' interpretations, and, second, that 'native speaker' interpretations are not necessarily monolithic and uniform amongst themselves. It is in thinking about the factors that might produce differences within and between 'insider' and 'outsider' interpretations that learners confront important sociocultural differences.

From the perspective of foreign language teaching, two important limitations of reader-response theory must be borne in mind. The first applies specifically to Fish's brand of reader-response theory: namely that it does not address the relationship between a text and the particular language in which it is written. Fish assumes an 'informed' reader, with well-developed linguistic and literary competence. Foreign language learners, by definition, have only partially-developed linguistic competence, and few have well-developed literary competence. Moreover, because they are coming to texts from different cultural worlds, they bring multiple rules of interpretation into play.

A second, more general, limitation has to do with the point made earlier about cultural learning from texts. If the 'authorly' role of the reader is played too assertively, the consequence would be that the expression of the 'foreign' culture (by the author through the text) would be obscured, and instead, the 'authorly' reader would freely impose his or her culture on the text. Although this commonly does happen in language classrooms, our goal should be to seek a balance between what Pearson and Tierney (1984) call 'thoughtfulness to self' and 'thoughtfulness to author' and what Widdowson (1984) calls 'assertive' and 'submissive' reading styles.

Despite these limitations, reader-response theory nevertheless offers a number of important insights for foreign language teachers. The first and most obvious implication is that individual students in a given class may produce substantially different interpretations—and these may differ significantly from those of native speakers—but they do not arise out of the blue, and they are not arbitrary. As we saw in the case of the ESL class reading the poem 'This is just to say' in Chapter 3, students see different things in texts because of differences in their backgrounds, in their past experiences, in their beliefs, attitudes, values, and so on. This point is supported by numerous schema studies showing the effects of cultural background knowledge on comprehension (for example, Kintsch and Greene 1978; Steffensen, *et al.* 1979; Johnson 1981; Floyd and Carrell 1987; Harris, *et al.* 1988). We therefore cannot think of students as a uniform, homogeneous, pre-understood group, just as we cannot assume monolithic homogeneity among 'native' interpretations. The pedagogic principle, then, is to explore multiple interpretations but also to attempt to understand how those interpretations reflect underlying cultural assumptions, beliefs, attitudes, and values.

That does not mean, however, that readers are free to construe texts any way they please. A second implication of reader-response theory is that readers must be familiar with the relevant interpretive constraints and must be responsible to the text, always ready to justify their interpretations based on the facts of the text itself. This point is of key pedagogical significance because it allows teachers and students to entertain multiple perspectives, without entering into endlessly relativistic discussions of texts. It also adds an important element to the design model presented in Chapters 2 and 3. If some interpretations can be said to be better than others (for example, by accounting more comprehensively for the facts of a text), then it is important to incorporate the *evaluation* of designs as a goal in literacy-based pedagogy. To this end, *rereading* and *reflecting* on texts become pedagogical imperatives.

A third implication is that because 'authentic texts' are texts written for a particular constituency, it means that even the 'native speaker/reader' will have difficulty reading a text when he or she is not a member of that constituency or intended readership, regardless of his or her native command of the language. We may talk about 'native-speaker' competence (linguistic, literary, cultural, or whatever) as if it were some established uniform state. But the whole problem of literacy, for native language as well as foreign language readers, is that this uniform competence is a fiction. All interpretation is partial because all competence is partial. Foreign language readers need not see themselves as hopelessly handicapped by their 'outsideness' with respect to the texts they read. On the contrary, their very outsideness can provide them with insights that would not necessarily occur to 'native' readers. When learners feel that the knowledge they can bring to a particular text is illegitimate or inappropriate, they will feel like keeping their interpretations to themselves. What teachers need to do, therefore, is to motivate learners to share their varied interpretations in order to make them aware of how *all* reading is mediated experience, and that many factors will contribute to the particular ways in which that mediation takes place during a given act of reading.

Design and reading

Reader-response theory and schema theory (discussed in Chapter 3) contribute in important ways to a view of reading as meaning design, as they take us beyond the linguistic design of the text itself to the cognitive and social dimensions of discourse. Both make clear the active role of the reader in creating meaning from textual, contextual, and knowledge-based resources. Whereas schema theory emphasizes the internal organization and activation of knowledge in the individual, reader-response theory emphasizes social constraints such as the situation of interpretation and the reader's membership in particular discourse communities.

To summarize in terms of the design model, reading is a dynamic rhetorical process of generating meaning from texts (i.e. realizing them as discourse) that draws on all of one's semiotic resources. Every text a reader encounters is the result of a particular act of design. It encodes particular reader-writer relationships, and a particular framing of a real or imagined world. Readers try to understand such relationships and such worlds by bringing whatever Available Designs they have (for example, knowledge of language, genres, styles, schemata, and so on) to the tasks of decoding, parsing, and interpreting, in order to produce some kind of meaning (i.e. designing, the innermost circle of Figure 2.3 in Chapter 2). The particular ways they do this will depend on their purpose (for example, getting a gist versus an in-depth understanding), the topic and how much they already know about it, their social role *vis-à-vis* the writer (for example, a student reading a professor's paper versus a professor reading a student's paper), and the physical situation (for example, a noisy bus versus a quiet library). These factors are represented by the second layer in Figure 2.3. The reader's interpretation of a text, along with any modifications to his or her existing knowledge (i.e. the original Available Designs that were used to make sense of the text), constitute the Redesigned.[5] To the extent that several readers share the same Available Designs, read for a similar purpose, and occupy similar social roles, their mental representations of the text will be similar. Conversely, when people apply different Available Designs to a given text, read for different purposes, or occupy different social roles, their interpretations will be more likely to diverge.

Finally, all of the above is influenced by the larger sociocultural context that has to do with the functions of reading in the home, school, and society, the social status of readers, and where and how reading is practiced in various contexts with various kinds of materials (the outermost layer of Figure 2.3). We are socialized to read in certain ways for particular purposes in particular settings, and to hold certain beliefs about texts. Reading Baudelaire in a French class is very different from reading the Koran in an Arabic class. We abide by certain interpretive conventions established within the discourse communities to which we belong and we gain entry into new discourse communities by learning their respective conventions through apprenticeship. In the remainder of the chapter we will consider how linguistic, cognitive, and sociocultural factors can influence how second language reading is performed (as well as how it is taught).

Reading in a non-native language

One of the most fundamental and self-evident differences between literacy in a first and second language is that the reader/writer of a second language has two languages at his or her disposal rather than just one.[6]

This fact begs a number of questions: Should we think of literacy as a 'universal' construct that underlies both first and second language use, or should we think of 'L1 literacy' and 'L2 literacy' as representing distinct sets of knowledge, abilities, and practices? What role might one's native language play in second language reading and writing? Assuming one is already literate in one's native language and has learnt the workings of the second language code, can literacy be assumed to be automatically available in the second language or is some sort of 'literacy mediation' necessary? Here we will be concerned with reading, but these questions will also be discussed in relation to writing in Chapter 6.

Investigation of these questions began in earnest in the 1970s. Goodman (1970; 1981; 1985) argued that the basic process of reading is universal, involving the formation, testing, modification, and confirmation of hypotheses based on features of the text itself as well as the reader's prior knowledge. Goodman's view found early support in a number of miscue analysis studies carried out in various languages (for example, Rigg 1977; Barrera 1981; Mott 1981) as well as other studies suggesting a positive correlation between native and foreign language reading (for example, Tucker 1975; Cziko 1976; Swain, Lapkin, and Barik 1976).

In the context of developing an argument for bilingual education, Cummins (1979; 1981) adopted this universalist stance, arguing that 'the literacy-related aspects of a bilingual's proficiency in L1 and L2 are seen as common or interdependent across languages' (1981: 23–4). That is to say, once one develops an ability to deal with 'cognitive academic' or 'context-reduced' uses of language, that ability does not need to be reacquired when one learns a new language. Calling this position alternately the 'Interdependence Hypothesis' and the 'Common Underlying Proficiency (CUP) Model', Cummins cited numerous studies of bilingual education programs, studies of learner age and language acquisition, and studies of home use of a minority L1, all supporting his claim that 'experience with either language is capable of promoting the proficiency that underlies the development of academic skills in both languages' (1981: 33).[7]

However, Cummins also made an important qualification to the standard universalist position. He posited a 'threshold level of L2 competence' (1976: 23) that bilinguals would have to attain in order for their linguistic interdependence to be fully realized. Cummins's threshold hypothesis was later supported by a number of studies that showed that people who were proficient readers in their native language were often unable to apply their well-developed reading skills when reading in a second language. Without a sufficient degree of language proficiency, their reading ability was seemingly 'short circuited' (Cziko 1978; Clarke 1979; 1980).[8] Cummins was careful to point out, however, that the threshold should not be thought of as static or absolute, but rather as variable according to factors such as the amount of time spent using the second language and the kinds of cognitive operations the learner needed to perform (p. 24).[9]

A number of studies have explored the fixity of the language proficiency threshold in the context of reading. Hudson (1982) found that by inducing relevant schemata through pre-reading activities, teachers could effectively override the threshold and facilitate comprehension in early stage language learners. Kern (1989) found that teaching discourse strategies could have a similar effect, and Devine (1988) found that students' theoretical orientation to reading (i.e. understanding reading as a meaning-based versus sound-based process) also seemed to mitigate the effect of the language proficiency threshold in second language comprehension. Most recently, Taillefer (1996) showed (as Cummins originally hypothesized) that the relative importance of second language proficiency varied with the type of reading task—the more difficult the task, the higher the language threshold.

The picture becomes more complex, however, when one considers certain other findings in second language reading research. First, it has been shown that many highly proficient bilinguals read 30 percent to 40 percent more slowly in their second language and that this difference is not related to any inadequacy in vocabulary or syntax knowledge (Favreau, Komoda, and Segalowitz 1980; Favreau and Segalowitz 1982). This finding suggests that L2 reading can remain less efficient than L1 reading well past a threshold point of language proficiency. Second, a number of studies have shown that reading in different languages can involve qualitatively different perceptual and processing strategies (for example, Cowan 1976; Tzeng and Hung 1981; Taylor and Taylor 1983; Bernhardt 1987; Koda 1987; MacWhinney and Bates 1989; Koda 1993), suggesting that transfer of L1 reading skills may not always facilitate L2 reading. Third, the influence of the native language on second language comprehension seems to vary according to the relationship of the two languages' orthographic and morphosyntactic systems (Gass 1987; Sasaki 1991; Koda 1996). Both the native language and the second language seem to play an important role in shaping the particular strategies that language learners use when reading second language texts, whether at early levels of L2 proficiency (Koda 1993) or at high levels of L2 proficiency (Kilborn 1989), and this L1–L2 interaction seems to be affected by the cognitive and linguistic requirements of the particular reading task (Koda 1996).

These studies suggest that successful second language reading is not simply a matter of transferring L1 reading abilities once a threshold level of second language proficiency is attained. Rather, as the design model elaborated in Chapters 2 and 3 predicts, the studies suggest that readers draw selectively upon Available Designs from both their first and second languages as needed *in particular acts of reading* to produce meaning—both at early and advanced stages of language learning. Thus, as Corder (1983) suggested, the term 'borrowing' may be more appropriate than the term 'transfer' in characterizing the role of the native language, as it focuses attention on learners' language use rather than on language structures.

Even 'borrowing', however, does not capture the full range of selective and strategic uses of the native language in second language reading. Consider the phenomenon of mental translation during second language reading (Kern

1994), here illustrated by the remarks of an English-speaking intermediate-level learner of French as she reads and then rereads part of a French text:

> [Section of text read:] *On simplifie leur culture et on la réduit à un petit nombre de caractéristiques qu'on attribue à tout le monde, comme s'il n'y avait pas de distinctions à faire entre les millions d'habitants d'un pays.*
> Okay, the first time, I tried to read this one for comprehension and I think my problem is that if it gets too long, for some reason my comprehension breaks, and so I read the first part for comprehension and then pretty soon I can't concentrate on it anymore, so I have to go back and read the whole sentence again. [rereads] Okay, when I read it the second time I got it. But for some reason I translated into English from here [*comme s'il n'y avait pas*]. I think it was because . . . Even though I'm totally familiar with all the words and I could have read it in French . . . again, I broke my concentration after about a line, and I had to read it again and I translated into English as I read. And this is probably the simplest part of the sentence, which is really strange, and I think it is because I have problems of keeping my concentration for more than one line.
> (Kern 1994: 447–8)

Here the student is not translating to figure out what the second half of the sentence means; in fact she is surprised that she has translated 'the simplest part of the sentence'. Rather, it seems that she is translating in order to maintain her concentration long enough to integrate and assimilate meaning that would be fragmented if it remained represented in French form. She states that if the sentence gets too long her comprehension 'breaks' and she loses her concentration, so she needs to reread the sentence from the beginning. From a cognitive perspective, her comprehension difficulties might be explained in terms of lack of automaticity in word recognition as well as working memory span limitations. That is to say, the reader may be expending effort in decoding words, thereby reducing the level of attention that is available for synthesizing the words' meanings.

How does her use of the native language help? Translation (here defined as a mental reprocessing of L2 words, phrases, or sentences in L1 forms while reading L2 texts) might facilitate cognitive processing and comprehension in at least two ways. First, given that familiar words can be stored in working memory faster and more effectively than unfamiliar words (Mewhort, Merikle, and Bryden 1969; Haber and Hershenson 1980), when the reader translates less-familiar French words into more-familiar English words she optimizes her short-term retention. Second, once words are translated into the native language, it may be that they can be more effectively synthesized into meaningful propositions by means of L1 chunking processes. Translation may thus allow the reader to establish a kind of mental scratch pad or semantic buffer, where phrase-level and text-level meanings can be represented and assembled in native language form, in order to optimize processing efficiency (see Kern, 1994 for further elaboration of this argument).[10]

The point of this example is that the native language provides not only a source of lexical and morphosyntactic structures to be 'transferred' or 'borrowed', but also an alternative processing space in which to design meaning. This alternative 'space' may allow learners to make use of well-established connections among procedural knowledge, declarative knowledge, and other Available Designs from their native language.[11] Again, then, the role of the first language in second language reading seems not to be an issue of wholesale *transfer*, but rather of selective and strategic *uses* of L1 linguistic and schematic resources to facilitate comprehension of L2 texts. The advantage of this characterization is that it gives greater agency to the reader, who is choosing among all available resources, both L1- and L2-related, in an attempt to fulfill particular purposes in particular contexts of reading as appropriately as he or she can.

But learners' tendency to draw on both first and second language resources is also influenced by the larger social context (i.e. the outermost ring of the design model shown in Figure 2.3). For example, Genesee (1979) has argued that the relative social status of the L1 and the L2 in the community, and parents' attitudes about reading, are key considerations. English-speaking children in Canadian bilingual education programs who are first taught to read in French are very likely to draw on French when they read in English because of the high-prestige status of their native language. If, however, the child's native language is less prevalent and less prestigious in the community, and the parents attach low value to it, the child may be less likely to apply skills developed in the non-native school language to the first language (p. 75).

Looking at second language reading from the perspective of the design model described in Part One allows us to reframe a question that has galvanized second language reading researchers since the early 1980s: Is foreign language reading a reading problem or a language problem? (Alderson 1984). As Alderson pointed out in 1984 and Bernhardt and Kamil (1995) were able to reiterate over a decade later, methodological limitations of many second language reading studies have prevented any definitive answer to this question. Even the findings of methodologically adequate studies (for example, Carrell 1991; Brisbois 1992; Bernhardt and Kamil 1995; Lee and Schallert 1997), however, indicate that *both* native language reading ability *and* second language proficiency play a significant role in second language reading.

By presenting reading as a social and cultural act involving cognitive and linguistic dimensions, the design model defines reading not in terms of universal and uniform processes, but rather in terms of contextually appropriate practices. From this perspective, we can expand the question 'Is foreign language reading a reading problem or a language problem?' to a question of broader scope and yet also of greater specificity: 'In what ways, and to what ends, do second language readers draw on the various linguistic and schematic resources available to them in particular contexts of reading?' Research implications of this question will be discussed in Chapter 10.

If reading is not just a psycholinguistic process but also a socially- and culturally-embedded practice, it follows that it is learnt through *apprenticeship* within discourse communities whose conventions are shaped by larger societal and historical forces. In the remainder of the chapter we will consider three examples from Japanese, Chinese, and Nigerian contexts.

Reading and teaching reading across cultural contexts

As Heath (1983) so clearly showed in her study of literacy practices in two communities in the Piedmont Carolinas, people's 'ways with words' can differ in very significant ways across contexts and across discourse communities. The same is true for learning to read in a non-native language. How one reads will certainly be strongly influenced by one's native language reading experience, but it is also influenced by the kinds of classroom practices into which one is socialized.

Consider, for example, Hino's (1992) discussion of the *yakudoku* tradition in foreign language literacy in Japan. *Yaku* means 'translation' and *doku* means 'reading', and the technique consists of translating a sentence word by word into Japanese, reordering the translated words in accordance with Japanese syntax, then recoding the sentence into normal Japanese syntax, as illustrated in Figure 4.1.

[Target language sentence] She has a nice table in her room.

Stage 1 [The reader makes a word-by-word translation]

She	has	a	nice	table	in	her	room
kanojo	*motteiru*	*hitotsu-no*	*sutekina*	*teburu*	*naka*	*kanojo-no*	*heya*

Stage 2 [Translated words reordered in accordance with Japanese syntax]

Kanojo	kanojo-no	heya	naka	hitotsu-no	sutekina	teburu	motteiru

Stage 3 [Recoding in Japanese syntax]

Kanojo-wa kanojo-no heya-no naka-ni hitotsu-no sutekina teburu-wo motteiru

---

Figure 4.1:   Three-stage process of the yakudoku *tradition of foreign language reading (Hino 1992: 100)*

Only individual lexical meanings are derived directly from the original text. A reader's understanding of a whole sentence or a whole text is therefore based entirely on the recoded Japanese forms.

Hino points out that although *yakudoku* was developed centuries ago as a way of reading Chinese texts, it remains the predominant way of teaching reading in foreign languages in Japan and, for many Japanese students of English, represents 'the' way to read in English: 'Once the English is transformed into Japanese, it is considered read. Conversely, if an English text has not been recoded into Japanese, 'reading' is not considered to have taken place . . . .' (p. 101). Hino adds that *yakudoko* also affects learners' conception of writing in English, which is seen as a matter of translating a Japanese text word by word into English, then reordering the words to agree with English syntax (p. 101). Although some educators claim that *yakudoko* offers certain benefits in terms of mental discipline and syntactic knowledge, Hino emphasizes its liabilities for learners, such as slow reading, fatigue, excessive emphasis on individual word meanings, and only approximate understandings.

Yakudoku is not prescribed by the Japanese Ministry of Education, it is commonly criticized in the Japanese TEFL journals, and yet it persists despite the disadvantages cited above. Hino explains that besides being easy to teach, the practice of *yakudoku* is deeply embedded in Japanese culture, linked to the very origins of writing in Japan. Precisely because it is such a longstanding cultural practice, breaking away from the *yakudoku* norm is exceedingly difficult. Hino concludes that in teaching foreign languages in Japan, it is best to incorporate *yakudoku* to focus on syntax, but to supplement reading instruction generously with a variety of techniques that support direct global understanding of the original language of the text. Instructional change, then, is dynamically negotiated at the juncture of professional discourse and larger sociohistorical forces.

Another example is provided by Kohn (1992), who discusses the literacy strategies of foreign language students in Chinese universities. He points out that although there are considerable regional differences, foreign language teaching practices in China tend to reflect a confluence of three traditions: Confucianism, Mahayana Buddhism, and pre-WWII British foreign language teaching techniques. Confucian tradition emphasizes the importance of knowledge and the authority of the teacher, while Buddhist tradition values the memorization of texts to demonstrate mastery of knowledge. British foreign language techniques of the 1920s and 1930s (imported via Soviet teachers of Russian in the 1950s) emphasized the close reading of texts, grammar analysis, and translation exercises. Today, as Kohn describes it, foreign language reading is taught both 'intensively' and 'extensively'. In intensive reading classes, students are asked to read slowly, to look up all unfamiliar words, to analyze complex structures carefully and to reread difficult sentences until they are understood (p. 121). According to Kohn, students tend to apply these same micro-level strategies when they read in their 'extensive' reading classes, paying little attention to global, text-level meaning. Kohn recalls his surprise when, having asked his students to write an analysis of a chapter from Nabokov's *Pnin*, they responded by copying passages verbatim from the textbook:

It seemed to me that in their experience, analyzing a story independently of the teacher's interpretation given in class was a very novel concept. Indeed, as I discovered later from observing other Chinese faculty members teaching the same students, extensive reading classes consisted of lectures on a literary subject by the teacher, from which lecture the students took verbatim notes, and repeated those notes on examinations. It was just the kind of behavior which might earn those students a reprimand, were they studying in an American university instead of a Chinese one.
(pp. 121–2)

Indeed, for Kohn's students, what is 'foreign' is not just the language, but also the pedagogical values of an American teacher who assumes that students will guess meanings from context, develop their own interpretation of a text, and volunteer their thoughts freely in classroom discussion. Jin and Cortazzi (1998) explore in greater depth the underpinnings of differences between Chinese and 'Western' cultures of learning, noting that educational culture in China is currently undergoing considerable change due to social and economic developments and that language instruction has become increasingly influenced by communicative approaches. Again, we see how broad changes in instructional practice occur within a larger sociocultural picture.

The third example highlights *awareness* as a key ingredient for change at the local level of language classrooms. Parry (1996) studied how Nigerian and Chinese ESL/EFL students' reading strategies related to the different ways that language and literacy are represented, used, and taught in the learners' home cultural communities. She found that her Nigerian students tended to be top-down oriented (they performed poorly, for example, on word-level tasks), while her Chinese students were more bottom-up oriented (i.e. they attended closely to textual detail). She explained these differences hypothetically in terms of the Nigerian students' communicative milieu (which she characterized as supporting a high tolerance of ambiguity) and the Chinese analytic writing system (characterized as requiring readers' precise knowledge of textual parts in order to understand the whole). Nevertheless, Parry acknowledged important individual differences within each of the cultural groups.[12] Moreover, she found that students could change their strategies if motivated and encouraged to do so. In her study, both the Nigerians and the Chinese became more flexible in their strategy use over time in the classroom. Parry attributed the change to 'constant practice in thinking about how they set about interpreting a text and explaining these processes in their interviews or essays' (pp. 687–8). Parry encouraged this metalinguistic and meta-interpretive thinking by asking students to talk about their reading strategies:

Because I was enquiring about their strategies and . . . soliciting information about where the strategies came from, the students became aware, as they had never been before, of what they habitually did, and this awareness made it possible for them to question their habits and thus to acquire greater flexibility.
(p. 688)

Here a focus on what is normally invisible because of its routinized nature— learners' habitual reading behavior—provides the impetus for reflection on familiar practices and consideration of new possibilities.

While it would be clearly wrong to deny that there is substantial overlap in certain aspects of literacy across cultures and languages, these three examples illustrate the point that it is equally wrong to view literacy as a monolithic and uniform phenomenon that can be automatically transferred to a second language once a certain proficiency in that language is acquired. These examples also remind us that reading pedagogy is as culturally-embedded as the reading process itself. Teachers and learners can have very different conceptions of what academic reading is, and consequently it can sometimes be difficult to implement pedagogical approaches that learners perceive as inconsistent with familiar cultural values or too far removed from familiar literacy practices. Yet it is precisely these differences that must be confronted in literacy-based language teaching. As Parry's study suggests, change is possible, and it is facilitated when learners are led to reflect on their own reading processes and to understand how their reading processes and their interpretations of texts are influenced by particular cultural assumptions, beliefs, attitudes, and values.

Conclusion

This chapter has presented reading as a dynamic, interactive process of deriving discourse from text. This process is not a monolithic and uniform one, however. On the one hand, reading is a socially-embedded activity involving reader-author relationships, shared assumptions, and conventions established by discourse communities. It takes place within an immediate context of situation, purpose, task, and social roles, as well as within a larger sociocultural context of values, beliefs, and attitudes related to literacy and education. On the other hand, reading is an individual and personal activity involving knowledge, imagination, and emotions. This double perspective allows us to account for broad commonalities in reading behavior within and across social groups as well as individual variation within those groups. It also has implications for the teaching of reading.

What are the principal things that foreign language students need to learn about reading? They need to learn that reading is not a generic, all-or-nothing affair (as implied in the classic teacher refrain 'Either you read it or you didn't!'), but rather a process whose particular product is contingent upon a variety of linguistic, cognitive, and social factors, including culture-specific goals and purposes for reading. They need to learn that reading is a recursive process, in which one can rethink one's interpretation in the light of new knowledge and experience. They need to recognize that the pragmatic rules of reading shift with the context of situation and purpose, that reading a newspaper and reading a poem are very different activities. In learning these things, students will also learn that words and texts are not containers of universally-shared meanings and that communication is not simply a question of information transfer.

As will be described in the next chapter, a literacy-based approach to language teaching provides learners with an opportunity to think about how text and context relate to one another. On the one hand, learners explore how a text's language invites them to develop particular contexts of interpretation—and how those contexts can be redesigned by manipulating textual features. On the other hand, learners explore how text-external, situational contexts—which can also be manipulated—predispose them as readers to interpret a given text in particular ways. Underlying this kind of pedagogical approach is the assumption that the more learners redesign meaning by manipulating both language and context, the more they expand their communicative capacity. We now turn to a detailed examination of how such teaching might be implemented in the language classroom.

Notes

1 See the section on rhetorical organization patterns in Chapter 3.
2 It may be that children's writing is convention-bound in its own ways. Note the striking similarity between Maria's story and one reported by Wells (1981), told by a schoolgirl about her name, Melanie:

> One day there was a M and the M played with the e and the e played with the l and the l played with the a and the a played with n and the n played with the i and the i played with the e and the e played with nobody and the e was very sad.
> (from Raban, cited in Wells 1981: 275)

3 In a sense, Fish's 'third context' is akin to Kramsch's (1993) notion of a 'third place' from which language learners can reflect upon the relationships among meanings and their expression in one's native language and culture, and in a second language and culture. One of the real benefits of classroom learning is that learners *expect* the new and unexpected, making them particularly receptive to the comparison of multiple perspectives (for example, multiple readings of a single text).
4 Fish is careful to point out, however, that interpretive communities are no more stable than texts. This is because 'interpretive strategies are not

natural or universal, but learned' (1980: 172). What this means is that rules of interpretation can be 'forgotten or supplanted, or complicated or dropped from favor' (1980: 172), ultimately leading to the production of new types of texts and new ways of reading them.

5 The Redesigned is thus somewhat akin to Iser's (1980) notion of the *virtual text*, which is always subject to redesigning upon subsequent readings, enriched by the listener/reader's fuller experience.

6 Here, I am excluding the case of child learners who are not literate in their native language, and who become literate for the first time in a second language (which happens not uncommonly, for example, in bilingual education). I am making this exclusion simply because in secondary and higher education contexts, the focus of this book, virtually all second language learners can already read and write in at least one language.

7 Cummins's model also predicts what *kinds* of skills might be more or less susceptible to transfer across languages. Language-specific skills like spelling patterns and grammatical rules, would be on the 'less-transferable' end of the continuum, whereas general cognitive processes involved in hypothesis-testing and synthesis of meaning would be much more transferable across languages. Genesee (1979) provides some evidence for differential transfer effect in English and French. He reported that English-speaking schoolchildren at various levels of a French immersion program performed comparably to their native-speaking French peers on tests of integrative skills (comprehension, use of context, synthesis of meaning) but performed less well than their native-speaking peers on *discrete-point* tests of vocabulary, orthography, and grammar.

8 It is well-established, for example, that people read more slowly in a non-native language, unless that language has become dominant through use (Kolers 1966; Macnamara 1967; Mack 1986; Kilborn 1989).

9 In addition to positing the variable nature of the threshold, Cummins (1976) entertained the idea of multiple thresholds.

10 Steffensen and Goetz (1997) explain learners' common habit of writing translations of words above the lines of texts they are reading, in similar terms. If learners are unable to process the syntax of what they are reading fast enough, they will be unable to retain words in working memory. Writing a translation above each word in the text therefore serves not only as a means to maintain word meanings in memory, but also to speed up processing (since they now process familiar words, easier to maintain in short-term memory).

11 It may be that these well-established connections also become expanded or transformed through their use in second language contexts.

12 Murray and Nichols (1992) and Spack (1997) also emphasize the importance of individual differences in cross-cultural literacy.

5 Teaching reading as design

Understanding texts written in a foreign language is a significant challenge for most students. Reading complex texts for which they are not the intended readers, language learners must learn to navigate through unfamiliar vocabulary, grammar structures, and cultural references. They must also learn to deal with frustrating silences—when cultural presuppositions remain tacit and keep the foreign reader at arm's length from understanding.

The challenge for the foreign language teacher is to provide appropriate guidance and support for learners' efforts. The question is, what is appropriate? Starting with the issue of vocabulary and structures, for example, a traditional question has been whether students should begin reading texts before they have learnt the vocabulary and grammar contained in them. Should, for example, a reading passage with lots of subjunctives be assigned before students have studied the subjunctive mood? Or, alternatively, should a text containing unfamiliar structures be simplified before it is assigned? These questions are rooted in an assumption that 'real' reading cannot occur until learners are familiar with all the elements that a given text contains—so that reading is in a sense an exercise in recognition of what one already knows. Certainly there are cases where text simplification is desirable, such as at the early stages of language learning, as a way to boost learners' motivation and to broaden the scope of their reading. It is not, however, a viable long-term solution for students who must be prepared to read texts written for native speakers. Moreover, a number of studies have shown that learners' language proficiency is not necessarily a good predictor of their comprehension of foreign language texts (Lee and Musumeci 1988; Demel 1990). What seems to be more important than simplifying texts is structuring learners' tasks and interaction to match their language abilities. Pica, Young, and Doughty (1987), for example, found that simplifying language input was less effective in improving ESL learners' comprehension than providing them with the opportunity to ask questions and clarify their understanding of the unsimplified version in an interactive context. Because language learners in academic settings ultimately need to learn how to read complex texts, a basic principle of teaching reading in a literacy-based language program is that students need controlled tasks, not controlled texts. In this chapter we will consider a number of structured tasks that not only focus students' reading purpose, but also allow them to confront and reflect upon reading difficulties in socially interactive ways.

Another issue is background knowledge. Our discussion of schema theory in Chapter 3 showed the crucial importance of background knowledge in reading comprehension. Faced with the impossibility of providing *all* potentially relevant information, however, teachers must make choices concerning *what* and *how much* background knowledge should be taught. Such choices are particularly difficult in the case of literary texts, since each element of background knowledge the teacher provides will highlight one aspect of the text and help students to develop an interpretation, but may blind students to other possible interpretations. Yet it is precisely that potential to redesign interpretations by considering new background information that makes the study of foreign texts so exciting. Learners can experience shifts in understanding as new knowledge is brought to light. The goal in literacy-based teaching, then, is not to present every possible piece of potentially relevant background information, but to allow students to see how additional background knowledge affects their interpretations, to see how context influences their particular designings of textual meaning. This suggests that background knowledge may be most effectively presented in stages—some before, some during, and some after reading—to sensitize readers to the effects of new information on their interpretations.

A closely related issue is that of text selection. It is often recommended that texts be chosen that deal with familiar topics in learners' home culture, so that background knowledge can compensate for linguistic difficulty. Like text simplification, this can be good advice for novice-level students. Reading texts that deal with familiar content not only stimulates motivation but also allows students to concentrate on vocabulary learning and reading fluency. Ultimately, however, academic language learners need to focus on texts whose information or underlying assumptions are unfamiliar. Besse (1984) has forcefully argued this point, suggesting that teachers adopt an intercultural perspective, focusing on cultural differences and their patterns, not just on discrete points of information. For example, after students formulate interpretive hypotheses (usually based on assumptions grounded in their native culture) the teacher guides them in analyzing what they themselves say or write about the text, in order to help them see the implicit assumptions they have made in its interpretation. In this way, Besse argues, students are encouraged to interpret 'authentic' texts as cultural outsiders, but also to understand in what ways a native speaker might interpret the text differently. In this kind of approach, language learners' incomplete knowledge of the second language and culture does not invalidate their readings of second language texts. On the contrary, their 'misreadings' can, with proper framing by the teacher, illuminate students' understanding of the reading process and, potentially, help them to increase their understanding of themselves and their cultural conditioning as reflected in their beliefs, attitudes, and assumptions.[1]

Another issue related to appropriateness of instruction has to do with the order of classroom tasks. In the traditional foreign language curriculum, reading, talking, and writing are relatively distinct phases of a linear instructional sequence. Students generally prepare for class by reading a text (which provides subject matter to talk about in class the following day). They talk about the text (or its general topic) in class, and then they are sometimes asked to write an essay about it, which is then submitted to the instructor for a grade. Sometimes students write notes or keep a reading journal, in which case the sequence by-passes discussion. Talking sometimes precedes reading, as in pre-reading activities. Rarely, however, does writing precede either reading or talking. The phases are typically discrete and sequential, rather than recursive, as illustrated in Figure 5.1.

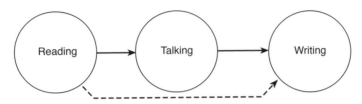

Figure 5.1:   Traditional linear relationship of reading-talking-writing

Most often that which *can* be done outside of class (i.e. reading and writing) *is*, in order to reserve class time for oral communication. This makes speaking the primary collaborative activity and maintains reading and writing as activities that students do chiefly on their own outside of class. There are a number of reasons why this traditional sequence of activity may be problematic when looked at from the perspective I have been outlining in this book. First, many students are not trained in the types of reading that teachers often tacitly expect them to do. Reading to identify thematic elements of a text, or to identify its underlying assumptions or ideological bias, for example, is not a well-practiced habit for most students. In fact, learners often need to be shown what teachers mean by these things before they can take the appropriate reader's stance and effectively do what teachers ask them to do. In other words, simply handing students a text to read will often not be enough—teachers may need to start off by leading students to recognize the kinds of textual phenomena, social interactions, information, and uses they hope students will ultimately recognize on their own when they read. First and foremost, this usually requires engaging learners in discussion (or even writing) *before* they read.

In sum, the problem with the traditional sequence of instruction is that students get little direct help with what they typically report to be the most difficult parts of language study—reading and writing. It is quite possible, in fact, that reading and writing are so often perceived as 'difficult' precisely *because* they are so often done outside of class, by oneself. Were reading and writing to be more frequently brought into the mainstream of classroom activity, made to be collaborative as well as individual activities, more integrated with speaking and with one another, they would perhaps not seem so difficult.

In literacy-based teaching the relationship between reading, writing, and talking is not linear, but overlapping, as shown in Figure 5.2.

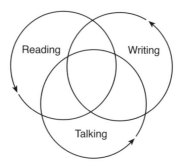

Figure 5.2:   *The relationship of reading, writing, and talking in a literacy-based curriculum*

It is the overlap that most clearly differentiates a literacy-focused curriculum itself from traditional curricula. Reading and writing overlap not only in the sense that students write formal essays about what they have read but also when students

- use writing to concretely represent their thoughts and interpretations of texts as they read—in the form of reading journals, summaries, diagrams, and so forth;
- write their own version of a topic or a theme *before* reading the target text, in order to be sensitized to the topic or theme before reading commences;
- write reflections on their own reading processes—their experiences, difficulties, and insights—as a component of their reports on their independent reading;
- read to improve their writing when they attend to linguistic, rhetorical, or stylistic elements in texts in order to incorporate them into their own work;
- actively and critically read their own and their peers' writing in the editing process.

A considerable number of the activities described in this chapter and in Chapter 7 involve combinations of reading, talking, and writing. The anticipated goal of working in these areas of overlap is not only enhanced skills, but also a greater awareness of language itself, of discourse processes, and of literacy practices. In this way, an overarching goal of literacy can not only bridge the traditional divisions among the 'four skills' of speaking, listening, reading, and writing, but also bridge the gap that too often separates the teaching of language from the teaching of literature.

Four curricular components

In organizing activities to accomplish these aims, it is useful to refer to four curricular components proposed by the New London Group (1996) for addressing the full range of learners' literacy needs. They are: situated practice, overt instruction, critical framing, and transformed practice.

Situated practice is immersion in language use. The focus is on communicating in the 'here and now', on learners' own lives and experiences, and on the spontaneous expression of their thoughts, opinions, and feelings. In terms of the design model presented in Part One, situated practice involves the use of Available Designs in a context of communication (i.e. the two innermost circles of the design model shown in Figure 2.3) but without conscious reflection, without metalanguage. The competencies involved correspond to Cummins's (1981) notion of context-embedded language use, or BICS (Basic Interpersonal Communication Skills). The other three curricular components, overt instruction, critical framing, and transformed practice, on the other hand, contribute to what Cummins called CALP (Cognitive Academic Language Proficiency), which tends not to develop automatically from social interaction but is of key importance to academic success. Situated practice is based on 'the world of learners' Designed and Designing experiences' (New London Group 1996: 83) and emphasizes apprenticeship, experience, pattern recognition, and socialization.

Overt instruction involves developing 'an explicit metalanguage of Design' (New London Group 1996: 83) so that various elements contributing to meaning can be identified, talked about, and learnt explicitly. In terms of the design model, overt instruction focuses learners' attention explicitly on Available Designs and their use. Pedagogically, it involves creating scaffolded learning activities, not just drills and memorization. Overt instruction therefore introduces an element of conscious control as well as a vocabulary to allow students to talk about the meaning design process.

Critical framing has to do with the reflective dimension of literacy instruction. Whereas situated practice focuses on the immediate 'here and now', critical framing involves stepping back and looking at the 'then and there' of communication. It involves drawing on the metalanguage developed through overt instruction to direct conscious attention to relationships among elements within the linguistic system as well as relationships between language use and social contexts and purposes. In terms of the design model, then, it involves learners thinking about relations and interactions among the three circles of design, communicative context, and sociocultural context shown in Figure 2.3. As suggested in Chapter 1, critical framing involves both cognitive (for example, Flower 1990) and social (for example, Freire and Macedo 1987) dimensions.

Transformed practice involves acts 'in which students transfer and re-create Designs of meaning from one context to another' (New London Group 1996: 83). In concrete terms, this means creating new texts on the basis of existing ones, or reshaping texts to make them appropriate for contexts of communication other than those for which they were originally intended. Writing an analytic essay about a text that has been read would be one common example of transformed practice. In terms of the design model, the focus is here on design processes, but now with an explicit awareness of both immediate and larger sociocultural contexts.

We can think of these four components as the 'basic food groups' needed to meet language learners' literacy 'nutritional needs', to borrow a metaphor from Schachter (1983). Situated practice and overt instruction have traditionally constituted the bulk of language teaching at the introductory and intermediate levels. Essential as they are, they are not sufficient for the development of students' critical or cultural understanding of language, literacy, and communication. In fact, the New London Group (1996) contends that 'both immersion and many sorts of Overt Instruction are notorious as socializing agents that can render learners quite uncritical and unconscious of the cultural locatedness of meanings and practices' (p. 85). Unfortunately, the complementary nutritional elements of critical framing and transformed practice are all too often either reserved for the elite in advanced level literature courses or not provided at all. A major goal of literacy-based language teaching, then, is to provide a well-balanced instructional 'diet' for all language learners at *all* levels of the curriculum.

In the rest of the chapter we will consider reading activities that represent each of the four curricular components. Although most of the activities in fact involve more than one component, I have nevertheless grouped them according to the component that I consider primary, and will show how they can be extended beyond the primary component (i.e. how a 'situated practice' activity can be extended to involve 'critical framing' as well). These activities aim (1) to focus on both process and product dimensions of reading, (2) to integrate reading with thinking, writing, and talking, and (3) to develop a wide range of literacy abilities from the early stages of language study. I have chosen to concentrate most of my discussion on activities for the introductory and intermediate levels, simply because this is where I believe the most important changes must be made in developing a literacy-focused curriculum.

Situated practice (immersion)

Situated practice has to do with learners' immersion in reading as an act of meaning design. Whereas traditional reading pedagogy tends to channel learners toward normative (i.e. 'native') interpretations of texts, the activities suggested in this section encourage learners to explore their spontaneous responses to texts, while also insisting on the importance of justifying their responses in terms of the text itself.

Apprenticeship in designing meaning: Directed Reading

One important aspect of the new vision of teaching reading during the early levels of language learning is to make students more aware of the kinds of mental activity they engage in when they read (see, for example, the discussion of Parry (1996) in Chapter 4). When reading in their native language, for example, fluent readers develop expectations about what they will encounter next in a text, based on their background knowledge as well as linguistic, graphic, and spatial features of the text. Writers take this into account as they construct texts, giving readers clear markers to guide their prediction process in the right direction (or tempting them to follow false paths in order to surprise them at the end). This is the 'discourse trail' discussed at the outset of Chapter 4. Most novice-level language students are not consciously aware of this meaning-prediction process—and understandably so, since their attention is generally focused on individual word meanings. Nevertheless, awareness of how they are predicting meaning can help them to take a larger view as they read, sometimes allowing them to cope with the limits of their vocabulary or syntax.

One teaching technique useful for guiding learners' thinking processes during reading and for enhancing their motivation is the Directed Reading-Thinking Activity (DRTA). Developed by Stauffer (1969), the DRTA encourages readers (1) to establish goals and to read purposefully, (2) to make inferences and predictions while reading, and (3) to evaluate the fit between information in the text and their own mental representations of the text.

In this activity, the teacher's role is to engage learners in a cyclical process of predicting, reading, and thinking by carefully selecting several stopping points in the text and asking two principal questions at each juncture: 'What do you think is going to happen next?' and 'Why?' The example below is from a first year French class reading a vignette by Alphonse Allais.[2]

Each student has a copy of the text, as well as a blank sheet of paper. The teacher asks the students to cover all of the reading selection except for the first two sentences.[3] (Alternatively, the teacher can use an overhead projector.) The teacher asks the students to read silently (or the teacher can read aloud as they follow silently).

Un jour je rencontre une femme à l'aspect pauvre qui tient à la main un petit garçon de quatre ans. L'enfant pleure.	[One day I met a poor looking woman holding a four-year-old boy by the hand. The boy was crying.]

[cover sheet]

The teacher asks (in French): *Based on what you've just read, what do you think this text will be about? Do you think this will be a story? an essay? a play?* These questions are intended to activate students' background knowledge related to both the content and the genre of the text. Below is a sample of students' responses:

Student 1:	C'est une histoire triste.	[It's a sad story.]
Student 2:	Oui.	[Yeah.]
Teacher:	Pourquoi?	[Why?]
Student 1:	Parce que 'pauvre' et 'pleure'.	[Because 'poor' and 'cries']
Student 3:	Oui, c'est . . . la femme est pauvre et déprimée.	[Yeah, it's . . . the woman is poor and depressed.]
Student 4:	Elle est probablement seule. Elle n'a pas de mari. Sa vie est difficile.	[She's probably lonely. She doesn't have a husband. Her life is hard.]
Teacher:	D'accord. Et qu'est-ce qui va arriver? Qu'est-ce qui va se passer?	[OK. And what's going to happen?]
Student 4:	Elle va rencontrer l'homme de sa vie?	[She'll meet the man of her life?]
Student 3:	Non, ça va être tragique.	[No, it's going to be tragic.]
Student 5:	Suicide peut-être? [laughter]	[Maybe suicide? (laughter)]

In the spirit of open and collaborative exploration, the teacher welcomes all contributions, even those that might seem 'off base', and encourages discussion of all proposed hypotheses.[4] In order to maximize participation, students can be asked to write down their responses before verbalizing them.

Once several ideas have been offered, the teacher tells the students to move their cover sheet down to the next predetermined point in the selection and read silently to find out whether they were right in their predictions. That is, students are asked to *monitor* and *evaluate* what preliminary meanings they have produced so far.

Un jour je rencontre une femme à l'aspect pauvre qui tient à la main un petit garçon de quatre ans. L'enfant pleure.

«Qu'est-ce qu'il a, ce petit ?»

—En passant devant un pâtissier, il a vu un gâteau. Mais ça coûte vingt-cinq francs. Je ne suis pas riche . . . C'est pour ça qu'il crie !

[One day I met a poor looking woman holding a four-year-old boy by the hand. The boy was crying.]

['What's wrong with the little one?']

[—He saw a cake as he was passing in front of a pastry shop. But it costs 25 francs. I am not rich . . . That's why he's fussing.][5]

[cover sheet]

When the students have finished reading the segment the teacher then asks *What do you think now?* or *Were you right?* These questions encourage students to assess the appropriateness of their earlier hypotheses and to make any necessary modifications. If modifications are made, the teacher should follow up by asking *What made you change your mind?* in order to focus students' attention on the specific words in the text that made the modification necessary, and on the logical and cultural connections the students have just made. As before, all ideas and comments are welcome regardless of their 'correctness', although now students are required (1) to explain the logic behind their statements, and (2) to support their hypotheses by citing relevant details from the text. These stipulations encourage students to reflect on their own comprehension and eliminate haphazard guessing.

Before continuing, the teacher asks: *What do you think will happen next?*, and elicits students' predictions that establish purpose and motivation for reading the next segment:

Student 2:	Il va acheter le gâteau.	[He's going to buy the cake.]
Teacher:	Qui?	[Who is?]
Student 2:	L'homme. Le narrateur.	[The man. The narrator.]
Teacher:	Et pourquoi vous pensez ça?	[And why do you think that?]
Student 2:	Parce que la femme dit 'Je ne suis pas riche.'	[Because the woman says 'I am not rich.']
Teacher:	Et c'est tout?	[Is that all?]
Student 2:	Non . . . aussi parce que l' enfant pleure . . . et parce que l'homme est sympathique.	[No . . . also because the child is crying . . . and because the man is nice.]
Teacher:	Et comment savez-vous qu'il est sympathique?	[And how do you know he's nice?]
Student 2:	Je crois . . . parce qu'il dit 'petit' quand il dit 'Qu'est-ce qu'il a, ce petit?' C'est sympathique.	[I think . . . because he says 'little one' when he says 'What's wrong with the little one?' That's nice.]

Note that this kind of questioning is simple, but it makes students accountable for their impressions. The student in this exchange had to think for a minute about why she thought the narrator was nice, but by scanning through the text she was able to give linguistic evidence for her claim. She could have also been asked why she thought the narrator was a man. It is this kind of sensitivity to the details of language—as logical, cultural, and informational indicators, not only as language structures *per se*—that students need to develop early on in their language study if they are to succeed at more advanced levels.

As the activity continues, students move their cover sheets to the next stopping point and read the exposed segment silently:

Un jour je rencontre une femme à l'aspect pauvre qui tient à la main un petit garçon de quatre ans. L'enfant pleure.

[One day I met a poor looking woman holding a four-year-old boy by the hand. The boy was crying.]

« Qu'est-ce qu'il a, ce petit ? »

['What's wrong with the little one?']

—En passant devant un pâtissier, il a vu un gâteau. Mais ça coûte vingt-cinq francs. Je ne suis pas riche ... C'est pour ça qu'il crie !

[—He saw a cake as he was passing in front of a pastry shop. But it costs 25 francs. I am not rich ... That's why he's fussing.]

—Allez lui acheter son gâteau, et rapportez-moi la monnaie !

[—Go buy him his cake, and bring me back the change!]

Je donne un billet de cinquante francs. Quelques minutes après, la femme revient avec l'enfant, qui a le sourire, et la monnaie.

[I gave her a 50 franc bill. Several minutes later, the woman came back with the child, who was smiling, and the change.]

[cover sheet]

The student is happy to see her prediction confirmed by the text. Here again, however, the teacher follows up her assertion by asking her to clarify exactly what she means.

Student 2: Ah! Il a acheté le gâteau!   [Ah! He bought the cake!]
Teacher: Qui? L'homme?   [Who? The man?]
Student 2: Oui ... non ... pas exactement. Mais il donne l'argent pour le gâteau.   [Yes ... no ... not exactly. But he gives the money for the cake.]

Some teachers may view this kind of clarification questioning as 'nitpicking', but it serves the important pedagogical function of consistently bringing students back to the details of the text to support their assertions and to tie communication to logical and cultural connections. In this way the teacher can maintain a open-spirited approach to interpretation, without letting the discussion degenerate into a *laissez-faire* free-for-all in which learners neglect the constraints on meaning imposed by the text itself.

The cycle of predicting, reading, and reflecting is repeated until the end of the text is reached (a total of four or five stopping points is optimal).[6] Although readers' predictions are often quite diverse at the outset, they become more similar towards the end of the reading selection as readers accumulate more and more textual evidence, and their mental representations of the text converge. Ideally, texts should be chosen that have a twist ending, so that students' expectations are challenged and the reading is enjoyable:

Un jour je rencontre une femme à l'aspect pauvre qui tient à la main un petit garçon de quatre ans. L'enfant pleure.

«Qu'est-ce qu'il a, ce petit ?»

—En passant devant un pâtissier, il a vu un gâteau. Mais ça coûte vingt-cinq francs. Je ne suis pas riche . . . C'est pour ça qu'il crie !

—Allez lui acheter son gâteau, et rapportez-moi la monnaie !

Je donne un billet de cinquante francs. Quelques minutes après, la femme revient avec l'enfant, qui a le sourire, et la monnaie.

Voilà qui va bien. Maintenant tout le monde est heureux : le gosse parce qu'il a son gâteau, vous parce que votre petit garçon ne pleure plus, le pâtissier parce qu'il a vendu un gâteau, et moi parce que je n'ai plus mon faux billet!

[One day I met a poor looking woman holding a four-year-old boy by the hand. The boy was crying.]

['What's wrong with the little one?']

[—He saw a cake as he was passing in front of a pastry shop. But it costs 25 francs. I am not rich . . . That's why he's fussing.]

[—Go buy him his cake, and bring me back the change!]

[I gave her a 50 franc bill. Several minutes later, the woman came back with the child, who was smiling, and the change.]

[Now everything's fine. Now everyone's happy: the kid because he has his cake, you because your little boy isn't crying anymore, the pâtissier because he sold his cake, and me because I no longer have my counterfeit bill!]

[cover sheet]

After briefly discussing students' reactions, the teacher should ask the students to reread the text without interruption, in order to consolidate their understanding and to clarify any unresolved questions. This is a good opportunity for students to identify and discuss textual clues they may have missed during their first reading. Of particular interest are those parts of the story that were misconstrued or falsely predicted, since they may be attributable to idiomatic expressions or cultural differences (for example, one student's thinking that the child is crying because he *has* something he doesn't want, after reading the utterance *Qu'est-ce qu'il a ce petit?*). Getting students to articulate their idiosyncratic predictions and understandings is an important step in developing their awareness of not only their own reading processes, but also those of their peers. And by hearing how their classmates attempt to resolve particular misunderstandings, students can expand their own problem solving repertoire.

Following this discussion of reading process, the text's content and themes can be explored in greater depth. It is here that the activity can be extended beyond situated practice to critical framing. Students can be asked, for example, to propose a few titles and to discuss the pros and cons of each proposal (for example, 'Le faux billet' would seem to nicely summarize the story, but it also gives away the ending). The text's relation to larger sociocultural realities can be discussed. For example, the sardonic cleverness of the narrator nicely reflects the French penchant for outwitting the system (codified in the French colloquial expression *'Système-D'*). Furthermore, the metaphor of 'counterfeit money' figures frequently in French literature, often extended to the general problem of distinguishing reality and semblance. In order to introduce students to this theme and enhance cultural learning in another dimension, the teacher could, for example, present Baudelaire's prose poem 'La fausse monnaie' about a man who tosses a beggar a counterfeit coin, and which ends with the following dictum: *'On n'est jamais excusable d'être méchant, mais il y a quelque mérite à savoir qu'on l'est; et le plus irréparable des vices est de faire le mal par bêtise.'* ['It is never excusable to be mean, but there is some merit in knowing that you are; and the most irreparable of vices is to do evil through stupidity.'] (Baudelaire 1989: 70). This could be compared, in turn, with one of Pascal's *pensées*: *'Jamais on ne fait le mal si pleinement et si gaiement que quand on le fait par conscience'* [One never does evil so completely and cheerfully as when one does it out of moral conscience.] (Pascal 1904: 440). Finally, students could be alerted to this key cultural theme in works such as Molière's *Tartuffe* or *Le Misanthrope*, which they might have already read in translation in other courses, and which they would likely encounter at more advanced stages of their French study, or in a world literature course. In this way connections can be established between elementary language study and later points in the curriculum.

In summary, the DRTA brings cognitive processes into the arena of social interaction. By making learners conscious of their own and others' expectations of a text, as well as their progressive reconciliation of those expectations to textual facts, the DRTA can foster an awareness of the communicative nature of reading and writing. Based on the notion of interactive discourse response, the activity helps learners to see that their developing representation of a text results from an ongoing 'dialogue' between the available textual evidence and their own knowledge of the world (as in the dialogic reformulation of the 'stigmergy' text in Chapter 4). Learners experience the contingency of meaning as they observe the ways their own mental representations shift and evolve as they are recontextualized, through continued reading and through juxtaposition with the ideas of their classmates. Learners can begin to take a 'writerly' perspective on their reading by paying attention to the particular uses of language that lead them to make certain inferences. Perhaps most important, they can learn that justification for their reasoning, rather than finding the single 'right' answer, is what counts most. In terms of the design model, then, the DRTA leads learners away from a 'one text = one meaning' conception of reading by focusing their attention on the dynamic interplay between Available Designs (for example, vocabulary, genre, style, background knowledge) and their contexts of use. It particularly emphasizes the development of learners' procedural knowledge by reinforcing a cyclical sequence of predicting, reading, and evaluating that can be applied to all types of reading. By involving public expression of cognitive procedures, the activity brings together both individual and social dimensions of reading.

Several caveats should nevertheless be kept in mind. Although this kind of guided reading activity can be used at all levels of language teaching, it is most useful during the early stages, when students are developing their ability to process multiple layers of meaning in the new language. One significant limitation of this particular guided reading activity for advanced learners is the fact that only relatively small chunks of text are presented at one time. While for novice-level students this is an advantage, since it limits the amount of language they need to attend to, for more advanced learners it can actively block the use of global reading strategies that require access to the entire text from the outset.[7] The DRTA is therefore best used as a *transitional* activity, to be abandoned in overt form once students have internalized the 'question/hypothesis testing' strategy and can apply it in their independent silent reading. Moreover, it should be used judiciously, not constantly, since one risk in relying too heavily on this (or any other) sort of teaching strategy is that of 'proceduralizing' reading, reducing it to a formulaic routine that is followed slavishly.

Readers' theater

Another way to bring the linguistic and the cognitive explicitly into the realm of the social is to have students perform their reading publicly. *Readers' theater* is a technique that makes reading a collaborative as well as individual endeavor. In readers' theater, students work together in small groups to convert short texts (or portions of longer texts) into 'scripts' containing multiple voices, which they then read aloud and (optionally) act out with minimal actions. Although the words of the original text cannot be modified, individual sentences or utterances can be divided among different voices. As an example, Figure 5.3 presents one possible scripting of the final lines of the Cisneros vignette that was presented in Chapter 3. (I have rewritten the text in script form for the purpose of illustration, but normally students would highlight the different voices with different colored markers on a photocopy of the original text.) The important point is that the members of each student team decide amongst themselves how many voices are needed, how to divide them up, and how they should be read aloud in performance.

Esperanza:	Once when we were living on Loomis, a nun from my school passed by and saw me playing out front.
Esperanza's narrator:	The laundromat downstairs had been boarded up because it had been robbed two days before and the owner had painted on the wood ...
Laundromat owner:	YES WE'RE OPEN
Esperanza's narrator:	so as not to lose business.
Nun:	Where do you live?
Esperanza's narrator:	she asked.
Esperanza:	There [Esperanza looks and points upwards]
Esperanza's narrator:	I said, pointing up to the third floor.
Nun:	You live *there*?
Esperanza and Nun:	*There.*
Esperanza:	I had to look to where she pointed
Esperanza's narrator:	the third floor, the paint peeling, wooden bars
Esperanza:	Papa had nailed on the window so we wouldn't fall out.
Nun:	You live *there*?
Esperanza:	The way she said it made me feel like nothing.
Esperanza and Nun:	*There.*
Esperanza:	I lived *there*.
Esperanza's narrator:	I nodded. I knew then
Esperanza:	I had to have a house. A real house. One I could point to. But this isn't it.
Esperanza's narrator:	The house on Mango Street isn't it.
Mama:	For the time being
Esperanza's narrator:	Mama says.
Papa:	Temporary
Esperanza's narrator:	says Papa.
Esperanza:	But I know how those things go.

Figure 5.3:   Sample readers' theater scripting of the end of the first vignette of Sandra Cisnero's The House on Mango Street

Through the scripting and performance process, each group effectively redesigns the original text, even though the actual words remain constant. Through these performances students actively *experience* how different interpretations can be derived from a single text.[8] Moreover, after performing their own scripted versions of the passage, the student teams can explain and compare their respective rationales for the particular interpretive decisions they made. By comparing their various redesigned versions with the original text, students can begin to get a sense of how the linguistic features of the text constrain meaning but also allow a certain freedom of interpretation within the parameters of those constraints. In this way, a critical framing dimension is added to an activity that focuses primarily on situated practice and transformed practice.

Readers' theater supports the goals of situated practice by stimulating oral discussion at the level of both small groups (during the preparation of the scripts) and the whole class (after the scripts have been performed). The transformed practice component of the activity (performing the text) allows for comparisons to be drawn among the various versions, which entails critical framing. 'The result of such discussions', Cazden (1992) has argued, 'is a richer classroom culture—a richer shared mental context of texts and activities involving them—that will make more likely not just more talk, but more talk of certain kinds' (p. 75). That is, talk centered on discourse and its interpretation. At the heart of this kind of talk is the *justification* of readers' interpretations based on the concrete facts of the text. Although novice learners are generally not capable of sustaining this kind of metadiscursive talk in the foreign language, they can nevertheless benefit from the language immersion that readers' theater provides. By reading, rereading, repeating, hearing, and performing passages of well-written language, learners can begin to internalize foreign language 'voices in the head'. As learners progress to more advanced levels, greater emphasis can be placed on comparing the specific differences across students' interpretations and how they might be justified by the language of the text.[9]

Reading journals

Assuming the availability of materials written in the foreign language, one of the best ways to get students immersed in reading *outside* of class is to assign independent reading. Students should be free to choose whatever reading material catches their interest, whether it be magazines, books, comics, newspapers, or another kind of text. For each text they read, they should write a reading journal entry in which they (1) cite a full reference of the text, (2) indicate why they chose it, (3) summarize the text, (4) express their personal response to the text, and (5) reflect on the process of reading it, noting details of what was difficult or easy, how they dealt with comprehension problems, and so forth. Novice learners will want to write these entries in their native language, but more advanced learners can write in the foreign language. It is important, however, that even the novice learners reflect on their reading processes and practices. Below is an excerpt from the reading journal of a student who had studied French for seven weeks, reading one of the *Tintin* series of picture books, popular among children and adolescents.

> I haven't read many comics and would likely be bored by similar stories in English, but the Tintin series offers a fun way to expose myself to new French words and expressions. There were many nouns, verbs and idiomatic expressions which I didn't immediately understand. I was able to deduce the meaning of many nouns and verbs, however, by their context or by way of the illustrations. Repetitive use of words and phrases also helped me guess at probable meanings. Exclamations and other expressions were more difficult to divine. Finally, a predictable plot complete with the expected melange of stereotypical adventure story, cops-and-robbers-type characters as well as familiar illustrations from this genre provided a good platform from which the French text could be interpreted in meaning and compared in style to a comparable story written in English.

It is this kind of sensitivity not only to the details of the text, but also to their own reading processes, that is important for teachers to encourage in their learners. In class, the teacher can discuss strategies that are commonly mentioned in students' reports, such as rereading, translating, inferring from context, and so on. In this way, the initial reading (situated practice) and the subsequent reflection on the reading process (critical framing) can lead into follow-up lessons focused on particular reading skills (overt instruction). As in the case of the DRTA and readers' theater, reading journals focus attention on Available Designs (vocabulary, genres, style, procedural knowledge, cultural knowledge) as they are put to use in communicative practice, rather than in isolation.

Overt instruction

In the overt instruction category we will discuss two broad areas of activities: focusing on relationships (i.e. lexical, syntactic, and discourse relationships) and teaching genres. Both areas establish a base for critical framing and transformed practice activities, which will be discussed later.

Focusing on relationships

As we saw in Part One, language is not a static stock of discrete elements, but has to do with relationships among elements, and relationships between language and context. Overt instruction can be very helpful in getting students to see and understand those relationships.

Word relationships

Given that words provide the basic 'raw materials' for designing meaning with language, it is not surprising that novice- and intermediate-level language learners often perceive vocabulary to be their biggest weakness. There is no doubt that vocabulary plays a crucial role in reading comprehension. The case of Gouin in Chapter 2 serves to remind us, however, that even memorizing the dictionary does not allow one to understand language in use. When teaching vocabulary, teachers need to think in terms of patterns anchored in a larger context. The goal should not be to teach words *per se*, but to teach word systems and relationships.

Attention to dictionary skills is very important for all language learners, but particularly for those learning languages that categorize and organize the lexicon in unfamiliar ways. It is often essential that students understand morphological relationships in order to use a dictionary effectively. In Arabic, for example, words are listed by their three-consonant roots. So various parts of speech related to learning, teaching, studying, schooling, threshing, effacing, flailing, and extinction would be grouped under their shared root *d-r-s*. Thompson-Panos and Thomas-Ruzic (1983) analogize the task of looking up a word in an Arabic dictionary to looking up the English word *misconceive* under the root *cept* (p. 613). In any language, attention to affixes is particularly important so that learners expand their knowledge of the lexical system, in addition to learning individual words. Attention to word derivation is also important—for example, analyzing how groups of words such as *write, written, writing, writer, writerly* relate to one another. This does not, of course, insure that students will be able to *use* all these words in their speech or writing, but it can at least significantly enlarge their recognition vocabulary in reading.

At the semantic level, it is crucial that students learn to become sensitive to the effects of words' level of specificity on meaning. Robinson (1993) provides the following example:

Where are you going dear?

	alsatian,	
I'm going to take the	dog,	for a walk.
	animal	

(p. 252)

'Dog' is the basic level, default choice. By specifying 'alsatian' the speaker implies that there is at least one other dog of a different breed in the household, whereas by choosing 'animal' the speaker conveys an ironic tone, possibly indicating dislike of the dog.

Students also need to attend to shifts in connotations and associations as words are used in different contexts. A good way to focus students' attention on how reading can affect their representations of word meanings is to give them a list of key words from a text they will soon read. Ideally, these should be familiar words that are rich in associations. For example, in preparation for reading Albert Camus's *L'Etranger* in a French class, students could be given the following list, and asked to jot down their first association with each word:

le monde	[the world]
la mer	[the sea]
bleu	[blue]
le soleil	[the sun]
la misère	[poverty]

The class can then be polled to see which associations were most commonly shared, and associations can be ranked in order of frequency. At a later time, after the students have finished reading *L'Etranger*, they can be given the same task again as a sort of post-test. The teacher then reminds them of associations they had made before reading the text, and the class can discuss the specific ways in which the reading may have affected their associations with the list of words.[10]

In terms of the design model, then, treatment of vocabulary in literacy-based teaching goes beyond dictionary definitions and attempts to establish linkages with other Available Designs such as background knowledge, genre, and style. In doing so it also focuses learners' attention on how contextual factors affect their interpretations of words (extending the focus into the middle circle of Figure 2.3).

Syntactic relationships

A major goal of teaching reading for academic purposes is to enable students to deal with structurally-complex texts. One component that is extraordinarily important in this regard is teaching students to see the 'big picture' of structural relationships within a text as a whole. The fact remains, however, that many sentences may be themselves difficult to understand because of their sheer structural complexity. Figures 5.4 through 5.6 show how teachers can focus learners' attention on different aspects of a given text, and help them to see the basic structures of complex sentences as part of a larger communicative picture. For the sake of showing how a single text can be analyzed for multiple structure types, we will examine the same Toqueville passage used in Chapter 3 (see Figure 3.3) to demonstrate co-reference patterns. In Figure 5.4, the teacher asks students if any phrases can be dropped out without affecting the basic structure of the sentences. On an overhead transparency the teacher shows how embedded clauses (generally marked off by pairs of commas) and modifying phrases can be bracketed off and temporarily ignored, modeling how a more experienced reader in the language might hierarchize information.

Excerpt from Alexis de Toqueville, *De la démocratie en Amérique* (vol 1, p. 2)

Ainsi donc, [à mesure que j'eetudiais la société américaine], je voyais de plus en plus, [dans l'égalité des conditions], le fait générateur dont chaque fait particulier semblait descendre, et je le retrouvais [sans cesse devant moi] comme un point central où toutes mes observations venaient aboutir.

Figure 5.4:   Bracketing off embedded clauses and modifying phrases to clarify the basic structure of sentences

In Figure 5.5, the teacher shows how the verb *donner* [to give] has three indirect objects or 'beneficiaries', which are underlined: (A) *l'esprit public*, (B) *les gouvernants*, and (C) *les gouvernés*. *L'esprit public*, in turn, is given (1) *une certain direction*, and (2) *un certain tours aux lois*, while the *gouvernants* and the *gouvernés* are given one thing each: *des maximes nouvelles* and *des habitudes particulières* respectively. Because the order of indirect object/ direct object is established in A and B, its reversal in C can cause students considerable comprehension problems until it is explicitly diagrammed.

Excerpt from Alexis de Toqueville, *De la démocratie en Amérique* (vol 1, p. 1–2)

Parmi les objets nouveaux qui, pendant mon séjour aux Etats-Unis, ont attiré mon attention, aucun n'a plus vivement frappé mes regards que l'égalité des conditions. Je découvris sans peine l'influence prodigieuse qu'exerce ce premier fait sur la marche de la société; (il donne) (A) à l'esprit public (A1) une certaine direction, (A2) un certain tour aux lois; (B) aux gouvernants (B1) des maximes nouvelles, et (C1) des habitudes particulières (C) aux gouvernés.

Figure 5.5:   Clarifying the structure of a complex verb complement

In Figure 5.6, a similar procedure is followed with a different passage to explicate an unusually complex five-part subject.

Excerpt from Alexis de Toqueville, *De la démocratie en Amérique* (vol 3, p. 6)

(1 Echapper (1a) à l'esprit de système, (1b) au joug des habitants, (1c) aux maximes de la famille, (1d) aux opinions de classe, et, jusqu'à un certain point, (1e) aux préjugés de nation; (2) ne prendre (2a) la tradition que comme un renseignement, et (2b) les faits présents que comme une utile étude pour faire autrement et mieux; (3) chercher par soi-même et en soi seul (3a) la raison des choses, (4) tendre au résultat sans se laisser enchaîner au moyen; et (5) viser au fond à travers la forme: tels sont les principaux traits qui caractérisent ce que j'appellerai la méthode philosophique des Américains. | Verbe principal |

Figure 5.6:   Clarifying the structure of a compound subject

The point in doing these exercises is not so much to teach students something new, but to 'remind' them of knowledge they may use only unconsciously when they read in their native language, so that it might be more consciously available in the less familiar context of the second language.

Berman (1975) proposes a technique she calls 'analytic syntax' to improve students' comprehension as well as their writing. This technique centers on the use of *structural paraphrase*, where the lexicon is essentially kept constant but reordered to create new phrases and sentences. Berman describes how the technique can be used to help ESL learners understand expository texts by focusing their attention on the following common structures:

– *Nominalization*. In expository texts where processes are frequently described by nouns rather than verbs, students can rewrite sentences, converting the nominalization into a more speech-like verb phrase (for example, 'after the decline of the Roman Empire' → 'after the Roman Empire declined'; 'there was no sharp division of labor' → 'labor was not divided up sharply' (Berman 1975: 246).
– *Reduced relative clauses*. The tendency for 'that/which' constructions to be deleted in English can often cause learners difficulty in understanding relationships among parts of sentences. Teachers (and students) can

rewrite reduced relative clauses, supplying the underlying 'that/which' construction (for example, 'the economic activities connected with the production of food . . .' → 'the economic activities *that were* connected with the production of food . . .'; 'property belonging to . . .' → 'property *that belonged* to . . .', p. 247).

- *Pronominal reference*. Students can identify the referent of each pronoun in a passage and then rewrite, substituting the full referent (for example, '*their* outlying fields' → 'the outlying fields *of the villages*'; '*it* was mostly able to produce enough for *itself*' → the *village* was mostly able to produce enough for *the village*', p. 247).
- *Sentence connectors*. Students can read for expressions such as 'however', 'furthermore', 'hence', and 'though' and categorize them according to function (for example, *and, so, but*) on the blackboard. They can then analyze their placement at the beginning, middle, or end of sentences and note how commas are used to set them off, and experiment with changing their position by rewriting the sentences. They can rewrite other passages, replacing *and, so, but* with other expressions in the same category (p. 248).
- *Whether X or Y*. Berman notes that 'whether' constructions are frequently misunderstood, especially in the form of 'whether or not'. She suggests that teachers show students how to use these structures by making the 'Y' component explicit (for example, 'Whether the workers on the land were slaves or *not*' → 'Whether the workers on the land were slaves or *free men*'.
- *Negation*. Predominantly written negation forms such as no/not any + noun, neither, and nor can often cause comprehension difficulties for students who are familiar primarily with the *-n't* negation form predominant in speech. Students can rewrite to clarify what is being negated (for example, 'women had *no* specially hard labor to do' → 'women *did not* have *any* specially hard labor to do'; '*nor* did the men lay specially hard tasks upon the women' → '*and* the men *did not* lay specially hard tasks upon the women, *either*', p. 249).

Berman does not recommend that teachers work through all these structure types in a given text, but rather that they focus on one of them when it is particularly prevalent in a particular reading passage.

Another approach in dealing with syntax is to have students play the role of 'editor' and rewrite passages they find difficult to understand. Students can identify a difficult passage, rewrite it as best they can in their own words, compare their rewritten versions, analyze differences among them, and compare them with the original text. Pearson and Tierney (1984) report that such rewritten passages are often better comprehended not only by the students who write them, but also by their peers as well.

Discourse structure relationships

In Chapter 4 we saw how the 'stigmergy' passage could be rewritten into a writer-reader dialogue format. This kind of transformation, proposed by Widdowson (1983), provides one effective technique for exploring the underlying discourse structure of difficult texts. Once students have seen the teacher redesign a text in dialogue form, they can take a difficult passage from their reading and try collectively to establish an explicit dialogic structure for it.

Paying attention to discourse markers is another useful strategy. As discussed in Chapter 3, discourse markers or signaling cues indicate relationships among structural elements of a text and can often serve as navigational signposts, directing the reader's attention to the most important ideas or information. Phrases such as 'the key point is' or 'of critical importance' fulfill this latter role, while 'on the other hand' and 'conversely' suggest contrast, 'one example is' indicates exemplification, 'furthermore' signals expansion, and 'as a result', 'therefore', and 'hence' mark consequence.

One way of developing students' awareness of these types of cues is through overt instruction, providing students with a list of common signaling words, grouped according to the type of relationship they indicate. A limitation of lists, however, is that they do not give learners a sense of how such markers are used in context. In addition to providing lists, then, teachers can (1) present plentiful examples of signaling cues embedded in texts, and (2) train students to recognize signaling cues as they read. The teacher can direct and guide the student in this effort by tailoring the type of questions he or she asks to the task at hand. For example, in developing students' ability to recognize time sequence relationships in a short story the teacher can ask about the order in which a particular sequence of events occurred. By attaching a 'How do you know?' to such a question the teacher forces the student to focus on the specific markers which led to his answer and allows other students, who may not have been able themselves to recognize all the signals, to learn the most important cues.[11]

Teachers' questions during class readings of texts are key in focusing students' attention on other dimensions of discourse organization as well. Raimes (1983) offers the following as sample questions:

– Which sentence states the main idea?
– Which sentences directly support the main idea?
– Has the writer used any listing words (first, next, etc.)?
– Which of the following did the writer do to support the topic: describe, define, divide into parts, compare, contrast, enumerate, explain, give reasons . . . ?
– How did the writer end the passage? What did the writer do in the ending—ask a question, summarize, introduce new material, point to future directions . . . ?

– Are any words repeated throughout the passage? Why do you think the
writer repeats those words?
– How many parts would you divide this passage into?
(Raimes 1983: 122).

Cohesion relationships

In Chapter 3 we saw how students can be guided systematically through a
densely cohesive passage by drawing lines to identify relations of coreference
(see Figure 3.3). Once students are familiar with basic cohesive devices, a
particularly fun and motivating way to help learners understand how
cohesive devices operate in a text is to assemble scrambled texts (O'Malley,
Chamot, Stewner-Manzanares, Kupper, and Russo 1985; Hedge 1988).
After choosing a very short story or a brief newspaper article to work with,
the teacher copies each sentence individually onto a separate strip of paper.
Cohesive devices can be highlighted or not, depending on the students' level.
The teacher tells students the topic of the story they will read, but tells them
that before they can read the story they first have to put it together. One
envelope of sentence strips is given to each pair of students in the class, and
students work collaboratively to assemble the story. Once they are done, the
students explain how the cohesive devices gave them clues to the text's
organization. See Chapman (1983) for additional ideas on teaching cohesion
in reading.

Coherence Relationships: Mapping

Mapping (Hanf 1971; Armbruster and Anderson 1982; Tierney, Readence,
and Dishner 1985) is a technique designed to help students understand
relationships among the ideas in a text by representing them visually. Unlike
outlining, which tends to lead to linear, chronological listing of content,
mapping allows learners to represent complex networks of relationships
among text elements. For example, differences between the 'real' and 'dream'
houses in *The House on Mango Street* text might be mapped as in Figure 5.7.

In this map, Esperanza's two houses are shown as mirror images of one
another, with contrasting thematic elements of reality/dream, temporariness/
permanence, suffocation/life, communalism/privacy, entrapment/freedom,
and poverty/hope situated around the periphery.
Although maps tend to look rather complex when they are completed, the
process itself is quite simple. In getting students started, the teacher asks
what the basic topic is. In this case it is houses, and specifically two houses—
the one on Mango Street and Esperanza's 'real' (ideal) house. These are
written on the blackboard and circled. What do we know about these
houses? Students call out features, which are written around the two

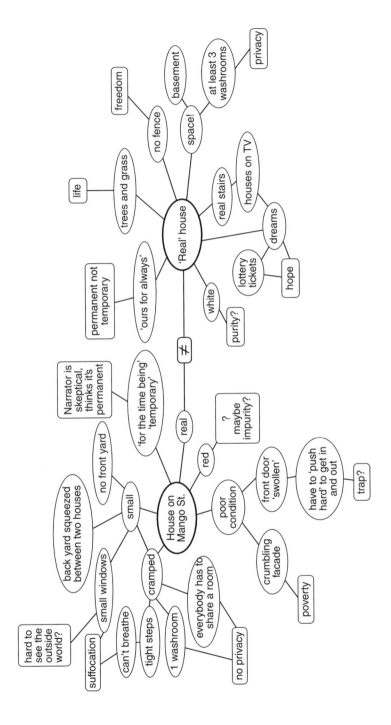

Figure 5.7:   Sample mapping of The House on Mango Street *vignette*

respective houses. Can we group any of these features into categories? 'Tight steps', '1 washroom', and 'sharing bedroom' are clustered around the word 'cramped'; 'windows' and 'yard' are clustered around 'small', and so on. Why might the writer have chosen to describe the front steps as 'tight' and the windows as 'so small you'd think they were holding their breath'? It's like suffocating, one student says. You can't see too much out of small windows, says another. The ideas are written on the board, put in boxes rather than circles to mark them as inferences. The process of associating textual evidence with thematic associations continues for both houses. Uncertainties are signaled with question marks, to be returned to at a later point (for example, whether the color red is significant or not). Students are often not aware of thematic elements in the text until they start seeing patterns of 'evidence' appear on the board. Consequently, although the finished product is useful as a memory aid, it is the engagement in the process of designing a map that is of greatest pedagogical value. Once students have been through the process a few times as a class, they can design reading maps in pairs or individually and then compare and discuss their maps. Mapping can also be used to organize ideas for writing, as will be discussed in Chapter 7.

Text–reader relationships

The *effects* of so-called 'equivalent' statements are always different. When we alter the linguistic form of an utterance (for example, 'one soldier remains unaccounted for' versus 'one soldier is missing in action') we also potentially change its reception. Teachers must be alert to such subtle but important differences in texture and be able to sensitize students to the effects of a writer's specific linguistic choices. The principal way to do this is by asking questions focusing on the writer's choices as students read a passage in class. When students read a newspaper article, for example, they can be asked to look at the writer's choice of words—do particular words reveal anything about the writer's attitude or bias toward the subject? Figurative language is particularly important to examine closely. For example, when a writer describes a character who 'talks like a book', what does that mean? Pearson and Tierney (1984) propose the following activity sequence for dealing with figurative language:

1 Have students select and/or compose literal paraphrases of figurative statements . . . .
2 Have them discuss the overtones that the expression carries with it.
3 Ask them to compare differences in image and emotion that are suggested by alternative figurative paraphrases (for example, John runs like a gazelle, John runs like a cheetah, John is greased lightning, John runs like the wind, and so forth).

4 Working with a group, have the students generate as many figurative paraphrases of a given idea as possible and then discuss differences in interpretation invited by each paraphrase.
5 Pick a selection (narratives and magazine articles and feature sports stories are prime candidates) that possesses a lot of figurative expressions. Peruse the text looking for examples. For each one discovered, discuss its literal paraphrase, its overtones, and the range of alternative expressions the author could have picked.
(Pearson and Tierney 1984: 166)

Nash (1986) provides excellent examples of paraphrases of poems and short literary texts, which help students to focus on exactly what it is about a text's 'literariness' that produces particular effects on readers. As Nash describes the process,

> The consciousness—sometimes embarrassed, sometimes humorous—of what is defective and awry in paraphrase creates a sharp focus on the text. The paraphrase is a vain attempt to reflect what is in the poem; the vanity becomes apparent to us, and we set about trying to identify and explain what we have missed. So a process of discovery begins.
> (Nash 1986: 74)

Nash recommends starting with proverbs (for example, 'It's the early bird that catches the worm') to keep text length limited. Citing student renditions such as 'If you get up early in the morning you will achieve your task' (p. 75), Nash notes that students never take such pieces of language as factual statements, even when they are not presented explicitly as proverbs. This opens the door for discussion about what it is that led readers to take the statement *literarily* rather than *literally* (p. 76). In aiming the discussion in this direction, the teacher appeals to students' knowledge of contexts and circumstances of language use (the 'context' circles of Figure 2.3), and how they influence the interpretation of particular configurations of Available Designs in texts.

Teaching genres: textual comparison

A principle in teaching genres is to work with multiple texts, in order to allow students to identify what is common to a group of texts of a given genre and what is variable within that same group (Johns 1997). To sensitize students to the effects of different genres on reader reception, pairs of texts can be chosen on a common topic or theme or rhetorical purpose to be compared and contrasted through classroom activities. Consider, for example, the following ESL lesson in which E. E. Cummings's poem 'next to of course god america i' is juxtaposed with excerpts from political speeches by Margaret Thatcher and Bill Clinton.[12] The primary goal of this particular activity was to familiarize ESL students with political rhetoric (and some of the cultural schemata commonly associated with it) through two different genres. A secondary goal was to spark learners' interest in poetry. Perhaps most important from a literacy perspective, it also serves a further goal of fostering critical reflection on certain kinds of language use in society.

Before distributing the poem to the students, the teacher begins with some questions to get students thinking about register differences in speech: How do the ways you talk depend on who you are talking to? Do you talk differently to the teacher than you do to your friends? In what ways? How does a store owner generally talk to you? A car salesman? The President giving a speech to the American people? Several students do their own imitations of these kinds of speech.

The teacher then shifts to a review of an earlier lesson about poetry, asking students how poetry is different from other kinds of texts and how it may need to be read differently. She then presents the Cummings poem on an overhead transparency, reading it twice: first in a normal voice, then with the tone and cadence of a rousing political speech.

> 'next to of course god america i
> love you land of the pilgrims' and so forth oh
> say can you see by the dawn's early my
> country 'tis of centuries come and go
> and are no more what of it we should worry
> in every language even deafanddumb
> thy sons acclaim your glorious name by gorry
> by jingo by gee by gosh by gum
> why talk of beauty what could be more beaut-
> iful than these heroic happy dead
> who rushed like lions to the roaring slaughter
> they did not stop to think they died instead
> then shall the voice of liberty be mute?'
>
> He spoke. And drank rapidly a glass of water

The teacher asks students what the differences between the two readings were and why they think she read the poem as she did. She then asks who they think the voices talking in the poem are. Students then copy down the poem in their notebooks exactly as it appears, as the teacher responds to their questions about vocabulary. On a second overhead transparency, the teacher then recopies the poem, breaking it into more recognizable phrases (for example, America I love you, land of the pilgrim's . . . , oh say can you see by the dawn's early . . . .). The teacher asks if any of these phrases are familiar, and if students can complete any of the elliptical phrases. They then examine the text of 'The Star Spangled Banner' (the national anthem of the United States), which provides some of the intertextual references. The teacher returns to the original poem to ask questions such as: Do the various elliptical phrases make any sense as they appear? Why are the phrases all run together? Why the quotation marks? What kind of person would talk like this? Why would he drink his water 'rapidly'? The teacher ends the lesson by having students read the poem aloud several times as a politician might and asking them what their opinion would be of someone who gave this speech: Would it be someone they would trust? What is it about what the person says that would make them trust or not trust him or her? What kind of attitudes do people have toward politicians in the students' own countries? Do they think most Americans would trust politicians who talked like this?

So far the curricular components that have been emphasized are situated practice and overt instruction, with the focus on genre characteristics and intertextuality. As the activity continues it incorporates critical framing as well.

The next day, the teacher distributes excerpts from real political speeches. The first excerpts are from former British Prime Minister Margaret Thatcher's speech to the annual conference of the Conservative Party, following the 1982 war with Argentina over the Falkland Islands:

> Unemployment will not be an option . . . [applause] and we must, we have got to do it together.
> Let all of us pause and reflect on what we who stayed at home owe to those who sailed and fought, and lived and died, and won.
> (Cohen 1994: 45–6)

The second excerpt is from U.S. President Bill Clinton's acceptance speech at the 1996 Democratic National Party Convention:

> My fellow Americans, 68 nights from tonight, the American people will face once again a critical moment of decision. We're going to choose the last president of the 20th century and the first president of the 21st century. But the real choice is not that. The real choice is whether we will build a bridge to the future or a bridge to the past, about whether we believe our best days are still out there or our best days are behind us, about whether we want a country of people all working together or one where you're on your own.
>
> Let us commit ourselves this night to rise up and build the bridge we know we ought to build all the way to the 21st century. Let us have faith and let us have faith, faith, American faith, American faith that we are not leaving our greatness behind. We're going to carry it right on with us into that new century, a century of new challenge, and unlimited promise . . . .
>
> My fellow Americans, after these four, good, hard years, I still believe in a place called Hope, a place called America.
>
> Thank you, God bless you.

The students' task at this point is to draw boxes around phrases in these excerpts that sound similar to some of the phrases in the e. e. cummings poem. They then discuss some of the similarities and differences between the poem and the speech excerpts, paying particular attention to students' judgments about what makes sense and what does not. Next, they can discuss the tone of the poem and the kinds of responses it evokes in them, focusing closely on the relationships between specific textual elements and their effects. The teacher concludes the lesson by explaining how political rhetoric is often constructed less to persuade people to believe certain things and more to let them fill in their own meanings so as to create a sense of ideological communion and shared goals (i.e. what the speaker means is what the individual member of the audience wants him or her to mean) (Cohen 1994). Together, the teacher and the students make sophisticated connections in language, context, and culture by exploring responses to political rhetoric.

In terms of the design model, the activity is meant not only to increase students' awareness of formal features of a genre, but also to help them understand how that genre connects to purposes, audience, social roles, and social practices in both communicative and larger sociocultural contexts (the middle and outer rings of the model in Figure 2.3). Examining relationships between Available Designs and such contextual factors is the same general goal of the critical framing activities to be discussed in the next section.

Critical framing

Critical framing involves distancing oneself from a text as well as from one's response to the text to examine the nature of the text-response relationship itself. In this section we will focus on two principal means for establishing this reflective stance: critical questions and summary writing.

Critical focus questions

In order to make students more aware of the significance of the lexical and structural choices writers make, even in mundane, non-literary texts, it is useful to explore the diction and syntax of journalistic texts in terms of their effects on reader reception. This can be most easily done through teacher-directed discussion. An ESL teacher might, for instance, raise the kinds of questions shown in Figure 5.8 during students' reading of a short newspaper article.

Such questions allow students to see how the reporter's phrases and discourse organization effectively 'naturalize' a terrible event, depersonalizing it and reducing it to routine and banal status. Once they are aware of the linguistic devices that have produced this effect, students can attempt to rewrite the newspaper article to reflect other possible perspectives. That is to say, the activity can be extended beyond critical framing to include transformed practice as well.

**Fruitvale BART
Shooting Delays
Train Service**

Oakland—A shooting at the Fruitvale BART station yesterday prompted a half-hour halt of train service as police searched for the assailants, authorities said.

A juvenile was shot once about 4 p.m. inside the station. He had been with a group of three other teenagers.

The victim, whose identity was withheld because of his age, was taken to Highland Hospital. His injuries were not considered life-threatening.

BART police ordered all trains to be stopped outside the station as they searched unsuccessfully for the two juvenile assailants.

(*San Francisco Chronicle*, May 29, 1997)

• In this headline, what is framed as 'given' information and what is framed as 'new' information? What is the effect of this phrasing?

• What is the effect of using the noun phrase 'a shooting' as the subject? What other options did the writer have? What would have been the effects of those options on you as a reader? What is treated as the most important piece of news in this sentence? How do you know?

• What do you associate with the word 'juvenile'? What might this imply about the person who was shot? What is the effect of using the passive voice ('was shot') instead of the active voice? Why do you think the writer specified 'was shot once'?

• Again, what is the effect of the passive voice?

• What is the implication of 'his injuries were not considered life-threatening'?

• How is this sentence ambiguous? How could the writer make it less so?

• What is the effect of using 'juvenile' to describe both the victim and his assailants?

*Figure 5.8:   Critical focus questions asked during the reading of a
newspaper article*

Summary writing

In Chapter 3, we saw in the 'Crickets' example the way summaries can be used as a critical framing activity involving discussion, analysis, and direct comparison of readers' interpretations. Because summary writing involves reconceptualization and transformation, it can involve a substantial cognitive load and can therefore be a difficult task for many students (Hidi and Anderson 1986; Kirkland and Saunders 1991; Sarig 1993). Kirkland and Saunders (1991) suggest giving students systematic practice in (1) making conceptual generalizations based on discrete textual details, (2) identifying the macrostructure of texts, and (3) transforming source text into a condensed form. They recommend starting with oral collaborative summary, moving to written collaborative summary, and finally to individual written summary. Within each stage, reading material should be at first concrete and then abstract. Throughout, the emphasis should be on thinking processes, with liberal use of mapping, underlining, and other forms of visual representation of readers' interpretations (see the section on mapping earlier in this chapter). In doing a summary, they recommend the following steps: (1) Read the assignment, (2) read the text to be summarized, (3) draw a diagram representing the meaning of the text, (4) formulate a summary based on this diagram, (5) reread the original text to check that the summary accurately reflects the main ideas, and maintains the same relative emphasis of some ideas over others, (6) check the summary against the assignment, and (7) write a final revision of the summary (Kirkland and Saunders 1991: 113).

Carter (1986: 114) points out that it is desirable to set a word limit on summaries (for example, 25–40 words for a short story) for three reasons. First, a need for brevity forces learners to make hard choices about what is most important—and comparison of students' choices demonstrates the point that summarizing is itself an act of *interpretation*. Second, when learners condense their expression by deleting, reorganizing, and reshaping their ideas, they are engaged in an act of *transformation* that allows them to integrate the development of both their language and interpretive skills. Third, in attempting to relate 'what happens' in a short summary, learners often come to see that a plot summary fails to capture the value of the text. This, in turn, can generate interest in not just *what* is narrated but also in *how* it is narrated. In this sense, summary can also be seen as an act of *realization*. As we saw in the 'Crickets' example in Chapter 3, written summaries can then be compared by writing them all on blackboards or large sheets of paper around the classroom. The teacher can guide students in their analyses of how their various interpretations overlap and differ in their design, asking them to discuss the effects of their particular language choices, and their reasons for making those choices.

Transformed practice

Both the 'critical questions' and 'summary writing' activities described above included elements of the fourth curricular component—transformed practice. In this category we are concerned with activities that involve reformulation and redesign of existing texts. It is important to note that essentially all writing based on reading is an instance of transformed practice, and therefore much of what will be presented in Chapter 7 might well have been included in this section. Here we will limit the discussion to two activity types: translation and dialogic transformations.

Translation

Seen in the light of a literacy-based pedagogy, the traditional activity of translation takes on new dimensions. Rather than simply a 'check' of mastery of lexical and syntactic structures, translation can, like summaries, be used as a way of comparing and contrasting parallel 'readings' of texts. Students can compare their own translations of crucial passages of either literary or non-literary texts; they can compare their own translations with published translations; or they can compare published translations with one another.[13]

One important benefit of translation (or discussion of translations) under the guidance of a teacher, is that it makes students distinctly aware of two things: (1) the importance of word choice in meaning design, and (2) the lack of simple one-to-one correspondences between expressions in the two languages. As they translate, students must closely analyze the particular context in which the expression is embedded, and then carefully weigh the semantic overtones of each potential rendering in order to find the most appropriate solution (Malmkjaer 1997). Translation therefore requires active confrontation of text-context relationships (i.e. critical framing), and these confrontations can be fruitfully discussed in class (adding a situated practice component to the activity).

Dialogic transformations

As exemplified in the Lewis Thomas 'stigmergy' example in Chapter 4, teachers can model the process of transforming an expository passage into a writer–reader dialogue. Once they understand the process, students can be given passages from their readings to transform into dialogues in order to expose underlying discourse relations. Although students should start with passages they already understand, this exercise is ultimately most useful as a way of working through passages whose vocabulary may be familiar but that nevertheless are not initially well understood. By collaboratively proposing, comparing, and analyzing discourse structures in discussion groups, learners can often come to comprehend passages that previously seemed opaque. Here (as in the Directed Reading-Thinking Activity discussed earlier) the goal is not necessarily to isolate a single, 'best' discourse structure, but rather to see how well various proposals can be justified in terms of the text itself. As in the case of critical questions and summary writing, the emphasis is placed on *relationships* (1) among Available Designs (vocabulary, genre, style, and so on), and (2) between Available Designs and particular contexts of interpretation.

Figure 5.9 summarizes the activities discussed in this chapter in terms of the instructional categories of situated practice, overt instruction, critical framing, and transformed practice. As mentioned earlier, most of the activities involve more than one category. Checkmarks indicate the primary focus of the activity, while those in parentheses indicate a secondary focus or potential extension, as described in the chapter. In designing an instructional sequence, teachers will want to insure that all four categories are represented, as demonstrated in the following section.

	Situated practice	Overt instruction	Critical framing	Transformed practice
DRTA	✓	(✓)	(✓)	
Readers Theater	✓		(✓)	✓
Reading Journals	✓		(✓)	
Focusing on relationships	✓	✓	(✓)	(✓)
Textual Comparisons	✓	✓	✓	
Critical Focus Questions	(✓)	(✓)	✓	(✓)
Summary Writing	(✓)	✓	✓	✓
Translation	(✓)		(✓)	✓
Dialogic Transformations	(✓)	(✓)	(✓)	✓

Figure 5.9:   Summary of reading activities organized by literacy-instructional category

Putting it all together: an outline of an integrative lesson

The following instructional sequence is offered as an example of an integrative lesson that brings together all four literacy instructional categories (situated practice, overt instruction, critical framing, and transformed practice), in order to maximize learners' understanding of a text. In Chapter 9, we will see how this same lesson outline can also be transformed into a heuristic reading test. The lesson will be based on Cisneros's vignette *The House on Mango Street*, which was presented at the end of Chapter 3. Grounded in a process-based approach to teaching reading for meaning (Swaffar *et al.* 1991), the goal is to start with students' global impressions of the text, then to delve more deeply into the textual details, and finally to return to a (now more refined) global understanding of the text.[14] The tasks outlined below are designed principally with novice and intermediate readers in mind, but can be adapted for use at more advanced levels as well.[15]

1 Linking form and intent

The first step in the heuristic sequence is to link text form and communicative intent at a global level. A natural starting place is genre. One approach, particularly useful for learners who have reasonably good oral skills but limited reading experience in English, is to begin by having students read not the targeted text, but a reduced and reformulated version which presents important information in a genre that is easy to process, such as a résumé or an information form:

Name: Esperanza Cordero
Address: 4006 Mango Street, Chicago, Illinois
Prior address: Loomis Street, Chicago
Occupation: Student (Catholic school)
Family: Daughter of Mr. and Mrs. E. Cordero.
               Eldest of four children.
               Brothers: Carlos, Kiki. Sister: Nenny.
Ethnic origin: Hispanic (Latina)

Treating this reduced and redesigned text as a reading passage, the teacher could ask questions to induce thinking about the social function of this particular genre, such as: Where would we be likely to encounter a text like this? What would its purpose be likely to be? Other questions would induce learners' awareness of the schemata that are activated, such as: What do you think of when you read the address 'Mango Street'? Why would the form include 'Prior address'? Can you infer anything else, something not stated here, about Esperanza based on this information? After this discussion students could then read the actual vignette by Cisneros (Figure 3.5), seeing some of the same information now presented in a personal narrative genre.

After scanning the Cisneros text, students can be asked questions such as: What kind of text is this? How do you know? What kinds of expectations do you have about this text (its content, its purpose)? Identifying the genre, purpose, and topic can lead to questions about students' impressions of the text's intended audience: Who was this probably written for? Why do you think so? What kinds of things might you be expected to know about already? Is this text the same as a personal diary entry? How might a diary entry be written differently? How is the relationship between writer and reader different in that case? How would it be different if someone else, such as the nun, were writing Esperanza's story? These questions take learners beyond a focus on isolated Available Designs in the text, and lead them to consider relationships between Available Designs and features of the communicative context in which they are being employed (i.e. critical framing).

2 Linking language to content

The next step is to establish the 'facts' of the text upon which an interpretation can be built. Although our interpretations and attitudes about a set of facts may change, the facts themselves do not, and if we have hopes of understanding a text we must first be clear on those facts. Content questions, true/false statements, multiple-choice completions, and informational grids are all useful techniques to help learners clarify the facts of a text. In any case, students should be asked to indicate the specific textual language upon which they have based their answer. Holding them accountable to the exact language of the text forces students to go beyond their vague hunches and encourages hypothesis-testing rather than random guessing.[16] For example, students could be asked to skim the first paragraph or page of the text and to find the words, sentences, or sections that tell something about the *who*, *what*, *where*, and *when* of the text. A student reading *The House on Mango Street* might produce a matrix resembling that shown in Figure 5.10:

	Hypotheses	Evidence and location in text
Who?	child? or adult thinking back on childhood. Catholic school girl? Latina? (names)	'we were six—Mama, Papa, Carlos, Kiki, my sister Nenny and me' (para. 1), 'a nun from my school' (para. 6)
What?	houses and feelings about them	title, first 5 paragraphs talk about houses they've lived in. Last 3 paragraphs talk more about feelings.
Where?	a city, in a poor section	'bricks are crumbling', 'no front yard, only four little elms the city planted by the curb', 'two buildings on either side' (para. 5) 'the laundromat downstairs had been boarded up because it had been robbed' (para. 6) 'paint peeling, wooden bars Papa had nailed on the windows' (para. 7)
When?	narrator's childhood. Seems modern, must be after 1950s.	mentions school (para. 6), T.V. (para. 4)

Figure 5.10:   Establishing the who, what, where, and when of a text

Grids such as these can be done in class, either individually or collaboratively in small groups, or they can be assigned to be done at home and then discussed in class. The focus is on situated practice, in that students are attending to the basic facts expressed in the text—facts which establish the groundwork for more interpretive and critical thinking about the text.

3 Linking form and meaning

The goal of the third step is to get students to look more closely at the particular linguistic choices that the writer made, to link formal text features to meaning. The targeted structures will of course depend on the particular text being read. In a newspaper article that makes strategic use of active versus passive voice, for example, students could be asked to underline all verbs, marking in red all those in the active voice, and marking in blue all those in the passive voice. They could then be asked to comment on the author's choices—are there significant patterns? Do the verbs in the passive voice contrast in some way with the verbs in the active voice? What effects might the choice of the passive versus the active voice have on the reader's interpretation of the information presented?

In *The House on Mango Street* text, students could be asked to analyze and comment on the author's use of definite and indefinite articles before the word 'house' (i.e, 'a house' versus 'the house')—which 'house' is being referred to in the two respective cases? What might be some possible implications of this choice? Or students might be asked to comment on the repeated italicization of the word 'there'. Students could begin by doing a readers' theater performance of the following excerpt from the text, exploring different stress and intonation patterns (a situated practice activity).

Where do you live? she asked.
There, I said, pointing up to the third floor.
You live *there*?
There. I had to look to where she pointed—the third floor, the paint peeling, wooden bars Papa had nailed on the window so we wouldn't fall out. You live *there*? The way she said it made me feel like nothing. *There*. I lived *there*. I nodded.

Afterwards, the teacher could ask critical focus questions. What does stress on the word 'there' connote in terms of the nun's attitude? In the process, the teacher can bring students' attention to the various conventions for representing speech and its prosodic features in written English. Why doesn't Cisneros use quotation marks in this text? Does it make a difference for you, the reader? If so, in what way? By focusing students' attention on the multiple voices within the text, the teacher can also facilitate discussion of the relationship between language and the sociocultural dimensions of the text (i.e. the outer circle of the design model in Figure 2.3). For example, in examining the exchange between Esperanza and the nun, one might argue that Esperanza's initial matter-of-fact use of 'there' as she points to her house is transformed by the nun's incredulous 'there?' into a new, shame-filled 'there', capturing in microcosm Esperanza's gradual socialization into and by institutions beyond her family.

The point of this stage of the sequence is to move from situated practice to critical framing, getting students to think about the possible implications of formal features of the text, linking formal analysis to interpretive activity. The goal is not for students to come up with 'the right answer' but rather to formulate a rationale for a hypothesis, based on concrete text-based observations.

4 Focus on organization of ideas

At this point we begin our return to a more global level of analysis, looking at the organization of ideas and information in the text. If students are reading an expository piece, they might be asked to identify the rhetorical functions of various sections of the text. In a text organized in a 'problem/solution' format, for example, students could be asked to mark the paragraph that presents the problem, then mark the paragraphs that present proposed solutions, indicating which is the author's 'preferred' solution and citing the linguistic evidence which led to this identification. Paragraphs or sections of fictional texts can also be analyzed for global information structures and 'mapped' in a variety of graphic formats.[17] Students reading *The House on Mango Street*, for example, could at this point be asked to map the descriptions of the narrator's 'desired' and 'real' houses in the middle two paragraphs of the vignette, as was shown in Figure 5.7, or to complete a two-column matrix as shown in Figure 5.11 below:

'Dream' house	'Real' house
a real house that would be ours for always; a real house with running water and pipes that work; has 'real stairs' inside, 'like houses on TV' a basement, at least 3 washrooms white with trees around it; big yard with grass growing without a fence house Papa talked about; house Mama dreamed about in stories at bedtime	Bricks are crumbling in places and the front door is so swollen you have to push hard to get in. ordinary hallway stairs only 1 washroom small and red with tight steps in front; no front yard, only 4 little elms the city planted by the curb

Figure 5.11:   Two-column matrix to contrast 'dream' and 'real' house in
The House on Mango Street

After organizing the information in this way, students could discuss the narrator's use of the word 'real' to refer to the ideal, dream house and to TV houses rather than to the actual house in which she lives. These two notions of 'house' could then be compared to their own personal (i.e. cultural) conceptions of what a 'house' really is, what it looks like, where it is located, and so on, leading in turn to a discussion of where such conceptions come from. The discussion again links the text's Available Designs to context, but now the focus is on the larger sociocultural context in which the text is embedded.

5 Transformation

With the fifth step we come full circle back to the level of a global 'sense' of the text, but by now it is no longer a vague, impressionistic sense, but one that is grounded in a detailed knowledge of the facts of the text. We are now interested in assessing students' global understanding through some kind of transformed practice. This might be a written summary, a thematic analysis, an oral retelling, a dramatization, a rewriting from a different point of view, or an expansion exercise—all activities that raise the cognitive complexity of the student's task while maintaining a focus on interpretation of the original text. Consider, for example, an expansion exercise for *The House on Mango Street*. Students could be asked to elaborate a selected portion of the text with sentences expressing states of mind, intentions, ideas, or relations that might have been suggested but not explicitly stated in the original. Taking the final section of the vignette, a student might expand the text as follows (with the student's additions in capital letters):

Where do you live? she asked. LIKE SHE REALLY DIDN'T KNOW.
There, I said, pointing up to the third floor, COMPLETELY INNOCENT.
You live *there*? SHE SAID, REALLY SURPRISED AND KIND OF SHOCKED.

There. I had to look to where she pointed—the third floor, the paint peeling, wooden bars Papa had nailed on the window so we wouldn't fall out. NOW I REALLY SAW IT—FROM THE NUN'S EYES. IT LOOKED AWFUL. You live *there*? The way she said it made me feel like nothing. I FELT SO ASHAMED. *There*. I lived *there*. I nodded, AND ALL I COULD DO IS LOOK DOWN AT THE GROUND. I JUST WANTED TO DISAPPEAR.

I knew then I had to have a house. A real house. A BRIGHT, WHITE ONE WITH INSIDE STAIRS LIKE ON TV, WITH A YARD AND A BASEMENT AND LOTS OF BEDROOMS AND BATHROOMS. One I could point to, AND SAY 'I LIVE THERE' AND BE PROUD. PROUD OF THE HOUSE AND PROUD OF ME, TOO. But this isn't it. *The house on Mango Street* isn't it.

Such an exercise, like summaries, retellings, dramatizations, and so on, allows students to put to use the linguistic details they have culled and organized in earlier stages of their reading, and to do so in a creative, expressive way that reflects their particular understanding of the text. Certain types of transformation activities, such as dramatizations and readers' theater, lend themselves to group collaboration, while others, such as rewritings and expansions, are better suited to individual work.

By now, the students have 'redesigned' Esperanza's story through discussion and interpretation. As a concluding activity they could then physically rewrite the text in a different form, either from a different point of view (using, for example, a third person narrative voice) or as a 'diary entry', or as an expository essay. The point here would then be to explicitly compare students' transformed texts with the original (and perhaps with the 'information form' text developed at the outset as well). If a student wrote a third person narrative which began:

Esperanza didn't always live on Mango Street. Before that she lived on Loomis Street, and before that she lived on Keeler Street. Before Keeler she lived on Paulina Street. She can't remember where she lived before that but she does remember moving a lot . . . .

The teacher would want to follow up with questions such as: 'What parts are difficult to "translate" into the new, third person, perspective?' 'Why?' 'How did you try to deal with those parts?' And when other students read this third-person narrative, the relevant question would be: 'How is reading this text different for you than reading the original version written from the perspective of "I/we"?' An important aspect of this kind of rewriting exercise is that linguistic demands are kept relatively low—students are provided the vocabulary and basic structure and manipulate only limited aspects of the text—and yet they can explore how even minor changes can significantly affect meaning. And in the process they are actively using words to create a coherent text, getting a feel of how they work together, rather than simply memorizing their meanings.

A second approach to teaching *The House on Mango Street*, appropriate for more advanced students who already have fairly well developed writing abilities, would be to reconfigure the instructional sequence, beginning not with reading but with writing. The teacher could ask students to write a 'showing not telling' (Caplan and Keech 1980) story in which they are to communicate through their narrative the idea 'I live in a house where I belong but where I don't belong,' *without* explicitly saying this. Below are the first lines of two examples:

> It is the house I grew up in. Since then, I've lived in many other places—college, abroad, my own apartment. I'm used to being the boss of my house. In the house where I grew up, though, I'm not the boss . . . .

> I have never liked it here, but I know it's not until I'm 18 that I'll be able to go out on my own. I used to wish I had been born into a different family, or in a different time, or at least in a different house. But this house follows me, is part of me. We understand each other, though I cannot wait to leave. I am different from everyone here . . . .

Students would then read *The House on Mango Street* to see how Cisneros handled a similar writing task, comparing their stories—and *the manner* of the telling—with hers. The purpose of beginning with writing in this example is to engage students with a problem of communication, allow them to puzzle their way through, and then provide them with an 'alternative solution' with which to compare their own. By manipulating the initial creative writing task, students can be sensitized to various elements of the targeted text to be read, such as its theme, genre, or style, making these elements more salient during students' actual reading (this point will be elaborated in greater detail in Chapter 7). Finally, these elements can be analyzed and discussed in written form (for example, in an argumentative essay). It is in this way that a curricular sequence evolves from the model I have been proposing to this point.

Conclusion

In the last two chapters, I have tried to argue that teaching reading in a foreign language should be based on a literacy framework that takes linguistic, cognitive, and sociocultural domains into account. Reading is not a matter of extracting fixed meanings from texts, nor is it a matter of making words mean whatever one wants. Texts are always embedded in social and cultural contexts, and only sometimes do these coincide with contexts that are already familiar to foreign language learners.

In a literacy-based language classroom teachers should be concerned with identifying and teaching reading *practices* as well as selecting and teaching *texts*. That is to say, close attention should be paid to the materials used. But also to the particular ways that students are led to deal with them.

To accomplish the goal of realizing discourse from texts, despite limitations in language ability and cultural background knowledge, we have considered a variety of activities that, as a group, address four different but complementary needs of the foreign language learner: (1) to be immersed in written language (situated practice), (2) to receive direct assistance in the complexities of reading L2 texts (overt instruction), (3) to learn not just to absorb information but to analyze and evaluate what they read (critical framing), and (4) to learn how to reshape or redesign texts through summarization, rewriting, or translation (transformed practice).

When students are encouraged to compare their readings—their working designs—amongst themselves, against those of their teacher, or perhaps even against those of native-speaker peers, they can become aware of the dialogic relationship between textual interpretation and culture, personal experience, attitudes and knowledge, and improve their ability to work in different frames of language use. By virtue of their distance from foreign language texts, language learners are actually in the privileged position of potentially seeing clearly what is so often invisible to 'intended' readers.

The next two chapters will continue to elaborate a core redefinition of teacher/student goals in literacy-based teaching, with a focus on writing.

Notes

1 Teacher guidance is obviously of key importance here. Texts whose cultural subtexts are relatively inaccessible to students are therefore probably best reserved for structured in-class reading activities, such as those discussed in this chapter. On the other hand, reading material having to do with familiar topics, written in a familiar genre, and relying on familiar cultural knowledge can be profitably read independently, outside of class. Both kinds of texts and approaches are necessary: the first highlights discourse and culture learning, whereas the second highlights vocabulary learning and reading fluency.

2 The procedures described here are essentially those proposed by Stauffer (1969), although several modifications have been added, including the use of the question 'why?' to follow-up on readers' responses, encouraging readers to provide concrete evidence for their statements. For another example of a DRTA, using Somerset Maugham's story 'The Man with a Scar', see Carter (1986).

3 Alternatively, one can begin by exposing any illustrations that accompany the text or the title (although it is often useful to withold the title so that students can propose their own title after reading the text).

4 Depending on course goals, students' verbal participation in the DRTA can be done in the native or foreign language. Swaffar, Arens, and Byrnes (1991: 69) point out that occasional use of the native language in discussing readings can be useful to identify conceptual misunderstandings that remain hidden if only the language of the text is used.

5 The text translation is offered in this example as an aid for those who do not read French, but the actual classroom activity does not involve translation. The amount of text read may range from a sentence to several pages, depending on (1) the nature and length of the reading selection, and (2) the relative reading ability of the students. Where one pauses to ask guided-reading questions should ideally be at pivotal points in the information structure of the selection (i.e. just before significant new information or a new event is presented). Students read the segment of text with the specific purpose of testing the various hypotheses that they proposed after reading the previous section of the text.

6 With longer texts, the first page or two can be broken into segments and read in class, as described above. Readied with predictions as to what will happen next, students can then continue reading subsequent pages at home. The DRTA can thus be used as a 'starter' activity in class to prepare students for reading extended works. Novels, for example, often contain important information in their first few pages; active prediction-making based on this information may facilitate students' interpretation of the novel at a later stage in their reading.

7 The DRTA can be profitably used at intermediate and advanced levels, however, in abbreviated form. When assigning a new text, to be read at home for the next class, the teacher can have students discuss the title and then the first paragraph of the text DRTA-style. This provides a preview of the text, awareness of some of the potential directions it might take, and opportunity to make hypotheses about the text, creating initial direction and motivation for their independent reading at home.

8 In fact, students can be asked explicitly, 'Does seeing and hearing this representation change your interpretation of the text? If so, how?' After seeing three or four readers' theater performances of a given text, students generally agree that their notion of what is 'in' the text has been considerably expanded. It seems that even the pre-performance discussion

leads to new perspectives. Students consistently report that the interpretations they end up representing in their performances are never ones they had in mind before working together in groups. Ideas piggyback on one another, creative experimentation leads to clever twists and fresh insights. During the performances, students are very attentive to how other groups have solved particular problems and are very appreciative of ideas they had not themselves thought of.

 9 For more on readers' theatre, see Cazden (1992), Cazden and Lobdell (1993), Kramsch (1984: 146–9), Ruddell and Ruddell (1995: 288–90), and Smith (1984: 126–7). Cazden (1992) discusses how readers' theater can be applied to explore the discourse structure of expository as well as narrative texts.

10 I am thankful to Professor John Rassias for this example.

11 See Neufeld and Webb (1984) for additional ideas for teaching signaling cues and transitions.

12 This activity was developed by Mimi Frede, a student teacher on a teacher certification program in English and ESL at the University of California, Berkeley in 1996.

13 See Jurasek (1993) for excellent examples of using multiple translations in content-based foreign language classes. See Lefevere (1992), Chapter 8, for an example of multiple comparisons of illocutionary strategies used in translations of Catullus's second poem.

14 The heuristic sequence I will describe is a direct application of the Hermeneutic Circle to reading instruction. Going full circuit around the Hermeneutic Circle involves examination of the whole as well as its component parts, and the relations between the two—how knowledge of the whole informs understanding of the parts and knowledge of the parts informs understanding of the whole. The point is that reading instruction must involve both macro-level and micro-level analysis, top-down and bottom-up processing, and allow them to inform one another.

15 For excellent foreign language examples of organized sequences of reading activities designed to help learners explore multiple dimensions of a German folktale and a Chinese poem respectively, see Kramsch (1985) and Cheung (1995).

16 An initial focus on the text itself also keeps cognitive demands relatively low, which may alleviate the anxiety that some students experience when they feel pressed to offer an immediate *interpretation* of a text.

17 See Swaffar, Arens, and Byrnes (1991) for extensive background on the design of matrices that help students to organize textual information in terms of themes and logical relationships. See Armbruster and Anderson (1982), Heimlich and Pittelman (1986), and Schultz (1991a) for descriptions, examples, and uses of idea mapping.

6 Writing as design

Writing requires reading for its completion, but also teaches the kind of reading it requires.

David Lodge (1977)

As the above epigram succinctly reminds us, reading and writing are intrinsically linked, complementary processes. Writers are their own first readers, and their ability to read closely is essential to their ability to write coherently. By the same token, the thought processes that writers go through in the act of writing promote a sensitivity to language that makes close, analytic reading possible. With this symbiotic relation between reading and writing in mind, we will focus in this chapter on writing and its importance in learning to design meaning in a non-native language.

If reading involves creating discourse from texts, writing involves designing texts to create a potentiality for that realized discourse. Like reading, writing involves the use of Available Designs—the residual voices and language forms we have internalized, our knowledge of rhetorical and stylistic devices, genres, formatting conventions, and so on—as resources in a dialogic negotiation between internal and external representations of meaning. Writers' moment-by-moment decisions concerning the choice and structuring of their words, and their placement in a visual field—what Vygotsky (1962) called 'deliberate semantics'—constitute the design process.[1] Sometimes, as when we write notes or lists, design is quick and formulaic—the graphic representation, reduced to a bare minimum, is meant simply to remind us of ideas, things, events, and so on. At other times, design is more deliberate, and we use writing not so much to record information, as to generate new ideas, to experiment with reconfigurations of language, to create fictional worlds. In formal academic writing, design involves the elaborate and recursive processes of planning, drafting, revising, and editing. Whatever the type of writing, the outcome is a textual product made possible by various Available Designs which are either reproduced or transformed into new resources for subsequent writing (the 'Redesigned').

What relevance might this have for foreign language learners, many of whom may never need to write in the foreign language after they complete their academic studies? From the standpoint of the literacy framework developed in Part One, writing is essential to academic language learning for a number of reasons. First, in designing meaning through writing, learners develop their ability to think explicitly about how to organize and express their thoughts, feelings, and ideas in ways compatible with envisioned readers' expectations. Working deliberately toward making one's thoughts understandable to others who may not share similar backgrounds is of course at the heart of communicative ability.[2]

Second, the concrete, visible nature of writing is of key importance in terms of the language learning process. Just as reading allows learners to focus their attention on relationships among forms, writing allows learners to create and reshape meaning through explicit manipulation of forms. Writing thus provides an excellent platform for learners to test hypotheses about the new language. By 'trying out' different words, syntactic structures, styles, and organizational patterns, and by considering the *effects* that such manipulations might have on meaning, learners can broaden their communicative potential in the language.[3] Thinking about the complex relations of forms and meaning in their own writing may in turn predispose them to be more sensitive to form/meaning relationships in the texts they *read* in the foreign language.

Third, like reading, writing provides *time* for learners to process meaning. Particularly at the early stages of study, many foreign language learners find writing easier and less anxiety producing than speaking, simply because they have time to think. When speaking, their attention is divided among many things, including the development of an idea, the mapping of that idea onto appropriate structures (and perhaps silent rehearsal of the utterance), and the monitoring of conversational turns so that they can find an appropriate place to interject their comments. While these processes operate smoothly when one is speaking one's native language, they are less efficient when one is learning a new language.[4] When writing, students need not worry about turns, or pronunciation, or keeping an idea (and its articulation) rehearsed in memory. They are free to take the time they need to get their message across in a form they find acceptable. Furthermore, when they are given the chance to express and respond to ideas in writing, students are often able to engage more effectively in subsequent oral discussions because their ideas have already been at least partially developed and articulated, allowing them to focus more attention on their oral delivery.[5]

Finally, writing allows learners' language use to go beyond purely 'functional' communication, making it possible to create imagined worlds of their own design. Symbolic play, and the recombining of elements in fresh, inventive ways can be highly motivating and can help to prepare language students to read poetry and other forms of literary expression with greater sensitivity.[6]

To illustrate the power that writing affords individuals in shaping meaning differently and in becoming aware of that difference, consider an informal experiment originally described by Osgood (1971) and subsequently adapted by Becker (1988) and Kramsch (1993). In a classroom or workshop, participants are asked to witness a simple event (for example, someone walking across the room and placing a book on a table) and then to write a one-sentence account of what they have perceived. Participants then share their sentences with the group. Below is a small sample of sentences produced by different individuals during a recent writing workshop:

Rick placed his books on the table.
The teacher crossed the floor and then slammed his books on the table.
The tall thin man took long, deliberate strides across the room and put his books on the table.
A pile of books crashed on the table.
You walked to the table and banged your books down.
The teacher is having a bad day.

Each of these sentences expresses a unique interpretation of a single event, and in so doing, creates a unique discourse world of relationships. Consider how the writers position themselves differently by the particular words they use to refer to the grammatical agent: 'Rick' and 'you' both suggest familiarity with the agent, but are addressed to different audiences. 'The teacher' creates a formal role relationship, whereas 'the tall thin man' positions the writer as a detached, 'objective' observer. 'A pile of books' removes the agent altogether. The verbs chosen ('placed', 'put', 'slammed', 'crashed', 'banged') characterize the agent as either calm or agitated. The last sentence does not directly describe the event at all, but reflects an inference about an underlying reality the observed event might signal.

What is remarkable about this experiment is that no matter how large the group, participants' sentences are invariably unique—even though they are all written about 'the same thing'. While both speech and writing involve making linguistic choices, then, the diversity of linguistic choice appears to be particularly striking in writing, when one is not influenced by others' expression. If participants had been asked to report orally what they saw (for example, 'You walked across the room and put your books on the table') they would quickly find it difficult and tiresome to differentiate their phrasings and perspectives: a few participants' utterances would seem to exhaust the expressive possibilities.[7] Writing, on the other hand, fully reveals learners' multiple and unique voices and provides a way to concretize and analyze differences in design of meaning. Explicitly exploring these differences through classroom discussion can be an effective way to raise language learners' consciousness of how their own personal voice is a function of particular choices they have made, and how their language use both reflects *and creates* social contexts (i.e. particular reader-writer relationships).

How does this example relate to the design model presented in Part One? Starting at the innermost circle of Figure 2.3 in Chapter 2, what the above writers are doing is drawing on a range of linguistic and schematic resources to design their own unique 'readings' or interpretations of an event they have witnessed. Drawing on the Available Designs of vocabulary and grammar, they make choices about how to represent what they consider key elements (for example, books, table, teacher) and the kinds of relationships that obtain among those elements (for example, placed, slammed, crashed). They draw on procedural knowledge as well as knowledge of the writing system and formal schemata as they inscribe their sentence on paper. They draw on metalinguistic knowledge (for example, knowing what a 'sentence' is) as well as genre conventions (for example, 'report' or 'narrative') and style conventions (what 'sounds' appropriate for the genre). They also draw on knowledge of stories when they interpret the event in terms of a larger, imagined whole ('The teacher is having a bad day'). Some elements are predictable; others not. The various sentences (i.e. designs) have points of commonality, but each one also takes a particular, unique perspective.

The circular arrow around the 'text' in Figure 2.3 represents not only the interaction of the various Available Designs in the creation of the text, but also the way the text itself influences how Available Designs are drawn upon. That is to say, once the writing process has begun, what has already been written will influence the writer's subsequent choices. This is particularly so in the case of syntax and style. As I write this very sentence I find myself mentally trying out various phrasings in search of one that sounds consistent with the wording of the preceding sentences. Most writers do not start out with fully-elaborated ideas on a topic before they begin writing. It is generally in the process of articulation itself, and in the subsequent reading of what one has written, that new relationships are seen and new ideas born—ideas which in turn become resources for the generation of further ideas in later moments of writing.[8]

Moving to the middle layer of Figure 2.3, all the above relations are embedded in a particular context of communication. In the case of the writing experiment above, this includes the physical situation (i.e. a classroom), a set of social roles (a teacher and students), a particular purpose for writing (obeying the teacher's request), a particular audience (oneself? the teacher? the class?), a topic (the observed event), and a task ('write to record what you observe') that will be more or less familiar to the particular writer.[9] Writing involves not only 'immediate' but also 'eventual' contexts of communication since the purposes for which one writes usually have to do with an anticipated, future act of communication (the reading of the text by a particular audience). The topic will influence the extent to which the writer's existing content schemata can be put to use, as well as the writer's choice of organizational patterns (Burtoff 1983; Schallert 1987). The writing task will influence the relative emphasis put on content versus form, and the degree to which genres familiar to the writer can be used. The situation of expression (which determines the availability of time, reference materials, and other resources) may influence the degree to which the writer plans and revises writing. Purpose and envisioned audience are key factors in global decisions about genre, style, diction, and formatting. They are also important in making decisions concerning what information needs to be explicit, what can or should be left implicit, and how information might best be organized for the intended reader (Nystrand 1987).

These dimensions of communicative context are in turn influenced by the broader sociocultural context, represented by the outermost circle of Figure 2.3. Here we are particularly concerned with the context of literacy practices in the learner's home language community, the target language community (which the learner may or may not wish to join), and the language classroom community, which in foreign language settings is a subset of the home culture educational community, but in second language settings is a subset of the target culture educational community.

The purposes and practices of literacy that one is familiar with in the context of one's home community and culture will be particularly influential in learning to write in a new culture and community. However, because of differences in functions and conventions of writing across cultures and discourse communities (as well as differences across schooling traditions), it cannot be assumed that being able to write in one's native language necessarily means that one can write effectively in a second language simply by virtue of learning a set of words and structures, or even a set of writing process skills. What must also be taken into account are epistemological considerations that not only underlie rhetorical conventions, but even more importantly frame what writing, reading, and learning are all about in a given community and culture.

To illustrate this last point, Ballard and Clanchy (1991) discuss the situation of Asian immigrant students in Australian universities, for whom the kind of critical analysis and evaluation typically required in reading and writing assignments can clash with the educational traditions of their home cultures. Underlying the demand for students to analyze, question, and critique ideas, Ballard and Clanchy argue, are the assumptions that (1) knowledge is socially constructed, not absolute, and (2) the goal of education is to train people to be independent learners and thinkers, capable of challenging existing knowledge. This 'extending' attitude toward knowledge contrasts with the 'conserving' attitude toward knowledge in many Asian cultures, where the reproduction and transfer of long-held knowledge from one generation to another is a primary educational value. Consequently, writing activities that involve questioning information in a text, challenging expressed points of view, and speculating about knowledge may potentially lead to difficulties and misunderstandings among some Asian students.[10] Furthermore, these cross-cultural differences in writing practices and approaches to knowledge can lead students and teachers to hold quite different attitudes about plagiarism (Pennycook 1996).

The danger, of course, in discussing epistemological and rhetorical differences is that it is easy to essentialize other cultures. One must not lose sight of the fact that individuals within any given culture (and especially those who are crossing cultural borders, as many learners of a second language are) draw on myriad influences, undergo continual change, and experience and use literacy in unique ways not always captured by cultural generalizations (Murray and Nichols 1992; Spack 1997).[11] Nevertheless, an awareness of difference among epistemological, rhetorical, and pedagogical traditions can often provide useful illumination when teachers try to understand language learners' writing development.

To elaborate on the point about pedagogical traditions, the classroom culture itself imposes its own particular conditions of appropriateness on writing and its uses. In foreign language classrooms, 'writing' encompasses a continuum of activities, ranging from tightly controlled copying and dictation exercises to freewriting activities. Some of these writing practices may seem to have little to do with 'real life' uses of writing in *either* the home or target culture, but are nevertheless judged to have pedagogical value. Carson (1992) adds that North American teachers' tendency to emphasize writing process and the expression of personal meaning may be alien to some Japanese and Chinese ESL students, who may expect more pattern practice and memorization work. Students' expectations and preferences concerning written feedback on essays from teachers can also vary substantially from those of native speakers (Chen and Hamp-Lyons 1999). What is important to recognize, however, is that cultures of learning often vary widely within a given societal culture. They can even vary widely within a given educational institution, as Atkinson and Ramanathan (1995) show in their discussion of the differences in writing pedagogy between an ESL institute and a mainstream composition program at an American university. Again, what is important in a literacy-based program is a clear understanding (on the part of both teachers and students) of the assumptions, purposes, and goals underlying what goes on in the classroom.

Crossing culture-literacy borders presents complex problems without simple solutions. The kind of literacy-based teaching argued for in this book (with its admittedly Western 'critical thinking' bias) attempts to ease these border crossings through forthright acknowledgment and examination of relevant epistemological, rhetorical, and pedagogical differences, with the assumption that improving students' understanding of the cultural underpinnings of literacy practices in both their home culture and the target culture is a key step toward developing their literacy and their communicative potential.

Writing in a non-native language

If the design model represented in Figure 2.3 outlines how texts, context, and the writing process interact with one another, it also provides us with a principled way of appreciating the complexities of writing in a second language. Reviews of second language writing research (for example, Dvorak 1986; Krapels 1990; Silva 1993) suggest that both first and second language writing involve essentially similar processes, but that second language writing is complexified by the addition of new resources and norms. Learning the structural elements of the new language, new rhetorical conventions, and perhaps even new uses of writing does not replace, but is added to what one already knows about writing from one's native language. To the extent that the language learner is less familiar with these new resources and less confident in their use, writing in a second language will be more difficult and less effective than writing in the native language. When learners' native language resources are more extensive and elaborated than those in the second language, learners will naturally tend to draw upon native language resources whenever they feel at a loss in the second language.[12] As learners gain experience in reading and writing in the second language, their repertoire of L2-based Available Designs will grow larger. However, rather than predict that learners will eventually shift to exclusive use of L2-derived Available Designs, the design model would suggest that *all* of one's Available Designs are potentially available in *either* L1 or L2 writing. Ultimately, then, the model predicts that learners will draw upon those literacy resources they deem appropriate to their communicative purposes, regardless of whether those resources were originally acquired in their first or second language.[13]

To examine how both L1 and L2 Available Designs are drawn upon in foreign language writing, let's first consider the case of vocabulary. In one of the few studies to examine foreign language writing processes at the novice level, Bland, Noblitt, Armington, and Gay (1990) found that in the early stages of learning to write in a new language, learners' thinking tends to be dominated by lexical rather than syntactic issues. Bland *et al.* identified three lexical search strategies that novice-level French students used in consulting an electronic dictionary/grammar reference, each of which relied on the use of L1 resources, but which reflected different degrees of sophistication in thinking about lexical meaning. Students were not limited to seeking one-to-one lexical correspondences, but developed creative ways of using paraphrase and circumlocution in their native language to find contextually appropriate French expressions.

At more advanced levels, many studies have shown how L2 writers will often draw on genres and rhetorical organization patterns that they originally learnt in their native language. This kind of use of the native language has been studied under the rubric of contrastive rhetoric (for example, Kaplan 1966; Purves 1988; Connor 1996). Although traditionally seen as a source of *interference* in learning to write in a new language, rhetorical resources acquired in one's native language can also have important facilitative effects on second language writing. Leki (1995), for example, describes Julie, a French ESL student who excelled in her English academic writing by judiciously employing the three-part, thesis-antithesis-synthesis organizational strategy she had learnt in secondary school in France. Julie did not always use this rhetorical scheme, which she sometimes found rigid and confining, but drew upon it under certain conditions, such as when she felt disorganized or when she found herself straying from the topic. This element of active *choice* of native language resources on the part of the writer has not been explored in most contrastive rhetoric studies. The important implication in terms of the design model of literacy is that Available Designs developed in whatever language (first, second, third . . .) are neither pre-emptive nor mutually exclusive, but can be used synergistically in attempts to solve particular communicative problems as they arise.

Analogous to the case of mental translation in second language reading (see Chapter 4), there is some evidence to suggest that language learners sometimes use their native language to facilitate the process of writing in a second language. Lay (1982), for example, noted that Chinese ESL students translated key words into Chinese while writing in English 'to get a stronger impression and association of ideas for the essay' (p. 406). She found that such language switches improved the quality of students' writing in terms of ideas, organization, and details. Whether or not a student switched to Chinese seemed to depend on the topic and its relation to the student's experience. Friedlander (1990) found that Chinese ESL students produced longer and better essays when they planned the essay in the language in which the topic was primarily experienced (i.e. when they used Chinese to plan a description of the Chinese *Qingming* festival and when they used English to plan an essay about difficulties in adjusting to the new cultural and educational environment of an American university). Friedlander hypothesized that a match in the language of essay planning and the language in which the topic has been experienced makes it easier for writers to recall and organize information.

Nevertheless, it is important to recognize that the manner and degree to which language learners draw upon their native language while writing in the second language seems to vary widely across individuals, tasks, and contexts (Jones and Tetroe 1987). Zamel (1982), for example, noted that the most proficient writer in her group of ESL students would write her essays in her native language and then translate them into English. As this student put it, 'When I write in my own language, I feel great because I can express my writing as part of myself. It's like painting' (p. 201). For the other students in Zamel's group, however, translation was considered a last resort, for as one student put it, 'It would be like being pulled by two brains' (p. 201).

Uzawa and Cumming's (1989) study on writing strategies in Japanese as a foreign language showed that how students perceive the writing task influences how they use their linguistic resources. When Uzawa and Cumming's students perceived a need to maintain the kind of standards they usually achieved in their native language writing, they tended to stretch their linguistic resources, using compensatory strategies such as rehearsing and organizing information in the native language, taking extra time to compose, seeking assistance on word choices or grammar, and revising texts extensively. On the other hand, when they needed to produce fluent text within a reasonable length of time and without excessive mental effort, the students tended to simplify their syntax, to 'borrow' specific lexical items verbatim from source materials, to avoid semantic elaboration, and to neglect concerns for their audience. Uzawa and Cumming concluded that the cognitive demands of second language writing tasks are at least as significant as contrastive rhetoric in accounting for illogical and incomprehensible texts.

If the immediate situational context of writing affects how L1 and L2 Available Designs are drawn upon, so does the larger sociocultural context represented in the outermost layer of Figure 2.3. Consider, for example, Bell's (1995) autobiographical portrait of her own experiences of becoming literate in Chinese. Bell explains that she and her Chinese tutor had very different tacit understandings of what literacy was about and how it should be taught. For Bell's tutor, the form of one's writing was considered extremely important since it was a direct reflection of one's self:

> The appearance of one's writing made evident to the reader the kind of personality one had and the degree to which balance and discipline were developed . . . This thinking was in direct contrast to my assumption that the content of what I wrote was the vehicle by which I displayed myself to others, while form was relatively unimportant.
> (Bell 1995: 696)

In Bell's efforts to learn Chinese, she found that most of her difficulties stemmed from her 'mistaken assumption that literacy in English and Chinese was differentiated only by the shape of the squiggles on the paper' (p. 701), which originally led her to approach Chinese literacy with the same strategies that had proved successful for her in English. She came to discover, however, that a surprisingly significant aspect of learning Chinese was learning a new way of thinking, a new set of values, a new way of presenting herself to the world—in other words, learning new Discourses in Gee's sense of the term. Bell concluded that:

> It is no doubt possible to learn to read and write in Chinese by methods which essentially allow one to transcribe English thinking via Chinese characters. Such an ability should not be confused, however, with developing Chinese literacy . . . . we need to think about the relationship between form and content and that between part and whole. We need to

become conscious of our notions of how progress is measured and how it is rewarded. We need to consider the human qualities which are valued in our society and explore how these are made manifest in our preferred literacy practices. We need to explore our own assumptions and recognize that much of what we used to consider an inherent part of literacy is actually culturally imposed.
(*Ibid.* 702)

As in the case of reading, the design model presents writing as a social and cultural act that involves cognitive and linguistic dimensions. Writing is thus most usefully defined not in terms of uniform, universal processes, but rather in terms of contextually appropriate practices. What is clear from the research literature is that the ability to write in a second language does not necessarily follow in any direct way from native language writing ability. Moreover, writing ability—whether in a first or second language—does not follow automatically from either speaking ability or general language proficiency. Writing, it seems, must be taught. The question is, how?

Three orientations to teaching writing

The design model represented in Figure 2.3 provides a useful metaphor for understanding the relationships among three well-established traditions in the teaching of writing, namely product-, process-, and genre-based approaches. Product approaches focus on the inner core of design: the interaction between texts and the structural resources needed to create them. Process approaches add elements from the middle layer of communicative context, and genre-based approaches address the outermost layer of sociocultural context. All three are widely represented in current teaching practices, with process approaches particularly favored in North America and the United Kingdom, and genre-based approaches predominant in Australia and New Zealand. Although these three orientations arise from fundamentally different theoretical bases and are often seen as mutually incompatible, I will argue that all three foci—textual features, writer processes, and social context—are essential in a comprehensive pedagogy of literacy. First, however, I will briefly outline the origins, characteristic practices, and underlying assumptions of the three orientations.[14]

Product approaches: focus on textual form

Product-oriented approaches, which characterized most writing instruction from the 1940s through the 1960s but which have by no means been abandoned today, emphasize the structural well-formedness of students' writing. Based on an autonomous text model, product-oriented teaching ascribes intrinsic value to a text primarily by virtue of its formal properties, placing less explicit emphasis on how well it addresses a particular audience and fulfills a particular communicative purpose. Instruction typically involves grammar study, error analysis, and practice in reworking problematic sentences or combining short sentences into complex sentences. Attention is also given to larger patterns of organization in students' writing. At the paragraph level, teaching is centered on the arrangement of topic sentences and supporting sentences, in inductive or deductive patterns, to fulfill particular functions such as comparison, contrast, illustration, definition, and so on. Instruction at the essay level is often focused on prescribed features or patterns for the introduction, body, and conclusion of essays in the four modes of description, narration, exposition, and argumentation. Model texts are commonly used to illustrate all levels of text organization. After reading a model text and analyzing its organizational structures in class, students imitate the model's structures in their own writing. Product-oriented instruction thus emphasizes the linguistic Available Designs in the 'inner core' of the design model in Figure 2.3. What it tends to emphasize less, however, are the cognitive and social dimensions of writing. For that, we turn to process- and genre-based approaches.

Process approaches: focus on the individual

During the 1960s attention began to shift away from texts to writers. New research evidence indicated that grammar instruction did not directly improve students' writing ability (Braddock, Lloyd-Jones, and Schoer 1963), putting in question one of the major tenets of product-based approaches. In 1966, British and American educators meeting at Dartmouth College called for greater emphasis on developing students' self-expressiveness in writing (Bizzell and Herzberg 1991). Moffett (1968) popularized the idea that writing was about thinking, and that learning to write was learning to think about increasingly abstract topics and to think about the communicative needs of increasingly broad audiences. In the UK, Britton and his colleagues (1975) emphasized the greater importance of expressive language use over the imitation of prescribed forms. Writing was no longer seen simply as a way of recording thoughts, feelings, and ideas after the fact, but also as a key means of generating and exploring new thoughts and ideas. Hence, instead of constraining students' writing by imposing prescribed patterns at the start, process-oriented teachers sought first to foster students' creativity, and then to guide them through the process of reformulating and refining their writing. Whereas product-oriented teaching was deductive and teacher-centered, process-oriented teaching was inductive and student-centered.[15]

Today, process-oriented writing classrooms are generally characterized by the use of collaborative brainstorming, freewriting, choice of personally meaningful topics, peer-group editing, and strategy instruction in the stages of invention, drafting, revising, and editing. What is modeled is not texts, but writers' processes. Grammar, spelling, and other issues of form come into play in the editing phases, but are not emphasized up front, so as to encourage students to express themselves freely. The expectation is that students will address issues of form naturally as they rework their ideas through cycles of drafting and editing. Murray (1978) explained this point as follows:

> During the process of internal revision, [writers] gather new information or return to their inventory of information and draw on it. They discover what they have to say by relating pieces of specific information and use words to symbolize and connect the information . . . . This naturally leads to the discoveries related to *form and structure*.
> (Murray 1978: 93)

Whereas product-based approaches emphasized linguistic Available Designs, we see here that schematic Available Designs (for example, stories, content schemata) are accorded primacy and are key in determining how linguistic Available Designs are used. Process approaches also emphasize procedural knowledge—focusing learners' attention on how to coordinate and integrate their use of linguistic and schematic Available Designs.

Over the last thirty years, the process paradigm has had a profound influence on writing instruction in both L1 and L2 settings and process-oriented teaching is still widespread in many parts of the world. The process paradigm has nevertheless been subject to a number of criticisms. First, while it acknowledges dynamic individual processes, it largely ignores the influence of sociocultural context on such processes. Second, it tends to favor students who are already familiar with a variety of culturally-appropriate academic genres over those who are not. The lack of explicit models can make it especially difficult for second language learners to discover the tacit expectations for various types of writing (Inghilleri 1989). Furthermore, as Horowitz (1986) noted, some students are not familiar or comfortable with the inductive orientation of process-centered instruction, and are much more at ease with a deductive approach.[16] Finally, process-oriented writing instruction has been criticized for letting idiosyncracies or inappropriateness be too easily swept under the rug of 'personal expression'. At stake is learners' understanding of links between form and communicative conventions that will allow them to construct meanings in ways that are appropriate within the immediate academic context as well as the larger societal context. It is this larger context, represented by the outermost layer of the design model in Figure 2.3, that is accounted for in genre-based approaches to teaching

Genre-based approaches: focus on social context

The third major orientation to writing instruction emphasizes the role that discourse communities play in shaping written communication. To summarize the discussion of genre as presented in Part One of the book: When we communicate we don't construct meanings in a completely idiosyncratic 'personal' fashion but within socially-determined parameters or constraints. These constraints are not universal, but are specific to particular discourse communities. In order to belong to a particular discourse community, we have to know its conventions. We learn these conventions through apprenticeship, by observing what established members say and do and by gradually appropriating features of these sayings and doings for ourselves. If we do not have practical knowledge of the conventions relevant to a particular situation, we may seem or feel communicatively inept, even if we otherwise have an excellent knowledge of the language.

Genre-based approaches to teaching writing focus on getting students 'in' to new discourse communities by making them aware of the characteristically patterned ways that people in the community use language to fulfill particular communicative purposes in recurring situations. For example, learners in an English for Specific Purposes (ESP) class might learn that writing an introduction to a research article typically involves three principle moves: (1) 'establishing a territory', (2) 'establishing a niche', and (3) 'occupying the niche' (Swales 1990: 141); or that writing a sales letter typically involves seven moves: (1) 'establishing credentials', (2) 'introducing the offer', (3) 'offering incentives', (4) 'referring to enclosed documents', (5) 'inviting further communication', (6) 'using pressure tactics', and (7) 'ending politely' (Bhatia 1991). It is argued that students in primary and secondary schools in Australia (Cope and Kalantzis 1993; Martin, *et al.* 1994) or in the United States (Delpit 1988) may be helped to cope with academic tasks and ultimately become empowered to cross barriers to social power by mastering scholastic genres such as reports, explanations, summaries, and argumentative essays.

Like product and process approaches, genre-based teaching has not been spared from criticism. One risk pointed out in Chapter 3 is that genres can be easily reduced to static formal recipes, taught in prescriptive fashion, reminiscent of traditional product-based teaching. As Cope and Kalantzis (1993) point out, if genre-based teaching is not done in a critical spirit, it can be oppressive rather than liberating. Furthermore, a number of scholars question whether one can really empower students simply by providing exposure and practice in various genres. Barrs (1994), for example, contends that it is only when one already occupies certain social roles that social power is conferred by the use of certain genres. Similarly, Dixon and Stratta (1992) argue that a writer's power comes not from producing generic forms, but from having an effect on people. Finally, little empirical research has been done on the outcome of genre-based writing instruction, particularly in second language contexts.[17]

By way of summary, Table 6.1 offers a thumbnail sketch of some of the characteristics of product, process, and genre orientations to composition instruction.

	Product	**Process**	**Genre**
Dominant theoretical/ disciplinary framework	structural linguistics; writing is a linguistic act.	cognitive psychology, constructivism; writing is a cognitive act.	social constructionism; writing is a social act.
Central focus	textual norms	writer's internal processes	audience needs and expectations
Learning to write is ...	imitating good models; adhering to prescriptive norms.	an evolutionary process; a discovery process of thinking, creating, and problem-solving; developing one's own unique voice; learning to invent, draft, revise, and edit recursively.	apprenticing in a new discourse community; learning to communicate with new discourse expectations and norms.
Instructional goals	formal accuracy, syntactic complexity, adherence to canonical organizational patterns.	individual creativity, fluency of expression, development of authentic voice, improvement through revision, learning through writing, self-reliance in the writing process.	Awareness of the conventional parameters of expectations for particular text types within particular discourse communities and the ability to conform to those conventions. Understanding these conventions in terms of social and psychological contexts.
Instructional techniques include ...	analysis and imitation of models, grammar study, sentence-combining, paragraph structure analysis.	prewriting activities, writing of repeated drafts, peer editing, journals, freewriting.	analysis of obligatory and optional rhetorical moves in various genres; creating new texts in a given genre.

Table 6.1:   Summary of product-, process-, and genre-based orientations to writing instruction

Linking this summary to the design model of Figure 2.3, we see that product approaches remain within the bounds of the inner circle, focused on 'linguistic' Available Designs. Process approaches lie partly within the inner circle (focusing on procedural knowledge in linking schematic Available Designs to linguistic Available Designs), but their focus also extends to the intermediate layer of communicative context (for example, focus on task, purpose, physical situation). Genre-based approaches, in turn, have a leg in each layer, from the Available Designs core ('genre' is one of the listed resources), to the communicative context layer (particularly audience and purpose), and the outer sociocultural layer (sociocultural practices in home, classroom, and target language communities).

The need to coordinate approaches

The teaching of writing in foreign language programs has tended to change more slowly than in English language teaching for native or non-native speakers. Traditionally product-oriented, foreign language writing instruction has nevertheless gradually incorporated features of process-based teaching over the last twenty years. Where it has not yet fully succeeded, however, is in addressing adequately the writing demands of advanced academic study of a language. As a consequence, students often find themselves ill-prepared to write essays in advanced-level courses in which they are held responsible not only for grammatical precision, but also for their ideas, their style, and their ability to develop a lucid argument (Schultz 1991b).

From the standpoint of a literacy-based curriculum, what is needed is an integrative, student-centered approach, solidly grounded in an Available Designs core, but that also attends to the interdependencies among textual products, cognitive processes, and sociocultural factors. That is, an approach that focuses on meaning as it is constructed *through* form in a cultural context.

The curriculum also needs to take developmental considerations into account, however, since not all Available Designs will be equally available at the beginning of language study. Assuming that students are already literate in their native language, for example, what they need most at the outset are linguistic Available Designs (knowledge of vocabulary and syntax as well as of the writing system). Techniques associated with the product approach, such as the use of models, grammar study, sentence-combining, and paragraph structure analysis, can be extremely useful at the early stages. What differs in a literacy-based curriculum, however, is the way in which models and structural analysis are framed. Rather than as absolute (and *acontextualized*) examples of 'goodness of form', models can be looked at as examples of a particular writer's solution to a particular communicative problem. They can be contrasted with other textual models that offer alternative solutions. Grammar analysis can also work contrastively, showing how different utterances might be expressed differently to achieve different effects for different audiences, and so on. In this way, class presentations can focus on questions of appropriateness, rather than on questions of correctness.

As students' knowledge of the language increases to the point where they can use it actively to communicate in the classroom, many techniques associated with process approaches can be incorporated to build learners' procedural knowledge, to integrate writing with the other language skills (through peer editing, for example), and to support fluency and creativity in writing (for example, freewriting, creative writing).

As students progress further through the curriculum, and as their declarative knowledge of the target culture grows, they are ready for tasks that involve critical thinking about particular content, genre, or stylistic issues. Here, genre-based approaches can be drawn upon to explore how various Available Designs might be managed differently as the context, purpose, or audience of a piece of writing change. For example, how might a student approach the writing of an exam differently from a course paper? What kinds of adjustments are necessary if the student's intent is to persuade rather than to report? What considerations need to be taken into account if students are writing about home culture topics to foreign pen pals, rather than to their teacher? How will an informal letter differ from a formal one? By shifting contextual parameters one at a time, students can not only gain insight into the complexity of writing, but also develop a sense of how to manage Available Designs flexibly.

Finally, a literacy-based approach to teaching writing underlines the dependency of writing upon reading. Writers read and reread their own writing to evaluate how well it does what they intend it to do. Students eventually need to become their own critics, able to analyze and reformulate ideas and their expression without relying on extensive teacher feedback. One of the important ways in which teachers can help students to write effectively, then, is to teach them to read with a 'writerly eye'. By that I mean teaching them to think carefully about the various texts they read, evaluate ideas and argumentation, and notice the particular ways in which ideas are expressed for a particular audience. By examining how form and meaning interact in particular texts, by keeping a record of their observations in reading journals, and by talking about these observations in class, teachers and learners can bring linguistic and cognitive dimensions of reading and writing into the realm of social interaction, where they can be analyzed, compared, and discussed.

Conclusion

This chapter has portrayed writing as a dynamic process of designing meaning through texts within a community. Writing is at once an individual, creative process and a socially constrained, normative process. As such, it is a key activity in fostering language learners' awareness of how purpose, audience, and context affect the design of texts. Furthermore, conventions of writing can be revealing of larger underlying cultural patterns, thus sensitizing students to new ways of thinking, new sets of values, and new ways of presenting themselves to the world. Product-based, process-based, and genre-based schools of writing instruction each address important parts of this picture, but I have argued for an integrated approach that attends to the interdependencies among textual products, cognitive processes, and sociocultural dimensions of writing. The next chapter will develop these general ideas more fully with concrete pedagogical examples.

Notes

1 Vygotsky (1962) described the dynamic relationship between thought and language as follows:

> The relation of thought and language is not a thing but a process, a continual movement back and forth from thought to word and from word to thought . . . . Thought is not merely expressed in words; it comes into existence through them.
> (p. 125)

2 Because writing is generally done in the absence of one's reader, it furthermore forces writers to elaborate and systematize their expression by providing the necessary contextualization, structure, and coherence to allow their reader to follow their meaning. In second language acquisition theory, Swain (1985) has discussed this point in terms of 'comprehensible output', arguing that the need to make logical relations explicit may induce learners to shift their attention from semantic to syntactic processing.

3 *Feedback* from teachers or other expert readers is of course essential for learning about communicative effects. Here again, the concrete nature of writing can facilitate the process. First, the teacher can often more easily analyze and reflect upon a written text. In many cases students' intended meaning is not immediately clear in a given instance, but can be eventually surmised when the teacher has a moment to reflect on the learner's words. Once this meaning is identified, the teacher can help students to formulate, in a more understandable way, what they are trying to express. This is considerably more difficult to accomplish in most types of oral interaction, when utterances tend to be more brief, and disconnected. The opportunity for reflection can be curtailed by the urgency of responding in real time. The issue of feedback will be discussed in Chapter 9.

4 In Chapter 8 we will see how synchronous online writing with networked computers offers a way to conserve the spontaneity, fluidity, and interactivity characteristic of face-to-face communication while affording

learners the time to process and reflect on the language they read and write.

5 On the importance of planning see, for example, Crookes (1989), Foster and Skehan (1996), and Wigglesworth (1997).

6 Consider, for example, the first paragraph of an 'apartment description' essay below, written in the fourth week of a beginning French class, in which the student's decision to shift the narrative point of view to that of the apartment itself, suddenly transforms a mundane description into a fun and interesting exercise in metaphor:

> *Bonjour, je suis l'appartement de Linda. Dans mon corps, il y a trois personnes. Toutes les personnes sont jeunes et occupées. Je ne suis pas très loin du campus. Dans mon corps, il y a une cuisine, une salle de bains, une salle de séjour, et deux chambres à coucher. Tous mes murs sont blancs. Sur mes murs, il y a beaucoup de grands tableaux intéressants. Je suis très joli parce que j'ai beaucoup de grands fenêtres. Alors, j'ai beaucoup de jolis yeux . . . .*
> *Je ne suis pas snob, mais* QUEL APPARTEMENT *!*

> [Hello, I'm Linda's apartment. In my body there are three people. All the people are young and busy. I am not far from campus. In my body there is a kitchen, a bathroom, a living room, and two bedrooms. All my walls are white. On my walls there are many interesting paintings. I am very pretty because I have many large windows. So I have many beautiful eyes . . . .
> I'm not a snob, but WHAT AN APARTMENT!]

7 It is important to clarify that I am not arguing that written language *per se* is somehow superior to spoken language in terms of fostering more varied and more creative expression. I am simply arguing that individual acts of meaning design will always be unique, and that writing is a practical way of getting students to design meaning individually in a classroom setting, and of allowing concrete comparisons to be made. If we could somehow isolate people's oral responses to a similar task, we would no doubt find a similarly rich variety of utterances. But once people hear models in others' utterances, they tend to converge rather than diverge in their expression.

8 It should be noted that all aspects of the writing process are also constrained and influenced by the learner's experience, cognitive maturity, learning style, and other variables at the level of the individual.

9 The task (and the individual's interpretation of the task) is key: on one occasion when I did the same experiment with another group, I phrased the directions as 'write one sentence describing what you see between the time I say START and the time I say STOP'. Although most participants focused on my actions, one participant wrote 'My left shoe has a spot on it.'

10 For an example in a Caribbean context of how aspects of literacy teaching appropriate in one culture may be inappropriate in another, see Irvine and Elsasser (1988).

11 Furthermore, the true source of a learner's particular writing behavior can often be difficult to pinpoint. Mohan and Lo (1985), questioning the assumption that Chinese EFL students' writing is influenced by an underlying 'indirectness' in Chinese language and culture, examined classical texts and modern works on Chinese composition and found 'no support for claims that the organizational pattern of Chinese writing differs markedly from that of English' (p. 515). They argue that the source of difference lies rather in teachers' greater emphasis on sentence correctness over rhetorical organization in many English language programs in China. Tucker (1995) describes mistakenly attributing an Afghani ESL student's 'flowery effusions' to stylistic conventions in her native language and culture. Tucker later learnt through interviews that the student's writing style was really an attempt to imitate Harlequin romances, of which she was an avid reader.

12 Students who have learnt multiple languages have multiple sets of Available Designs at their disposal. One student of mine, who speaks Japanese as his native language, who learnt English as a foreign language in Japan, and who now studies French as a foreign language in the United States, regularly uses all three languages in his first drafts of his French essays. As he writes, certain thoughts come to mind in each of the three languages, and a substantial part of his rewriting efforts go into reworking the 'Japanese' and 'English' ideas into French form. He feels that his French writing would be much more limited if he only allowed himself to write in French from the start.

13 See discussion of Cummins's 'Common Underlying Proficiency' hypothesis in Chapter 4.

14 My summaries attempt to capture product-, process-, and genre-based approaches as they are typically represented *in theory*. The reality of instructional practice is far more complex, and therefore these summaries will not likely correspond in all respects to what is actually done in a given product-, process-, or genre-based classroom. For a comprehensive overview and intellectual history of the development of composition studies, see Nystrand, Greene, and Wiemelt (1993).

15 In second language classrooms, Zamel (1976), McKay (1979), and Raimes (1979) were among the first ESL writing specialists to call for an emphasis on writing processes. The process writing movement has had a significant impact on the way writing is taught in ESL as well as foreign language classrooms. Textbooks commonly include 'staged' writing assignments that walk students through the steps of brainstorming for ideas, organizing them in schematic formats, writing a first draft, then revising. In foreign language contexts, whereas writing used to be done

almost exclusively for the purpose of reinforcing other language skills, it has increasingly come to be seen as a way of *using* the language for creative personal expression. Consequently, in process-oriented foreign language classrooms greater emphasis has been placed on the formulation of original ideas, with lesser concern attached to grammar and spelling.

16 The implicitness of the process approach can also pose problems for evaluation, where vestiges of a product orientation are often evident. Although students are encouraged to discover form and structure naturally, teachers often cannot recognize the structure of a student's essay if it does not conform to their own culturally formed but not explicitly articulated expectations. As Inghilleri (1989) puts it, 'when no structure is perceived, it is often assumed that the text has no structure' (p. 393). Students' compositions are thus still often seen as failed native speaker writing rather than as developing transitional efforts at communication (Barrs 1994). Thus when instruction is process-oriented and yet evaluation is essentially product-oriented, students can be confused about what is most important.

17 In one of the few empirical studies on genre-based writing instruction in a second language context, Henry and Roseberry (1998) compared genre-based and traditional approaches to teaching Malay-speaking English students to write tourist brochures. After six hours of instruction, the genre group outperformed the control group on both a motivation index (measuring the degree to which the brochure motivated the reader to visit the described location) and on a texture index (which provided information on 'conjunction, conjunctive reach, specificity, connectivity, topic, and topic shift' (p. 151)). The genre group did not, however, score better than the control group on a measure of genre-specific textual moves, suggesting that students in the control group may have been able to induce obligatory and optional features of the tourist brochure genre simply from reading the six model texts used in the study. Clearly, more empirical research is needed in the area of genre-based instruction, and particularly research that provides thick description of students' classroom activities, their interaction with the teacher, their writing processes, and the texts they produce.

7 Teaching writing as design

Writing in the foreign language classroom encompasses a continuum of activities, ranging from tightly controlled transcription exercises (for example, copying and dictation), to freewriting activities in which students write down whatever enters their mind without editing or pausing (see Figure 7.1). In between these two extremes lie the most common writing activities: completing workbook exercises, taking notes, keeping journals, composing essays, and perhaps some translation and creative writing.

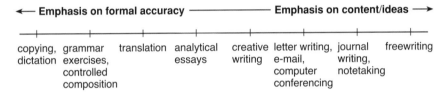

Figure 7.1:   *Continuum of writing activity types in language teaching*

As teachers know, there is a place for all of these activity types in language teaching. Although beginners will certainly tend to do tasks primarily at the left end of the continuum (especially when the writing system is a new one), with structured help from the teacher they can engage in more creative tasks as well (for example, cinquain poetry and dialogue journals, discussed later in this chapter). In academic programs, where discussing ideas, supporting opinions, and constructing coherent arguments are at the heart of the curriculum, essay writing is particularly important. As shown in Figure 7.1, writing analytical essays lies at the midpoint of the continuum, and involves striking a balance between an emphasis on formal conventions and an emphasis on original ideas.

Each of these activity types carries its own degree of demand on the language learner, and requires different degrees of attention to the Available Design elements that were shown in Figure 2.2 (Chapter 2). Transcription exercises, such as copying or dictation, focus on handwriting, spelling, and punctuation. Workbook exercises generally emphasize grammar, vocabulary, and mechanics. Controlled composition tasks, which involve performing transformations and substitutions (for example, rewriting a paragraph to pluralize all singular nouns and pronouns or to change all present tense verbs to an appropriate past tense form), focus attention on grammar and sometimes style. Journal writing emphasizes content schemata; translation emphasizes vocabulary, grammar, and style. More complex writing activities, such as composing formal essays, involve the full range of all of these elements, and especially knowledge of genres.

Based on the design model, a literacy-based approach integrates the teaching of Available Designs (elements of product- and genre-based instruction) with the teaching of design itself (process-based instruction). As in the case of reading (Chapter 5), it does this through a teaching agenda that incorporates four curricular components: situated practice, overt instruction, critical framing, and transformed practice. In the following sections we will examine activities that highlight each of these components, as well as activities that integrate more than one component.[1]

Situated practice (immersion)

Situated practice has to do with the learner's immersion in writing as an act of meaning design, and is a key ingredient in the development of writing ability. Although this point may seem self-evident, foreign language instruction has traditionally not immersed students in writing as meaning design, but rather in writing as grammar practice. While the latter approach definitely has its place in helping students to understand and master language forms, it does not go far enough in fostering learners' expressive and communicative abilities. In this section, we will consider letter writing, journal writing, freewriting, and creative writing as examples of immersion techniques. In terms of the design model, the principal goal of these activities is to give students extensive practice in using Available Designs to express personal thoughts and ideas, encouraging the development of fluency and automaticity in writing.

Letter writing

Writing letters either to native speakers or to other language learners is an excellent way to introduce students to writing. Foreign contacts for pen pal correspondences can be found through various online organizations,[2] but speakers of the foreign language can frequently be found in the local community as well, and such individuals often welcome the chance to communicate with learners of their native language. Letter writing corresponds well to the goals of communicative language teaching because it provides an authentic purpose for writing, it entails the use of a wide range of functions (for example, greeting, asking questions, explaining, clarifying, apologizing, expressing agreement and disagreement), it integrates reading and writing, and it motivates learners to pay attention to form (because they are addressing a 'real' audience). Depending on the content of the exchange, letter writing can also support cultural enrichment (see Chapter 8). When pen pals are unavailable, students can correspond with peers in other sections of a language course. For example, during a unit on 'providing advice', students in two different classes might write 'Dear Abby' (or 'Chère Françoise') letters in which they describe real or imagined personal problems, and then sign with a pseudonym. After exchanging letters, students in the other class write back individual responses with comments and/or advice. Such activities create an audience other than the teacher and provide a clear purpose and motivation for writing.

Journal writing

Journal writing is another 'immersion' technique, the principal goal of which is to encourage a writing 'habit' and to develop fluency, as well as to improve students' motivation and attitude toward writing. Journals are typically of two types: 'personal' journals, in which learners write diary-like accounts of day to day experiences and thoughts, and 'intellectual' journals, in which students reflect on readings, lectures, class discussions, their own ideas, or their ongoing writing projects. While both types encourage students to write freely and expressively, the personal type usually has language production as its chief goal and therefore emphasizes immersion, whereas the intellectual type serves more as a tool for reflection and therefore incorporates critical framing.

Blanton (1987), describing the use of personal journals in an ESL setting, recommends starting class sessions with five minutes of journal writing, in which students write about whatever is on their mind. The teacher writes along with the students, but neither teacher nor students read aloud what they have written. A more common practice is to assign journals as out-of-class assignments, that are handed in at regular intervals. In either case, to encourage students' fluency, teachers should not correct students' journals, but respond by expressing personal reactions, similar experiences, and the like.[3] 'Dialogue' journals—a variation in which students and teachers write directly to each other in an ongoing written conversation—provide an excellent medium for students to use a variety of language functions (asking questions, describing, expressing personal feelings, and so on) as well as a good way for teachers to get to know their students better. They are, however, time-consuming for teachers and may be impractical in a large class.[4]

Spack and Sadow (1983) describe the use of intellectual journals in an ESL context: students wrote one journal entry per day of class, from a half to two pages in length, which was regularly collected and read by the teacher, but not corrected. The teacher in turn regularly wrote a journal entry to the class which usually cited certain student journal entries (edited for readability). Spack and Sadow reported that journal writing became easier the more students wrote in their journals, and that students came to understand writing as a way of exploring, developing, and sharing ideas. Students' journals also provided valuable feedback on what students had and had not understood from their readings, lectures, and class discussions, and therefore served an important diagnostic purpose. For teacher-student journal writing focused specifically on students' readings of texts, see Walworth (1990).

Freewriting

Freewriting is a technique of the 'expressive' school of process writing pedagogy, in which students are asked to write about a topic without stopping, even if they must simply repeat the last word or sentence until a new thought comes to mind. The technique is associated with Peter Elbow, who in his book *Writing Without Teachers* (1973), argues that concern with diction and sentence structure is misplaced in the initial stages of the writing process, when it can interfere with thinking. When writers are freed from worry about form, Elbow contends, they can most creatively discover what they have to say about a subject and develop their own unique voice. A variation on freewriting is 'looping', in which learners write non-stop for a specified period of time on a given topic, then stop and read what they've written and summarize it in one new sentence. They then continue, repeating the sequence several more times.[5]

   Freewriting can be very useful in generating ideas for essays, but it is also useful in the context of reading instruction. For example, students can be asked to freewrite about a topic, theme, or image that will be treated in a text they are about to read. This allows their knowledge, expectations, and assumptions to be made concrete, facilitating direct comparisons across students and, eventually, with the text itself.

Creative writing

Brief creative writing tasks can give students the chance to play with the language, to adopt fresh perspectives, and to explore different emotions in writing. Especially at early levels, however, it is important to provide constraints to make tasks manageable. *Cinquain poetry* is one example of a highly constrained, yet fun activity, in which students often surprise themselves with what they are able to produce. It can be done from the earliest stages of language study, either in small groups or individually, and involves writing within the constraints of the following formula:

1 noun	subject
2 adjectives	description of the subject (can be noun and adjective if desired)
3 verbs	action of the subject
4 words	expressing an emotion about the subject
1 noun	restatement of the subject with a different word

(Allen and Valette 1994: 321–2)

Below are examples from ESL and Spanish:

> Lion
> Angry beast
> Killing, eating, living
> They hunt you unthinkingly
> King

> Lluvia
> Agua cayendo
> Saltando, bailando, duchando
> ¡Qué alegre pareces tú!
> Diversión
> (Allen and Valette 1994: 322)

Another possibility is to present short expressive and exploratory tasks that allow students to invent situations and microworlds. These can provide a welcome antidote to frequent analytical writing. Below are five sample assignments that students can write in their journals or hand in as separate papers:

1 Assume the identity of a person whom you've studied in class. Try to imagine what they would write in a given situation.
2 Go somewhere where you've never been before (it could be a different city or a place you never go within your own home, such as under your dining room table), take note of all the sensory information that you're taking in. What new perspective does this give you on the geography of that place?
3 Create a dialogue between two famous people who might not normally be in the same room together (for example, Jacques Pepin and Julia Childs; Wonder Woman and the Terminator; Jean Paul Sartre and René Descartes).[6]
4 Choose a painting, photograph, or film and walk into it. Describe who you meet, what you see, and how the experience affects you. Thinking of *Alice in Wonderland*, you might ask yourself how perspective and proportion work to change your entire experience of the setting.
5 Deprive yourself of one of your senses for a short while. Describe what you experience when you do that. What do the rest of your senses do to compensate? How do they become heightened? How does the world change?[7]

As mentioned in earlier chapters, the literacy-based curriculum is concerned with texts in a broad sense: written, graphic, spoken, and multimodal. This range of text types allows teachers to deal with issues of interpretation even in introductory-level classes without having to use materials that are overly complex linguistically. Photographs and other visual artwork, for example, are especially useful for linguistically-simple interpretive and discourse-transforming activities. A particularly motivating and enjoyable use of writing is to create descriptions, narrations, and inventions based on visuals (see, for example, Maley, Duff, and Grellet 1980). In order to make this kind of writing a collaborative class activity, Raimes (1983) proposes the following task sequence: As a prewriting task, students work together in small groups to brainstorm words and phrases that describe the picture. Students then each write a paragraph describing the picture. Next, the group members combine elements of their paragraphs and write one that represents the whole group, with as many details as possible. The activity can then be extended into narrative: students invent a narrative (past or present, depending on learners' level) based on the picture. These narratives can then be read to the group or to the whole class.

A critical framing dimension can be added to this creative writing activity by comparing students' descriptions. How did they deal with organizing their subject? What aspects of the scene did they focus on? in what order? what was highlighted, what was downplayed? what details were included or left out? What was their opening sentence, and how did that affect what came next? (Raimes 1983: 123). Students' use of generalizations and supporting details in their descriptions can also be analyzed (Raimes 1983). Pairs of sentences can be presented, such as 'The house is very spooky' and 'The house is dark'. What images come to mind as students read each sentence individually? Which leads students to elaborate more? Which raises more questions? What happens when the two are read together? Students can analyze their own descriptions, noting the proportion of generalizations to supporting details and then rewrite their descriptions to maximize the vividness of their writing.

Visual-based writing activities can also involve transformed practice. Consider, for example, Brandelius's (1983) activity for beginning-level French students based on Pierre-Auguste Renoir's impressionist painting 'Le déjeuner des canotiers'. The teacher begins by showing the painting on a poster or slide and letting students look at it silently for a minute. The teacher then asks students to take out a sheet of paper and label three columns: adjectives, nouns, and verbs. Students are asked to write down all the nouns, adjectives, and verbs they can think of that apply to the painting, listed in the appropriate columns on their sheet. Students then work in groups of four to share their lists and to develop a compilation which each group member copies down. The teacher then assigns each member of each group a number from one to four and students regroup by number (i.e. all the ones form one group, all the twos form another, and so on). Each student announces the number of adjectives, nouns, and verbs his or her group has, and the student with *smallest* number in each category begins, so that all get a turn to speak. Students add new words to their lists, until all students in each group have identical compiled lists. The teacher then asks the students what could be done with all these words, into what context(s) they could be inserted.

Students brainstorm proposals (for example, story, poem, song, skit, description of the image, advertisement), which are written on the board. The next day the students form new groups, this time based on their genre interest (i.e. 'poem', 'skit'), and work together to design whatever they want with the words on their common list. When the projects are completed, each group presents its final product to the class. At this point the teacher can return students' attention to the original painting and ask in what ways the images influenced their final product, and in what ways the words themselves led them in new directions they had not anticipated when they first looked at the painting alone.

One benefit of working with non verbal texts in this way in the early stages is that students can be introduced to basic principles of interpretation without having to deal with heavy linguistic demands. Because students work exclusively within their collective linguistic limits, they are less likely to become intimidated or frustrated. Moreover, their cultural interest is often piqued (for example, in Renoir or impressionist painting in this case) through their in-depth attention to the visual work and their active use of language to redesign it.

Overt instruction

Many aspects of students' writing can benefit from direct instruction. While product-approach teaching emphasizes a sequence of mastery which begins with sentence grammar, followed by paragraph structure, then idea development and essay organization, literacy-based teaching treats these as interrelated issues that must be addressed in parallel rather than in series. Before students can meaningfully deal with sentence grammar, for example, they need to have something to say. In this section we will consider several ways in which overt instruction can help students to generate ideas, to organize and express them in ways that will meet the expectations of their reader, and to edit their writing effectively.

The initial step in writing is figuring out what to say. Once students are beyond the beginning level of language study, they often need help in developing an idea that is sufficiently complex for them to write about at some length. Classroom discussion, brainstorming, and freewriting are all commonly used techniques to help students generate initial ideas on a topic. What these techniques do *not* generally do, however, is help students to identify relationships among ideas. One technique particularly useful in this regard is mapping.

Mapping

Mapping, described in Chapter 5 as a reading comprehension technique, has also been embraced by process-oriented composition teachers as an effective way to help students develop and organize their ideas before they begin writing.

Schultz (1991a), for example, illustrates how mapping can be used collaboratively in a foreign language classroom to analyze a French short story and to formulate the thesis and outline of an essay. After discussing the text, the teacher targets a particular theme and solicits ideas from the class. As students contribute observations, interpretations, and textual evidence in brainstorming fashion, the teacher writes them on the board in random order (i.e. not yet attending to placement or connections). When the flow of ideas slows down, the crucial part of the activity begins: the teacher asks the students to think about relationships among the various elements on the board. In response to students' comments, the teacher then draws lines and arrows to form and connect idea clusters. The teacher also asks what ideas seem irrelevant and should be erased. Once relationships have been mapped, the teacher asks students to try to develop a generalization that could serve as the focus of an essay. Once this generalization is established, the students and teacher use the map to integrate abstract interpretive statements and supporting evidence into a standard hierarchical outline format.[8] Once students have had the experience of being guided through a mapping activity several times in class, they can be encouraged to develop maps, individually or in collaboration with others, when they plan their essays. Schultz points out that mapping is a particularly useful technique in one-on-one teacher-student conferences.[9]

Teaching genres

As teachers know well, students can benefit greatly from explicit attention to expectations and standards for their work. This is especially important in teaching students to write in a new language. Learners need to know what the specific expectations are for a given kind of text if it is going to be considered an 'effective' piece of writing. Genre-based teaching is designed to address that need.

To take the argumentative essay as an example, students need to know that proving one's case effectively in many Western academic settings ideally involves considering alternative perspectives and revealing their limitations. Whereas students are usually good at stating opinions and producing lists of observations, they often have difficulty understanding what constitutes an 'analytical argument'. Schultz (1995) describes explicit steps in teaching intermediate-level French students to develop and test an argument via what she calls an 'XYZ' formula, in which 'Y' represents the interpretation the student wishes to argue, 'X' represents opposition to 'Y', and 'Z' represents evidence for 'Y'. The structure of the formula, then, is: *Although X . . . nevertheless Y . . . because Z.* A student writing an essay on Flaubert's novel *Madame Bovary* might produce a thesis statement something like the following: 'Although Emma Bovary may at first seem morally reprehensible, nevertheless the reader sympathizes with her desire to rise above her situation, because the circumstances of her life are so mundane and hypocritical.' Schultz points out that such a statement, while in itself awkward, serves as a test of the arguability of the student's interpretation as well as a mini-outline for the essay.

The potential risk in genre teaching, of course, is that it can become reduced to a survey of 'cookbook'-style rhetorical formulas. While teaching specific generic routines is an important starting point, a literacy-based approach aims for broader goals. Because the number of potentially relevant genres is limitless, what is needed is a discovery approach to genres in which students first become aware of the importance of genres in communication, and then are taught how to identify the characteristic features of genres by themselves.

Flowerdew (1993) moves teachers in this direction through his process approach to teaching genre, which involves the following six activity types:

1 Using the results of existing genre analyses to familiarize students with the notion of genre and to acquaint them with the kinds of genre features that have been studied.
2 'Metacommunicating'—that is, talking about instances of genres, their social function, and their communicative effects.
3 Doing genre analyses on texts (for example, identifying features of a newspaper feature headline genre and relating them to communicative functions).
4 Concordancing—seeing how key words are used in multiple texts, both within and across genres.[10]
5 Doing 'online' genre analyses of parallel texts as learners write their own text (i.e, using multiple similar texts as models, identifying common features that need to be included, pieces of language that can be appropriated without plagiarizing).
6 Translating texts, attending to genre-specific differences across the two languages.
(Flowerdew 1993: 309)

What Flowerdew is advocating, then, is not a slavish imitation of prescribed models but rather an acknowledgment that writers in a discourse community naturally echo and adapt one another's words, and that an explicit awareness of genres can help language learners to identify which features of a genre-specific group of texts will be most generalizable. Flowerdew's activities go well beyond overt instruction, incorporating critical framing (activity types 2, 3, and 4) and transformed practice (activity types 5 and 6).

Use of models

Although sometimes maligned by proponents of process-based teaching, the use of models is extremely important in teaching writing, and particularly second language writing. There is, however, a crucial difference in the way models are conceptualized and used in traditional product-based teaching and in literacy-based teaching. In product-oriented approaches, models serve as ideals that are to be emulated in structure and style. Writing exercises are typically mechanical in nature, and they are evaluated in terms of strict adherence to a pre-established norm. In literacy-based teaching, on the other hand, models are not treated as ideals, but as resources for students' design of meaning. Models are valued as examples of how a particular writer has approached a particular writing problem for a particular audience.[11] They allow analysis of diction, style, organization, syntax, and the communicative effects these might have on intended readers. For example, in writing a letter of apology, students could first consider an informal letter written to a friend ('I'm really sorry that . . .') and then compare that with a formal letter conveying greater social distance between writer and reader ('We regret to inform you that . . .') in order to become aware of the social implications of linguistic design choices (Watson 1982). Students can thus be led to discover what it is about a particular piece of writing that makes it more or less effective in a particular context, rather than being asked to imitate it because it embodies some absolute notion of 'goodness'.

Models, moreover, need not be of 'professional' quality to be useful. In fact, other students' writing can often be the most useful kind of model for students to examine, since it is not so far removed from their own ability-level and presents certain problems that they themselves may have tried to overcome. Thus the model text is not portrayed as inherently 'better', but as a means to help learners see ways to enhance their own writing. The model thus operates within a student-centered framework rather than within a text-centered framework, and serves as a tool not just for overt instruction, but also for critical framing and transformed practice.

Revising and editing

To most students, 'revising' means checking verb conjugations, agreements, accents, and spelling. Two important parts of teaching writing are expanding students' notion of revision and explicitly teaching them how to edit their writing.

Teaching revision is best approached through class discussions of student essays (presented anonymously) that go step by step through the formulation of ideas and thesis statements, paragraph organization, style, and grammar (Schultz 1991b). During these discussions the teacher can demonstrate thinking processes by asking the kinds of questions he or she thinks about when writing, out loud. This kind of 'open window' into a more experienced writer's thought processes is where learning writing can become truly an apprenticeship. Below we will briefly consider paragraphing strategies, sentence combining, and rereading as three examples of topics that could be treated in such discussions of revising and editing.

Paragraphing strategies. When students draft and revise essays, explicit knowledge of common patterns of information organization can afford them expressive choices. Patterns can be presented by comparing parallel versions of a paragraph (for example, ascending versus descending order of importance of points; topic sentence at the beginning versus at the end versus in the middle) within the context of surrounding text, so that students can see how well each option serves to link the preceding and subsequent paragraphs. The emphasis should be on familiarizing students with various possible permutations and discussing their relative effectiveness in a particular discourse context rather than in any kind of absolute terms.

Raimes (1983) suggests giving students a paragraph with the first and last sentences missing. Depending on students' level, they can either select from teacher-provided options or they can write their own sentences to complete the paragraph. They can then discuss their choices in comparison to the original writer's choice. This extends the activity to the level of critical framing, since students must reflect on the appropriateness of linguistic choices in relation to particular parameters of communicative purpose and context. Once students have done this with published material, they can do the same activity with their own writing, in order to gain a clear sense of what options they have open to them when they rewrite a previously drafted essay.

Sentence and Discourse Markers. Just as sentence- and discourse-level markers are important to students' understanding of the texts they read, they are also important elements in the texts that students write. In addition to the reading activities discussed in Chapter 5 (for example, assembling scrambled texts), written exercises can be used as supplementary practice in becoming familiar with signaling cues.[12] For example, students can be asked to consider the possible meaning relationships between two clauses and fill in an appropriate conjunction:

We'll have a picnic _____ the weather is nice.
_____ the nice weather, we can't have a picnic.
We can't have a picnic _____ the weather is nice.

The goal of exercises like this is not for students to come up with 'the right answer', but to discuss in class how various answers relate to different situational contexts—to show that coherence has to do with *situation models* in the mind, not just words on a page (de Vega 1996). For example, one can complete the last item with, among many other possibilities, 'unless', 'until', 'even though', or 'even if'—each signaling a different relationship between the weather and having a picnic. What is important for students to understand is that the signaling cues they choose as writers influence their reader's ability to design an appropriate situation model. This awareness is less likely to be fostered by overt instruction than by critical framing. It is, therefore, important that students be required to reflect on the pragmatic implications of various solutions, rather than simply to accept a single appropriate answer.

Sentence Combining. Sentence combining is a technique designed to increase the syntactic complexity of students expression.[13] It involves taking two or more simple sentences and combining them through the use of relative pronouns, conjunctions, or other devices (for example, He told me the news. I fainted. → I fainted *when* he told me the news).

The use of sentence combining exercises has long been a topic of debate among composition specialists. Although product-based studies in foreign language and ESL contexts confirmed that sentence-combining increased the complexity of students' sentences (Monroe 1975; Kameen 1979; Cooper and Morain 1980; Cooper, Morain, and Kalivoda 1980; Cooper 1981), it was not clear that it improved the overall quality of students' writing (Zamel 1976; 1980). Is sentence combining strictly a mechanical technique, far removed from issues of inventing and expressing meaning? Johnson (1992) investigated this question by asking advanced-level ESL students to 'think aloud' as they did various types of sentence-combining tasks. Johnson's analysis revealed that the students were 'most frequently engaged in restating content, constructing meaning, and planning' (i.e. thinking about relationships between form and meaning). Johnson concluded that sentence-combining exercises 'may be particularly well suited for helping second language writers to focus on the arrangement of logically connected information and plan their revisions according to global or abstract features of written text structures' (p. 70).

In my own experience, I have found that sentence combining is most beneficial to students when it is done as part of reworking their own writing, rather than as an isolated activity using third-party examples. The example below is from a discussion of editing techniques in a first-year French class that focused (anonymously) on one student's essay draft. The student's original draft began with the following four sentences:

> *Je suis étudiant à Berkeley. Je me spécialise en chimie. Mes parents habitent à Palmdale. Mon père est médecin et ma mère travaille dans une banque.*

> [I am a student at Berkeley. I am majoring in chemistry. My parents live in Palmdale. My father is a doctor and my mother works in a bank.]

Presenting these four sentences on the blackboard, the teacher then modeled how relative pronouns (which the students had already studied) could be used to combine certain propositions into single sentences (effectively 'reminding' students of how that particular grammatical resource can be used):

Je suis étudiant à Berkeley, où je me spécialise en chimie. Mon père, qui est médecin, et ma mère, qui travaille dans une banque, habitent à Palmdale.

[I am a student at Berkeley, where I am majoring in chemistry. My father, who is a doctor, and my mother, who works in a bank, live in Palmdale.]

Next, the teacher pointed out how in certain types of writing (such as journalistic writing) propositions are frequently combined through clause reduction rather than relative pronouns:

Un étudiant à Berkeley, je me spécialise en chimie. Mon père, médecin, et ma mère, banquière, habitent à Palmdale.

[A student at Berkeley, I am majoring in chemistry. My father, a doctor, and my mother, a banker, live in Palmdale.]

It is important that such models not be presented as universally recommended formats, but rather as stylistic resource options for (1) varying sentence length and complexity, and (2) highlighting or downplaying particular pieces of information. What the student eventually opted for in his rewritten composition was a mix of the above possibilities that incorporated a new relative clause (*où mon père travaille*) that had not been previously modeled:

Un étudiant à Berkeley, je me spécialise en chimie. Mes parents habitent à Palmdale, où mon père travaille comme médecin et ma mère travaille dans une banque.

[A student at Berkeley, I am majoring in chemistry. My parents live in Palmdale, where my father works as a doctor and my mother works in a bank.]

The student was very pleased with his newfound stylistic sophistication, and his subsequent compositions showed a greater variety of sentence structure. In sum, especially when treated as an editing technique in the context of students' own writing, sentence combining can help students to write more flexibly and with greater confidence by making them aware of available syntactic and stylistic options.

Rereading. Finally, the importance of students' rereading their own writing in the revision process cannot be overstated. It is in rereading their drafts that students become most keenly aware of what they are trying to say. As Zamel (1982) reports, rereading led her ESL students to 'hear' their ideas more objectively, allowing them to evaluate and communicate them more effectively. But in order to be most effective, writers' reading needs to be analytical and critical. Teachers' questions and comments on students' initial drafts are crucial in this regard, as they can shift emphasis from formal accuracy (what students often assume to be the most important dimension of writing) to issues of content development, organization, and stylistic appropriateness (see 'Responding to student writing' in Chapter 9).

Sometimes rereading of one's own writing is best done after reading other texts within the genre, for purposes of stylistic refinement. Below are reflections of an advanced level French student talking about his first draft of an essay:

> In this case, I think this was better than average, but definitely not the best. What I'd probably have to do with this is read in French for a lot, then go back and look at it and then try and fine-tune my style to, you know, what I'd consider a standard French. And I usually do that by reading, like reading criticism or an article. I like reading journalism, and then trying to pick off of those structures and usually that's about what will do it . . . .

Through reading, the student is looking for appropriate Available Designs to incorporate into his own writing. Here, reading might serve either to remind the student of structures he already knows but has simply not thought of, or to introduce him to new structures that might be well suited to his own writing.

Critical framing

We have seen that many of the activities that have been proposed can be extended to include critical framing, that is, conscious attention to relationships between linguistic forms, and social contexts and purposes. Below we will consider several examples of activities that have critical framing as their central focus.

Sensitization through reading

In order to make students more aware of the significance of the lexical and structural choices they make in their own writing, it is useful to explore the effects of the particular ways that other writers design meaning in texts. In Chapter 5 we considered the kinds of sensitizing questions an ESL teacher might raise as students read a short newspaper article ('Fruitvale BART Shooting'). The same procedure can be done with students' own writing as well. This involves the teacher's picking one or two pieces of writing, copying the text after removing the student's name, and developing a series of questions that focus students' attention on key features that give clues to the writer's attitudes, point of view, and purpose (or, as the case may be, on the lack of such features). Once they are aware of such clues, students can attempt to rewrite the piece of writing to reflect other possible perspectives. This rewriting phase extends the activity to include transformed practice as well.

Shifting contextual parameters

Moirand (1979) offers the following activity (Figure 7.2) to structure students' learning of how language varies within a given situational context according to the different social roles, different attitudes, and different communicative intentions that might be operating. The task involves the systematic manipulation of roles, attitudes, and intentions in the writing of a note to an upstairs neighbor whose bathroom is leaking.

Communicative frame	Social role and relations	Attitude	Acts	Utterances/ Sentences
In an apartment building in Paris, water from a fourth floor apartment is leaking into a neighbor's third floor apartment. The third floor neighbor leaves a note on the fourth floor neighbor's door.	a) neighbors who have never seen one another before	A) neutral	1) 'INFORM'	. . .
	b) neighbors who know one another	B) kind	2) 'WARN'	. . .
	c) neighbors who often fight with one another	C) aggressive	3) 'THREATEN'	. . .
	d) neighbors who are good friends	D) whiny	4) 'ASK'	. . .
	e) the third floor neighbors are the in-laws of the man in the fourth floor apartment, ..., etc.	etc.	5) 'BEG'	. . .

Figure 7.2: Moirand's 1979 'upstairs neighbor' activity

Each student (or group of students) writes a number of notes with different permutations of the matrix parameters: social role, attitude, speech act type. These variations on a common situational theme can then be analyzed and compared in terms of the relationships between the chosen language forms and the communicative context (Moirand 1979: 105). Working with grids like this, which incorporate a metalanguage for classifying various dimensions of communication, can help learners to internalize a set of analytical tools that can be applied widely as they read and write.

Peer-group response/editing

A development of both process- and social-constructionist perspectives on composition, peer editing involves students' exchanging of essay drafts followed by pair- or small-group discussion of the essay's strengths and weaknesses and suggestions for improvement. Peers' comments typically include the following kinds of responses: 'What I like is . . .', 'What it seems you're trying to say is . . .', 'What I'd like to know more about is . . .', 'Where I got a little confused was . . .', 'Where I felt I was left hanging was . . .'. Most importantly, peer editing sessions allow writers to ask for advice concerning whatever they might be struggling with in writing the essay, as in the following brief excerpt of a computer-mediated peer editing session in a third-semester college French class. The students were discussing their in-progress drafts for an essay on Albert Camus's story 'L'Hôte':

Elizabeth:
Comment est-ce que je devrais organiser ma deuxieme paragraphe pour la rendre plus specifique?

Mary:
Dans ce paragraphe, tu as plusieres idees, et toutes tes idees sont bonnes. Mais ce paragraphe ne discute pas seulement un sujet, comme le professeur a dit 'une idee par paragraphe . . .' Mais, il faut que tu n'elimines pas aucune idee!

Elizabeth:
(Une idee pour chaque paragraphe) Je m'excuse.

Mary:
Pour organiser les paragraphes des composition, normalement, je cherche pour les idees centrales de mon these, c'est-a-dire, les grands sujets que je veux discuter. Dans ta composition, tu discute en detail les differences entre la societe des francais et celle des Arabes. Voila deux paragraphes dans laquelles tu pourrais montrer que Daru est exile de la societe comme un prisonnier. Tu parle aussi des mauvais temps et de la nature, peut-etre un autre paragraphe. Est-ce que ces suggestions t'aideraient a organiser ta composition?

Elizabeth:
How should I organize my second paragraph to make it more specific?

Mary:
In this paragraph you have several ideas, and all of them are good. But this paragraph doesn't address just one topic, like the teacher told us 'one idea per paragraph . . .' But you shouldn't get rid of any of your ideas!

Elizabeth:
(One idea per paragraph) Sorry.

Mary:
To organize paragraphs in a composition I normally look for the central ideas of my thesis, that is, the main subjects I'm going to discuss. In your essay, you discuss in detail the differences between French and Arab societies. Those could be two paragraphs in which you could show how Daru is exiled from society like a prisoner. You also talk about bad weather and nature; maybe another paragraph. Could these suggestions help you to organize your essay?

As Mary and Elizabeth read and respond to one another's writing, they both help and learn from one another, giving each other ideas to improve their writing. Knowing that a classmate will read one's draft also motivates students to take greater care in their writing. Furthermore, as is evident in the example above, students learn to use a metalanguage (a key component of critical framing) for talking about texts and the writing process.

The standard format for peer editing is for students to work in groups of two or three, to exchange drafts, read and comment upon them, and then meet in class to discuss their responses to the ideas and organization of the draft, as well as attend to style and grammar issues. Peer editing lends itself to a number of variations, however. The use of computers for electronic conferencing, as in the example above, is a variation that allows students to keep a written record of their exchanges (see Chapter 8 and Schultz 2000). Brannon and Knoblauch (1982) propose that the student-author write a paragraph-by-paragraph analysis of what he or she was trying to accomplish in the piece of writing. A peer reader then writes a parallel paragraph-by-paragraph account of his or her responses to the essay, so that the author can then directly compare the intended and achieved effects of the writing. Leki (1990) proposes a less time-consuming alternative, in which the student-author answers specific questions, such as those listed at the begining of this section, and then compares his or her answers with those of a peer reader, or the teacher. Finally, when access to the Internet is available, students can exchange essays with members of other classes, either in the same country or abroad, to get 'outside' responses to their writing.[14]

Research on the degree to which peer editing leads to improved student writing has had mixed results. While peer editing seems to make a significant contribution in some settings (for example, Clifford 1981; Nystrand 1986), its effectiveness seems to vary according to a wide range of variables such as student background, teacher beliefs and investment, the degree of structured guidance available to students, and the degree to which students are held accountable for their feedback (Grabe and Kaplan 1996).

In second language contexts, the question arises as to whether students will trust peers' comments since their classmates are just learning the language, like themselves. Furthermore, the ideological underpinnings of peer group work may be in direct conflict with mainstream educational beliefs in the students' home culture (for example, Hudson-Ross and Dong 1990; Carson 1992). In a small study involving four intermediate-level ESL learners from four different countries, Nelson and Murphy (1993) found that subjects tended to incorporate peers' comments into their final drafts when their interactions were interactive and cooperative, but to a much lesser degree when there was little interaction or when learners interacted defensively. Such variability in learners' incorporation of peers' comments should be expected and seen in a positive light, since ultimately it is the writer's choice to agree or disagree with peers' comments, and slavish incorporation of other readers' suggestions can often weaken, rather than strengthen, students' writing. Grabe and Kaplan (1996) conclude from their review of peer-editing research that the activity is most beneficial when students are highly motivated, when they are carefully trained and assisted in peer-response procedures, when they are given plentiful examples of supportive feedback, and when teachers closely monitor students' feedback (p. 387).

Transformed practice

Transformed practice involves redesigning texts, often with the goal of adapting them to suit new contextual parameters. It also involves creating new texts on the basis of existing ones. In this sense, all writing that is focused on the analysis of texts that have been read (the most common type in academic writing courses) is a form of transformed practice. We will consider below a few specific examples of other types of writing activities that involve transformed practice.

Experimental syntax and reformulation

As a way of promoting learners' communicative flexibility, Pike (1988) argues for the use of 'experimental syntax'—systematic, patterned restructuring of narratives, poems, and other texts—to 'force the student to use different grammatical forms to paraphrase the same referential material' (p. 222). As Pike describes it, 'When the same story is told forwards, backwards, or "inside out," grammatical usages of conjunctions, verb forms, or phrase and sentence arrangement must change in order to preserve the original referential content in the face of such grammatical sequence changes' (p. 222).

Such modification of grammatical structure inevitably involves altering the meaning, however subtly. The potential value of this kind of activity lies precisely in identifying the ways in which meaning *is* altered and what effect the changes might have on the reader's reception. Thus one pedagogically-desirable aspect of this kind of activity is that it allows close examination of the effects of various grammatical changes (i.e. a critical framing component), while keeping vocabulary and topic demands constant. Pike adds that redesigning small texts is a good way to teach conjunctions and special phrase forms without having to teach much linguistic theory.

Redesigning stories

Kramsch (1985) recommends the practice of having students write 'intratextual variations' of texts they have read as a way to sensitize them to the relations between textual language and the contexts they create. For example, students can be asked to begin telling the story at a middle episode and tell the beginning as a flashback. Or they can tell the story in a different way (for example, through dialogue between characters, through the eyes of a different narrator, through letters between characters, or a character's diary entries). Again, discussion should focus on what effects such transformations might have on readers' interpretations. Kramsch notes that 'The very reconstruction of the text by the students makes apparent to them better than any analysis by a teacher some of its stylistic features' (p. 363).

A particularly challenging form of intratextual variation is rewriting a literary text from a different narrative point of view. Herman (1986) points out that this task involves far more than making certain grammatical changes. For example, content changes as a function of the new narrator's age, sex, status, and role in the story. If the original narrator was omniscient but the new one is not, what is the extent of the new narrator's experience and awareness? What must be left out of the original telling? What must be modified? In what ways? What must be made overt in other characters' speech and actions if the narrator is no longer omniscient? Herman adds that a particularly creative exercise is to have an inanimate object (for example, a phone, a wall) become narrator. The goal, as Herman describes it, is not so much literary analysis *per se*, but rather the understanding that a close examination of textual relationships can bring, as well the creative enjoyment of reconstructing a literary text.[15]

Stylistic reformulation

Many language learners (and some teachers) assume that 'style' is something that grows automatically out of grammatical mastery. It does not. Many foreign language students spend considerable amounts of time working on the formal accuracy of their essays, only to feel at the end that their writing, although grammatically 'correct', does not sound very native-like.[16] Stylistic reformulation is a technique designed to focus intermediate and advanced level learners' attention on stylistic elements of their expression, a dimension of writing often neglected in foreign language classes.

Cohen (1990) describes the technique as follows. In the 'pre-reformulation' stage, students write a text, which they submit to their teacher for general feedback on ideas, topic development, grammar, and so forth. They then rewrite the text, incorporating the teacher's recommendations. In the 'reformulation' stage, a native speaker of the language (or the teacher if he/she is a native speaker) rewrites either the entire paper (if it is short) or the beginning portion of it (if it is long), to make the style more 'native-like', while remaining as faithful as possible to the original content and organization.[17] Finally, in the 'post-reformulation' stage, the student and native speaker compare the original and reformulated versions, looking first at discourse functions (for example, ways of questioning, asserting, and qualifying statements), then at text cohesion (for example, use of conjunctions, deictic pronouns, repetitions, and synonyms) and discourse coherence (for example, topic development), then finally at the vocabulary and syntax of the two texts. From the point of view of literacy-based teaching, this discussion is the most valuable part of the exercise, since it provides an opportunity to identify the specific differences in linguistic choices, to discuss the reasons for those choices, and to evaluate their respective communicative effects for readers. The point is not to show that the native-speaker reformulation is necessarily 'better'—in fact, students may ultimately prefer certain aspects of their original versions—but rather to make students aware of what choices are available to them and to sensitize them to the communicative effects of those sets of choices. In other words, the focus expands from 'what I will SAY' to 'what my text will DO'.

Several variations on the reformulation technique have been proposed. The teacher can assign the whole class a common writing task and give only one student's composition to a native-speaker for reformulation. The original and the reformulated version are photocopied and distributed to the class for discussion. All the students then rewrite their compositions, attempting to make use of the newly introduced stylistic options (Hedge 1988). Alternately, students can all reformulate a single student composition (written by a former student, for example) and then compare their reformulations to one written by a native speaker (Schultz 1994). A third variation is to use more than one reformulation of a particular piece. One written by an expert native-speaking writer, and another by the teacher, for example, making a three-way comparison possible (Swales 1990: 221).

However implemented, stylistic reformulation is one way of making learners explicitly aware of Available Designs and the process of redesigning, in a manner that does not separate linguistic structures (and the cognitive processes brought to bear on their use) from particular social and communicative contexts.

Genre reformulation

Reformulation can be extended to genre as well. Whereas stylistic reformulation is focused on reworking the surface features of texts at the same time as keeping the text's purpose and audience constant, genre reformulation is focused on reframing the text's purpose and audience. Caudery (1998) provides a comprehensive discussion of the rationale, techniques, potential benefits, and drawbacks of genre transformation exercises. The basic procedure is to have students read a text of a particular genre, discuss its content, purpose, and intended audience, identify the formal features that suggest that purpose and audience, and then create a new text, based on the same information or ideas, but designed for a different purpose and audience. For example, students might take an encyclopedic entry on a city they would like to visit and write a letter to their parents that attempts to persuade them to allow the student to visit the city. Or a passage from a novel might be transformed into a playscript with stage directions. Or a public health report on the dangers of smoking might be rewritten so as to be understandable to schoolchildren. Or a short story might be composed based on a simple aphorism, proverb, or poem. For example, intermediate to advanced level French students could take the 'Chinese philosopher's' pithy definition of love in Mammeri's *La colline oubliée* ('On se veut, on s'enlace; on s'en lasse et on s'en veut' [One desires, one binds, one tires, one begrudges] (Mammeri 1952: 22)) and elaborate each phase of this 'love story' formula in the form of a short story. They would then compare their stories and the original aphorism, and discuss the effects of reading one versus the other. They could then try the reverse process of transforming short stories they have read into aphorisms or poems, again discussing what is gained and lost in the transformation process.

Inventing story continuations

An adaptation of the surrealist game *le cadavre exquis* (Brotchie 1993), this activity involves students' writing the continuation of a story to which they have only read the first few lines.[18] The teacher divides the class into groups of three to five students, and all are given a long sheet of paper with the first few sentences of a story printed at the top. (This activity is particularly useful when the story is one that students will soon be reading in class.) Each student begins to write a logical continuation to the story. After five minutes or so, students fold their paper back so that only the most recently composed portion is visible. Papers are then passed and the process begins again. When each story reaches the last member of the group, the teacher asks students to write a conclusion. Each student then reads the completed, surrealist tale to the members of his or her group. In order to extend the activity to include a critical framing dimension, the teacher and students can compare versions the following day, analyzing how the first (original) section constrains topical and stylistic possibilities but also leaves open many options. When the students then read the complete story they see how 'another author' worked within the same constraints as they did to create an original story.

Using writing (and reading) for speaking

Early on in this book, it was suggested that effective oral communication generally requires 'literate' sensibilities about the particular ways a language can be used for particular purposes, in particular settings. Our final example of a transformed practice activity involves using writing as a transformative step between reading and speaking in the development of content-based oral reports and role-play activities.

Cortese (1985) describes an experimental intermediate-level EFL course in

Italy that focused on developing a content-based project on American Indians. Students first did preliminary background reading in Italian, and then chose books in English from a teacher-prepared bibliography according to their particular disciplinary interests (for example, anthropological, economic, historical, political perspectives). Students had one month to read the book and to prepare an oral report on its main topics and lines of argument, as well as the writer's attitudes as reflected in the text. Because students' oral performance had previously consisted mostly of brief utterances, however, Cortese realized that students needed training in discourse planning and cohesion devices before they could effectively deliver their reports. She addressed this need by having students write and peer edit successive drafts of their oral presentations. Through the writing process, Cortese observed that her students became more aware 'that problems of meaning derived only to a limited extent from lexical items or lack of grammatical accuracy' (p. 15) and that writing allowed them to deal in a concrete way with the transition from speaking in brief utterances to producing extended, connected discourse. After their written exposés were completed, the teacher's role shifted from one of facilitator to that of explicit language trainer: common problems ranging from diction to syntax to rhetorical organization were dealt with systematically by taking several examples of each problem from students' writing, and reworking the samples with the whole class. Following the oral reports, the students then did a simulation of a United States Supreme Court hearing concerning a land claim. This simulation involved a wide range of testimony role plays. Students worked together in small groups, wrote out their speeches, and videotaped their final performance for evaluation purposes. Cortese notes that providing students with these project-oriented reading and writing tasks had brought her students to a new level of expressive sophistication in their speaking:

> The variety of speech acts which the students could handle in connected discourse was substantially greater than at the beginning of the course. But it was the ability to convey point of view and illocutionary force, to match verbal behavior to its intended effect, and to use codes appropriate to the interacting partner . . . that was most rewarding, as one could see the participants actually *doing* things with words.
> (Cortese 1985: 22)

Figure 7.3 summarizes the activities described in this chapter in terms of the instructional categories of situated practice, overt instruction, critical framing, and transformed practice. Checkmarks indicate the primary focus of the activity, with those in parentheses indicating secondary foci or potential extensions, as described in the chapter. As in the case of the reading activities in Chapter 5, teachers will want to insure that all four categories are represented in an extended instructional sequence.

	Situated practice	Overt instruction	Critical framing	Transformed practice
Letter writing	✓		(✓)	
Journal writing	✓		(✓)	(✓)
Freewriting	✓			
Creative writing	✓			(✓)
Mapping	(✓)	✓	(✓)	
Teaching genres		✓	(✓)	(✓)
Use of models		✓	(✓)	(✓)
Revising and editing	(✓)	✓	(✓)	
Sensitization through reading			✓	(✓)
Shifting contextual parameters			✓	
Peer-group response	(✓)		✓	
Experimental syntax	(✓)		(✓)	✓
Stylistic reformulation	(✓)		(✓)	✓
Genre reformulation	(✓)		(✓)	✓
Inventing story continuations	(✓)		(✓)	✓
Writing for speaking	(✓)	(✓)	(✓)	✓

Figure 7.3:   Summary of writing activities organized by literacy-instructional category (parentheses indicate potential inclusion in the category, depending on task framing)

A sample teaching sequence

The basic curricular sequence recommended for literacy-based teaching is · one that works from exploration of meaning, through social interaction, to the internalization of those processes of exploration within the individual, eventually leading to learners' greater independence as readers and writers. This explains why most of the examples in this book are in-class examples, even though one of the biggest virtues of reading and writing is that they can be done *outside* of class: students need first to be *prepared* for independence. The teaching example below illustrates this process-internalization sequence, and, as in the 'Mango Street' lesson sequence presented at the end of Chapter 5, shows how reading and writing can be integrated throughout.

Teaching Tennyson's 'Mariana'

A basic problem, shared by teachers of native- and non-native speakers alike, is getting students to write about thematic elements in literary texts when students have great difficulty *seeing* thematic elements in the first place. Taking Alfred Lord Tennyson's poem 'Mariana' as an example, Booth Olson (1984) observes that when teachers simply ask their students to write an essay about a theme like 'setting as a reflection of character' the results tend to be very disappointing and both students and teacher are frustrated. Booth Olson outlines an excellent example of how teachers can address this problem by systematically guiding students through a series of thinking/writing/reading activities that culminate in an analytical essay on the theme of 'setting as a reflection of character'. Although her example is designed for native-speakers, the basic activities and structure of the lesson can be readily adapted to second and foreign language contexts.[19]

The first step is to sensitize students to the targeted theme. Instead of starting with the literary text, Booth Olson starts with popular culture, selecting a television show that her students know and in which setting plays a key thematic role. She chooses 'Magnum P.I.,' a light detective show now in syndication, which takes place in Hawaii.[20] With the teacher asking guiding questions about the setting and the main character (for example, Where does the show take place?, What do you associate with Hawaii? What about Magnum? What do we know about him? What kind of car does he drive? What color is it? Red? What do you associate with red?), students collaboratively produce a cognitive map that shows relationships among elements of the story setting, associations with those elements, and characteristics of the protagonist, Magnum (Figure 7.4). While this is primarily a situated practice activity, teachers' questions that lead students to reflect on the associations and relations that they propose can push the activity to a critical framing level.

After seeing how setting mirrors character in a familiar television show, students next see how setting can be interpreted to reflect character in their own personal settings—in their homes. Students are asked to draw five columns across a sheet of paper. In column 1 they are to list four or five items in or around their home. In column 2 they then write down what they think these items say about themselves to other people. They then fold the paper over so that column 1 is juxtaposed with column 3 and column 2 is hidden (see Figure 7.5). They pass the paper to the classmate to their right, who then reads the list of items and interprets what those items say about the person who chose to list them. After writing down his or her interpretations, this student then folds the paper over so that column 1 is now juxtaposed with column 4, passes it to the person to the right, and so on until at least three people have interpreted the significance of the household items, without seeing other people's interpretations. At this point the papers are returned to

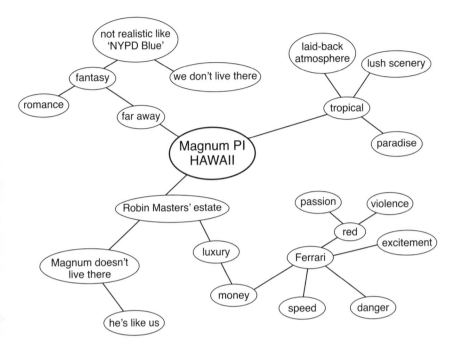

Figure 7.4:   Settings as a mirror of character (Booth Olson 1984: 35)

the original writer and everyone reads the interpretations of their list of
household items, followed by discussion. Again, this is primarily situated
practice, although it is possible to move the activity to the level of critical
framing by requiring students to reflect on *why* they interpreted particular
settings as they did.

Next, Booth Olson has students move on to do some actual writing in the
form of a 'showing, not telling' activity (Caplan and Keech 1980) in which
they write creatively to 'show' (i.e. communicate to a reader) without
explicitly saying the following: 'The state of her house made it clear that she
had long since stopped caring about herself.' In doing this, students are
essentially put in Tennyson's shoes, needing to think of some way of getting
this impression across to a reader through verbal description. After writing
for 15 minutes or so (they need not have fully completed their writings)
students read aloud what they have written, so that the class can hear the
diversity of ways in which the basic communicative problem can be
approached. This activity involves transformed practice as well as situated
practice, since students must transform a straightforward descriptive
statement into a rich descriptive *narrative* that indirectly expresses the same
proposition.

Column 1	Column 2	Column 3	Column 4	Column 5
Items in or around my home (brief description)	What I think these items say about me to others	What these items *do* say about me to others (Response 1)	What these items *do* say about me to others (Response 2)	What these items *do* say about me to others (Response 3)
1 A wilted house plant that didn't get enough sun	That I'm absent-minded and have a brown thumb.	Busy, and plants are low on priority list.	Wants greenery but no time, little attention to spend on plant, over-extended.	Well-intentioned but neglectful. Lets things go (and maybe him/herself) go.
2 A mountain bike—kind of muddy, taking up space	That I like the outdoors and live in a crime-ridden area.	Wish you had more time to ride... 'Once upon a time I was really active...'	Considers toughness and outdoor adventurer a status symbol, wants bike to stand out.	Once physical, athletic, full of vitality. Now stuck in own clutter.
3 A computer on my desk/ kitchen table	That I'm a student with a *small* studio.	Student in a small apartment or sharing a room.	Working on writing a lot of the time, work more important than eating.	Work is important—crowds out pleasures like eating.
4 Framed pictures of friends and family	That I'm close to friends and family.	Family/ friends important in life.	*Has* family, likes people. Picture-taking family.	Nostalgic, living life vicariously through others.

Figure 7.5:   Interpretations of personal settings (based on Booth Olson 1984).

At this point, having worked with the theme of 'setting as a mirror of character' in terms of a familiar television show, their own personal living situation, and their own creative writing, students are primed to read Tennyson's 'Mariana'. The teacher distributes copies of the poem and reads it aloud to the class, while students follow on their written copies, underlining words and phrases that describe the setting and that also seem suggestive of Mariana's psychological state. Students then paraphrase the poem, identify themes, and the teacher asks students to cite evidence from the poem to support their statements. To systematize students' observations, a chart can be filled out, similar to the one they had earlier done on their own personal settings (see Figure 7.6).

Items in the landscape that say something about Mariana	What these items mean to me	What Tennyson might be trying to say
Rusted nails, broken shed, weeds	Neglect	Mariana has let things fall apart. She no longer cares about appearances.
Unlifted hatch	Isolation, loneliness	No one comes but also Mariana doesn't go out.
Lonely moated grange	Not a real moat—not on a farm	Mariana builds a moat of isolation.
Sluice with blackened waters	Stagnation	Instead of being a symbol of life, water is a symbol of death-in-life.
Poplar tree	Life? Death? Lost love?	Something is calling to Mariana. It's 'wooing' her; but she refuses to listen.
Casement-curtain	Refusal to face life	Mariana purposely shuts out light and hope.
The blue fly sung in the pane	Entrapment	Mariana is imprisoned in her own mind. She is haunted by the past; the present is only waiting; and the future is death.

Figure 7.6 : Interpretations of textual references (Booth Olson 1984: 38).

At this point students can begin to plan analytical essays on the poem. They can use their observations outlined in Figure 7.6 to develop a thesis statement (as discussed earlier) and then to think of three alternative ways of writing an introduction to their essay (for example, beginning with a quote, stating the whole thesis or just part, or providing descriptive background). Students' multiple introductions can then be read aloud and discussed in terms of their potential effects on the reader. This stage of the lesson thus involves both transformed practice and critical framing. Students then draft their essays, exchange their drafts for peer editing, revise their drafts, and submit the final essay.

Again, the assumption is that this kind of guided practice in a social context will eventually lead students to internalize general strategies that they will eventually be able to call into practice on their own as they read and write outside of class.

Conclusion

Students sometimes see writing primarily in terms of following rules—grammar rules, spelling rules, outlining rules, organizational rules—to the point that writing seems like a pre-existing form into which they need to mold their ideas. It is hoped that through the kinds of writing activities outlined in this chapter, students can come to see constraints in a new light: as resources that establish broad limits on what they can do, but that also create new pathways for personal expression. As Cohen (1994) reminds us, 'The rules of rhetoric as cultural products are nothing without their actualisation in the mouths of creative individuals. They are brought to life by the self' (p. 50). The more students can be made aware of their acts of writing as particular solutions to a communicative situation, seeing writing not merely as 'language practice' but as a personally meaningful activity, the more interest they will take in writing.

Part Three will discuss further dimensions of writing and literacy-based teaching. In Chapter 8 we will consider a number of ways in which computer technology has introduced new possibilities for using writing for communication and learning. Chapter 9 will explore ways of evaluating students' reading and writing performance within a literacy-based framework, and Chapter 10 will discuss implications for teacher and student roles, teacher education, and research.

Notes

1 For many more examples of techniques that can be used to develop writing in conjunction with other communicative skills, see Hedge (1988), Hillocks (1995), Raimes (1983), and Zamel (1983; 1985; 1992).

2 See, for example, web sites for the Comenius Group's E-mail Key Pal Connection (at *http://www.comenius.com/keypal/index.html*), Who? Where? Pen Pals (at *http://whowhere.com/PenPals*), Pen-Pal Connection (at *http://alberti.crs4.it/pen-pal/*), and Pen Pal Exchange (at *http://www.iwaynet.neet/~jwolve/pal.htm*).

3 In cases where students specifically request correction of their journals, teachers can either provide written corrections, or go over journals with students in individual conferences (Peyton and Reed 1990). In a study of sixty intermediate-level Spanish students, Kepner (1991) found that surface grammar corrections had no effect on students' error rate in their journals, but that teachers' message-related comments affected students' use of higher-level propositions in their journals.

4 For more on dialogue journals, see Peyton and Reed (1990), Peyton and Staton (1993), and Staton and Shuy (1988).

5 See Belanoff, Elbow, and Fontaine (1991) for extensive examples of the use of freewriting in classrooms.

6 See Boyer, *et al.* (1990) for more along these lines.

7 I am thankful to Ann Delehanty for these creative writing tasks.

8 Whereas students are usually able to produce lists of observations, they often have difficulty moving to analysis and interpretation in their writing. Shaughnessy (1977) observed that the problem is not simply one of making abstract statements, but rather one of moving back and forth between abstract generalizations and concrete cases in an essay (p. 240). As can be seen in the map in Figure 5.7, mapping can help students to clearly differentiate generalizations from concrete evidence and to visualize the relationship between the two.

9 For more idea-generation techniques, see Spack (1984) and Cowan and Cowan (1980).

10 Concordances (lists of examples of immediate linguistic contexts for a chosen word or phrase from a corpus of texts) can be assembled collaboratively by students, or via inexpensive concordancing software programs (for example, *MonoConc*). For example, a group of newspaper articles downloaded from the Internet can be analyzed with a concordancer to find every instance of the word *would*, in order to give examples of how modals are used in news reports versus editorials.

11 Instructional sequence is of key importance here. In traditional product-oriented writing lessons, the model text is read, analyzed, and then emulated, in that order. The model text is both starting point and end goal. In literacy-based teaching, on the other hand, models are used as parallel texts to students' own writing—read before, during, *or after* their own writing efforts.

12 See Zamel (1983) for many excellent suggestions for teaching signaling cues in writing.

13 Francis Christenson (1967) and William Strong (1973) were the earliest proponents of sentence combining.

14 Sharing writing with native speakers assumes, of course, a reciprocal agreement about writing topics that will be of relevance and interest to both groups.

15 In a later article, Herman (1988) describes another rewriting technique, 'retrograde writing' in which the events of a narrative passage are rewritten in reverse (i.e. from the most recent to the earliest), while maintaining logical relationships among the textual elements. As in the shifting of point of view exercise, the goal is not the final product, which is usually more awkward than the original, but rather the process of paying close attention to the original, analyzing relationships, and thinking about how to reconstruct the elements within new constraints. For other reformulation ideas based on the principle of employing novel constraints, see the various books written on the French group OULIPO (Ouvroir de Littérature Potentielle), such as Oulipo (1973) or Motte (1986).

16 The importance of style in communication should not be underestimated. Thompson-Panos and Thomas-Ruzic (1983) discuss Arabic stylistic devices, which are often perceived as 'overassertive' or 'exaggerated' to readers of English. Repetition, frequent use of superlatives, redundant pronouns, rephrasing, and other devices are highly valued in all forms of communication in Arabic (and the authors point out that when such repetition and exaggeration are insufficient, misunderstandings often arise—sometimes to the degree that meanings opposite to those intended are taken). Just as teachers of Arabic need to alert their students to these kinds of important stylistic differences, ESL teachers in turn need to be sensitive to the influence that their students' native language stylistic conventions may have on their English speech and composition.

17 While the text's organization may itself sometimes seem distinctly 'non-native-like', Cohen points out that it is important not to overdo the reformulation (i.e. to keep students' papers recognizable as 'their own'), for students' motivation derives from seeing how their own writing has been 'dressed up' in native style.

18 I am thankful to Peter DeDomenico for introducing me to this game.

19 See Schultz (1995) for an example of a two-week unit plan that systematically addresses learners' analytical thinking, reading comprehension and, writing development in an intermediate-level French class.

20 Finding movies and television shows that all students are familiar with is admittedly easier in foreign language teaching contexts (where students tend to share similar cultural backgrounds) than in second language teaching contexts (where students tend to come from a wide range of cultures). In the latter case, the teacher will likely need to find popular culture examples drawn not from learners' past home culture experience, but from their current, second-culture experience.

PART THREE

8 Computers, language, and literacy

> . . . we are drowning in information . . . . In such a society, the scarcest commodity turns out to be not information but the human attention needed to cope with it.
>
> Richard Lanham (1993)

Our conceptions of literacy are intimately tied to technologies of writing. From stone tablets and papyrus scrolls, to paper and the printing press, and now to computers, technological advances have always created new possibilities, as well as challenges,[1] for literacy development. 'Technologies are not mere exterior aids', contends Walter Ong, 'but also interior transformations of consciousness, and never more than when they affect the word' (1982: 82). Not only 'interior' transformations, but also profound social transformations arise from changes in the ways writing is produced and disseminated. The transition from vellum to paper between the twelfth and fourteenth centuries in Europe, for example, had a significant impact on literacy practices. The relatively high cost and scarcity of vellum books had meant that reading was most often a public event, with the text delivered orally to gathered groups of people. As Donald Howard puts it, '. . . almost everyone's experience of a book was chiefly the experience of seeing the precious object at a distance on a lectern and hearing someone read aloud from it' (Howard 1976: 63). As paper books were introduced and became increasingly available, reading became a more widespread, yet also a more individual and private, practice. The solitary reader, as Howard describes, 'could possess his own books, pick and choose what to read, stay up late with a candle, skip, select, compare, turn back, and reread. He had more power over the book—could stop reading to think, could write notes in the margin' (p. 65).

With the advent of widespread computer use and global communications networks, technology continues to affect how we read, how we write, and how we use written language to learn and to communicate with others. In the first part of this chapter, we will consider how reading and writing are 're-mediated' through word processing, hypertext, and multimedia, and how this re-mediation can affect not only our reading and writing processes, but also our conceptions of texts and narratives themselves. In the second part of the chapter we will explore how networking applications such as synchronous conferencing and electronic mail create new opportunities for social interaction on both local and global scales, and what implications these opportunities might have for language and literacy development.

It is important to clarify from the outset that I do not wish to suggest that literacy-based teaching depends on the use of computers. Access to computers (and especially access to the Internet) varies tremendously across institutions and societies, and is especially rare in developing countries. It is nevertheless clear that where computers are available they are being put to use in a variety of ways to support language learning, and it behooves us to understand the potential benefits and limitations of those uses.

Reading and writing with computers

As we have seen in earlier chapters, literacy involves familiarity with the conventions of texts—how they are arranged and structured—and knowledge of how to use those conventions to design meaning. Reading and writing electronic texts draws upon many of the same conventions used in printed texts, but also involves acquiring additional conventions that are both procedural and conceptual in nature. On the procedural level, readers and writers must become familiar with the conventions of text display and navigation through the use of keyboards, mice, visual displays, text viewing software, operating systems, and so on. On the conceptual level, they must become familiar with conventions associated with new forms of texts (for example, multimedia documents) and new ways of arranging and structuring textual material (for example, hypertextual links). Reading and writing with computers therefore adds layers of complexity to an already complex process.[2]

Let's begin by considering some of the characteristic differences between texts in paper and electronic media. Paper texts are static and self-contained. They are generally organized in a continuous linear sequence of units such as paragraphs, sections, and chapters, but are usually presented in discrete, rectangular blocks of writing, surrounded by white margins, on pages. The pages are bound in such a way that we cannot change their physical order, but we can easily flip through the pages to go from one location to another, and, because pages are usually numbered, we can easily find our way back to a particular location. One can look at a paper text and immediately have a sense of its length by assessing its thickness.

Electronic texts, on the other hand, are dynamic and malleable. Readers can adjust the size and style of the typeface as well as the spacing and length of lines of text to suit their own preferences, and writers can easily move chunks of text from one location to another and make editing changes without disrupting the visual flow of the document. Electronic texts are also virtual. Whereas paper texts can be seen in their totality, long electronic texts can only be viewed one 'window' at a time. Furthermore, because electronic texts are often interconnected with other texts in broad networks, it is sometimes unclear where the exact boundaries of a given text lie. The interlinking of texts and text fragments also makes possible new forms of narrative, in which multiple alternative episodes and conclusions exist in parallel, giving readers an unprecedented sense of control over story events and outcomes. Finally, because electronic texts allow writing to be combined with voice, graphics, sound, and video their creation and interpretation draw upon multiple representational systems.

In the following sections, we will explore in greater depth some of the features and conventions associated with three widely-used digital technologies—word processing, hypertext, and multimedia—and consider the implications of these technologies for reading, writing, and learning languages.

Word processing

Word processing software is probably the computer tool most commonly used by language learners. It allows writers to move and edit text easily, to reformat documents quickly, and to produce a professional-looking product that incorporates special characters, orthographic accents, multiple typefaces, tables, and graphics. Outline programs can help to organize the overall structure of documents, while automated spelling- and grammar-checking routines can help to reduce surface errors.

Some scholars (for example, Tuman 1992) argue that word processing has not changed our notions of literacy in any fundamental way—that it merely automates certain writing tasks and helps us produce a neat, legible manuscript. While this may be true when the final product is a paper text, the literacy implications of word processing may be most plainly seen when the written text is designed to be read on a screen rather than on a page. As Selfe observes:

> . . . the writers in our classes who compose their texts for reading on computer screens have invented and exploited a new set of literacy skills that their teachers never imagined. Using different fonts, font sizes, symbols, highlighting, and graphic elements, they have not only adjusted their writing to the conventions of the screen and the computer, but have also reconceptualized the content of their assignments in terms of these conventions. It seems possible that the grammar of the computer, the word-processing package . . . [has] changed the way in which writers think and express thought.
> (Selfe 1989: 13)

It is also during the writing process itself that the possibilities offered by word processing seem most significant. Besides moving text easily, writers can shift instantaneously from an outline view to a full display of a word processing document. They can use 'hidden' text to write notes to themselves or to keep track of deleted paragraphs that they might use elsewhere. They can use color to visually indicate the logical structure of their writing (for example, marking thesis statements in one color and supporting evidence in another, or using two colors to show contrasting points of view within a paragraph). They can use different typefaces to convey a 'formal' or 'casual' or 'playful' feel to the text. Recent word processing packages even include 'animated text' features, allowing writers to make selected portions of text 'blink', 'shimmer', 'sparkle', or to be surrounded by 'Las Vegas lights'.

Does all this help students produce better academic writing? Research studies have been inconclusive in determining whether the use of word processing software improves students' overall writing quality, although certain aspects of writing seem to be positively influenced, such as students' attitude toward writing, the length of their essays, and the reduction of surface errors (Hawisher 1989; Laing, van den Hoven, and Benessiano 1991). On the other hand, certain aspects of the writing process may be negatively affected. Selfe (1989), for example, cites a number of studies showing that people read more slowly and less accurately on a computer screen, and that they have more difficulty getting an overview of the text and finding specific information (p. 9). This reading difficulty has important implications for writing. Haas (1989), for example, interviewed students who wrote with computers and found that writers frequently printed out their writing because, as they put it, 'seeing it on the screen really isn't seeing it' (1989: 17). Haas also found that although computers make small editing changes easy, reading from a computer screen can make detecting the need for such changes more difficult. Similarly, although moving large chunks of text to reorganize a piece of writing may be technically simple, many writers 'get lost' in the process when they are working exclusively online because of a difficulty to represent the overall structure and meaning of the text when viewing it on a screen (1989: 23). In sum, there are significant limitations to using computers for writing that we are only beginning to understand, and that have not yet been incorporated into theories of writing. In terms of the Available Designs model illustrated in Figure 2.3 (Chapter 2), we can see from Haas's research that procedural knowledge is a key area of difference between writing with computers and writing with pen and paper.

The question of 'better writing' is itself problematic, however, for if, as Ong suggests, a new technologizing of the word brings about transformations of use, then the criteria for what 'good' writing is will presumably need to be revised.[3] Perhaps even more significant than questions of 'improvement' or 'effectiveness' is the question of how the use of word processing may affect the way people view texts. To speculate for a moment, it seems plausible that experience in using word processing applications might render people more sensitive to the malleability of words, to their visual appearance, to their rhetorical charge—both on- and off-line.[4] If so, this sensitivity might extend to broader issues of reception and audience when they read and write.[5]

The jury is still out on these issues. But we should not lose sight of the fact that what makes us look at rhetorical conventions is not so much the type of text (printed versus electronic) as our reading goals and purposes (i.e. the communicative context layer of the design model shown in Figure 2.3). As Bolter (1991) has argued, digital technology supports 'every form of reading and writing from the most passive to the most active' (p. 238). The challenge for language teachers is to structure appropriate and varied tasks that focus learners' attention on conventions, and that make their reading and writing meaningful.

Hypertext

Whereas word processing preserves the kinds of text organization that characterizes printed texts, hypertext does not. Hypertext is 'non-sequential writing' (Nelson 1981; Landow 1992) that allows information to be organized in multi-linear strands. In hypertext, chunks of text are linked electronically to other chunks of text in associative webs, as illustrated in Figure 8.1.[6] Hypertext is relevant to language teaching in two principal ways. First, it is commonly used as an infrastructure for tutorials and other instructional software, and second, it is the architectural underpinning of the World Wide Web.

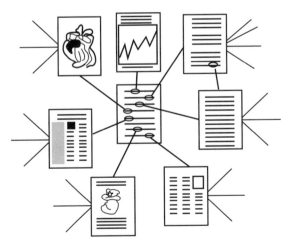

Figure 8.1: Texts connected by hypertextual links

The multi-component nature of hypertexts requires new strategies in writing and reading. For instance, if this book were written in hypertext it would not have chapter-length units of text. Instead, it would consist of many topic modules, linked to a topic index. This index would group topics in some logical fashion, but there would not necessarily be a 'beginning' and an 'end' with a clearly mapped path leading from one to the other. Within each module, words or sentences referring to ideas or concepts elaborated upon elsewhere would be linked to the appropriate modules. So it would be entirely up to the reader at a given point in time whether to explore a side issue in greater depth or to continue on with the point of the module at hand. In hypertext there is no standard reading sequence, no 'next page' determined by the author, even though the author does ultimately restrict the range of possibilities by the number and location of links that are created.[7]

In the following three sections, we will examine how hypertext has been used in foreign language contexts both to support print literacy (through reading tutorials), and to extend literacy into the digital realm (through reading and authoring on the World Wide Web).

A hypertext tutorial

Because hypertext is about making explicit relational links between pieces of information, it has been seen as a natural way to facilitate the reading of foreign language texts. As an example of a hypertext reading tutorial we will examine *French Reading Lab I* (Romeiser and Rice 1992). The reader begins by selecting a story to read (out of three by Guy de Maupassant). A scanned image of Maupassant appears, along with a number of 'buttons' along the bottom of the screen. These buttons allow the user to read an introduction to the chosen story; to begin reading the text; to get background information on Maupassant and on the Naturalism movement; or to take tests (called 'activities'). As one reads the story, one can select unfamiliar words (by clicking on them) to access their dictionary definitions, which appear in a separate window on the computer screen. Some words and idiomatic expressions are given more lengthy glosses. After working through the reading, one can check one's understanding by doing the 'activities', answering a list of true-false statements about the story or completing a fill-in-the-blank test.

In many ways, tutorial programs like *Reading Lab I* seem to be making good use of technology. They allow learners to work at their own pace, they provide a 'smart' dictionary that picks the contextually appropriate meanings, they supply background reference material on command, they offer immediate feedback on the accuracy of the learner's understanding, and they give the reader a sense of interaction with the computer and the text. And, above all, they put the learner in control.

One limitation of many tutorial programs, however, is that they are predetermined, closed systems. Although they often provide the illusion of objective comprehensiveness, they are not unbiased resources, but rather reflect the software designer's particular choices, based on a particular reading of the text. Tutorials supply the 'right' definitions and translations and the 'essential' background information about the life and times of the author. They test the 'important' factual information from the text. Not only have all the choices and decisions about relevance been made by someone else, but also the very ease of getting answers at the touch of a button may work against the learning process. By providing so much information so easily, such programs can in effect make reading a very one-way process of receiving the fruits of someone else's work. Because the computer package is 'comprehensive', learners have little incentive to explore dictionaries, and may consequently miss out on exposure to secondary word meanings that may have significance in the context of the story and that may enrich their vocabulary as well. Although users must actively decide where to click next, their reading experience nevertheless can be relatively passive. Close-ended tests convey the idea that reading is about absorbing information, rather than imagining other worlds. In presenting a finished reading product, such programs seem to neglect the notion that the very process of doing the work oneself—of making connections between context and word meaning, between word meaning and text meaning, of developing one's own representation of the text—is what leads to reading pleasure and, arguably, to language learning as well.

Other hypertext projects are based on a more open-ended architecture, allowing teachers or students the possibility of annotating texts themselves or linking various complementary or opposing texts in creative ways. For example, *Annotext*, a hypertext authoring system developed by Otmar Foelsche at Dartmouth College, allows complete electronic dictionaries to be linked to texts, such that clicking on any word in a source text brings up a list of its definitions. Students can also link their reader-response journals (see Chapter 5) to texts, allowing a number of responses to be visually juxtaposed with the original reading passage, to facilitate the comparison of interpretations.[8] Video footage from staged versions of a theatrical text can be linked to the written script so that by selecting a portion of text, the reader can immediately access the various filmed stagings of that particular scene. Digitized recordings of songs, lectures, and poetry readings can also be linked, allowing readers to follow the written text visually while listening to the oral performance. Such quasi-authorial uses of hypermedia seem to offer a very promising means of making learners aware of intertextuality and textual difference. In the next two sections we will see how the World Wide Web can be used as a resource for both accessing texts and designing one's own hypertextual and hypermedia environments.

Reading on the World Wide Web

Currently the most talked-about computer resource, the World Wide Web is an information system that links computer servers around the world via the Internet. Within a given Web document a reader may find dozens of hypertext links to other documents at various locations around the world. Although the World Wide Web is still dominated by English-language sites, it is rapidly becoming more linguistically diverse (Marriott 1998). Using multimedia technology, web documents can incorporate text, graphics, sound, or video.

For language teaching, the World Wide Web has so far been mostly used as an informational resource: students can 'visit' the Louvre, read Chinese magazines, see images of festivals in Córdoba, hear the Japanese national anthem, see the latest cover of *Der Spiegel*, read Nepalese poetry, hear excerpts of the latest pop hits in Russia, and so on. Because Web documents can be manipulated like any ordinary computer file, students can cut and paste text, graphics, sound, and video into their own personal documents. They can then use these collected excerpts in class presentations on selected topics. For example, during the 1995 presidential elections in France, a Web page included up-to-date regional election figures, photos, and biographical information on all of the candidates, excerpts from their campaign speeches, detailed descriptions of their party's political platform, candidates' views on the economy, foreign policy, immigration, and so on. With access to similar web sites, students in foreign language classes can work in groups to prepare a summary handout on political candidates, for use in presentations on national elections or as preparation for a classroom debate.

The astonishing diversity of information available on the World Wide Web is, however, as problematic as it is attractive. First, there is the issue of quantity: a search for a given topic on the World Wide Web may produce hundreds or even thousands of 'hits'. Consequently, web users must learn techniques to narrow the search field. Even then, one may have to scan a dozen web sites before finding what one is looking for. Search engines are far from perfect and sometimes cannot find the desired location at all, so that the user must try to find it indirectly by meandering through related web sites. 'Information browsing' thus takes on much greater importance than in paper literacy (Tuman 1996). Second, there is the problem of quality. Anyone with access to an Internet server can publish anything on the World Wide Web. There is no gatekeeping mechanism to assure production standards or accuracy of information. A third, and related, issue is cultural authenticity. It is often assumed that whatever sites one finds in a given language will be representative of the particular culture. As a keynote speaker at a recent language teaching conference phrased it: 'What could be more authentic than a World Wide Web page?' But critical reading on the Web requires asking *who* designed the web page and *for whom*. Even non-commercial web sites are often covert forms of advertising, and many sites that deal with national cultures offer little more than propaganda. Such sites may be useful in a language teaching context precisely because they present an opportunity for critical reading. All too often, however, learners are encouraged simply to browse and gather information, without critical evaluation of the source and purpose of the information gathered.

These issues of quantity, quality, and authenticity all point to the essential need for teaching online research skills and for providing guided practice in the critical evaluation of online information. In thinking about how to organize instruction, it is useful to refer back to the four curricular components, discussed in Chapters 4 to 7: situated practice, overt instruction, critical framing, and transformed practice. After showing students the basics of how to use a web browser to navigate within and across sites (overt instruction phase), teachers can begin by giving students a set of questions and a short list of web addresses where answers to the questions can be found (situated practice phase). After collecting their answers the students can reconvene to discuss their findings. If any discrepancies in information are found, the class can return to the particular sites in question to evaluate the sources of information: Who created the web site? For whom was it likely designed? Is the web site a primary or secondary source of information? What clues can be identified that might allow one to distinguish the relative authority and quality of the particular web sites from which the discrepant information was derived? This constitutes the critical framing phase.

A second instructional sequence can then follow, beginning with familiarizing students with various web search engines and indices (overt instruction). The teacher can provide a given topic, students can search for relevant web sites, and their findings (and search techniques) can be discussed—again with a focus on evaluating the relative quality and usefulness of the information on the respective web sites (situated practice and critical framing). Finally, students can work in small groups to develop content-based presentations or reports based on research involving the World Wide Web as well as other resources (transformed practice). These projects might include a 'research method' section in which students discuss how they located and evaluated information on the topic, how they dealt with any problems or discrepancies they encountered, and so forth. These kinds of activities not only familiarize learners with practical use of the World Wide Web but also support more broadly the goals of a literacy-based curriculum—communication, knowledge of conventions, cultural knowledge, interpretation, collaboration, problem solving, and reflection.

Authoring on the World Wide Web

Because the World Wide Web is also an authoring environment, it has enormous potential as a site where language learners can create their own collaborative projects. I will illustrate by describing a World Wide Web project that a class of second-semester French students initiated in 1994. My students had been corresponding via e-mail with students in France, and were surprised to learn that many of the French students had never heard of Berkeley—and those that had, imagined it to be full of blond surfers. Eager to disabuse their French colleagues, my students wanted to do more than just describe what Berkeley was like in e-mail messages: they wanted to *show* their French pen pals the sights and sounds of Berkeley and give them a sense of what it was like to be a student there. Since the World Wide Web was coming into vogue at the time, I suggested that my students develop a multimedia document that would allow their French correspondents, as well as others throughout the French-speaking world, to see what Berkeley was like—through their eyes.[9]

Our first task was to decide on content: what to include in this Web document? The students brainstormed about all the possible aspects of their lives that could be portrayed, and then collectively narrowed the list down to the following: (1) general information about the Berkeley campus—its location, its academic programs, its student body, and so forth, (2) the Campanile—the campus bell tower, (3) Telegraph Avenue—cafés, boutiques, and street vendors, (4) the Underground—a student arcade, (5) Sproul Plaza—where activists congregate, (6) dormitory life, and (7) fraternities and sororities. They chose to call the document 'Découvrir Berkeley!'

The class split into teams to work on each of these areas. Each team had to decide how to divide up the informational load for their topic: what should be represented in text? in video? in sound? Given the need for conciseness, students had to decide what was essential and what was peripheral to their particular topic. My principal role was to consistently remind students to think about how to represent their topic to a group of French peers who did not necessarily share a good deal of cultural common ground with them. In the case of the team working on 'fraternities and sororities', for example, the students had started out by writing: 'Le système grec est très important à Berkeley' (The Greek system is very important at Berkeley). The group was momentarily taken aback when I pointed out that *le système grec* would not at all convey the idea of 'the Greek system' as it is understood in an American college context. Nor could concepts like 'pledge', 'mixer', or 'hazing' be simply translated, as these social practices had no direct analogues in the French-speaking world. Such points, while obvious to language teachers, often go entirely overlooked by students, who sometimes see their writing simply as a neutral conduit for conveying 'objective' or 'generic' information. Consequently, a good deal of thought had to go into (1) identifying what kinds of knowledge the students presumed (and therefore did not explicitly communicate) when they wrote to members of their own culture, and (2) devising explanations that did not presume knowledge that their French readers might not share. In this way, reflection upon cross-linguistic and cross-cultural concerns—as part of an effort to avoid ambiguities and potential misunderstandings—became an integral part of learners' language use.

Students collaboratively wrote multiple drafts of essays on their particular topic, which I read and commented on. When the teams were satisfied with their texts, they shifted their attention to how they might use video and sound to enhance their descriptions. Deciding in advance what to film, and from what angles, students shot their video footage, showing extraordinary creativity in their filming. One important question that arose in organizing the introduction was how to visually represent a link between Berkeley and France. The ingenious solution was to open 'Découvrir Berkeley' with a scanned photograph of the Campanile and San Francisco Bay, with a somewhat blurred 'tricolore' (blue, white, red of the French flag) digitally superimposed on the sky portion of the image (shown in black and white in Figure 8.2).[10]

Figure 8.2:   The first screen from the Découvrir Berkeley! *web page*

Such projects thus require learners to extend their 'design' focus beyond words to graphics, audio, and video. Students must think not only about which modes might best lend themselves to the expression of particular meanings, but also about how the chosen information and representational modes combine and interact with one another to produce an overall communicative effect.

More recently, student projects have included collaborative cross-cultural investigations of social topics such as graffiti, police brutality, fashion, and the representation of youth in the media in both France and the United States. The goal of projects like these is to give students the opportunity to use their language and literacy abilities to explore a topic of genuine interest, to communicate with others, and to design and develop (with teacher guidance) a web-published product that can then in turn serve as a learning resource for other students. Perhaps most important, from a literacy standpoint, is the extent and depth of learners' thinking as they attempt to represent through language and other symbolic means, their own personal experience to members of another cultural community. By being encouraged to take on the role of the other, by taking a 'readerly' perspective on their own language use, students come to a greater awareness of how meaning can be constructed differently in different cultures. It is this kind of thinking that lies at the heart of a literacy-based approach to language teaching. Of course, it is not the technology itself that brings about this kind of thinking—that will always remain the special responsibility of the language teacher—but technology can nevertheless provide a useful catalyst for engaging in cross-cultural problem solving.[11]

New forms of narrative

Another development that grows out of multimedia and hypertext is the new kind of participatory narrative that Murray discusses in her (1997) book *Hamlet on the Holodeck*:

> Every day, and particularly every night, thousands of people forsake real life (RL) and meet in virtual space 'in character' (IC) to play out stories based on favorite books, movies, or television shows. This new kind of adult narrative pleasure involves the sustained collaborative writing of stories that are mixtures of the narrated and the dramatized and that are not meant to be watched or listened to but shared by the players as an alternate reality they all live in together.
> (Murray 1997: 44)

Central to Murray's argument is the notion of the 'multiform story', a playing out of multiple versions of a single story (as, for example, in the Frank Capra film *It's a Wonderful Life*). Murray's conception of the multiform story involves a complete rethinking of authorship, which is no longer a matter of writing a permanently fixed text, but rather a matter of inventing and arranging a core set of narrative algorithms that can give rise to multiple, varied performances. Computers are the ideal stage for multiform stories, because they make it easy to juxtapose elements in different permutations in order to bring about multiple perspectives and interpretations.

Because they are immersive and participatory in nature, the new cyberstories would seem to offer considerable potential for foreign language teaching. A first-generation multimedia narrative specially designed for intermediate and advanced French students is the highly acclaimed *A la rencontre de Philippe* (Furstenberg, Murray, Malone, and Farman-Farmaian 1993), developed by the Athena Language Learning Project at the M.I.T. Laboratory for Advanced Technology in the Humanities (and of which Murray is a co-author). Using interactive videodisc technology, *Philippe* incorporates full motion video, sound, graphics, and text, and allows learners to 'walk around' and explore simulated environments by following street signs or floor plans (see Figure 8.3).

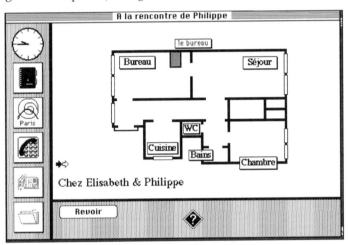

Figure 8.3:   A la rencontre de Philippe. *Clicking on the 'arrows' activates the corresponding view on the videodisc player, allowing the user to visually explore all corners of Elisabeth and Philippe's apartment (Furstenberg, et al. 1993)*

The storyline goes as follows. Philippe, a young journalist, and his girlfriend, Elisabeth, have had a fight and Elisabeth has asked Philippe to move out of her apartment. Philippe asks the player to help him find a place to live, or maybe to help him patch up his relationship with Elisabeth. In the process of helping, the player visits Philippe's current apartment, reads rental listings from *Le Figaro* (see Figure 8.4), listens to messages on an answering machine, takes notes, leaves messages for others, uses a map to navigate through Paris, visits rental agencies to read posted rental announcements, and so on. The program is designed to put learners' problem-solving skills to the test, and the player's decisions at various junctures determine the plot and eventual outcome of the story (the story has seven different endings). Filmed in Paris, the video footage creates a sense of realism, and the branching of the storylines maintains the player's interest. To help the learner to understand the sometimes challenging spoken French, the program provides optional comprehension tools, such as transcriptions of all audio segments and a glossary, as well as a video album that includes most of the items one would use in a communicative approach such as expressing feelings, saying hello, goodbye, gestures, and so forth. Students can easily create their own custom video albums, which they store on their own computer diskettes.

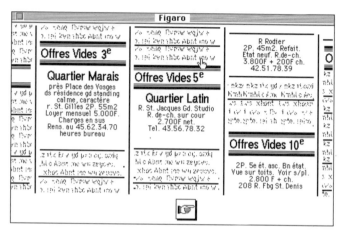

Figure 8.4:   A la rencontre de Philippe. *Apartment listings in* Le Figaro *(Furstenberg et al. 1993)*

Multimedia programs such as *A la rencontre de Philippe* are ambitious and impressive. One may wonder, however, to what extent the skills these programs develop (and require) correspond to those used either in classroom communication or in real life. Although a learner using *A la rencontre de Philippe*, for example, determines the direction and outcome of the story through his or her decisions, and is addressed directly by Philippe, he or she operates very much as a solitary agent, with no real communicative exchange, and with no real identity in the story. Moreover, the listening, reading, and writing involved are strictly a matter of remembering and recording factual information. Like the hypertext reading tutorial, we are once again dealing with a closed system, albeit a much more complex and engaging one, in which the learner acts in a principally consultative mode. While this kind of computer product certainly puts the learner in an active stance, and provides an effective illusion of communicative interaction, it does not offer the possibility of genuine negotiation of meaning and ultimately turns the learner back upon himself or herself.[12] Furthermore, as Wrigley (1993) points out, the qualities of privacy and independent learning that such software offers may in fact work against communicative ability if learners are deprived of the social support they need to develop confidence in their language use.

These limitations aside, *A la rencontre de Philippe* has much to offer in support of literacy-based teaching. As a highly engaging game, it lends itself to repeated use (i.e. rereading, discussed in Chapters 4 and 5) in a way that books generally do not. This repeated use gives learners a chance to pay close attention to spoken, written, and visual clues (and perhaps to notice and reflect on cross-cultural differences). Furthermore, by allowing learners to create their own custom-designed video albums, the program makes it possible for learners to save particular video segments in order to study them at a later time or in order to redesign the story itself (see Chapters 5 and 7 on redesigning stories).

As in the case of hypertext, the most exciting potential for cybernarrative would seem to lie in students' own use of authoring systems to create their own multiform narratives. To imagine an ideal scenario (in which students have access to the requisite software and hardware), students could, in a first phase, develop multimedia stories about personal experiences, using text, images, and voice-overs, which they could share over the Internet with native-speaker pen pals. In a second phase (in a subsequent course, for example) they could then develop alternative endings to those stories. In a third phase, the foreign pen pals could create their own alternative endings, which could then be compared with those developed by the learners themselves. Murray's claim is that 'By experiencing such interwoven stories as one unit, we can enhance the kaleidoscopic capacity of our minds, our capacity to imagine life from multiple points of view' (Murray 1997: 160–1). Given that a large part of foreign language teaching is ultimately about getting students to see the world from a different, 'foreign' perspective, her claim seems well worth exploring as authoring tools become more accessible.

Word processing, hypertext, the World Wide Web, and multimedia games can be valuable resources for language learning, especially when they are used under the thoughtful guidance of a teacher. What these applications do not provide, however, is a means for genuine communicative language use with other people. For that, we will need to turn to other applications of computer technology that link individuals via local and worldwide networks.

Social interaction via computers

As we enter the twenty-first century, computers are being increasingly used to facilitate, not replace, human contact. The Internet, characterized in a recent U.S. court decision as 'the most participatory marketplace of mass speech that ... the world ... has yet seen' (Lewis 1996: A1), not only provides access to an ever-expanding body of published information, as we saw earlier, but also allows the creation of unique learning communities. The most profound effects of computer technology on literacy and language learning will likely arise not from language pedagogy software, but from the new forms of information dissemination and social interaction made possible by local and global computer networks. The implications of networked communication for language learning are important not only because computer networks potentially expand the number and diversity of people one can communicate with, but also because they influence the ways in which people use language to interact with one another.

In the rest of this chapter, I will discuss three types of networked communication that can potentially, with a teacher's guidance, broaden language learners' literacy and metacommunicative awareness.

Synchronous communication

As we saw in Chapter 6, writing in ESL and foreign language teaching has traditionally been seen as a linguistic exercise. Students generally write for a limited audience (their teacher) and for a limited purpose (to display their mastery of grammar and vocabulary). Recently, however, many language teachers have adopted more social and developmental perspectives on writing, emphasizing collaboration among learners at various stages of the writing process. The use of networked computers, many teachers have found, can promote this collaboration in unique ways.

Local area networks

Local area networks consist of interconnected computers located at a particular site. With the addition of communication software, local area networks provide groups of individuals an electronic 'space', somewhat akin to a bulletin board, in which information, ideas, opinions, and questions can be posted and responded to in real time. Often used in business settings to improve the productivity of meetings, local area networks tend to encourage both the free exchange of ideas and critical feedback—presumably because they allow many of the conventions and constraints of oral face-to-face communication to be suspended. Unlike oral conversation, for example, in which speakers' turns follow one another sequentially, synchronous networked communication allows people to express their ideas simultaneously, increasing the flow of ideas and reducing the likelihood of domination by one party. Because communication is written and contributions can be made anonymously, a certain distance is created between participants and the ideas expressed that may contribute to an atmosphere of critical receptivity.[13] Synchronous conferencing thus combines the temporal immediacy of spoken interaction (as with the telephone) with the social distancing allowed for by writing. In terms of the medium/mode distinction mentioned in Chapter 1, it incorporates many features of spoken *mode* within a written *medium*.

One type of network application that has caught the attention of language teachers is synchronous conferencing, commonly known as 'chat'.[14] Unlike electronic mail exchanges, in which the posting and the reading of messages may be separated by hours or days, chat occurs in real time, allowing all members of the discussion group instant access to each message as soon as it is sent. In the classroom, students and teacher typically sit at individual computer terminals linked together electronically (for example, in a computer lab). The teacher presents a writing task, which appears in a 'class assignment' window on all students' computer screens. To begin writing, students open a second, 'session' window. The bottom half of this window is the editing buffer where students compose their comments. Once a message is completed, it is 'published' by being sent to the other members of the discussion group (which can range in size from two or three students to the entire class). Messages appear in the top half of the session window, appended to previously posted messages, on all participants' screens. Participants read the posted messages and can respond to whichever ones they choose. Their responses are in turn 'published' to all members of the discussion group. This is an ongoing process in which one may compose and send a message at any time, even as other group members' messages are arriving. When new messages appear on the screen, the reader can scroll backward through the file to review earlier comments. Each posted message is identified by the participant's name or alias, although complete anonymity is possible by allowing all students to log in as guests. Just as in oral classroom discussions, the teacher can choose to participate actively or to observe students' exchange of ideas. At the end of the session, the transcript of this text-based discussion can be printed and then distributed to the students at the next class meeting. This transcript can serve as the basis for subsequent oral discussion, composition drafting, grammar analysis, or other activity.

The obvious question at this point is: why would a group of people hold a 'discussion' in writing, when they could simply talk? The point of using synchronous conferencing is not at all to replace talk, but to supplement it with discussion that is governed by a different set of conventions and constraints, in which some of the normal rules of interactional discourse within a group are destabilized. That is, to open up new possibilities for an alternative, or even oppositional, discussion.[15] What chat offers is an entirely different medium of interaction that offers participants the possibility to voice their thoughts at will, without interrupting other participants' thoughts or expression. By virtue of being *written*, all participants' comments are available throughout the discussion for rereading and response—the most recently posted message need not be the first to be addressed. Participants can pursue independent threads within the context of a main discussion (much like small group discussions) and unobtrusively change from one thread to another.

To illustrate, consider a brief excerpt of a chat session that took place during the third week of a second-semester French class. This excerpt illustrates not only the dynamics of student-to-student interaction, but also the potential for exploring individual and cultural variation among classmates. The topic was differences between family generations, and students were asked in what specific ways they and their parents were different or alike. Alda and Billy are ethnic Chinese, Kang is Cambodian, Claudia is Anglo-Saxon. I am the instructor. (Intervening messages from other conversational threads have been edited out in order to make the excerpt more readable.)

> Alda: Je pense que je suis comme mes parents en un sens, nous sommes toujours heureux. Mais en general, nous sommes tres differents. Peut-etre c'est parce que je deviens adulte aux Etats-Unis, et ils habitaient aux autre pays la plus grande partie de temps. Ils aiment les traditions chinois, mais je n'en aime pas trop.
>
> Rick: Alda, est-ce que vous participez aux fêtes chinoises, même si vous ne les aimez pas?
>
> Alda: Prof. Kern, hier, c'etait le premier d'annee au calendrier chinoises. Je suis retourne chez mes parents, et nous avons celebre. Les premieres trois jours de la nouvel annee sont tres importants. Il me faut celebrer. Je n'en aime pas la tradition trop, mais je (et peut-etre tous les enfants chinoises) aime le premier d'annee. C'est parce que les adultes donnent des poches rouges. Et il y a beaucoup d'argent.
>
> Kang: Alda, est-ce que tes parents parle à toi en chinois et tu parle aux parents en anglais? Moi, mes parents ne me parle pas en anglais, mais je leur parle en anglais en meme temps. C'est un peu bizarre.
>
> Billy: Alda, Est-ce que vous êtes chinoise? Si vous êtes chinoise, avez-vous célébré la nouvelle anneé chinoise hier? Avez-vous reçu beaucoup d'argent de votre famille?
>
> Kang: Alda, pourquoi 'tu n'aime pas trop' de traditions chinois? Que penses-tu a la NOUVELLE ANNEE de Chinois?
>
> Claudia: Alda- J'aime les traditions chinois. Mon petit ami est chinois.
>
> Kang: BONNEE ANNEE POUR LES ETUDIANTS CHINOIS!!!!!!!!!!!!!!!!!!!!!
> !!!
>
> [Alda: I think that I'm like my parents in a way: we're always happy. But in general, we're very different. Maybe it's because I grew up in the U.S., and they lived in other countries most of the time. They like Chinese traditions, but I don't like them too much.
>
> Rick: Alda, do you participate in Chinese holidays, even if you don't like them?
>
> Alda: Prof. Kern, yesterday it was the first of the year in the Chinese calendar. I went home to my parents' house and we celebrated. The first three days of the new year are very important. I have to celebrate. I don't like tradition too much, but I (and maybe all Chinese children) like the first of the year. That's because the adults give red pockets. And there's lots of money.
>
> Kang: Alda, do your parents speak to you in Chinese and you speak to them in English? My parents don't speak to me in English, but I talk to them in English at the same time. It's a little bizarre.
>
> Billy: Alda, Are you Chinese? If you're Chinese, did you celebrate Chinese New Year yesterday? Did you get lots of money from your family?
>
> Kang: Alda, Why don't you 'like too much' Chinese traditions? What do you think about Chinese NEW YEAR?
>
> Claudia: Alda- I like Chinese traditions. My boyfriend is Chinese.
>
> Kang: HAPPY NEW YEAR FOR CHINESE STUDENTS!!!!!!!!!!!!!!!!!!!!!!!!!!
> !!!]

(Kern 1995b: 458–9)

One notable aspect of chat sessions is the structure of participation and its effect on the way topics are explored. Here, for example, Alda's initial answer to the question stimulated five responses (posted *at the same time*) that introduced three new subtopics: Chinese New Year, differences in loyalty to Chinese traditions, and differences in the use of Chinese and English in Asian students' families. Unlike oral discussion, which proceeds linearly from one comment to the next, the written chat interaction develops in multilinear and associative fashion. Furthermore, the structure of participation is not determined by the teacher, but collaboratively, by the group. The typical pattern of classroom discourse, consisting of a teacher-initiated topic, student reply, and teacher evaluation of the reply (Mehan 1985) is rendered inoperative: a participant's message is directed to the entire group or to a specific addressee, but it is rarely produced for (or in the expectation of) teacher appraisal. Moreover, the teacher has no mechanism by which to allocate the floor, which is equally available to all group members at all times. As a consequence, many student comments surface that might never be heard in a normal classroom discussion. Claudia's and Kang's final messages in the exchange cited above, for example, would most likely be deemed inappropriate in an oral classroom discussion. But it is precisely the personal nature of such contributions that leads students to remark that they learn more about their classmates from written chat discussions than they do in oral interaction. For example, following the session cited above, Kang wrote in a composition (here translated into English): 'Every Friday after the computer lab session I feel closer to my classmates. Because when we discuss different subjects on the computer I can start to understand their ideas, their situations and, above all, their personalities.' Whether this effect is due to the difference in the participant structure, or to the written medium of chat sessions, it seems to be a valuable aspect of networked synchronous discussion.

Perhaps the most obvious feature of written chat discussion is the level of student participation. A transcript of a fifty-minute elementary language class session with 15–20 students typically runs about twelve pages of single-spaced text. Advanced-level students generally produce much longer transcripts. In a study comparing students' written chat and oral classroom discussions on the same topics, I found that students had over twice as many turns, produced two to four times more sentences, and used a much greater variety of discourse functions when working in synchronous conferencing than they did in their oral discussion. Furthermore, the distribution and direction of turns differed radically in the two conditions, with much more direct student-to-student exchange in the synchronous conferencing condition (Kern 1995b).

Synchronous conferencing not only stimulates writing production, but can also vary social roles and interactional conventions for teacher and students. Teacher authority takes a different form when mediated by the written format of synchronous conferencing discussion. The teacher cannot control turns by calling on students, nor is there any guarantee that students will respond to the teacher's questions or comments. Students can send messages at the same time without worrying about 'cutting someone off' in the middle of an utterance. By immersing learners in writing—their own, their peers', and their teacher's—use of networked conferencing can contribute to the creation of a 'writing community' that provides a real sense of audience and that allows peer collaboration to extend beyond group planning and peer editing to the composing process itself.

Furthermore, synchronous conferencing supports 'readerly' writing: participants not only 'read to write' (by paying close attention to others' points in order to respond) but also 'write to be read' by others. As one student remarked, 'When I send something, and I see it pop up on the screen, I'm thinking about how someone might disagree with my statement. I come up with a kind of counter-argument. I kind of answer myself by thinking about it.' This is what readerly writing is all about: writing while thinking in terms of the ways one's writing can be interpreted by a reader, or a variety of readers.[16]

Networked communication also affects language use. The kind of language produced in chat sessions is a natural outgrowth of students' social interaction, and its form reflects that context. Spelling and grammatical accuracy may suffer, but not to the point of incomprehensibility. Like speech, written chat exchanges are characterized by direct interpersonal address, rapid topic shifts, and frequent digressions. Similarly, the *functions* expressed in chat frequently overlap with purposes normally associated with speech. Writing becomes a channel for lively, spontaneous exchange of thoughts, feelings, and ideas—as useful in developing social relationships and entertaining others as in informing, explaining, and persuading. Writing is not done just to display language knowledge or for teacher validation, but for a variety of other communicative purposes.[17]

The written form of synchronous conferencing discussion may also heighten students' awareness of the structure of their own communication by distancing them from it and allowing them to review the discourse visually to find patterns and progressions. Because session transcripts can be printed out and reviewed, synchronous conferencing makes it possible to reflect on and analyze direct interpersonal communication. In other words, synchronous conferencing affords the possibility of adding a recursive dimension to the immediate act of communication (Swaffar 1991). Of course, the degree to which students actually engage in analysis and reflection will be strictly a function of the teacher's creation and management of precise, well-structured learning tasks; it will not result simply from the use of certain technological tools.

The differences between classroom discussion and networked conferencing outlined above suggest how written spontaneous exchanges can supplement classroom talk. Reconfiguring conventions of interaction and language use, opening new pathways for collaboration and consciousness of one's own linguistic output, and shifting the interpersonal classroom dynamic, can all have potentially salutary effects on learners' language and literacy development.[18] It is important to bear in mind, however, that the extent to which learners engage in negotiation of meaning is less a function of synchronous conferencing itself than of the kind of tasks learners are asked to perform.[19] And not all activity types lend themselves equally well to synchronous conferencing work. Warschauer (1999), for example, points out that while activities involving 'reflective exchange of ideas' (p. 70) tend to work well, those that require making group decisions or arriving at a consensus do not.

In terms of literacy development (and specifically academic literacy), it is important to remember that while synchronous conferencing and academic writing share the same medium, they differ significantly in mode, and therefore highlight different aspects of written communication (see Table 8.1). Questions of 'effectiveness' therefore need to be framed in terms of specific goals. Grammatical accuracy, stylistic refinement, global coherence, and sustained, logical development of one's ideas are more likely to be fostered in traditional academic writing. Synchronous conferencing, on the other hand, tends to encourage fluency (in terms of both speed and quantity of language production), lively interactive responsiveness, a blending of 'orate' and 'literate' language forms and communicative devices, and the collective voicing of multiple perspectives on topics. Given these differences, it would be unwise to assume that the use of synchronous conferencing would directly improve learners' ability to write a formal essay. Nevertheless, the complementarity of the two modes of written communication suggests ways they might be exploited in tandem in a literacy-based curriculum. In principle, at least, synchronous conferencing is well suited to the invention stages of a writing project (for example, the rapid generation of ideas through collective brainstorming) as well as certain aspects of the revision process (for example, the collection of multiple reader responses and peer editing

Academic writing	Synchronous conferencing
• Formal accuracy	• Fluency of self-expression
• Global coherence	• Interactive responsiveness
• Reinforcement of canonical written discourse conventions	• Blend of 'orate' and 'literate' forms of communication
• Uninterrupted personal exploration of an idea	• Juxtaposition of multiple voices, perspectives

Table 8.1: Features of written communication highlighted in academic writing and in synchronous conferencing

feedback). The presumed advantage of using synchronous conferencing for these activities is that learners obtain a full written transcript of what are normally evanescent oral activities (i.e. 'speech as text'), which can be subsequently analyzed, discussed, and reflected upon, both in and out of the classroom.[20]

Social encounters in cyberspace

Although the particular synchronous conferencing activities described above took place over a local area network in a language laboratory, other synchronous communication environments are Internet-based, allowing participants to be geographically distant from one another. Internet Relay Chat (IRC), for example, allows one to 'chat' with other individuals worldwide. Participants can make appointments to meet at a particular time on a particular 'channel' (there are well over 5,000 channels, such as ***#espanol, ***#francais, ***#malaysia) in order to carry on a written conversation in real time.

Similar to IRC, but offering more elaborate communication environments, are MOOs (Multiple user domains Object Oriented). Based on spatial metaphors, MOOs are organized as geographic locales and are divided into 'rooms' where participants may congregate and interact.[21] Users can create and 'own' their own rooms, as well as various objects within them (for example, a blackboard, a cup, a glove). Once created, objects can be manipulated and shared with others. Participants navigate from room to room by typing directional commands (for example, 'north', 'west') or by 'teleporting', which allows immediate transport to rooms not adjacent to one's present location. To represent themselves in this virtual space, users create characters with names and detailed descriptions. Controlled by simple commands, each user's self-defined character can perform actions (for example, looking, knocking, moving) or can 'emote' (smile, frown, etc.). Because users can extend themselves in cyberspace through movement and through construction of new rooms, MOOs are dynamic social environments that are continually growing and evolving.

MOOs created specifically for language learners and teachers include: schMOOze University for ESL/EFL, the MOO Français for French, MundoHispano and ArdaMOO for Spanish, MOOsaico for Portuguese, MorgenGrauen and UNItopia for German, Little Italy for Italian, and SvenskMUD for Swedish.[22]

To illustrate, let's visit schMOOze University, a place where learners of English as a second or foreign language can meet and have written conversations in real time. After connecting,[23] I am greeted by the following message:

You have connected as a Guest to schMOOze. We want our Guests to feel welcome here, so as a Guest you can give yourself a name and description. This way you won't be an anonymous guest, but yourself. —schMOOze Management.

After typing in a name and a description of my character, I am told that I am at the Entrance Gates, a location described as follows:

> The Entrance Gates
> ― ― ― ― ― ― ― ―
>
> These are the entrance gates to schMOOze University. To the north you can see a carved stone archway leading to the tree lined mall of the campus. Guests and new players might want to head directly to the Beginner classroom by typing CLASSROOM.
>   To find out where things are on campus, just type MAP.
>   <==The campus clock tower reads 10:01 a.m. EDT==>
> You see a newspaper, Suggestion-Box, Mission Statement, map, and TREASURE HUNT here.
> Obvious exits: North and Classroom
> Welcome to schMOOze! Please type HELP MANNERS before continuing.

Social protocol is very important in MOOs. When I type 'help manners' on my computer I get the following information:

> RESPECT OTHER PEOPLE. Citizens here are of all ages and come from many different parts of the world. Please do not offend others with your language or actions.
> ALWAYS BE POLITE. It is always polite to ask permission before entering someone else's home. Please use the verb KNOCK <player> before @joining someone.

I am now eager to meet someone, so I type '@who' to find out who else is present and where they are. I see that someone called Hang has just logged on and is in another room. After 'knocking' and being invited to enter, I join Hang in his own room, called PAT SIN RANGE, which is described on the screen as follows:

> PAT SIN RANGE in the north east of Hong Kong which consist of eight mountains. On 10 FEB 1996, there was a terrible forest fire. Five students and teachers die in that fire. The teachers are very courage since they protected students but lose their life. However their fame will never die. So i make my room as this name to celebrate them.
> Obvious exits: out
> Hang is here.
> Rick [Guest] has arrived.
> Hang asks, 'hi where are yuo.. you from?'

I respond, and my utterance appears in the second person on my computer ('You say, 'Hello Hang, I'm from California.'"), but in the third person on my interlocutor's computer ('Rick [Guest] says, 'Hello Hang, I'm from California.'"). We continue our conversation for fifteen minutes or so, talking about the fire, about Hong Kong, and about California. At one point I tell Hang that I am a novice MOO user, and Hang gives me some procedural directions.

> Hang says, 'type @who then you can see whom in the moo'
> You say, 'Thanks, Hang'
> Hang says, 'you are welcome'
> Hang says, 'if you want to join anyone who now in another room, you need type knock <the name of player> and then a.. obtain . . . after their consent you type @join <the name of player>'

Now at this point there is a long 'silence', and I am suddenly not sure how to read the intent behind Hang's messages. Is he simply picking these commands at random, and telling me about them for my future reference? Or is he ending our conversation and indirectly asking me to leave his room? In the absence of extralinguistic cues I feel lost. Not knowing exactly what to say at this point I finally ask: 'Are you staying here for a while or are you leaving?' Hang responds straightforwardly, 'I will stay here now,' which still leaves me wondering whether I ought to be staying or be leaving myself. It is not until Hang's 'non verbal' message comes that my lingering doubts are allayed:

> Hang smiles
> Hang says, 'you try to type :smiles'
> :smiles
> Rick [Guest] smiles
> Hang exclaims, 'you success!'

And I indeed felt successful, having learnt to interact not only verbally but 'visually' as well. It is this kind of communicative contact and cooperative learning, mediated exclusively through writing, that makes MOOs so intriguing and engaging. Although a native speaker of English, I felt I still had much to learn about communicating in this new environment; the feeling was very much like that of visiting a foreign country for the first time. The intricacies of new conventions loomed large in my mind. Fortunately, in Hang I had found a patient guide.

Because MOOs are constructed by their regular users, they tend to engender a strong sense of community among participants. 'Regulars' become well known to one another, and very soon a group history develops, with shared values and interactional norms. Rooms, or locales, give structure to what would otherwise be a vast electronic space, and offer a stable, familiar place to which one can return as often as one likes, and where one can meet both familiar as well as new 'faces'. The locational stability of MOOs, the possibility of creating and controlling one's own character, room, and objects, and the exhilaration of spontaneous communication with people from different parts of the world can, for some, offer a comfortable sense of social integration that may be lacking in their 'real' lives. Small wonder that some dedicated enthusiasts allegedly spend most of their waking hours in MOOs.

The virtual encounters made possible by online environments are ideal contexts for role-playing and acting in situations that may be outside the realm of one's personal experience. Participants can leave their 'real' identities aside and construct new virtual ones at will, becoming entirely textual beings, interacting with others in a silent, writing-mediated world. Consider this debriefing exchange between a female Asian student and her teacher following an interactive written role-play in which the student took the role of a male character in a story the class had been studying:

Teacher:	What is your reaction to speaking in the voice of one of the characters?
Student:	I feel really good. The sense of I am the man of the house and I have all the power. Everybody is below and they better not dare to question my authority. I feel good.
Teacher:	It's interesting that taking on a masculine role gave you a sense of power! Do you think that if you adopted a male pseudonym regularly it would help you to speak in a different way?
Student:	Yes, it definitely will.[24]

It may be that the construction and reconstruction of identities made possible in online virtual environments will give voice to learners' 'other language' selves, creating an inner dialogue that may lead to greater self-understanding and perhaps self-transformation.[25]

From a literacy standpoint, MOOs create a bridge between written and oral communication. Although the mode of verbal exchange in a MOO is decidedly 'interactive' or 'conversational', it is nonetheless mediated by writing. Movements, actions, and gestures are initiated by written commands and are represented to participants as narrative statements, sometimes elaborated by the computer itself (for example, when Wendy types :smiles it might appear on the computer as 'Wendy smiles beguilingly to show you her white teeth'). The basic vocabulary and punctuation conventions of narrative dialogue are introduced automatically (and therefore made available as 'language input' for learners). For example, when one types a question mark at the end of a 'say' command (for example, *say How are you?*), what appears on the screen is You ask, 'How are you?' Typing an exclamation point (for example, *say I'm fine!*) produces *You exclaim, 'I'm fine!'*. Descriptions of guests, permanent characters, robots, locales, rooms, and objects are all provided in writing, as are navigational instructions, help files, behavior code policies, and so forth. Because MOOs are based on a spatial metaphor, they create their own 'virtual' context for interaction. Participants know, for example, where they are and what the room looks like, who is there with them, what they look like, and what they are doing. The interpretation of utterances and actions can often be facilitated by this jointly constructed, virtual context.

Of course, all this means that students have to learn a new set of conventions in order to navigate and communicate in a MOO environment. For example, they must learn a considerable number of MOO commands if they are to become 'fluent' participants, adding a layer of complexity to an already complex process of verbal interaction. Some teachers may see this as a significant obstacle, although in my experience students generally learn the commands they need very quickly. Moreover, the need to focus explicitly on a new set of rules and conventions in the MOO microcosm may (when the link is identified by the teacher) contribute to learners' understanding of the importance of rules and conventions in all varieties of discourse in the larger macrocosm of their verbal communication.

Some teachers may also object that learners both produce and are exposed to many grammatical errors when they interact in MOOs. Research on errors in learner-learner oral discourse has shown that error rates are no greater when learners interact with their same-level peers than when they interact with more competent speakers (for example, Porter 1983, cited in Long and Porter 1985). Whether this holds true when learners interact in writing and *read* their peers' spelling and grammar errors remains to be researched, although Pellettieri's (2000) study suggests that it may be the case.

In sum, MOOs bring geographically dispersed people into a common virtual space. Within that space, they use language to overcome the limits set by the technology. They create their own rooms and artifacts through verbal description. They address the lack of visual clues that accompany face-to-face communication by introducing them linguistically. And of course they enter into relationships and negotiate common rules of social conduct through language. In the process, they fabricate a textual reality resistant to the actual reality of individuals sitting in front of keyboards and luminescent screens. It is perhaps the MOO's seemingly infinite potential for re-creation of the self in interaction with others that attracts people to the medium and motivates them to return.

It is the very extremity of this potential, however, that raises questions in many teachers' minds about the contribution that MOOs might make to students who must learn to function in 'real' language contexts. As summarized in Table 8.2, writing in a MOO is quite different from traditional pen and paper writing. To what extent can such manifestly 'created' and protean textual environments support general learning goals?

As is true for all of the other uses of technology discussed in this chapter, whatever real learning students derive from participation in a MOO will result more from their teachers' involvement than from their mere use of the technology itself. What MOOs provide is a communication laboratory that yields a written transcript of all interactions. Merely participating in MOO encounters (i.e. situated practice) may or may not enhance learners' ability to communicate in non-MOO contexts. What is more likely to contribute to students' learning and communicative ability, however, is their *reflection* on their written interactions (i.e. critical framing): how the MOO's particular discourse conventions were used to certain effects, how misunderstandings developed or were avoided, how 'emotive' and 'non verbal' messages contributed to the interpretation of verbal exchanges, how the 'definition' of a room and the configuration of its space might have affected the interaction of its visitors, and so on. Because communicative interactions *and their contexts* are encoded in written form, MOOs offer an ideal opportunity to take explicit notice of the choices that participants make in their efforts to design meaning. In the above exchange, for example, students could consider

Pen and paper writing	MOO environments
• Writer supplies and controls all text	• Writer's input is transformed by MOO (i.e., not an exact input-output match)
• Formatting and punctuation are entirely writer's responsibility	• Formatting and some punctuation handled by the MOO
• Imagined, anticipated interaction with reader	• Interactive environment (even in the absence of an interlocutor, one's writing allows one to navigate through locales, meet robots, etc.)
• Overt response from reader (if any) is deferred well past the moment of writing	• Expectation of immediate response to writing (either from other participants or from the MOO itself)
• Allows one-to-one or one-to-many communication	• Allows one-to-one, one-to-many, and many-to-many communication

Table 8.2:   Comparison of features of written communication via pen and paper and MOO technologies

Hang's choice to make his room a memorial to celebrate the teachers who lost their lives in the Pat Sin Range fire. Would an American student in Hong Kong likely have created such a room? How might the room description influence the discourse within the room? What is the effect when Hang 'nods' (instead of speaking) when I introduce myself? What might I have done to clarify Hang's communicative intent (for example, if he had not smiled and taught me to smile)? The teacher's structuring of tasks that demand such reflection is essential, for although the experience of using a MOO may be enjoyable, it will probably not in itself lead to increased sensitivity to cultural differences or to greater metacommunicative awareness.

Can MOOs contribute to learners' academic writing ability? Perhaps when used as a tool for invention and revision as described in the above section on synchronous conferencing. Of greater significance, I believe, is their potential to expand students' imagination by allowing them to design virtual worlds in which they can represent themselves (or their personas) exclusively through language and, in so doing, become more sensitive to the subtleties of their own and others' language use.

Intercultural exchanges via e-mail: toward multiple perspectives

Another way in which computer technology can support a social interactional basis for reading and writing is by facilitating intercultural partnerships between language learners and native speakers. As Sussex (1996) notes, the Internet is 'bringing about a renaissance in epistolary' (p. 56). With increasing frequency, groups of language learners are sending letters, photos, and cultural artifacts to one another in order to develop ongoing lines of communication and to deepen their knowledge of one another's culture.[26] This kind of exchange can of course be done via standard mail, although electronic mail is quickly becoming the preferred medium of written exchange due to its speed of delivery (creating a sense of communicative immediacy), the ability to attach sound and graphics files, and its much lower cost.[27] To illustrate, I will cite two examples from content-based e-mail projects designed to promote cross-cultural dialogue between American students of French at Berkeley and French students of English at the Lycée Frédéric Mistral in Fresnes, France.[28]

The first example is from an introductory French class at Berkeley. Members of the two classes had been introducing themselves and describing their respective environments when one of the French *lycéens* remarked in an e-mail message: 'I am glad to hear that there are suburbs in the U.S. too.' Quite puzzled by this comment, my students followed up with questions. One strand of this discussion, an exchange between Virginie and Andrew, is presented below. Virginie begins by saying that suburbs in France are plagued by violence and wonders if the same is true in the United States. Andrew replies that in fact American suburbs are generally calm places and that violence in America is most concentrated within major cities. Having identified this contrast, Virginie and Andrew collaboratively explore how economic and historical forces came to produce different social realities, eventually widening the scope of their discussion to issues of racism at the end.[29]

Message from Virginie:

. . . Before I went to high school I was in the secondary school Guy Maquet. There, there were a lot of problems of violence. For example a teacher received a death threat and had to be taken home by the police. Even my father was punched in the face! But the administration did nothing. And violence exists not only in schools but everywhere. This is one of the biggest problems in the suburb. Is there a lot of violence in the suburbs of the USA too?

Response from Andrew:

Virginie, Pour répondre à ta question de la violence aux banlieues aux Etats-Unis: Je pense qu'on voit la majorité de la violence aux Etats-Unis au centre des villes principals. Les banlieues sont souvent calmes et ils ont moins de gens que les villes principals. Generalement il y a plus de problemes au centre des villes.
   A bientot, Andrew

[Virginie, To answer your question about violence in suburbs in the U.S.: I think that one sees the most violence in the U.S. in the heart of major cities. Suburbs are usually calm and they have fewer people than big cities. There are generally more problems in the center of cities.]

Response from Virginie:

Thank you for your letter and for having answered my question. In fact I didn't suspect that there was more violence in the center of American cities than in the suburb. It is the contrary here, in France, where violence stays a big problem although the government tries to fight against it. I think one of the causes of this violence is that the people who live in the suburb are generally poorer than the people who live in the center of cities because of the high price of the apartments there. For example the average price of a square meter in Paris was F 24,600 in 1991 and it was F 7,392 in Saint Denis (in the suburb). Maybe the people who live in the suburb find a way to express their anger to be poor and they reproach society for it. But it is a vicious circle, isn't it? I mean when you find shelter in violence, you become a delinquent and then you won't find a job and you will be excluded and you'll stay poor. Can you explain the reasons why violence is a bigger problem in the city centers than in the suburbs in America? What sort of people are delinquents?

Response from Andrew:

Virginie,

Comment ça va?

Je pense que tu as raison quand tu dis qu'il y a un rapport entre la violence et l'état d'etre pauvre. Les gens pauvres ne sont pas contents avec leurs vies quand ils voient que le reste des gens a plus d'argent et ils ont des vies moins dures. Mais la violence n'est pas une bonne réponse. Les gens pauvres ne réussissent pas à changer leurs vies. C'est vraiment un 'vicious circle.'

Aux Etats-Unis les gens qui habitent aux banlieues ont generalement assez d'argent. Et puis ils ne sont pas generalement d'un groupe qui est part de la minorite, je veux dire qu'ils sont principalement blancs. Au centre des villes principales les gens sont plus pauvres, la vie est plus dure, et il y a plus de problemes. Au passé, quand les villes étaient plus jeunes, les centres des villes étaient plus agréables et plus chic. Mais les villes ont changé. Les immigrants, quelqufois très pauvres, sont arrivés aux Etats-Unis et ils et les gens des Etats-Units qui étaient pauvres d'aborde ont commencé à habiter les centres des villes. Les gens plus riches ont quitté les centres des villes et maintenant ils habitent autour des centres des villes ou aux banlieues. Alors malheureusement, maintenant les villes sont divisées et generalement plus de gens qui ne sont pas blancs habitent au centre où il y a plus de violence et plus de problemes.

[Virginie, How are you? I think you're right when you say that there's a relationship between violence and the state of being poor. Poor people are not content with their lives when they see that everyone else has more money and easier lives. But violence is not a good answer. Poor people don't succeed in changing their lives. It's really a 'vicious circle.'

In the U.S. people who live in the suburbs are mostly well off. And they are generally not minority group members, that is to say, they are generally white. In the center of big cities people are poorer, life is harder, and there are more problems. In the past, city centers were nicer and more chic. But cities changed. Immigrants, sometimes very poor, arrived in the U.S. and they and the poor people who were already there began to live the city centers. The wealthier people left the city centers and now live around the city center or in the suburbs. So unfortunately, now cities are divided, and generally more people who are not white live in the center, where there is more violence and more problems.]

Response from Virginie:

Andrew,

How are you? Thank you very much for your letter. It is very strange, in my opinion, because in France most poor people live in the suburb and it is the opposite in the USA. For a long time, lots of poor people used to live in the center of Paris. (I take this example because it is the city I know the best). But after the reign of Napoleon and especially after the work of Haussmann, lots of rich houses were built and life in the center of Paris became too expensive, that's why the poor migrated to the suburbs, but they didn't go too far in order not to be too far from their job. Nowadays, one of the characteristics of suburbs is that immigrants live there. And these people do low paid jobs and are quite excluded. In fact racism exists in France and it is one of the causes of violence. Does racism exist in the USA too?

Letter exchanges, because they are dialogic in nature and therefore prime the reader's expectations, provide an extraordinarily motivating means of developing learners' reading comprehension—particularly at beginning levels, when learners' confidence in their ability tends to be low. Because they involve a 'real' audience, letter exchanges also motivate learners to write clearly and accurately. Witness, for example, the quality of Andrew's writing after only three months of studying French. What is interesting about this example is that the students themselves define the topic and the discourse that surrounds it. Instead of passively listening to a teacher lecture about differences between the French *banlieue* and American suburbs, students are able to experience the surprise of finding out that *la banlieue* and 'suburbs' can have very different connotations. This surprise motivates them to ask questions, to pay close attention to their peer's responses, to think through potential explanations, and tends to make their learning more memorable. The teacher would ideally develop this particular example further in class discussion by considering cultural conceptions of space in America and in France, and how they are played out differently in demographic patterns (for example, expansion into open territory versus centralization), but this teacher-led discussion would grow out of students' own initial inquiry and would therefore likely be perceived as immediately relevant to their interests.

The second example is from a second-year, intermediate-level French conversation class at Berkeley corresponding with another group of students from the Lycée Frédéric Mistral, in the spring of 1997. Both groups had recently viewed the French film *La Haine*, which depicts the experiences of three boys living in the housing projects of a Parisien suburb, and which touches on issues of racism, violence, gang culture, and the influence of American culture. The students' task was to discuss their impressions of the film with one another via e-mail. While space limitations preclude my presenting all of the messages that constitute the discussion, I have chosen several messages that reflect the overall tenor of the discussion. We will begin with a message from the Berkeley students, summarizing their questions:

A qui de droit:

   Je vous écrire de la part de la classe Français 13, instruire par Julie Sauvage, a UC Berkeley. Récemment, nous avons regardé le film <<Le Haine>> en classe. Le contenu de ce film nous a choqué car il y avait des images de France que nous ne voyons pas d'habitude ici aux Etats-Unis. Alors ce film était un peu deroutant pour nous. J'éspere que vous ou votre class peut nous aider avec notre confusion. Voici une liste de questions sur <<Le Haine>> que nous avons preparé:

1. *Est-ce qu'il y a des ressemblances entre la situation a la banlieue de Paris dans la film et la vraie situation?*
2. *Est-ce qu'il y a beaucoup de problems entre les jeunes français et la police?*
3. *Est-ce qu'il y a des émeutes à la banlieue de Paris?*
4. *Est-ce que la plupart de jeunes français déteste la police?*
5. *Est-ce que c'est difficile a obtenir un arme à feu en France?*
6. *Est-ce que c'est difficile a obtenir des drougues (comme marijuana) en France?*
7. *Pourquoi est-ce que vous pensez que les jeunes americains ignorent des problemes sociaux en France?*

8.   *Est-ce que vous pensez que la situation a la banlieue de Paris est en plus mauvais etat que les ghettos des Etats-Unis?*
En addition a repondre a nos questions, beaucoup des eleves dans notre classe veulent correspondre regulier. Répondez s'il vous plait!!!
~Nat Chadwick

[To Whom It May Concern:
     I am writing you on behalf of French 13, taught by Julie Sauvage, at UC Berkeley. Recently we saw the film <<La Haine>> in class. The content of this film shocked us since there were images of France that we don't normally see here in the U.S. So this film was a bit unsettling for us. I hope that you or your class can help us with our confusion. Here's a list of questions on <<La Haine>> that we've prepared:
1.   Are there similarities betweeen the situation in the suburbs of Paris in the film and the real situation?
2.   Are there many problems between young French people and the police?
3.   Are there riots in the suburbs of Paris?
4.   Do most young French people hate the police?
5.   Is it hard to obtain firearms in France?
6.   Is it hard to get drugs (like marijuana) in France?
7.   Why do you think that young Americans are not aware of social problems in France?
8.   Do you think the situation in the Paris suburbs is worse than in the ghettos of the U.S.?
In addition to answering our questions, many students in our class want to correspond on a regular basis. Please write back!!!]

Over the following three weeks numerous replies came from France. Among the first was from Sandrine, Delphine, and Sophie:

Dear Nat,
You shouldn't generalize, because there are three sorts of suburbs at least. For example Sandrine lives in a very good suburb, in which all is quiet; Sophie lives in an area where violence is rising and Delphine lives in a suburb where violence is widespread: a bookseller was killed without any reason four months ago. However the situation in France is certainly better than the situation in America. As a matter of fact, delinquents have more difficulty getting arms than in the USA. Moreover, areas resembling the American ghettos don't exist in France. If you go to France, you will never see an area like Harlem, where violence is great. We don't really know if we can get drug easily, so we can't give you much information about that. The police are present in areas where there are many Muslims, because, like in the USA, there are immigrants who find it hard to integrate into our society. And to assert themselves they turn to violence and sometimes to drug. But we think the police have much more problems than the young: these days, a lot of policemen have committed suicide. So we can confirm that the suburbs you saw in 'La Haine' are not like this in reality.
          Sandrine, Delphine and Sophie

Other students from France wrote that they thought the film was actually quite representative of life in the *banlieue*, but nevertheless still agreed that the situation in America was worse than in France, based on 'the impression we get through TV reports about the Bronx or LA'. Sabrina, Emilie, and Isabelle in fact proposed that American culture played a contributing role in France's problems: 'It's not a reproach, but we think that the American violence is one of the reasons which made violence develop in France.'

Although the French students believed that American films and television accurately represented 'the real American problems', French films were seen as slightly deceptive for all their artistry. As Marie, Severine, and Sebastien wrote, 'French films don't usually portray French society as it really is. We think we must imagine France as a country where you can eat well and visit the Eiffel tower or enjoy green landscapes.' France's penchant for comedies or historical period films, Céline and Stéphanie added, was probably why 'American teenagers don't know about the real situation in France.'

Nat and Eric, responding to Sandrine, Delphine, and Sophie's letter, wrote:

Chere Sandrine, Delphine, et Sophie,
   La premiere chose que vous ecrivez dans votre lettre etait: <<You shouldn't generalize>>, ou en francais, <<Vous ne devriez pas generaliser>>—ca, c'est incroyable. Innocemment, ma class de francais vous a posé des questions pour mieux comprendre la vérité de la situation à la banlieue francaise. Tout que nous recevions de vous etaient des reactions nationalistes! Vous ne disiez rien sauf des choses comme: <<The situation in France is certainly better than the situation in America>>, et, <<If you go to France, you will never see an area like Harlem where violence is great.>>
   Avez-vous visité Harlem? Pouvez-vous dire franchement que vous connaissez bien les problemes sociaux des Etats-Unis? Avez-vous habité a Harlem ou Brooklyn, ou 'the Bronx', ou Oakland, ou Richmond, ou Compton, ou Long Beach, ou ici a Berkeley? Comment est-ce que c'est possible que vous connaissez la situation des ghettos des Etats-Unis quand vous n'avez jamais habité ici? D'ou avez-vous obtenu votre information—Des films americains? Si je ne me trompe, vous etes coupable de faire des generalizations, pas nous. Et ca, c'est un peu hypocrite.
   En plus, Christelle, une autre etudiante qui nous a ecrit, a dit que <<La Haine>> etait d'aider les gens du monde a comprendre la realite de la banlieue de Paris. Alors, qui a raison?
—Nat et Eric

[Dear Sandrine, Delphine, et Sophie,
   The first thing you wrote in your letter was: <<You shouldn't generalize>>, or in French, <<Vous ne devriez pas generaliser>>—that is incredible. Innocently, my French class asked you some questions in order to better understand the truth of the situation in the French suburbs. All that we got back from you were nationalistic reactions! You didn't say anything except for things like: <<The situation in France is certainly better than the situation in America>>, and, <<If you go to France, you will never see an area like Harlem where violence is great.>>
   Have you visited Harlem? Can you frankly say that you know the U.S.'s social problems well? Have you lived in Harlem or Brooklyn, or 'the Bronx', or Oakland, or Richmond, or Compton, or Long Beach, or here in Berkeley? How is it possible that you know the situation of U.S. ghettos when you've never lived here? Where have you gotten your information—from american films? If I'm not mistaken, you are guilty of making generalizations, not us. And that is a little hypocritical.
   What's more, Christelle, another student who wrote us, said that <<La Haine>> was to help the people of the world to understand the reality of the Paris suburbs. So who's right?]

The confrontational tone of this message raises a number of questions. Is it constructive for students to be so verbally aggressive? Should the teacher intervene to avoid causing possible offense to the French students?

Electronic communication seems to foster bald, sometimes confrontational messages more than normal written correspondence—perhaps because of the rapidity of response or the perceived ephemeralness of the medium, or perhaps because of a perception that letter writing is more formal and e-mail is more conversational. In any event, students sometimes do need guidance in formulating appropriate messages. E-mail may obscure important sociocultural differences. As Rice (1996) has pointed out, for example, e-mail communication tends to level the perceived social status of participants (for example, messages to complete strangers are often written in a friendly, familiar register). This may raise problems in cross-cultural communication when one of the cultures emphasizes social distance more than the other. Furthermore, given the absence of paralinguistic and other contextual cues, learners may have difficulty determining where the other group draws the line between public and private topics, when it is appropriate to use a familiar register, and so on. This is an area where teachers can help learners to become sensitive readers and interpreters—not by directly controlling the interaction through editing students' messages, but rather by making students aware of the range of communicative options available to them, and helping them to anticipate the potential effects of each option.

Exchanges such as that between Sandrine, Delphine, and Sophie and Nat and Eric can serve to illustrate to students that the letters they write are real texts—open to others' interpretation and analysis—just like the 'official' texts they read in their classes. Students are certainly engaged in communication. But has the communication led to any new understanding?

In terms of the four curricular components discussed in Chapters 4 to 7, this e-mail exchange has so far involved *situated practice* but no *critical framing*. In neo-Vygotskian terms, there has been *interaction* between people with different points of view, but there has been no '*appropriation* of one view by the other, leading to cognitive change' (Newman, Griffin, and Cole 1989: 60). What is needed, at this point, is the creation of what Vygotsky called a 'zone of proximal development',[30] a dialogic space in which the processes of analysis and interpretation are modeled and co-constructed by the teacher and students together. The teacher's crucial task is to lead follow-up discussions, so that the chains of texts that students produce can be examined, interpreted, and possibly *re*-interpreted in the light of class discussion or subsequent responses from native speakers. How is each group representing its own culture and that of the other group? What are these representations based on? (for example, what is the basis for comments by either group about, say, Harlem or the Bronx?). Focusing on the communication itself, what is it about the particular content, organization, and phrasing of Nat's original letter that may have led the French students to react as they did? What is the implicit generalization that Sandrine, Delphine, and Sophie are referring to and how are its traces manifested in the language of Nat's letter? What are the specific elements of their reply that Nat and Eric find objectionable? Why can't one simply separate the ideas from the way they are expressed in words? How might the discourse of Nat's letter have constrained and shaped the writing of letters responding to it? What are some of the alternative expressive options each author might have chosen, and how might each of these alternative choices have affected the other group's reading? The point is to show students that what they 'intend' in their writing is in fact only one particular reading, and that their words may not be read the same way by people operating within different cultural contexts. Indeed, as it turned out, Delphine felt that she had been misinterpreted by Nat and Eric :

> Dear Nat and Eric.
> I want to answer your letter which surprised me. To my mind, you didn't understand what we wrote. Now, to answer your questions, I have never been to America and all what I know is taken from books and films. The films we see, show us a bad image of the States. In American films, we always see violent actions and in the books we see photos . . . . And to my mind, we are not 'hypocritical' like you wrote; we only wrote what we thought. I'm waiting for an answer from you to know what you think about my last letter.
>   Delphine.

By bringing native speakers into the act, getting them to engage in an ongoing dialogue with language learners about not only content, but also the particular ways in which that content is communicated and read, teachers can foster the development of learners' metacommunicative awareness, essential to their literacy in the foreign language.[31] An important point that this exchange brings to light, however, is that intercultural understanding is, in practice, difficult to achieve, and often has to pass through a phase of conflict, suspicion, and doubt, with each side clinging to its own cultural values. Contrary to the assumption that intercultural understanding is a simple function of cultural awareness, which emerges spontaneously from exposure to a given culture, we find here that exposure and awareness of difference seem to reinforce, rather than bridge, feelings of difference. Cultural intolerance must be acknowledged as a cultural fact and explored through discussion that frames opposing perspectives critically.

Logistic and pedagogical challenges

Like any use of technology, e-mail for language learning entails certain logistic and pedagogical challenges. First, finding a partner class that has access to the Internet can be a significant source of frustration. While this is becoming easier each year, it is still one of the major obstacles to incorporating e-mail into the curriculum, especially for the less commonly taught languages.[32] It is important to recognize, however, that exchanges with native speakers are not the only worthwhile e-mail projects. On the local level, electronic mail lists provide an excellent medium for out-of-class discussion of readings, films, or 'meta-discussions' of earlier face-to-face discussions (for example, Bernhardt and Kamil 1998). Collaborative projects can also be profitably pursued by pairs of foreign language classrooms across the country (for example, Barson 1991).

A second potential challenge, particularly acute for languages that use non-roman scripts, is the technical compatibility of computers on both the sending and receiving ends. Both sets of computers must often use the same software package and be specially configured in order to display the appropriate characters.

On the pedagogical side, one challenge is to make e-mail use interesting and worthwhile for students. The novelty of electronic pen pal exchanges can quickly fade, and without a teacher's guidance students sometimes lose interest after a few sets of messages. Projects such as investigating family histories (Kern 1996), studying water pollution in Brazil and California (Ullah, Sodrel, Maldonado, Callegaro, and Fredo 1998), and developing a collaborative newsletter in Guatemala and Wisconsin (Schmolze 1998), in which whole classes explore a content area together, tend to maintain student interest far more effectively than mere 'conversation' between individual pairs of students.[33] The second, and biggest, pedagogical challenge is going beyond 'situated practice' (i.e. communicative interaction) alone and incorporating 'critical framing' discussion (as mentioned above) or 'transformed practice' activities (such that learners transform what they have learnt from their e-mail exchange by applying their knowledge in a new context).

It is too early to know exactly what effects intercultural e-mail projects will have on student learning. While a number of descriptive accounts of projects have been published (for example, Lunde 1990; Avots 1991; Barson 1991; Soh and Soon 1991; Tella 1991; Rosenbusch 1992; Tella 1992a; Tella 1992b; Cononelos and Oliva 1993; Suozzo 1995; Warschauer 1995a; Kern 1996), there have not yet been any in-depth data-based investigations of what students actually learn in these projects. Nevertheless, a number of potential benefits of class e-mail exchanges seem apparent:

- *Contact with real people.* Rather than dealing only with abstract generalizations, learners can explore cultural differences within the framework of personal connections with real individuals.
- *Motivation.* Interaction with native speakers is motivating and fulfilling. It provides a real purpose for learning vocabulary and grammar, and fosters deep personal involvement with the language. The dialogic format of letter exchanges can facilitate learners' *prediction* of meaning because what one correspondent says and asks will create certain expectancies to be satisfied by the other correspondent's response.
- *Metacommunicative awareness.* With the teacher's help, students can analyze the course of an e-mail exchange, noting how particular messages were interpreted, the communicative effects of particular

phrasings, what questions were not responded to, how those silences might be interpreted, and so on.

– *Critical thinking.* By comparing what they learn through their e-mail exchanges with what they learn through teachers, textbooks, and other media, learners can evaluate information in a framework of multiple perspectives. For example, when American learners receive detailed personal accounts of life in twenty different French families, they can suddenly see the limitations of global generalizations in textbook portrayals of 'the French family.'

– *Better understanding of one's own culture.* Responding to questions about their lives and their world (and doing so in a way that makes sense to someone who does not necessarily share the same cultural background and values), forces learners to reflect and think critically about their ordinary experience in relation to the other group's reality.

These goals can be contrasted with those of traditional academic writing assignments, as shown in Table 8.3. E-mail exchanges complement, but in no way replace, the kinds of academic writing tasks that students must also learn to do (see Chapters 6 and 7). They can potentially broaden learners' communicative range, enhance motivation, and develop written fluency. Because e-mail is asynchronous, it also allows greater time for reflection than either synchronous conferencing or MOOs. As we saw in the e-mail exchange above, however, whatever critical reflection is achieved will be due primarily to the teacher's involvement and guidance, not to the nature of the e-mail environment itself.

Academic writing	Electronic mail
• Normally limited audience (teacher)	• Contact with real people outside the classroom
• Often limited communicative purpose (display of competence)	• Wide range of communicative purposes (informing, persuading, etc.)
• Tends to be perceived as relatively permanent and 'on record'	• Tends to be perceived as relatively ephemeral and disposable
• Intensive, recursive process that fosters elaboration and development of ideas	• Emphasis on speed and succintness of expression
• Adherence to formal norms (language, genre, style) generally plays more important role	• Adherence to formal norms tends to be relaxed (for example, mixing of oral/ written genres, grammar/spelling mistakes)

Table 8.3:   Comparison of features of written communication highlighted in academic writing and e-mail exchanges in foreign language classrooms

Conclusion

Over the past decade, we have witnessed a shift in perspective concerning the role and function of computers in language teaching. Whereas computers were first viewed as drill and test machines, well suited to improving learners' mastery of language forms, they are now often used as a medium for quick, casual communication, in which formal accuracy is of secondary importance. Originally intended for independent use outside of class, computers have increasingly been used *collaboratively* and *in* class. Once thought to be a means of replacing certain teacher functions, computers have proven to be of far greater pedagogical value when their use is thoughtfully structured and guided by teachers. In short, the current trend in the use of computers in language teaching is toward providing increased, rather than decreased, human contact. This humanization of technology is consistent with the humanistic goals of communicative language teaching, and has important consequences for literacy.

First, computer environments can foster the development of sociocognitive literacy in a number of ways. Worldwide networks allow learners to have ongoing contact with geographically-distant peers and to form learning communities that cross local and national boundaries. Although some have argued that computer networking will create a homogeneous global village in which differences in race, gender, religion, and nationality are made invisible and therefore neutralized, networked communications have so far tended, if anything, to accentuate the rich and fascinating diversity of human experience, rather than its commonality. The motivation that real interpersonal contact provides may lead learners to read more, to write more, and to think more about what they read and write.

Second, the process of negotiating meaning across linguistic and cultural boundaries exercises learners' communication skills and can enrich their knowledge of the other's culture. But it also provides a context in which learners can view their own culture from another group's perspective, potentially leading to better *self-understanding*.

Third, by altering traditional classroom discourse structures, electronic conferencing not only allow some learners greater opportunity to communicate but may also increase their awareness of those very classroom discourse conventions (and the power relations reflected in them) by providing an alternative set of conventions in which to operate. In this respect, local-area-networked discussions might provide an effective platform for critical pedagogy approaches. Furthermore, because learners' communication is written (and therefore recursive) it may facilitate reflection *during* communication as well as afterwards, therefore contributing to learners' metacommunicative awareness.

Fourth, because the World Wide Web brings together different modes of expression, representing information in text, images, or sound, it can introduce a new dimension to learners' literacy. Classroom analysis of Web documents can raise important questions of symbolic representation—how the choice of a particular medium may influence reception, the implications of combining media, and so on—and thereby broaden learners' textual competence. It seems a certainty that the ability to read and write in multimodal electronic environments will become an increasingly common literacy requirement in the workplace, as well as in classrooms. If this is the case, the language teacher's task is not simply to teach language via computers, but also to teach how to read, write, and communicate effectively in computer environments.

Media pundit Marshall McLuhan popularized the idea that we shape our technological tools and then they shape us. As language educators, we stand at a critical juncture. The increasing ubiquity of computers in educational institutions, as well as in society in general, will undoubtedly have profound effects on the ways we read, write, and communicate with other people. It is imperative that we attempt to understand the nature of new technologies in order to take a stand on which uses of technology will likely serve our goals and which will not. Our decisions should be based on thorough knowledge of our local setting and instructional needs, as well as on an understanding of the capabilities and limitations of the available technologies. Teachers, not technology, are the key to improved language learning and cultural understanding. Nevertheless, it can be hoped that technology will help us to achieve that end by opening up new and productive connections to other peoples and other worlds.

Notes

1 This chapter is an elaborated version of a previously published chapter (Kern 1998).

2 Selfe (1989) describes these layers of conventions as 'grammars' of computers.

3 See, for example, Hawisher and Selfe (1991) and Lanham (1993) on rhetorics of electronic writing.

4 Lanham (1993), for example, has argued that whereas traditional printed texts invite readers to look THROUGH them, to become immersed directly and unselfconsciously in the world of the text, electronic texts, by virtue of their malleability, temporarily destabilize the reading process, inviting readers to alternate their attention between the textual surface and the textworld—to engage in reading that moves constantly back and forth between looking AT a text and looking THROUGH it (p. 5).

5 For recent research on this shift in emphasis see (Beach and Lundell 1998; Garner and Gillingham 1998; Myers, Hammett, and McKillop 1998).

6 By extension, the term hyper*media* refers to the linking of text, sound, graphics, and video documents.

7 It is important to recognize, however, that hypertext does not, as it is often

claimed, turn reading into a 'nonlinear' process. Although readers may take alternate paths in their reading of a text's parts (as they often do with standard texts as well), the reading of a given chunk of text on the screen remains sequential and linear.

8 An anologue in the commercial world is the provision for individual readers to publish their own book reviews on booksellers' World Wide Web sites (see, for example, the feature 'Write an online review and share your thoughts with other readers!' within the *www.amazon.com* website).

9 It is important to acknowledge that undertaking a web design project requires extensive local technical support in terms of both material and personnel. On the material side, one must have access to a web server, access to a multimedia workstation, access to a range of multimedia software, as well as tape recorders, video cameras, and so forth. Of particular importance is the availability of knowledgeable technical support staff who can do HTML (Hypertext Markup Language) programming or train students to do it themselves. The 'Découvrir Berkeley' project could never have been implemented without the generous support of the Instructional Technology Program on the Berkeley campus.

10 The 'tricolore in the sky' idea was that of Jeff Rusch. 'Découvrir Berkeley' can be found at *http://www.itp.berkeley.edu/french*

11 For an in-depth profile of a class web-authoring project in a heritage language (Hawaiian) context, see Chapter 4 of Warschauer (1999).

12 Chun and Brandl (1992) point out that student-computer interactivity will be possible only when Artificial Intelligence with full parsing capability is available for computer-assisted language learning products.

13 On the negative side, this distance can also lead to inappropriate behavior ranging from 'flaming' (insulting messages) to silliness. The teacher's role is crucial in establishing clear ground rules for appropriate behavior in computer-mediated communication.

14 Examples of synchronous conferencing programs for local area networks are *Aspects*, *CommonSpace*, *InterChange* (part of the *Daedalus Integrated Writing Environment*), *Conference Writer*, and *Forum*. Synchronous conferencing is also available on wide area networks through chat software such as *Internet Relay Chat* or *TALK*, and virtual environments such as MOOs, which will be discussed later in this chapter.

15 Oral classroom discussion does not, of course, preclude the possibility of shifting the rules of discourse—in fact, a teacher's ability to lead effective discussions, always involves flexibility in opening/narrowing the floor, increasing/lessening guidance, and so on. What synchronous conferencing provides, however, is a discourse environment that, by virtue of the constraints it imposes, engenders rules of interaction that are difficult to achieve in oral classroom discussions, allowing discussions to be restructured in a way that seems 'natural' for both students and teachers.

16 In using the phrase 'readerly writing' I am not alluding to Roland Barthes' notion of 'readerly' and 'writerly' texts (Barthes 1970). What I am calling 'readerly writing' is writing that takes an anticipated reader's views, beliefs, preconceptions, and informational needs into account—in other words, producing a maximally understandable text for a particular envisioned reader. Barthes' use of 'readerly texts', on the other hand, refers to texts that place the reader in the relatively limited position of either accepting or rejecting them—texts that do not invite 'writing' on the part of the reader.

17 Chun (1994) reports that learners engaged in synchronous written discussion gave more feedback to one other, and exhibited a broader range of their sociolinguistic competence in greeting and leave taking, requesting confirmation or clarification, and apologizing, than in their oral classroom discourse.

18 Although relatively few studies have examined the effects of synchronous conferencing in language classroom settings, those that have indicate that students tend to be more voluble, to interact more with one another, and to be more candid in their comments than in oral, face-to-face discussions (Beauvois 1992; Kelm 1992; Kern 1995b; Warschauer 1996). A notable finding in these studies is the consistently high level of student motivation and the increased level of participation among the perennially 'silent' students in a class. The syntactic complexity of learners' language production, and the range of discourse functions used, also appear to be greater during synchronous conferencing sessions than in oral discussions (Chun 1994; Kern 1995b). Pellettieri (2000) shows that learners negotiate both meaning and linguistic form in conferencing sessions, but underlines the importance of the task-type in determining how much negotiation (and learning) takes place. Finally, two studies by Beauvois suggest that participation in written chat may improve low achieving students' attitude and motivation (1992) as well as their speaking ability (1998).

19 In her study of intermediate-level Spanish students, Pellettieri (2000) found that 'tasks that involve vocabulary beyond the repertoire of the learners, and that involve ideas, concepts, or items outside of their real-world expectations, can increase the quantity of negotiation produced' (p. 83).

20 The evaluation of synchronous conferencing for these purposes is an area in need of research. The only study I am aware of that looks at these issues in a foreign language context is Schultz (2000), who found that peer editing led to more content and style changes in advanced-intermediate French students' draft revisions when it *alternated* between synchronous conferencing and face-to-face formats than it did when either format was used exclusively.

21 'Room' is a somewhat misleading term, since players' personal locales may be a garden, a mountain top, a swimming pool, or any other environment they can imagine.

22 Telnet addresses for these MOOs are as follows:

schMOOze University (EFL/ESL):	schmooze.hunter.cuny.edu 8888
Le MOO Français (French):	moo.syr.edu 7777
MundoHispano (Spanish)	europa.syr.edu 8888
ArdaMOO (Spanish)	telnet lince.las.es 7777
MOOsaico (Portuguese):	moo.di.uminho.pt 7777
MorgenGrauen (German):	mud.uni-muenster.de 23
UNItopia (German):	infosgi.rus.uni-stuttgart.de:3333
Little Italy (Italian):	little.usr.dsi.unimi.it 4444
SvenskMUD (Swedish):	svmud.lysator.liu.se 2043
Virtual Classrooms MUSH	risky1.ssg.comp.uvic.ca 6250

A most useful starting point for exploring MOOs is the following World Wide Web address, where one can find orientation information, a list of common commands, and direct access to over twenty different MOOs and associated World Wide Web sites:
http://www.itp.berkeley.edu/~thorne/MOO.html

23 One can connect to MOOs via Telnet. For MOOs that allow guests, type *connect guest* at the login prompt, and follow the instructions. For MOOs that require a permanent character, follow online instructions in the MOO introduction. Basic MOO commands are as follows:

@who	find the location of others on the MOO
@knock [name]	knock on [name]'s door to see if you may enter
@join [name]	join another player in a room
look here	read description of the room you are in
look me	read description of yourself
look [name]	read description of other player
say [message]	say something to other players in room
@quit	log out

24 I am grateful to Maggie Sokolik for this example from her ESL class in 1994.

25 As one example of how a MOO interchange might be used in conjunction with the reading of a literary text, after reading a novel, students can take on roles of particular characters and interact online in improvised encounters on the MOO. Although this is often done as a face-to-face oral activity, the fact that students get a printed transcript of their role play allows them to go back to examine and reflect on their interaction, to compare the particulars of their discourse with that of the 'real' characters in the novel, and to analyze the specific ways in which their discourse might reflect similar and different representations of the

characters (keeping in mind the 'foreign' cultural context in which they have read and interpreted the novel).

26 Although e-mail exchanges are relatively recent in language teaching, global community learning projects are of course not new. They are part of a long tradition of classroom partnerships, perhaps best exemplified by Célestin Freinet's *Mouvement de l'Ecole Moderne* (Modern School Movement), established in Europe in the 1920s. Freinet, a French school teacher in Bar-sur-Loup (Provence), initiated an exchange of student writing and 'cultural packages' (consisting of local artifacts, flowers, fruits, fossils, post cards, photos, figurines, and so forth) with a partner class in Brittany (Freinet 1981: 39). This first interschool exchange led to other school partnerships, and gradually the Modern School Movement grew to include some 10,000 schools around the world (Cummins and Sayers 1995: 126). Freinet's collaborative pedagogy, based on social interaction and community engagement, also encouraged reflection on learning and practice. The feedback from learners and teachers at other sites allowed learners to consider different perspectives on common questions, problems, and issues.

27 The cost of e-mail transmission is low. The cost of computer equipment is, of course, significant. This brings us back to the important issue of differences in access to technology alluded to at the beginning of the chapter. While some institutions enjoy well-equipped and well-supported computer labs, many others are hard-pressed to make any computers available to students and faculty. Such inequities are not easily resolved, but their resolution certainly begins with the consolidated and persistent efforts of teachers to inform administrators of their needs for adequate computing facilities and support.

28 See Kern (1995a) for background on this project and examples from a second-semester class.

29 The e-mail messages presented here are written in each participant's foreign language. The two teachers who organized this exchange decided this arrangement would be the most fair and advantageous to both groups of students. The downside of this decision, of course, is that students do not receive 'input' in the target language.

30 Vygotsky's idea of a 'zone of proximal development' refers to the 'distance between the actual developmental level as determined by independent problem solving and the level of potential development as determined through problem solving under adult guidance or in collaboration with more capable peers' (Vygotsky 1978: 86). While Vygotsky specifies that one's peers should be 'more capable,' Forman and Cazden (1985) contend that collaboration with equally skilled peers can be very beneficial, particularly when they take on complementary roles.

31 Many teachers are justifiably concerned that their students cannot discuss such issues in the target language. It may be that at beginning

levels, a 'text lab' could be established outside of the regular class meeting times (for those programs that use only the target language in beginning language instruction). Students would start by discussing texts in their native language. The teacher would provide vocabulary and structures as needed to facilitate the gradual transition to greater use of the second language in these discussions.

Nor is the particular language that students use to write their e-mail messages necessarily a critical issue. For beginning students, use of their native language will allow them to deal with much more sophisticated cultural issues than would otherwise be possible. What is important is close attention to the details of language use in the texts they receive and create, and consideration of how those details contribute to reader interpretations, in whichever language the messages are written. It is important that even beginning learners, who lack the linguistic wherewithal to cope with elaborate discussion in another language, be able to participate in this kind of project, for they will learn a great deal about the other culture (as well as about their own) while they are learning the rudiments of the language.

32 Below are a number of resources for finding partners for e-mail exchanges.

To find partner classes (not individual pen pals), consult the following resources:
- IECC (Intercultural E-Mail Classroom Connections), a collection of related lists serving over 7,650 teachers from more than 82 countries. See their web site at *http://www.Iecc.org*
- eMail Classroom Exchange (*http://www.iglou.com/xchange/ece/index.html*), a website designed to facilitate finding partner classrooms for e-mail exchanges at primary and secondary education levels.
- Orillas (*http://dune.srhs.k12.nj.us/WWW/IDEAL/html/orillas.html*), an international clearinghouse for promoting long-distance collaborative teaching partnerships. Using e-mail and computer-based networking, paired classes can develop international and cross-cultural projects such as dual community surveys, contrastive geography projects, and comparative oral history and folklore studies.
- The International Writing Exchange project (*http://www.hut.fi/~rvilmi/Summer98/iwe.html*), organized by Ruth Vilmi of the Helsinki University of Technology, has brought together classes from various countries. Teachers can obtain information on finding partner classrooms at the web site.
For individual pen pals, consult the following resources:
- The E-mail Key Pal Connection (*http://www.comenius.com*) for native English speakers and ESL/EFL learners worldwide.
- The International E-Mail Tandem Network (*http://www.enst.fr/tandem/*), funded by the Commission of the European Union, is

made up of a number of bilingual 'subnets,' in which language learners from different language backgrounds work together to help each other learn. Each subnet includes at least one bilingual discussion forum as well as a database, which allows learners to access teaching and learning materials and publish their own documents. Languages represented at the time of this writing include: Danish, Dutch, English, French, German, Italian, Polish, Portuguese, Russian, Spanish.

– The Europa Pages Web Site (*http://www.europa-pages.co.uk/index. html*), which has a section 'International Pen Friends' designed to help individuals find native speaker pen pals in a foreign language.

– The Web of Culture Web Site (*http://www.worldculture.com/contact. htm*) has an international list of individuals seeking pen pals. As in the case of the Europa Site, it is very easy to add one's own name to the list of people seeking contacts.

– Dave's ESL Email Connection (*http://www.pacificnet.net/~sperling/ guestbook.html* for teachers; (*http://www.pacificnet.net/~sperling/ student.html* for students).

– The Penpal-L list. Subscribe to penpal-l@unccvm.unc.edu by sending a one line message: 'subscribe penpal-l [your name]' to LISTSERV@ unccvm.unc.edu.

For further ideas, as well as general information on using e-mail in language teaching, see Warschauer (1995a). For a list of network-based language learning project descriptions, see Warschauer (1995b).

33 For more on paired classroom projects, particularly at the elementary and secondary level, see Harasim, Hiltz, Teles, and Turoff (1995); Hart (1987); and Levin, Kim, and Riel (1990).

9 Evaluating learners' performance

The susceptibility of language to precise measurement seems to be in direct proportion to its fragmentation . . . .

Daniel Horowitz (1991)

Ultimately the vexed question arises: how are we to evaluate what students have learnt and what they are able to do? This question is significant, for our response to it will influence what students perceive to be important about learning a language. In the educational settings with which I am most familiar (universities in the United States), what 'counts' in a language course is what contributes directly to a grade. What is evaluated constitutes the *de facto* curriculum, and how it is evaluated reflects the *de facto* philosophy of learning and teaching, regardless of what the teacher or course description says. Thus reading tests that only measure recall of factual content in effect define reading as a factual recall task. Grading essays on the basis of the number of grammar errors sends a message that producing error-free sentences is what foreign language writing is all about.

Over the last fifty years, while language teaching goals have expanded from instilling automatic, accurate speech patterns to developing broad communicative abilities, language assessment practices have struggled to keep pace. Tests generally constitute the primary form of assessment, and in many academic programs language tests have tended to remain focused on discrete grammar forms and isolated language skills (Magnan 1991). The development of 'proficiency testing' in North America in the 1980s, best represented by the Oral Proficiency Interview (Buck, Byrnes, and Thompson 1990), was an impressive move toward performance-based assessment of learners' ability to use language to accomplish a variety of communicative functions, but it did not go far enough. The grammar-structure checklists of traditional tests had been expanded to include functions and contexts, but still surprisingly little emphasis was placed on meaning.[1]

Before proceeding further, a brief explanation of terms is in order. Following Strickland and Strickland (1998), I will make a distinction among assessment, evaluation, and grading. Assessment, as used here, is the process of collecting and measuring information relevant to student learning and performance. Evaluation is a subsequent phase of analyzing, interpreting, and judging the results of assessment. Evaluation need not be a subjective opinion based on a vague instinctive feeling. Ideally it is interpretation that is solidly grounded in the 'text' of a student's performance. Finally, grading is a way of reporting the results of *either* assessment or evaluation with numbers, letters, or percentages.[2] Grading is not the only reporting option, however, and written comments or reports are common alternatives.

In literacy-based teaching, we are certainly interested in assessing students' knowledge of syntax and vocabulary as well as their ability to use language to fulfill particular communicative functions. But we are interested in these things within the larger context of evaluating how learners create and interpret meanings—drawing not just on their language skills but also on the full breadth of their experience and knowledge. We are interested in learners' ability to articulate analyses of texts and contexts, and the new understandings generated by those analyses. We are interested in their ability to reflect on relationships between form and function, between locutionary expression and illocutionary force, between language and culture. In short, we are interested in evaluating learners' ability to use language as a tool of creative and critical thought.

Educators must also recognize, of course, that they themselves are using these exact same abilities when they assess and evaluate students' performance. Interpretation is not only the object but also the means of assessment and evaluation.

The interpretive nature of assessment and evaluation

Educational assessment and evaluation are *interpretative* endeavors, not purely objective science. And the interpretive dimension extends to all phases of the assessment/evaluation/reporting process. Testing, for example, involves interpretation on the part of test-designers, test-takers, test-scorers, and test-users alike.

Reading tests, in particular, involve complex interactions among multiple readers, writers, and texts. Spolsky (1994) has shown how reading tests involve multiple layers of interpretation and introduce multiple reader/writer roles. As shown in Figure 9.1, what we are ultimately interested in when we test reading—a student's interpretation of an author's text—is deeply embedded within a cascading series of interactions among four writers, four texts, and three readers.

The real-life outcome of the test, whatever it might be, is thus based on an interpretation of an interpretation of an interpretation of a text, with some degree of error introduced at each stage. The task designed by the test creator (text 2) is particularly influential on the test outcome. Text 2 normally reflects the test designer's own interpretation within the range of possible readings of text 1, as well as his or her interpretation of how text 1 relates to learning and assessment goals.[3] As Devine (1987) has pointed out, however, the student

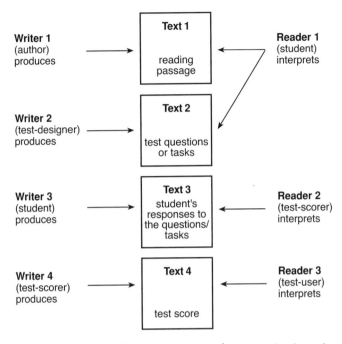

Figure 9.1:   Four levels of writer-text-reader interaction in testing (based on Spolsky 1994)

may well have different, and possibly better, ideas about text 1 than the test designer did. The more the test designer's operational interpretation of text 1 differs from the student's interpretation of text 1, the less likely it is that the test score will accurately reflect the student's understanding of the original text.[4] As Spolsky puts it, the basic problem is that text 4, the test score, 'attempts to squeeze too much information into itself' (1994: 148).

Spolsky offers no simple solution to this problem, but stresses the importance of setting 'very precise contextual constraints on the task' (1994: 151) so that explicit statements can be made about what precisely the test attempts to test in order to prevent the interpretation of the learner's test performance from being overgeneralized.

Spolsky's point brings us to the important concerns of validity and reliability. Validity has to do with the degree to which a form of assessment does what it is meant to do, such as measure learners' reading comprehension or writing ability. An assessment measure is said to be valid when learners' assessed performance can be accurately generalized to their performance in other (non-assessment) contexts. But Spolsky's model reminds us that the problem extends beyond the assessment measure itself to the *interpretations* of assessment results (i.e. evaluation).[5] Reliability, on the other hand, has to do with the degree to which the assessment of learners' ability is affected by measurement error—that is, the degree to which the measurement varies because of factors *other than* the particular ability being assessed. Thus, how students feel on the day of the test, how they react to the content matter of the test, how tasks are worded, how long the test is, and how much time is allowed can all affect reliability. One of the most important factors contributing to reliability is consistency of scoring within and among individual raters—and this is where Spolsky's model is again useful, because consistency of scoring is based on some *interpretation* of what an 'acceptable' response is.

The relationship between validity and reliability is one of dynamic tension. In order for a test to be valid it must be reliable, but this is a question of degree. The more valid a measure is, the less reliable it tends to be, and the greater the reliability of a measure, the less valid it tends to be. Traditional essay tests tend to have high validity but low reliability, whereas 'objective' discrete-point tests are highly reliable but tend to be less valid. As Bachman points out, however, the reliability/validity distinction is ultimately a function of perspective:

> A writing test that is scored largely on the accuracy and completeness of the content . . . might be an unreliable and hence invalid measure of writing ability, but a valid measure of the test taker's knowledge of a given subject matter. The recognition of this ambiguity, this lack of a clear-cut distinction between reliability and validity for all times and places, leads to a better understanding and appreciation of the fact that the way we interpret language test scores depends upon the uses for which the test is intended.
> (Bachman 1990: 227)

Once again, we see that interpretation lies at the heart of the assessment/evaluation process.

Three desiderata for literacy-based assessment and evaluation

In thinking about how to evaluate learners' language and literacy abilities in the light of this and earlier discussion, three key points come to mind. In order to be valid and meaningful, assessment and evaluation must be (1) based on a broad view of language and literacy, (2) multidimensional in nature, (3) highly integrated with teaching and learning. Let us briefly consider each of these points in turn.

1 *Assessment and evaluation must be based on a broad view of language and literacy.*

As we saw in Chapter 2, language is not just a conduit for the transmission of pre-existing meanings. As a corollary, communication and literacy are not simply a matter of decoding linguistic texts. Rather, communication and literacy have to do with the complex process of realizing texts as discourse, which involves the application of sociocultural as well as linguistic knowledge in particular contexts of use.

Our first step in assessing and evaluating language and literacy, then, is to consider ways to broaden the goals of evaluation beyond learners' language knowledge *per se*, to include cognitive, cultural, and social goals as well. The seven principles outlined in Chapter 1 can help us to identify the scope of our task in evaluating learners' performance in a literacy-focused language program. Put briefly, we are concerned with evaluating learners' ability to use language, literacy conventions, and cultural knowledge thoughtfully in communicative acts. By 'thoughtfully' I mean two things. First, I mean it in a cognitive sense, referring to thinking, interpreting, solving problems, as well as reflecting on these processes. Second, I mean 'thoughtfully' in a more social sense of being considerate and respectful of others—of taking social responsibility for one's use of language across lines of cultural difference (Brown 1991).

In moving toward evaluation that includes cognitive and social dimensions, the notion of *context* becomes extraordinarily important. Because communicative ability and literacy are relative, context-dependent constructs, we must pay close attention to the particular tasks, purposes, and settings that are operative when we assess and evaluate learners' performance. Just as an in-class essay will not capture all that is involved in using written language, so an interview will not be suited to assess many aspects of a learner's spoken language ability. Moreover, communication events such as 'reading a story', 'writing a letter', 'having a conversation' all take on particular requirements when they are performed in the context of a *test*. How learners interpret the task, what criteria they think the tester is looking for, how they perceive their role and the role of the tester, will have a significant impact on how they approach the task, and ultimately on their performance. Consequently, it is important that assessment not be limited to tests, but that it include samples from a broad variety of language and literacy activities that learners are involved in during the course of their study.

2 Assessment and evaluation must be multidimensional in nature.

'The fundamental flaw of objective modern language testing', Spolsky writes, 'has been to presuppose that language proficiency is measurable and unidimensional, in the sense that the speed of a runner or the weight of a shot-put is measurable on a single defined dimension' (1995: 357–8). Extending the Olympic sports analogy, Spolsky notes that while certain events such as races, shotput, or weightlifting are timed or measured with objective precision, other events, such as diving, skating, or gymnastics are judged subjectively by a panel of judges. Should language proficiency be measured or judged? Spolsky's argument is that different aspects of language proficiency lend themselves to different approaches to assessment and evaluation. When one looks at literacy, for example, certain dimensions such as visual recognition, text recall, spelling and writing mechanics lend themselves more to discrete-point measurement, whereas interpretation, inference, analysis, and synthesis are all more easily judged than measured. The complexity goes even farther when one realizes that what one is evaluating is often not overt, but must be inferred.

As was suggested at the beginning of the chapter, however, judgment need not be seen as divorced from measurement. Rather, they can be parts of an integrated system, such that the standards of measurement can be usefully applied to judgment and the richness of judgment can enhance measurement. We will see how this integration can be operationalized in the case of performance-based reading and writing tests later in this chapter.

Because language and literacy are multifaceted, our approach to assessment and evaluation must also be multifaceted. Just as we aim for multiple perspectives on texts in the classroom, we must aim for multiple perspectives on our students' performance. In order to produce a composite profile of students' abilities, we need to have a range of multiple and varied indices of performance whose patterns we can analyze and interpret.

In reading, for example, assessment limited to performance on a single reading passage cannot lead to a valid, generalizable evaluation of learners' reading ability. As Bernhardt and Kamil (1995) have argued, what is needed is an aggregate measure involving analysis of a student's reading across a variety of contexts—reading texts that vary in genre, content, length, and linguistic difficulty; reading texts that are assigned versus texts of the student's choice; reading texts for different purposes. Similarly, in writing, assessment must involve multiple writing samples of different types, on different topics, for different purposes, and in different settings (for example, writing done out of class as well as in-class timed writing).

As a continuous undertaking, rather than a 'one-shot' affair, assessment and evaluation should attend as much as possible to process as well as to product, and ideally attempt to interpret product *in terms of* process. This is where students' journals and their reflection reports on their reading (see Chapters 5 and 7) can be particularly useful.

Finally, in assessing communication and literacy we need to look not only at what learners can do in solo performance but also at what they can do in collaboration with others—such as peers, teachers, or other speakers of the language. From a Vygotskian perspective this means we need to look at the top as well as the bottom of learners' 'zone of proximal development' (i.e. look at what they are capable of doing with the assistance of a more experienced individual or their peers as well as what they are capable of doing alone).[6] It is therefore important to establish a variety of learning and assessment contexts—some individual, some collaborative—in order to observe the full range of students' abilities.

3 Assessment and evaluation cannot be divorced from teaching and learning.

As Shohamy (1990) and others have been at pains to point out, assessment and evaluation should not only be consistent with the particular teaching approach but it should also contribute to teaching and learning (sometimes called a 'washback' effect). In other words, as well as being meaning-oriented, assessment and evaluation should be pedagogically-oriented.

Here it is important to make a distinction between *formative* and *summative* evaluation. Formative evaluation is process-oriented. Its goal is to provide ongoing feedback during a process so that the process can be improved. Comments and suggestions for improving an essay draft, or diagnostic grammar quizzes, or 'think-aloud' reading interviews are just a few examples of formative assessment activities that can help teachers and students to identify those aspects of learning that are going well as well as those where extra attention may be needed. Summative evaluation, on the other hand, does not lead to instructional modification but simply states students' measured performance or achievement at the end of an instructional unit, a course, or a program. How learners perform on a final exam or a standardized test, for example, does not generally lead to adjustments in instruction. The difference between formative and summative assessment/evaluation is thus analogous to the difference between a thermostat and a thermometer. Both measure temperature, but the thermostat is designed to trigger either a heater or an air conditioner when certain temperatures are reached, whereas the thermometer is designed simply to display the temperature.

In foreign language education, classroom-based assessment and evaluation have traditionally been predominantly summative in nature. In literacy-based language teaching, it is essential that formative evaluation also play an integral role. Shohamy (1990) recommends that teachers make greater use of observations, interviews, questionnaires, portfolios, and project materials in order to 'obtain a broader and more extensive picture of the language of the students' (p. 389) as well as to provide diagnostic information which can be discussed in student-teacher conferences. Traditional form-based exercises, quizzes, and tests also clearly have their place, but the ideal in a literacy-based program is to emphasize their use as formative rather than summative measures. One option is to correct but not grade students' form-focused work, providing students feedback without penalizing them for errors.[7] The problem with this option is that it can reduce certain students' motivation to study the material as well as their sense of achievement. With such students in mind, a more viable option might be to grade grammar exercises, quizzes, and tests, but to weight the grades lightly compared to students' more skill-integrative work such as their writings, project materials, and portfolios. In this way teachers can take advantage of the motivating value of grades while still emphasizing the principally diagnostic role of exercises, quizzes, and tests. Another option, which lends itself particularly well to composition work, is to respond in detail to the first several assigned essays in a course but not grade them, so as to give students a clear idea of what is expected before they submit subsequent essays for grades.

Assessment and evaluation can be further integrated into teaching and learning when students play an active role in the evaluation process. Portfolio analyses, to be discussed later in this chapter, are perhaps the most obvious case of student involvement, but other options exist as well. For example, in oral exams, students can establish their own groups and topics, which they discuss with or without the teacher's participation. In reading and writing, students can be taught to reflect on their own thought processes and behavior and to write up these reflections as part of major reading and writing assignments. These 'inside stories' can be extremely illuminating to the teacher and can contribute significantly to a comprehensive portrait of students' performance. For the students, the articulation of such reflections encourages greater self-awareness and understanding of their own strengths and weakness—key factors in developing their ability to direct their own learning and to seek help from others.

When assessment activities are also viewed as teaching and learning activities, the notion of 'teaching to the test' is seen in a new light. Traditionally viewed as a problem either of 'giving away the answers' or of excessively restricting the scope of teaching activities, 'teaching to the test' can in fact be desirable—as long as the test is a good one (Oller 1991). The problem with teaching to the test comes when the test is not consistent with one's instructional goals. Because teachers will tend to teach to the test if the stakes of the test are perceived to be high enough (Madaus 1988), it is essential that high-stake tests reflect the real goals of instruction and encourage thinking rather than simply language skill mastery.

Rethinking the assessment and evaluation of reading and writing

So far we have seen that when creativity, interpretation, and critical thinking are concerned, learners' language performance has tended to be judged subjectively and globally. It is perhaps not surprising, then, that learners' performance in these areas tends to be neglected in large-scale assessment efforts that focus on the most reliably measured aspects of language performance. In order to address the full range of abilities involved in literacy we must find ways to integrate thoughtful evaluation with reliable assessment techniques so as to strike an appropriate balance of validity and reliability. In the following sections we will consider a number of ways in which learners' capacity to use language thoughtfully, creatively, and critically might be reliably assessed and evaluated.

Assessing and evaluating reading

In the literacy framework discussed in this book, reading is much more than deciphering texts. It is a multidimensional process that requires a multidimensional approach to teaching and testing. We are not just concerned with learners' verbatim reproduction of information (for example, their 'proposition recall') but also (and primarily) with their understanding of the pragmatic implications of the ways that informational content is presented. What is important, in other words, is *interpretation*, getting at the communicative value of texts.

Despite the emphasis on the importance of 'the reader' in recent years, many reading tests still operate on the principle that meaning is text-immanent, and that the reader's job is to find the same meanings that the test designer found.

The problem with testing comprehension via discrete-point, 'right/wrong' item types is that they test only whether students are able to think what we want or expect them to think (i.e. what we ourselves have thought), and they do not lead to an accurate assessment of what students really are thinking as they read. In fact, 'forced choice' item types such as true/false and multiple choice usually produce the most problems among the *best* readers, who invariably find some logical flaw or are confused by the only partial adequacy of the possible answers provided.

On the other hand, a caveat needs to be mentioned about holistic testing as well. Testing reading involves a good deal more than testing only 'global comprehension' in the sense of gist or main idea. During the 1980s, when cognitive psychologists were talking about the importance of 'top-down' (expectation-driven) processing, second language educators often promoted broad holistic comprehension measures over those that focused on the linguistic 'facts' of texts. This imbalance sometimes had unfortunate consequences by lowering expectations and standards. What is needed are assessment measures that maintain a balance of top-down and bottom-up aspects of the reading process, so that some latitude is given for variation in learners' interpretations, but also so that students are held accountable to the text itself.

Assessing and evaluating reading in a literacy-focused program requires more than checking students' ability to arrive at a normative comprehension product. It involves paying attention to the processes by which learners design meaning. That is to say, we are interested in finding out about the particular ways that learners (1) make connections among textual elements, and (2) interpret those connections in terms of their own knowledge, attitudes, and beliefs.

Reading tests should, then, do the following things:

1 *Assess readers' understanding of pragmatic implications (i.e.
   illocutionary force) as well as informational content*

This involves assessing their ability to perceive meaning relationships across
sentences, to identify textual organization, to make inferences, and to apply
their understanding to their own experience.

2 *Provide opportunities for students to link comprehension to production*

Integration of writing into the assessment of reading is of key importance
because it promotes active design of meaning and permits concrete
representation of interpretive processes. This is a controversial point since it
is sometimes seen as undesirable to confound skills in testing situations (i.e. if
you use writing to test reading then you are not getting a 'pure' assessment of
the student's reading ability). But in a literacy framework in which reading
and writing are seen as tightly interwoven, complementary processes of
meaning design, such confounding is less problematic. Therefore, while it is
fully justifiable to include sections that attempt to isolate reading
comprehension by not involving language production, it is also justifiable
(and I would argue more ecologically valid) to include test sections that
require writing.[8]

3 *Allow for individual differences in responses*

Continuing along the lines of point 2 above, reading tests should involve
individual, meaningful expression. The point is not just students' ability to
think what the teacher or tester has thought about a text, but what the
student himself or herself thinks. What is crucial, however, is that learners be
able to justify and support their interpretations by citing specific textual facts.

   What kinds of assessment techniques will allow learners to express their
own understanding of a text they have read? That is, how can we minimize
the constraints imposed by Spolsky's 'text 2' in order to allow students to
maximally apply their own knowledge and experience to the interpretation
of a text? Below I will revisit several of the teaching activities presented in
Chapter 5 to show how they might also serve as assessment techniques. I will
then propose one kind of heuristic test that can assess multiple aspects of
reading (i.e. process as well as product) and serve both diagnostic and
evaluative purposes.

Adapting reading activities for assessment

Wesche (1983) offers a useful framework for analyzing communicative tests.
She posits four components: (1) stimulus material (for example, a text), (2) a
task posed to the learner, (3) the learner's response, and (4) scoring criteria.
Within Wesche's framework, what distinguishes teaching activities (for

example, the kinds of reading activities discussed in Chapter 5) from reading assessment tools is the absence of the fourth component—scoring criteria. In order to adapt instructional activities for assessment use, then, our principle task is to develop a scheme for grading students' performance.

Let's consider the first activity presented in Chapter 5, the Directed Reading-Thinking Activity. The DRTA can be done in writing (to assess the individual working alone—i.e. looking at the 'bottom' of Vygotsky's zone of proximal development) or orally in small groups of learners (for a collaborative context, i.e. looking at the upper reaches of a learner's zone of proximal development).[9] In either case, there are three basic performance goals with which we are concerned: a learner's ability (1) to generate hypotheses, (2) to support hypotheses with data from the text being read, and (3) to adjust established hypotheses that are contradicted by textual information. The first two goals are universal for any DRTA; the third goal is contingent on the learner having previously established a hypothesis inconsistent with textual information, and therefore may not always apply.

Given these criteria, the student's written or oral performance on a DRTA can be analyzed by the teacher, who writes up descriptive feedback on the performance, noting both strengths and weaknesses in terms of the three performance goals. This analysis can then be used in at least two ways. First, and ideally, the report can be a contribution to a reading portfolio (see the section on portfolio analysis later in this chapter). Second, if a score or grade is needed, the student's performance can be measured on a three-point scale for each of the two 'universal' performance goals. A score of 3 would represent clearly demonstrated ability to generate reading hypotheses with the particular text in question. A score of 2 would indicate some ability to generate hypotheses, but also some inconsistency of response. A score of 1 would indicate minimal hypothesizing based on the text in question. A similar procedure could be followed for the second performance goal (for example, 3 = consistently able to demonstrate textual support for hypotheses; 2 = sometimes, but not always, able to demonstrate textual support; 1 = seldom able to demonstrate textual support). Combining these scores would yield a rudimentary five-point grade scale, for example, 6 = excellent, 5 = good, 4 = fair, and 3 or 2 = no pass. In any event, because learners will read different texts differently, it is essential to include a *series* of DRTA-assessments over a period of time, using a variety of texts. This allows learners the chance to improve performance and not to be penalized if a particular text is too difficult. Repeated administration is also important in that it extends the total score range beyond the overly limited five-point range.

Similar development of scoring criteria could be applied to other pedagogical techniques described in Chapter 5, such as the dialogic transformation of texts (à la Thomas's 'stigmergy' passage), reading journals (which lend themselves particularly well to reading portfolios), mapping ideas of a text, paraphrasing and summarizing texts, and translation exercises. In the following section we will see how a series of reading activities can be integrated in a reading test.

Heuristic tests: guiding the reading process

The heuristic reading activity sequence presented at the end of Chapter 5 provides a model for *testing* as well as teaching. The goal of a heuristic reading test is to lead the student to focus on both form and meaning at various levels. The basic organizational scheme is to start with students' global sense of a text, then to delve more deeply into the textual details, and finally to return to a more refined global understanding of the text. The six-step sequence below, demonstrated with Cisneros's *The House on Mango Street*, is sufficiently general to serve as a framework for either a written test situation or a one-on-one 'think aloud' reading assessment interview (to be described later). I should emphasize that the scoring scales are offered as examples of the *kinds* of scales that teachers might want to explore; teachers will certainly need to adapt these ideas as they apply them in their own teaching contexts.

Whatever scoring system is used, it is important that teachers using a particular test establish clear scoring criteria in line with assessment goals. For example, if a teacher takes off a large number of points for grammar mistakes in a student's written summary of a text, which is nevertheless fully adequate in terms of its content, the grade will not accurately reflect the student's comprehension, as it was intended to do, but rather his grammar usage. Designing test items is therefore only part of the tester's task; it is essential that those using the test have an appropriate understanding of how students' responses are to be interpreted *vis-à-vis* the particular objectives of the test situation. That is to say, in terms of Spolsky's framework, there must be a common agreement on goals between Writer 2 (the test designer) and Reader 3 (the test-user). Of course, Reader 1 (the test taker) must also have a clear understanding of the rubrics or evaluative criteria being used if the results are to be valid.

1 Linking form and intent

Students can begin by writing answers to global questions that link form and communicative intent. Here, we are interested in readers' ability to get an initial sense of the genre, style, and content of a text and to generate expectations about the purpose of the writing. Using *The House on Mango Street* as an example, students could be given the following questions:

> Scan the text and answer the following questions:
> 1 What kind of text do you think this is—a personal diary? a story? a report? What specific things in the text make you think so?
> 2 What do you think this text will be about? Why?
> 3 What do you think the writer's purpose might be?

In the first question we are interested less in students' genre label than in their reasons for choosing it. One option for scoring is to use a simple 3-point scale (3 = good match between genre and text features cited; 2 = partial match; 1 = poor match). In the second question we are again interested in the consistency between the answer and the given reasons, so the same scoring rubric can be used. The third question is more open-ended and is intended principally to prepare the student for closer reading. Nevertheless, the answer can be scored in terms of its consistency with answers given to questions 1 and 2 (for example, 3 = good consistency; 2 = partial consistency; 1 = poor consistency). Of course, if a question is not answered at all it is scored '0'.

2 Linking language to content

The next step is to establish the 'facts' of the text upon which an interpretation can be built. Content questions, true-false statements, multiple-choice completions, and informational grids are all useful techniques to help learners establish the *who*, *what*, *where*, and *when* of the text. Figure 5.10 (Chapter 5) exemplified an informational grid for *The House on Mango Street*. There are eight cells in the grid, and, again, scoring ought to focus on the quality of the connections between hypotheses and evidence, rather than on whether a particular hypothesis is deemed 'correct' or not by the teacher. Teachers could therefore use the 3-point scale proposed above for each pair of cells, yielding a total of 12 possible points for the item (but teachers can adjust point values to weight certain sections of a test more or less heavily, according to their particular instructional emphases).

3 Linking form and meaning

Here is where the question *why* is added to the above list. The focus here is getting students to think about the possible implications of formal features of the text. Again, the goal is not so much getting 'right' answers but rather getting learners to formulate a rationale based on specific textual evidence. One question for students reading *The House on Mango Street* could be: 'The word "there" is repeated six times in the dialogue between Esperanza and the nun and in the paragraph that follows. Why is "there" repeated so many times? Why is it italicized five of the six times? Do the italics signify the same thing each time? If not, explain how they differ. What is your interpretation of the significance of the word "there" in terms of the whole reading passage?' (As mentioned in Chapter 5, another set of questions could ask readers to examine the use of articles ('the', 'a') used with the word 'house' to see if they notice any tendencies and if they can speculate on their possible significance.) Scoring can be based on the quality of explanation (3 = cogent, complete, and well articulated rationale; 2 = partial rationale; 1 = unsupported rationale).

4 Focus on organization of ideas

Attention now shifts to the more global concern of how ideas and information are organized in the text. Referring to the map in Figure 5.7 (Chapter 5), students might be provided with the two central nodes and a few secondary nodes and given these directions:

> Complete this map to show how specific pieces of information in the text relate to the two central nodes (house on Mango Street and 'Real' house). Be sure to include any associations and interpretive ideas that come to mind.

Two scores could be used: one to reflect the number of pieces of information included (for example, 3 = all relevant pieces of information; 2 = most relevant pieces of information; 1 = few relevant pieces of information), and another to reflect the associational and relational nodes created (for example, 3 = relational/associative nodes are plentiful and appropriate; 2 = nodes are moderate in number and appropriate—or nodes are plentiful but only some are appropriate; 1 = nodes are few and/or inappropriate).

5 Transformation

Here we are interested in the learner's ability to use the reading passage as a resource in producing some new text. This might be a written summary, a thematic analysis, a rewriting from a different point of view, or an expansion exercise that allows students to maintain a focus on interpretation, to apply what they have learnt in earlier stages of the test, but that raises the cognitive complexity of the student's task. Using *The House on Mango Street* expansion exercise shown in Chapter 5, we could again use double scores: one for number of expansions (3 = frequent; 2 = moderate; 1 = few), and another for the appropriateness of the expansions, with 'appropriate' meaning justifiable in terms of the text (3 = all or most expansions are pragmatically appropriate; 2 = some are appropriate but others are not; 1 = more than half are not appropriate).

6 Self-evaluation (coda)

One of the principles listed in Chapter 1 is that literacy involves not only reflection about text meaning but also reflection on one's own reading and writing processes. As described in Chapter 5, one way to assess such reflection is to have students write down their reflections about their own reading experience, as a coda to the sequence described above. What difficulties did they experience while reading? How did they try to overcome them? What did they learn from reading the text? Below is one example of a beginning French student reflecting on her reading of an article from *Paris-Match*, which she had just summarized:

I really enjoyed reading this article because it surprised me how much I could comprehend without knowing the meaning of every single word. There was never an instance where I did not understand an entire sentence. I could usually translate one section and then from that, I would make a logical assumption on what the unknown part was talking about. Even when I was unsure of the verb tense, I could usually guess what the infinitive was and define the word. I feel proud and excited that I can comprehend an article that was not specifically designed for elementary French students but rather was written for native French people. Although I did not grasp every idea expressed, I was able to attain a tone and basic summary of the story. In conclusion, this was a very gratifying and pleasurable activity because it reinforced how much I have actually learned and can apply to the real French world.

Students often report that having to write about their own subjective experience of reading over time gives them a real sense of their own progress as learners and readers in the foreign language. Such reflective reports can obviously be of diagnostic value to teachers as well, providing a good starting point for student-teacher conference discussions.

How to evaluate such reflections? As a contribution to a test score, dual 3-point scales could be used to assess the extent of reflection (3 = extensive; 2 = moderate; 1 = minimal) and the judged quality of reflection (3 = very perceptive; 2 = moderately perceptive; 1 = minimally perceptive). However, a response written by the teacher should also accompany this portion of the test, summarizing the teacher's own reflections on the students' comments. The teacher may additionally wish to comment on the student's overall performance on the test.

At this point a total score could be devised, by placing the total possible number of points on a percentage scale. If, for example, our 'Mango Street' test came to 45 points total, the grading scale would be as follows:

41–45   = A
36–40   = B
31–35   = C
27–30   = D
below 27 = F

The above cycle of activities has been demonstrated in written form, but it could also be done orally in the form of a 'think-aloud' interview between teacher and student. The 'think-aloud' interview is a research technique that encourages learners to verbalize whatever thoughts are going through their mind as they read. It is particularly useful for revealing the particular ways learners go about solving comprehension problems, and therefore is a powerful diagnostic measure. Because it is an extremely time-intensive procedure, however, the think-aloud is not generally practical for assessing all students in a class. Rather, it is probably best reserved as a supplemental diagnostic tool for the few students who seem to be having the greatest difficulty in reading.[10]

A common question about this kind of assessment sequence is whether students should write in the foreign language or their native language. Research on novice and intermediate-level foreign language readers suggests that they are able to bring more of their background knowledge to summarization tasks when they write in the native language as opposed to the second language (Lee 1986; Wolf 1993). Furthermore, novice language learners do not yet have the linguistic wherewithal to write responses in the second language that accurately reflect the full range of their cognitive abilities. Finally, if summaries are written in the same language as the text students will sometimes copy directly from the text without fully understanding the meaning of what they are copying. For these reasons it may be advisable for recall/summary tasks to be done in the students' native language when possible. However, there are also significant advantages to having students write in the target language: There is no linguistic disjunction in thought, it is desirable for students to reformulate and rework the language of the text, to appropriate parts of it for themselves, and in ESL settings where the teacher may not be familiar with many of the native languages spoken by the students, it is a practical necessity to have students respond exclusively in English. In sum, use of the native language for recall and summary tasks makes it possible to assess reading in cognitively challenging ways, and is therefore recommended for novice-level students. But once learners have developed sufficient ability in the target language, it is preferable (at least for pedagogical purposes) to have students use the target language in such tasks.

Assessing and evaluating writing

Evaluation involves *responding* to and (most often) *grading* students' writing, based on some kind of *assessment* criteria. Responding to student writing is a formative activity, aimed at providing feedback to students at various stages of their writing process in order to help them improve their writing and to enhance their motivation. Grading is more summative in nature and is often a key contributing variable to important decisions such as course grades, program admissions, placement, advancement, exit requirements, and so on. We will address responding and grading in turn.

Responding to student writing

Prior to the process-writing movement, responding to student writing was virtually synonymous with grading. The teacher corrected grammar and spelling mistakes and assigned a grade to a single and final draft. The underlying assumption was that students would then study the corrections so as not to repeat the same mistakes in a future essay. Process-oriented approaches to teaching writing, discussed in Chapter 6, broadened the scope of response considerably. Not only was response deemed appropriate at multiple stages of the writing process—from brainstorming, to drafting, to revision, to final editing—but also it was extended to include peers' responses as well.

The question of how best to respond to students' writing is sometimes framed dichotomously in terms of content versus form (Fathman and Whalley 1990). Whereas product approaches focused teachers' attention on surface grammar errors, process approaches focused attention primarily on content development. Most teachers recognize the importance of addressing *both* form and content. The problem, however, is that too often their comments do not address the *relationship* between content and form.[11] Comments such as 'awkward', ' not clear', 'watch your organization', 'poor connection', or simply '?', are too vague to guide the student toward making a specific series of changes.[12] On the other hand, extensive surface correction done by the teacher in order to make an essay less awkward, less unclear, and so on, does not help the student learn *why* such changes might be desirable.

What is called for in literacy-based teaching is teacher comments that draw a clear picture of the linkage between form and content, so that students can understand exactly what it is that makes their expression 'unclear', 'awkward', and so on (for example, 'When you say X here, it makes me think Y. Is that really what you're saying?', 'In paragraph 2 you said X, but paragraph 5 says Y, which contradicts X. Can you write one transition that makes this opposition explicit and then another transition to show how it leads to Z, which you talk about in paragraph 6?'). An important function of teacher comments is to make students aware of linguistic and organizational options available to them at specific points in their text (for example, 'You could elaborate idea X further in this paragraph, then present idea Y in the next paragraph, then contrast the two ideas, or you could break down X and Y into component points and contrast each point successively in one long paragraph. Which do you think will communicate your point better?').

A particularly useful form of response is *a narrative account of what the teacher was thinking* while reading the student's piece of writing. In the following example, the teacher tells the student that his stance on the issue of smoking in public places is not clear, but indicates what specific parts of the essay led to confusion.

> When I was reading your introductory paragraph I thought that you were really in favor of smoking in public places because you used the phrase 'unfortunate discussion.' In the second paragraph, when you said 'people who don't smoke have rights too,' I realized that wasn't the case. But then in paragraph 4 when you referred to non-smokers' 'unrealistic requests,' I began to wonder again where you stood on the issue . . . .

Such commentary can help students to become aware of how the particular words and organizational strategies that they have chosen affect their reader's understanding in ways they might not have anticipated.[13]

The extent to which students can assimilate such comments is, of course, variable. With beginning and intermediate-level students it may be best to focus on only one or two important issues in one's comments to avoid overwhelming the student. At advanced levels, however, feedback can be more thoroughgoing. As suggested by the following remarks of a graduate student looking back on her earlier French studies, students often vary in their receptiveness to feedback, and particularly corrective feedback, at different stages of their study:

> My first two years of high school French were drenched in red. All my errors in written French were quantified and emphasized to the point where I dreaded the thought of taking the next French test or quiz. I cannot say that I willingly used tests as a learning tool.

But then later as an undergraduate:

> Red-drenched papers were a condition I could better accept as an undergraduate student writing critical essays in French. I was extremely invested in conveying my literary analysis in the manner I would expect to do in English; thus, the style of comprehensive stylistic and grammatical error correction felt necessary to me.

It may well be the case that recognition of the communicative importance of linguistic form is a prerequisite for benefiting from written feedback and correction.

In recognition of students' needs for encouragement, it is important that teacher 'comments' not always be synonymous with teacher 'criticism'; teachers should express what they see as good about a piece of writing as it is right now, as well as offer suggestions for improvement. Finding positive things to say about a student essay is sometimes a far greater challenge than exposing its faults, but those positive comments will go a long way in motivating students to confront their weaknesses and to work toward improving their writing.

Another format for providing feedback is *teacher–student writing confer-ences*. Conferences are one-on-one meetings, normally conducted outside of class, that focus on the student's overall progress as well as specific issues in the student's current writing assignment. Alternatively, they can be short (5–10 minute) in-class 'mini-conferences' focused on a particular aspect of the student's current essay (Grabe and Kaplan 1996). A number of studies suggest that the feedback that students receive in conferences tends to be more focused and understandable than the written comments they receive on their essays (for example, Carnicelli 1980; Zamel 1985).

What seems to be crucial to the effectiveness of writing conferences is planning for focused objectives and active participation on the part of both the student and the teacher (Freedman and Sperling 1985). To this end, Reid (1993) proposes a student planning form to be filled out by the student before a writing conference, as shown in Figure 9.2:

REVISION PLANNING CONFERENCE

1. I thought the best part of my essay was . . .
2. I thought the weakest part of my essay was . . .
3. According to your [i.e. the instructor's] comments, the strengths and problems in the essay draft are as follows:

STRENGTHS   PROBLEMS

a. _____   a. _____

b. _____   b. _____

c. _____   c. _____

4. Based on the feedback, here is my plan for revising this essay (list specific steps you intend to take and specific paragraphs you intend to revise):

a. _____

b. _____

c. _____

5. Three questions I want to ask you [i.e. the instructor] are:

a. _____

b. _____

c. _____

(Reid 1993: 222–3)

Figure 9.2:   Revision planning conference

Reid also recommends that at the end of each conference the student and teacher agree on one or two specific changes that are most important to make so that the student has a concrete plan of action upon leaving the conference.

Peer-group response. Feedback from one's peers, as discussed in Chapter 6, can be a particularly important supplement to teacher response because it tends to be very supportive, consisting of 'friendly' (as opposed to 'authoritative') suggestions for improvement. Moreover, it gives the writer the chance to ask questions that might not be easily asked of a teacher, such as Does my argument make sense to you? When I was writing this I had trouble with . . . . Do you have any ideas about how I could better deal with that? What do you want to know more about? What needs to be developed more?

Besides in-class peer editing sessions, another way to elicit peer response is to have the student author write a paragraph-by-paragraph analysis of what he or she was trying to accomplish in the essay. A peer then reads the essay and writes a paragraph-by-paragraph account of his or her responses, so that the author can then directly compare the intended and achieved effects of his or her writing (Brannon and Knoblauch 1982). Leki (1990) proposes a less time-consuming alternative, in which the student writer answers specific questions, such as those in the previous paragraph, and then compares his or her answers with those of a peer reader or the teacher.

Grading student writing

Grading can apply to routine writing assignments as well as to tests. Traditionally it is only the final writing product that is graded, although in some process-approach classrooms the grade may reflect the degree of improvement from initial drafts to the final product.

How to grade student writing? The most common way is to assign a single (holistic) grade, perhaps along with some kind of response (for example, comments and suggestions for improvement). Hamp-Lyons (1991c) argues, however, that students writing in a second or foreign language have 'a special need for scoring procedures that go beyond the mere provision of a single number score' (p. 241). That is because second language writing development is typically uneven. Sometimes a high degree of fluency is accompanied by a lesser degree of accuracy, or vice versa. Sometimes the ideas expressed are very sophisticated, but their organization leaves the reader dissatisfied. The fact that all aspects of writing competence (vocabulary, grammar, familiarity with patterns of analysis, rhetorical strategies, knowledge of genres, and so forth) do not develop at the same rate suggests the particular need for second/foreign language learners to have specific feedback on a variety of dimensions of their writing.[14] Gaudiani (1981), for example, suggests the following sequence, moving from global to local issues:

1 Start with global meaning issues. What is this piece of writing about? What is it trying to do? Is it understandable? Is it interesting? Do the expressed ideas make sense?

2 Next consider text-organizational issues. Is this piece of writing easy to follow or does it demand unusual effort on the reader's part? Does the organization of ideas seem logical?

3 Finally deal with diction and grammar mistakes, focusing in particular on those that make meaning and organization unclear.

As suggested by these procedural steps, it is essential to consider more than grammar when grading student writing. In the first year of language study, writing grades might be based half on content and half on form. From the second year on, however, grading should take a broader range of areas into account. So-called 'analytic' scoring schemes establish categories (based on some theory of writing) that allow a variety of dimensions of students' writing to be assessed ('ideas', 'organization', 'vocabulary', and 'grammar' are common categories). The problem with such categories is that while they apply fairly well to certain kinds of writing (for example, academic expository essays), they are difficult to apply to many other kinds of writing.

A solution consistent with the design model of writing set forth in Chapter 6 (which emphasizes the *appropriateness* of a piece of writing in achieving a particular purpose in a particular context) is to use a broader, more flexible set of criteria such as those shown in the left-hand column of Figure 9.3. As in the case of the scoring scales presented earlier in the section on reading evaluation, this analytic scoring instrument is offered as a general model, to be adapted and refined according to individual teachers' needs and preferences.

Criteria	Score	Descriptor
Task/Content appropriateness (How well does the writing accomplish its purpose?)	30–27	**Excellent to very good:** Thorough and complete response to the task; thorough treatment of the subject; information is relevant and accurate; interpretation is cogent and well supported.
	26–24	**Good:** Adequate response to the task; adequate treatment of the subject; information is mostly relevant and accurate; interpretation is sound and mostly well supported.
	23–21	**Fair:** Less than complete response to the task; treatment of the subject is acceptable but may be inconsistent; information is sometimes irrelevant and/or inaccurate; interpretation may be sometimes inconsistent with facts.
	20–18	**Inadequate:** Response does not address the task; incomplete and inconsistent treatment of the subject; information may be often irrelevant and/or inaccurate; interpretation may be inconsistent with facts.
	17–0	**Unacceptable:** Disregard or lack of understanding of the task; minimal treatment of the subject; information and interpretation are irrelevant.
Rhetorical appropriateness (How well does the organization of the writing take its intended audience into account?)	25–23	**Excellent to very good:** Communicates effectively; fully consistent with constraints of the particular genre; expression is appropriately organized and sequenced; relations among text sections are clear to the reader.

	22–20	**Good:** Communicates adequately; generally consistent with constraints of the particular genre; expression is mostly well organized and sequenced; relations among text sections are mostly, but not necessarily always, clear to the reader.
	19–18	**Fair:** Communicates somewhat adequately, at least some of the time; constraints of the particular genre are sometimes neglected; organization and sequencing sometimes difficult to follow; relations among text sections are sometimes unclear.
	17–16	**Inadequate:** Communication is ineffective; the point is unclear; constraints of the particular genre are not adhered to; organization and sequencing are puzzling to the reader; relations among text sections are unclear to the reader.
	15–0	**Unacceptable:** The reader does not understand at all; there is no apparent point; no regard to genre constraints; little or no discernable organization.
Language appropriateness (How well does language use suit the context of communication?)	25–23	**Excellent to very good:** Thoroughly and consistently appropriate use of language for the given genre and context of communication.
	22–20	**Good:** Generally appropriate use of language for the given genre and context of communication.
	19–18	**Fair:** Inconsistent appropriateness of language for the given genre and context of communication.
	17–16	**Inadequate:** Inappropriate use of language for the given genre and context of communication.
	15–0	**Unacceptable:** Offensive use of language.
Formal appropriateness (How well does the writing meet genre-relevant norms for formatting, spelling, neatness?)	20–18	**Excellent to very good:** Layout, spelling, verb conjugation, accents, agreements, punctuation, capitalization, and neatness fully meet norms for the genre.
	17–16	**Good:** Layout, spelling, verb conjugation, accents, agreements, punctuation, capitalization, and neatness generally meet norms for the genre.

	15–14	**Fair:** Layout, spelling, verb conjugation, accents, agreements, punctuation, capitalization, and neatness partially meet norms for the genre.
	13–12	**Inadequate:** Layout, spelling, verb conjugation, accents, agreements, punctuation, capitalization, and neatness generally do not meet norms for the genre.
	11–0	**Unacceptable:** Layout, spelling, verb conjugation, accents, agreements, punctuation, capitalization, and neatness consistently do not meet norms for the genre.

Figure 9.3   Example of analytic scoring scale (adapted from Tribble (1996))

The scoring scale is based on 100 points to facilitate interpretation and reporting (100–90, Excellent to Very Good; 89–80, Good; 79–70, Fair; 69–60, Inadequate; below 60, Unacceptable). The task/content appropriateness category has been weighted most, rhetorical and linguistic appropriateness are weighted equally, and formal appropriateness is weighted least.[15] A student who has written a paper that is 'very good' in terms of task/content appropriateness and rhetorical appropriateness (27 and 23 points respectively), on the low end of 'good' for language appropriateness (20 points), and on the high end of 'good' for formal appropriateness (17 points) would thus earn a total score of 87 out of 100 points on the paper. If necessary this score could then be converted to a letter grade. It is essential, of course, that the student see the assessment of all four components (not just the overall score) and that explanatory comments accompany the scores.

Because analytic scoring scales are operationalizations of writing theories, they are only as good as the theories on which they are based. Consequently, teachers and test users must always be aware of the implicit assumptions that assessment scales (including the one above) make about writing, and stand ready to judge for themselves the appropriateness of those assumptions. Furthermore, as Bailey (1998) has pointed out, as our understanding of writing evolves, we must be prepared to effect corresponding changes in the ways we evaluate writing.

Writing tests

Hamp-Lyons (1991a) distinguishes between 'direct' and 'indirect' writing tests. Whereas direct tests involve actual writing of continuous text that is read by teachers, indirect tests focus on discrete elements related to writing (especially grammar and vocabulary knowledge) and are scored objectively according to a pre-established key.[16] In the context of literacy-based teaching we are interested in direct tests of writing.[17]

Direct writing tests typically consist of writing of a timed, in-class essay in response to a level-appropriate task involving a familiar topic. The essays are then read by the teacher and scored either holistically (a single grade assessing the overall quality of the essay, based on a set of exemplars) or analytically (a set of scores for multiple dimensions such as illustrated in Figure 9.2). Options do exist, however. Grabe and Kaplan (1996), for example, propose that on the first day of the exam, two hours be allocated for students to write, and then on the second day, that one hour be allocated to editing and producing the final essay. In this way, testing is made to be consistent with process-oriented approaches to writing instruction. Another option is to have students write a variety of short essays focused on a given theme during the final week of instruction, varying the genre or task type (for example, a reading summary, a comparison of two texts, an argumentative essay, and a written self-evaluation). Such an approach broadens the scope of the writing test to include a variety of different types of writing.

Given the interconnectedness of reading and writing in all academic areas and levels, Johns (1991) proposes a number of ways to incorporate reading into academic writing tests in order to make them more consistent with what students normally do when they write.[18] First, reading can be incorporated to test students' audience awareness by having them redesign a text for a particular audience with particular characteristics. For example, a graph could be used as a common information source for writing two reports to different audiences, each requiring a particular interpretation of the data (Johns 1991). Second, in order to focus on the key academic genre of argumentative writing, Johns recommends that students be given two texts representing differing points of view and that they be asked to argue for one of the sides after summarizing both. Evaluation in this instance could focus on the degree of balance in their summaries, their ability to maintain an objective stance, and the persuasiveness of their argument (p. 174). Third, in order to assess students' ability to conceptualize, Johns recommends giving students two short readings discussing the same concept(s). Students are asked to identify the concept(s) and to discuss and illustrate them by means of 'real world' examples (p. 175).

Johns recommends that the balance of reading/writing skills should vary with curricular level, so that beginning students should do proportionately more reading, with relatively simple writing tasks. Intermediate-level students would do more complex, analytical writing tasks with less reading proportionately. Advanced students could work with several texts, synthesizing concepts across multiple sources.

Faigley, Cherry, Jolliffe, and Skinner (1985) provide a particularly interesting example not only of how reading can be incorporated into a deductive writing task but also of how students' writing can be assessed in terms of specific task demands (commonly called *performance assessment*). The reading/writing task is presented in Figure 9.4 and the performative scoring rubric in Figure 9.5.

Deduction Task

Assume the following regulations regarding academic cheating apply to the situation below. Cheating on a test includes:

1 The use during a test of materials not authorized by the person giving the test.
2 The possession during a test of materials not authorized by the person giving the test.
3 Copying from another student's paper.
4 Collaborating with or seeking aid from another student during a test without authorization.

Students guilty of cheating automatically fail the course and are subject to more severe penalties.

Charlie Roberts had had trouble with Zoology all semester, and now that the final was approaching, he began to get desperate. One day he approached his friend Jack Cline and suggested the two attempt to exchange answers during the test.

Not wanting to offend Charlie, Jack never explicitly refused to cooperate with Charlie in the scheme. He was decidedly uneasy about it, however, and attempted to compromise by offering Charlie his class notes to use in preparing for the test.

During the test, Charlie was caught using a set of class notes and automatically failed both the test and the course.

When the professor examined the notes Charlie had used during the test, he discovered they belonged to Jack. As a result of the discovery, the professor also failed Jack, claiming that he too had cheated on the test.

Jack felt he was innocent and followed the university's procedures for appeal to the Faculty Disciplinary Committee, which is responsible for making a decision in cases involving academic cheating. You are the student member of that committee.

The chair has asked you to prepare a written statement on whether Jack is innocent or guilty that will be presented before the Committee. Defend your opinion on the basis of the university regulations on cheating.

Figure 9.4:   *Academic cheating deductive writing task (Faigley, et al. 1985: 130–1)*

Deduction Scoring Rubrics   Task 1: Academic Cheating

Rate individual papers on each of the variables described below.
(1 = Least effective; 4 = most effective)

A Meeting the Demands of the Rhetorical Situation

1 The writer does not identify him/herself as a member of the university disciplinary council *and* does not identify the task at hand.

2 The writer does not identify him/herself as a member of the university disciplinary council *or* does not identify the task at hand.

3 The writer identifies him/herself as a member of the university disciplinary council and provides an introductory statement that describes the task at hand.

4 The writer identifies him/herself as a member of the university disciplinary council and provides an introductory statement that describes the task at hand. In addition, throughout the paper, the writer makes occasional reference to the audience, acknowledging that he/she is leading them through an argument and that the council as a whole is responsible for making a determination on Jack's guilt or innocence.

B Discussing the Regulations Regarding Academic Cheating

1 The writer neglects to discuss some of the regulations as outlined in the writing task.

2 The writer mentions the regulations, but merely reiterates them verbatim from the writing task.

3 The writer discusses all of the regulations regarding academic cheating, but does not demonstrate his/her understanding of them.

4 The writer discusses all of the regulations regarding academic cheating as outlined in the writing task in such a way as to demonstrate his/her understanding of them. It is also clear from this discussion of the regulations that the writer is summarizing the regulations for the audience.

C Relating the Regulations to Jack's Behavior

1 The writer ignores the regulations themselves and merely retells the story of Jack and Charlie.

2 The writer alludes to the regulations, but does not relate any particular regulations to Jack's behavior.

3 The writer relates one or two regulations to Jack's behavior.

4 The writer relates all the regulations to Jack's behavior, stating the particular sections that apply.

D Drawing Conclusions from the Regulations as Applied to Jack's Behavior

1 The writer draws no explicit conclusions regarding Jack's behavior.

2 The writer expresses a personal opinion that Jack is innocent or guilty, but does not state that the disciplinary council must make a final recommendation regarding Jack's case.

3 The writer concludes that, overall, Jack is innocent (or guilty) of the charges brought against him and states that the disciplinary council must make a final recommendation, i.e. that Jack should be exonerated or disciplined.

4 The writer draws explicit conclusions from the discussion of the regulations regarding academic cheating as applied to Jack's behavior and clearly states that the disciplinary council must make a final recommendation. These conclusions result from syllogistic reasoning, e.g.: Cheating consists of 'X'; Jack did (or did not) do 'X'; therefore, Jack did (or did not) cheat.

*Figure 9.5:   Scoring rubrics for academic cheating deductive task
(Faigley, et al. 1985: 133–4)*

Allaei and Connor (1991) report on the use of Faigley *et al.'s* 'cheating' prompt and assessment rubric in an ESL context. Below is one student essay:

> The way that the professor treated Jack was so strict and obviously unfair. According to the listed rules we clearly see that Jack was innocent:
> 1. Jack didn't use the materials during a test.
> 2. Jack didn't have the materials with him during a test (The professor didn't catch anything at Jack).
> 3. Jack didn't copy anything from another student's paper during a test.
> 4. Jack didn't work together or ask for help during a test.
> Although the professor discovered that Charlie was using Jack's notes but this fact didn't violate the rules because Jack gave Charlie before a test to study, Jack didn't give Charlie during a test, so he didn't do anything wrong.

From the facts above, Jack was innocent and the professor should review the case and give him good grade. Jack is good student. He's very helpful. (Allaei and Connor 1991: 235)

Allaei and Connor (p. 235) report that this essay was scored by two raters as shown in Table 9.1 (1 = least effective; 4 = most effective):

	Rater 1	Rater 2
Meeting the demands of the rhetorical situation	1	1
Discussing/using the source text material	4	2
Linking the given text source material to the problem at hand	4	4
Drawing conclusions	3	3
	12	10

Table 9.1: Essay scoring results (from Allaei and Connor (1991))

Raters 1 and 2 both agreed that the essay did not meet the demands of the rhetorical situation (the writer neither identified himself as a member of the university disciplinary council nor did he identify the task at hand). They differed in their judgments concerning the student's use of source text material, however. Rater 1 considered the writer's summarization and discussion of the regulations complete. Rater 2 considered that the writer merely reiterated the regulations verbatim from the writing task (which he clearly did not). Finally, both raters agreed that the essay linked all the regulations to Jack's behavior, that a conclusion was drawn and a recommendation made, but that syllogistic reasoning was not clearly evidenced.

Allaei and Connor point out that a performance assessment approach is particularly useful if the writing component focuses on a particular type of writing (for example, deductive reasoning), but that if one is trying to assess a wide range of types of writing, it is somewhat impractical. One would need a sizable battery of tasks in order to get a comprehensive profile of learners' abilities—and this would be very time-consuming and expensive). For better or for worse, performance assessment does not take writing mechanics into account, and thus would need to be supplemented by some other evaluation component that addresses grammar and mechanics. Nevertheless, Allaei and Connor point out that a real strength of performance assessment is that it allows teachers to systematically evaluate students' ability to address particular audience specifications and it provides a good deal of descriptive information about students' writing, making it very useful for diagnosis and instruction.

Portfolio assessment

Portfolio assessment has been used for some time in Britain and parts of Australia, and is becoming increasingly widely used in North America as well. Consisting of a self-selected group of texts that the student has written over an extended period of time, a portfolio can include: writing samples (analytic writing and creative writing, including successive drafts), reading response journals, vocabulary journals, daily journals, or pen pal letters, as well as statements by the student about (1) the goals of writing the included pieces, (2) the rationale for their inclusion in the portfolio, and (3) reflections on the process of writing them. Portfolio assessment therefore acknowledges the broad variety of kinds and purposes of writing, and leads teachers and students away from the notion that a single piece of writing, produced in the context of a test, could ever represent something as complex as a student's ability to write in a new language.[19]

The primary goal of portfolio assessment is to keep assessment in line with teaching and learning practices, grounded in real use of language. It is a dynamic, student-based process that engages learners in an ongoing cycle of assessment and evaluation (gathering materials and reflecting upon them). When it includes a student-teacher conference, portfolio assessment provides a good opportunity for dialogic exploration of learners' particular strengths and weakness, learning progress, and future goals. Consequently, it is a process that goes beyond assessing language performance *per se*, since it involves cognitive, social, and motivational dimensions as well.

Hamp-Lyons and Condon (1993) cite studies that substantiate claims that 'the benefits of portfolio assessment are real, and the indications are that its potential has hardly begun to develop' (p. 176). But they also point out that portfolio assessment requires ongoing maintenance and change in response to the insights that it brings (and that it must be viewed critically). Based on a study of raters' 'reading logs', they found that the broader-based corpus of student writing provided by portfolio assessment makes evaluation more complex rather than easier. The juxtaposition of texts alone invited comparisons, and required very close reading. Second, they found that different genres did not produce contrasting results (as they had assumed they might). No rater said, for example 'This student can write an effective narrative, but has a good deal of trouble with more complex forms of discourse' (p. 181). But Hamp-Lyons and Condon did find that impromptu versus revised writing produced rating differences across genres. They also found that readers do not generally read all the portfolio materials with equal attention. In fact, most readers came up with a tentative score while reading the first of four papers (and some after only one or two paragraphs of the first paper). Hamp-Lyons and Condon's recommendations include (1) that students should perhaps only include two pieces of writing, and place their best material first, not last, (2) that readers be asked to respond to questions about *all* the texts in the portfolio (for example, in the case of comparing two drafts, 'Specify the strengths present in this text which make it better than the first text' (p. 184), and (3) that multiple drafts must be included if writing process is going to be taken into account.

One significant drawback of portfolio analysis is that it is a very time-intensive process for teachers. Stowall and Tierney (1995) note that some teachers see portfolio assessment as just more record keeping and work. It also poses certain challenges in grading: How to deal with the uneven quality of work within the portfolio? How much of the grade should be allocated to 'progress' and how much to the actual quality of the work? How to avoid being too 'lenient', given that the portfolio presumably includes only the best work of the student? This introduces the problem of reliability. Specialists in educational measurement and psychometrics point out that the broader the range of students' choice options, the lesser the reliability of the assessment. Inter-rater reliability has been shown to be low in some studies of portfolio assessment, although a number of other studies have reported inter-rater reliabilities in the .80 to .90 range (Koretz, Stecher, Klein, and McCaffrey 1994).

One way to improve the reliability of portfolio assessment would be (1) to specify as explicitly as possible what kind of materials should be included, (2) to establish explicit criteria for evaluation, and (3) to provide readers with training and practice in the application of such criteria or rubrics. Herman, Gearhart, and Aschbacher (1996) offer comprehensive general guidance in all three of these areas and, within a second language context, Ferris and Hedgcock (1998) offer useful practical examples. I will summarize key points below.

In terms of what should be included in portfolios, Herman *et al.* (1996) stress the need for teachers to identify priority goals for their students' learning and then to determine what tasks would most appropriately reflect those goals. As one example, Ferris and Hedgcock (1998) present two sample checklists used in their first year college ESL composition course (COMP 120). One is for midterm portfolio collection and the other for the end-of-semester collection. For the midterm collection, they specify that students should include the following items:

- Paper 1 (including all intermediate drafts, a peer response worksheet from at least one classmate, cover sheets/self analyses, and all written instructor feedback)
- Paper 2 OR Paper 3 (including all intermediate drafts, a peer response worksheet from at least one classmate, cover sheets/self analyses, and all written instructor feedback)
- One of your three timed writings (including instructor feedback). In addition, you may optionally include a revision of this timed writing.
- One to two pieces of informal, personal, or self-selected writing (eg, a journal entry, a reading response, a letter to your instructor or a peer, a poem, an editorial for the campus newspaper)

– A one-page self-assessment of your performance and progress over the first 7½ weeks of COMP 120. Please use the *Midterm Self-Assessment Guidelines* to compose this document, which should review your work and change as a writer. If you wish to receive a provisional, in-progress grade, please include this request at the end of your self-assessment. (Ferris and Hedgcock 1998: 252)

At the end of the semester, Ferris and Hedgcock's students' portfolios are to include the following items:

– Three revised papers (each including intermediate drafts, at least one peer response worksheet, cover sheets/self analyses, and all written instructor feedback);
– Two of your six timed writings (including instructor feedback). You may also optionally include a revision of one of these timed writings, with an appropriate cover sheet . . . .
– Two pieces of informal, personal, or self-selected writing related to the course, to another course, or to activities outside of your school (for example, a journal entry, a reading response, a letter to your instructor or a peer, a poem, an editorial for the campus newspaper)
– A two-page self-assessment of your performance and progress in COMP 120. Please use the *Final Self-Assessment Guidelines* to compose this document, which should review your work and change as a writer and should explain why you have given yourself the grade you have indicated. If your instructor has asked you to revise your self-assessment since your Final Conference, please include your initial draft as well.
(Ferris and Hedgcock 1998: 253)

The 'final conference' mentioned at the end of this checklist occurs several weeks before the end of the course. During this conference, the student discusses with the instructor a draft of his or her two-page final self-assessment (submitted in advance of the conference), as well as any other materials that the instructor might wish to discuss.

If focusing on goal priorities determines what should go into portfolios, it also informs the process of establishing scoring criteria. This process begins with two questions: 'What kind of performance are we trying to measure and what domains of students' knowledge and skill are to be assessed?' (Herman, *et al.* 1996: 36). In terms of performance, students' demonstrated achievement is generally the main focus, although decisions must be made about whether the student's degree of progress should also count, and, if so, how much.[20] The question of 'domains' requires thinking about the degree to which things like language knowledge, content knowledge, and meta-cognitive abilities come into play in the chosen writing tasks, and how much relative weight they should be given in the portfolio. Once the criteria are established, a decision can be made to use either holistic or analytic scoring schemes (see 'Grading student writing' above).

To give an example of how portfolio grading operates in one classroom, Ferris and Hedgcock (1998) use either 'satisfactory' or 'unsatisfactory' labels to grade students' writing during the semester, relying extensively on written and oral comments for detailed feedback.[21] 'Satisfactory' means the piece of writing has sufficient merit to go into a portfolio (Ferris and Hedgcock say it equates to a grade of at least 'C'), but the very generality of the grade encourages students to revise, in the hope of maximizing their final grade. 'Unsatisfactory' pieces of writing are not adequate for inclusion in the portfolio and need to be resubmitted after they have been rewritten. It is only at the end of the semester, when the complete portfolio is evaluated, that a letter grade is assigned. Grading is done collectively, with each portfolio evaluated independently by two instructors, based on benchmark portfolios in order to maximize reliability.[22]

Clear criteria, descriptive rubrics, and the use of benchmark portfolios can all improve consistency of scoring, but teachers' training and practice are also of crucial importance. Herman, *et al.* (1996) suggest explicit training on the meaning of the chosen criteria and extensive practice in applying them to actual portfolios. When collectively scoring portfolios, teachers also need some kind of system for monitoring the consistency of their scoring (for example, rescoring previously scored portfolios, scoring a portfolio by two raters). In their ESL writing class, Ferris and Hedgcock (1998), address both training and consistency issues (1) by using benchmark portfolios as models, and (2) by pairing less experienced teachers with more experienced instructors and having them exchange their sets of portfolios, so that each portfolio receives two grades. When discrepancies arise they are discussed and any unresolved differences are arbitrated by the course supervisor. Although Ferris and Hedgcock admit that this system is labor-intensive, they are confident that it 'reduces instructor bias, increases reliability, and lends face validity to the feedback that students receive . . .' (p. 255).

Portfolio assessment challenges traditional testing practices that are well-entrenched in schools and colleges. The use of portfolio assessment is more than adding a new technique to a set of established practices. It requires rethinking what assessment and evaluation are about and rethinking the respective roles that teachers and students play in the assessment/evaluation process. As Stowell and Tierney point out, 'implementing a portfolio approach will involve more than simply the introduction of another assessment tool. With the introduction of portfolios come some major shifts in teacher professionalism, the role of classroom-grounded assessment data, and student empowerment' (Stowell and Tierney 1995: 93). If, for example, the evaluation of portfolios is based upon a tallying of surface errors (i.e. used as a new technique within a traditional form-focused framework), then it will not serve usefully. The point is that it is not just the assessment *techniques* used, but how the results are evaluated and utilized, which is directly tied to the teacher's understanding or philosophy of language learning and teaching.

The transition to the use of portfolio assessment can therefore be a long one. It is probably not the kind of change that can be 'tried out' for a semester with any degree of success, but rather a change that requires patience and commitment on the part of both teachers and administrators.

Conclusion

Like language, assessment and evaluation can be characterized as a system of choices. Like language use, the assessment and evaluation practices we choose both shape and are shaped by social contexts. If we as language educators are serious about making students more mindful readers and writers, then we need to pay particular attention to the ways in which we assess and evaluate reading and writing. Our task involves, first, taking into account both our instructional context (who our students are, what our goals are, what our resources are) and the assessment choices available to us and, second, making decisions that will bridge the two appropriately.

Like language use, evaluation relies on interpretation. In order to arrive at the best interpretations possible of learners' abilities, it is imperative that educators look beyond single assessment measures, and look for broad patterns across multiple measures, both quantitative and qualitative.

Finally, like language use, assessment and evaluation potentially contribute to language learning itself. Our goal should be to maximize that potential by integrating formative as well as summative modes of assessment and evaluation into the curriculum.

Notes

1 In the Oral Proficiency Interview, the object is not to assess *what* the learner says as meaningful communication, but rather whether certain key functions (such as asking questions, narrating in past/present/future time frames, hypothesizing, supporting opinions, and so on) are being accomplished in the language. Subject matter is a vehicle for assessing functions, and at the most advanced levels of proficiency, learners are expected to be able to hypothesize and support opinions in several topic domains. However, neither the particular thoughts and ideas that learners express, nor the manner in which they are developed is deemed relevant. In fact, OPI interviewers are advised to switch topics if they hit upon a 'hothouse special'—a topic with which the interviewee is particularly at ease and knowledgeable.

2 I say that grading can follow *either* assessment or evaluation because there is often no phase of evaluative reflection between collecting and scoring data, and the reporting of a grade.

3 In the case of certain standardized tests, text 2 may actually reflect neither the test designer's nor any other single real reader's interpretation of text 1,

but rather may have been derived as a statistical composite from a pool of many test-takers' responses (Spolsky 1994).

4 An analogous situation exists in writing tests when the writer's understanding of the writing task differs from that intended by the test designer. Ruth and Murphy (1988) distinguish between the *given task* (prompt, topic, question) that normally involves instructions on *what* to write about and *how* to write about it, and the *constructed task* (the writer's mental representation of what he or she is being asked to do). Because of the 'linguistic, cognitive, and social reverberations' that writing prompts may trigger in writers, Ruth and Murphy point out that the degree of congruence between 'given' and 'constructed' tasks is subject to considerable variabililty (p. 7). Not only do students differ amongst themselves in their interpretations of a task, but students and teachers will often differ as well. Thus, Ruth and Murphy conclude that 'the success of students' performance may depend not only on their ability to match their evaluators' *interpretations* of the task elicited by the topic, but also on their ability to match their evaluators' expectations about what a *successful completion* of the task would entail' (Ruth and Murphy 1988: 181).

5 This point is well reflected in the American Psychological Association's definition of validity: 'the appropriateness, meaningfulness, and usefulness of the specific *inferences* made from test scores' (cited in Bachman 1990: 243, my emphasis).

6 See Note 30 in Chapter 8 for Vygotsky's definition of zone of proximal development.

7 Rivers (1983) takes this idea further, advocating testing as a *recursive* activity, in which students have the chance to repeat a test as many times as they wish, until they achieve the goal of mastery. As Rivers puts it, when students 'feel ready to match the criterion, they test. Note that *they* test: It is not we who test them. If necessary, they later retest. When satisfied that they have matched the criterion, they move on' (p. 142). Such a model obviously assumes unusually self-motivated and conscientious learners.

8 As Swaffar, Arens, and Byrnes (1991) have argued, an integration of reading and writing can promote learning through assessment:

> The bridge between comprehension of factual or ideational content and extended production of language is tacitly ignored. Yet it is precisely in the process of connecting these two capabilities, not only in choosing the best paraphrase, but also in being able to generate one as well, that student learning appears to be considerably enhanced . . . .
> (Swaffar, *et al.* 1991: 159)

9 See Chapter 8, Note 30, for definition of zone of proximal development.

10 For more information on think-alouds, see Ericsson and Simon (1984), Block (1986), and Pressley and Afflerbach (1995).

11 This may help to explain the mixed results of research on the effects of teacher feedback on students' writing. For research on feedback in native language writing instruction, see Hillocks (1986); for research in second/foreign language contexts, see Cardelle and Corno (1981), Semke (1984), Zamel (1985), Cohen and Cavalcanti (1990), Fathman and Whalley (1990), Leki (1990), Kepner (1991), Ferris (1995), and Ferris and Hedgcock (1998).

12 Chen and Hamp-Lyons (1999) provide an interesting discussion of Hong Kong EFL student writers' reactions to such comments.

13 In giving this kind of response teachers also 'practice what they preach' by modeling the principle of 'supporting claims with textual evidence', which is central to literacy-based teaching.

14 An explicit accounting of multiple components also reduces the effects of the teacher's professional bias. Hamp-Lyons (1991b) found in earlier studies that readers of ESL/EFL academic writing varied in their responses depending on their situation/role: subject matter specialists were most concerned with accuracy and coherence of *content*. Writing specialists, on the other hand, were most concerned with *rhetorical* aspects of the writing. Hamp-Lyons studied the verbal reflections of four raters with backgrounds in Applied Linguistics and ESL/EFL teaching, and found that they looked primarily for a convincing discourse structure in students' writing: '. . . they respond from their own sets of values, and do not try to respond to student writing as they think subject specialists would' (p. 143).

15 Teachers will vary weights according to their particular emphases. In the first criterion rubric they may also wish to separate 'content' from 'task', although in practice the two are often so imbricated with one another that this may introduce scoring difficulties.

16 Hamp-Lyons (1991a) points out that the grading of indirect writing tests is in fact no more 'objective' than that of direct tests. But the interpretation involved in determining the 'right' answers is done ahead of time by the test designer, so that no decision is needed on the teacher's part at the time of scoring the test.

17 It is important to note, however, that not all researchers accept the 'direct' and 'indirect' distinction. Messick (1994), for example, argues that direct tests are an impossibility.

18 Johns (1991) insists, however, that test-designers specify the intended purposes for reading, as well as the intended purposes and audience for writing, on the test (for example, will the reading be summarized? analyzed and critiqued? compared to other texts? used strictly as an information source?).

19 There is a growing literature on the use of portfolio analysis in secondary and higher education (for example, Belanoff and Dickson 1991; Tierney, Carter, and Desai 1991; Calfee and Perfumo 1996; Yancey and Weiser

1997). For a particularly good overview from an ESL perspective, see Chapter 8 of Ferris and Hedgcock (1998).

20 Progress can most easily be taken into account in scoring by weighting later writings more heavily than earlier ones.

21 Ferris and Hedgcock point out that students do, however, have the option to request a traditional letter grade once they have received a 'Satisfactory'.

22 As part of their self-assessment during the 'final conference', students themselves participate in the grading process by assigning a grade to their own performance and justifying their decision.

10 Rethinking language and literacy teaching

We began this book with the notion that learning a language is more than learning the elements of a new linguistic code. While learning these elements is certainly essential, equally important is understanding that communicating in another language often involves shaping one's expression differently, thinking differently, indeed sometimes seeing the world differently. I have argued that foreign language learners can best begin their exploration of another language and culture by reading, discussing, and writing texts. Reading and writing, as framed in this book, are not just language skills, but also cognitive and social practices that provide learners access to new communities outside the classroom, across geographical and historical boundaries. This is the rationale for a language curriculum based on the organizing principle of literacy. In Parts One and Two we considered the notion of design as a heuristic metaphor to guide language educators in their decisions about what to teach and how to teach it. In this final chapter we will explore the implications of this argument for instructional goals, student and teacher roles, teacher education, and areas of future enquiry.

Goals of a literacy-based curriculum

Throughout the book I have argued for extending the goals of language teaching beyond linguistic knowledge and beyond the functional ability to communicate, by considering cognitive, cultural, and social dimensions as well. Literacy-based teaching assumes the primary importance of developing communicative ability in a new language, but it also emphasizes within that general goal, the development of learners' ability to analyze, interpret, and transform discourse and their ability to think critically about how discourse is constructed and used toward various ends in social contexts. It thus emphasizes communication (both oral and written), but communication that is informed by a metacommunicative awareness of how discourse is derived from relations between language use, contexts of interaction, and larger sociocultural contexts. In Chapter 9 this was characterized as 'thoughtful' communication, both in the cognitive sense of critical reflection, and in the social sense of respectful, responsible use of language across lines of cultural difference.

The seven principles of literacy outlined in Chapter 1—interpretation, collaboration, conventions, cultural knowledge, problem-solving, reflection, and language use—and the design metaphor elaborated in Chapter 2, provide some guidance in identifying what and how to teach, in order to support this general goal of thoughtful communication. Language, conventions, and cultural knowledge form the basic *Available Designs* to be taught, as discussed in Chapter 3, and they are taught in conjunction with the *design processes* of interpretation, collaboration, problem-solving, and reflection, as illustrated in Chapters 4 to 7. These design processes are operationalized through the kinds of activities presented in Chapters 5 and 7, which were distributed across the four instructional categories of situated practice, overt instruction, critical framing, and transformed practice.

Like most language curricula, the literacy-based curriculum places Available Designs squarely at the center, but, unlike most language curricula, it also directs learners' attention to *relationships* among Available Designs (i.e. within the inner circle of Figure 2.3), as well as relationships between meaning design and context (i.e. relationships across all three circles of Figure 2.3). It is therefore a curriculum concerned with rhetoric in the sense that it aims to prepare learners to deal with multiple forms of language use in multiple contexts (some perhaps quite different from those learners are familiar with), and to foster some awareness of how the forms and contexts interact in the process of making meaning. Moreover, it attempts to establish this as a common orientation across introductory, intermediate, and advanced levels of language study.

A literacy-based curriculum is thus neither purely structural nor purely communicative in approach, but attempts to relate communicative to structural dimensions of language use, as summarized in Table 10.1 below.

Structural emphasis	Communicative emphasis	Literacy emphasis
Knowing	Doing	Doing and reflecting on doing in terms of knowing
Usage	Use	Usage/Use relations
Language forms	Language functions	Form-function relationships
Achievement (i.e. display of knowledge)	Functional ability to communicate	Communicative appropriateness informed by metacommunicative awareness

Table 10.1:   Summary of goals of structural, communicative, and literacy-based curricula

Adopting literacy as an organizing principle of language teaching entails subtle but important changes in curriculum. Instructional objectives shift from an emphasis on conversation for conversation's sake or the delivery of linguistic and cultural facts, to the development of learners' ability to interpret and critically evaluate language use in a variety of spoken and written contexts. Instructional activities emphasize interdependencies between speaking, listening, reading, and writing skills, and focus students' attention on the interactions between linguistic form, situational context, and communicative and expressive functions. The study of language and the study of literature are treated as mutually dependent, not mutually exclusive, activities.

Such a vision of foreign language education is not new. Breen and Candlin described it well twenty years ago, in their seminal article, 'The Essentials of a Communicative Curriculum in Language Teaching':

> [The language classroom] can become the meeting-place for realistically motivated communication-as-learning, communication about learning, and metacommunication. It can be a forum where knowledge may be jointly offered and sought, reflected upon, and acted upon. The classroom can also crucially serve as the source of feedback on, and refinement of, the individual learner's own process competence.
> (Breen and Candlin 1980: 98)

In practice, however, Breen and Candlin's vision has not been realized in most communicatively-oriented language programs. Generally speaking, the goal of communication has been well met, but the goals that can be uniquely and best served in language classrooms—reflection and metacommunication— have yet to be adequately addressed. One reason may be the predominant focus on oral communication in many language programs. Speech, fleeting and evanescent, does not lend itself easily to developing learners' metacommunicative awareness. For reasons outlined throughout this book, I believe that a greater emphasis on written communication, well integrated with the development of oral language ability, is more apt to foster reflective, metacommunicative goals.

A second impediment to the realization of these goals has been the tacit espousal of 'near-native proficiency' (i.e. communicative skills approximating an educated adult native-speaker norm) as the ultimate aim of many communicatively-oriented language programs. There is growing recognition in the foreign language teaching profession that such an aim is at once too ambitious and too limited.[1] It is too ambitious in the sense that it is unrealistic to try to achieve native-like mastery of the phonology, morphology, syntax, semantics, and pragmatics of a foreign language within the relatively short time span of most academic study programs. On the other hand, it is too limited a goal in the sense that a second 'monolingual competence' effectively reduces language learning to mere skill acquisition. Instead, as Cook (1996) and Kramsch (1997) argue, language teaching should aspire to developing individuals' ability to mediate between the different perspectives and different meanings born of two languages and cultures—a capability far beyond that of a monolingual native speaker.

Kramsch (1998) suggests that this aim requires a shift from 'native speaker' to 'intercultural speaker' norms:

> ... it would make more sense to view speakers acquiring over their lifetime a whole range of rules of interpretation that they use knowingly and judiciously according to the various social contexts in which they live and with which they make sense of the world around them. That, one could argue, is the characteristic of a 'competent language user': not the ability to speak and write according to the rules of the academy and the social etiquette of one social group, but the adaptability to select those forms of accuracy and those forms of appropriateness that are called for in a given social context of use. This form of competence is precisely the competence of the 'intercultural' speaker, operating at the border between several languages or language varieties, manoeuvering [sic] his/her way through the troubled waters of cross-cultural misunderstandings ....
> (Kramsch 1998: 27)

From the perspective of the pedagogical model presented in this book, such a shift is not so much a matter of changing *what* is taught. The basics of language teaching—the Available Designs of language, conventions, and cultural knowledge—remain central. Rather, it is a matter of changing teachers' and learners' *stance* toward what is taught. This involves a shift in teacher and learner roles.

Roles of teachers and learners

The notion of apprenticeship has long characterized student and teacher roles in foreign language teaching. What has changed, however, is the *focus* of the apprenticeship. In the days of grammar-translation and later structural/audiolingual language teaching methods, students were apprentices to 'philologists' or 'linguists'. The communicative competence models of the 1980s made the native speaker primordial, and students often apprenticed with the ultimate aim of developing 'near-native' competence. In literacy-based language teaching, students are neither apprentice philologists, nor apprentice native speakers, but rather apprentice discourse analysts and intercultural explorers.

One of the biggest challenges in promoting a 'thoughtful communicative' mindset is establishing teacher and student roles that allow for critical analysis of classroom communication itself. The role that typified structural approaches to language teaching (and one that is still often expected by students) is the traditional 'authority' role: the teacher is the one who is always right, the one who has the knowledge the students need to acquire, the one who manages and controls everything that happens in the classroom. This role tends to polarize responsibility for learning. If the students do not learn, it is either because the teacher did not teach things correctly, or because the students are too lazy or not smart enough. The learner role that complements an authoritative teacher role is one of deference and relative passivity.

A more contemporary teacher role, born of communicative, 'learner-centered' language teaching, is represented by the well-known motto, 'The teacher is the guide on the side, not the sage on the stage'. The idea is that the teacher designs and organizes learning activities, and then gets out of the way, so that students can go about their business of communicating and learning. Responsibility for what happens in the classroom (including student learning) is therefore shared: the teacher is there to organize, to motivate, to provide assistance and feedback, but the students must play an active participatory role which involves a considerable degree of self-motivation, self-direction, and co-operation.

Unfortunately, neither of these sets of teacher and learner roles is likely to engender the kind of classroom culture that fosters critical thinking and metacommunicative awareness. What is needed to accomplish these goals is a recasting of teacher and learner roles inherited from both structural and communicative approaches.

The 'three Rs' of literacy-based teaching

Given the centrality of the design processes of interpretation, collaboration, problem-solving, and reflection in the literacy-based curriculum, teacher and learner roles can be characterized by the 'three Rs' of *responding, revising*, and *reflecting*. As we saw in Chapter 9, these three Rs of literacy-based teaching are also at the heart of assessment and evaluation methods that are capable not only of producing valid grades, but also, and more importantly, leading to improved reading and writing.

Responding

The first of the three Rs, *responding*, means both 'to give a reply' and 'to react'. Both meanings come into play when one reads, writes, and talks. In reading, readers respond to a text in the sense of 'reacting', based on how well the text meshes with their knowledge, beliefs, values, attitudes, and so forth. Readers also respond in the sense of 'replying' or participating in a dialogic exchange with the writer, by filling in discourse that the writer has left implicit in the text (see, for example, the Lewis Thomas 'stigmergy' passage in Chapter 4). It is therefore important to bring students to a realization that their understanding of a text cannot occur without some kind of response on their part. Of course, during the process of discussing a text, other students' (and the teacher's) responses become 'secondary texts' to which one also responds—and these 'secondary' responses will ultimately influence one's response to the 'primary', written text.

Writing involves responding in both concrete and abstract ways. On the concrete level, one may respond to a letter, to a teacher's assignment, or to an exam question, by writing. On a more abstract level, the processes of inventing, planning, redesigning, and evaluating what one wants to say involve responding to a complex array of factors, including the task demands, the ultimate purpose of the writing, the identity of the addressee (and the writer's relationship to the addressee), and limitations in the extent of one's Available Designs. From this perspective, every text that students write is a response, as is every text they read. A literacy-based approach to teaching thus encourages learners not only to respond to the texts they read, but also to have some sense of how the texts they read are themselves responses to something. This involves attention, then, not only to Available Designs (i.e. the inner circle of Figure 2.3), but also to the particular contexts of their use.

In a literacy-based curriculum, responding is as important for teachers as it is for students, and teachers are called upon to respond in ways that go well beyond error correction. If design of meaning is the central issue, then teachers need to respond to the particular meanings that learners create, allowing them to assess how well their expression fits their communicative intentions. In the following exchange in an introductory-level French classroom, for example, the student's first two utterances would likely be considered 'incorrect' in a structure-based teaching situation. In fact, however, the student's first two utterances are perfectly grammatical—they simply do not communicate what the student wants to say.

Student: [*describing other student*] Elle n'est pas une voiture.
Teacher: Oui, ça c'est sûr. Je vois qu'elle n'est certainement pas une voiture.
Student: Ah . . . Elle n'a pas une voiture.
Teacher: Elle n'a pas une voiture. D'accord. C'est-à-dire qu'elle a deux ou trois voitures?
Student: Non . . . Elle n'a pas . . . de voiture.
Teacher: Pas de voiture. D'accord, j'ai compris.
[Student: She is not a car.
Teacher: Yes, that's for sure. I see that she is certainly not a car.
Student: Ah . . . She doesn't have one car.
Teacher: She doesn't have one car. OK. In other words she has two or three cars?
Student: No . . . She doesn't have . . . a car.
Teacher: No car. OK, I get it.]

Here the teacher's responses make clear to the student what he is really saying, allowing him to make adjustments until there is a good match between his intentions and the response that he gets from the teacher.

Similarly, teachers' responses to students' written work are crucially important in that they allow students to see where they have been successful in communicating what they intended to communicate, and where their expression may have fallen short of their intentions. An exclusively form-based response (i.e. spelling and grammar correction) does not provide learners with sufficient feedback in this respect. What is most needed, as described in Chapter 9, is the kind of response that shows learners how their writing has been interpreted, where their meaning is not clear, and how content, organization, and expression can be improved. It is largely through teacher modeling that students will develop their ability to respond not only to others' texts, but to their own as well.

Revising

The second of the three Rs, *revising*, is often associated exclusively with writing. Literacy-based teaching, however, incorporates revision in a wide range of language activities. At the level of the lesson plan, as well as at the level of curriculum, literacy-based teaching emphasizes rereading, rewriting, rethinking, reframing, and redesigning language. The point is not to repeat, but to *redo* within a different contextual frame, purpose, or audience, in order to develop learners' ability to reflect on how meaning is designed differently in different situations. Tierney and Pearson (1984) discuss the importance of the revising process in reading as follows:

> If readers are to develop some control over and a sense of discovery with the models of meaning they build, they must approach text with the same deliberation, time, and reflection that a writer employs as she revises a text. They must examine their developing interpretations and view the models they build as draft-like in quality—subject to revision.
> (Tierney and Pearson 1984: 41)

As we saw in Chapter 3, rereading is a way to fine-tune interpretations and make connections that were not at first obvious, but it is also a way to better understand the reading process itself. By evaluating their responses to reading from various angles, readers can experience the contingencies of meaning that accompany shifts in context. If readers remain bound to a view of reading as remembering as much as possible from a single pass through a text, they not only limit the richness of their reading experience, but also hold themselves back from fully developing their communicative potential as language users. One implication of this view is that in-depth reading of fewer texts may be more beneficial to language learners than superficial reading of a large number of texts (although there should certainly be a place for extensive reading too, as an out-of-class activity, based on learners' interests). And it is in-depth reading that most requires the careful guidance of a teacher.

Writing, of course, benefits tremendously from revision. But what is most significant from a language teaching perspective is not the quality of the final draft, but the effects of the revising process itself on the stance that learners take toward their writing, the kinds of questions they ask themselves, and their capacity to reshape their expression (and perhaps even their intentions) flexibly.

The teacher plays an important role in providing specific purposes for revision. Simply giving students more time to read or write will probably not be enough. Students need some kind of structure (for example, comparing one draft or reading with another, *with a specific purpose in doing so*). The purpose might come from class discussion or from students' journals, but will most often require urging by a thoughtful teacher.

Speaking ability can also be enhanced by revision and redesigning. Kramsch (1993) illustrates how a simple activity of one student narrating a story to another can be developed into a series of exchanges that allow students to express and experience multiple meanings, based on the same content. Kramsch's technique involves systematically varying parameters of context, such as the setting, the participants, the ends, the act sequence, the key, the instrumentalities, the norms of interaction, and the genre. By working through such contextual manipulations, students become aware of their effects on language and meaning (Kramsch 1993: 94–8).

Reflecting

The third R, *reflecting*, takes us back to the point made in Chapter 4 concerning the importance of evaluation of designs (including responses and revisions) as a goal in literacy-based pedagogy. From the standpoint of receptive language use (i.e. listening, reading, viewing), reflecting might involve questions such as the following: What might be this person's intentions? What does this particular manner of expression (use of language) imply about the speaker/writer's beliefs and attitudes about the topic, about me (the reader/listener), and about our relationship to one another? Are other signs (for example, body language, gestures, situational context, text formatting) consistent with or in opposition to the semantic meaning of what has been said or written?

From the standpoint of expressive language use (i.e. speaking and writing), reflecting might involve questions such as: In what ways might the other person interpret what I say if I say/write it like this? What am I assuming that he or she knows or believes? Is it appropriate for me to say this, given my social role *vis-à-vis* my interlocutor/reader? What might be communicated (about me, about our relationship to one another) by the very act of communicating this?

Imbricated in all of these questions are issues of cultural norms and cultural knowledge (i.e. relationships across the three circles of Figure 2.3). In reflecting on culture, teachers must concern themselves with the target culture to which learners are being exposed, but also with the culture(s) that learners themselves bring to the language classroom, and the relationship between the two. As Jin and Cortazzi (1998) have pointed out, the culture learners (and teachers) bring to the foreign language classroom is more than just a background influence. It shapes what happens in the classroom, including how teachers and students interact and how they evaluate one another's roles and performance (p. 98). Jin and Cortazzi recommend that language learners

> become more aware of their own cultural presuppositions and those of others in order to build a bridge of mutual intercultural learning. The process of raising cultural awareness implies a willingness for classroom participants to challenge their own assumptions.
> (p. 99)

This is, one might add, a role requirement for teachers as well as students.

Literacy-based teaching calls for a classroom culture that looks self-consciously at the roles that are played out in classroom communication. Teachers need to model this critical stance through the questions they ask, the issues they raise, the way they themselves respond to students' questions, comments, and retorts. They need to guide their students in looking at their own interaction as a text in itself.

Consider one example of how reflection might bring to light certain cultural presuppositions in the context of an intermediate-level French conversation class. After reading and discussing two newspaper editorials on smoking in public places (one in a French-language newspaper published in the U.S. for students and the other from a newspaper published in France), students invent skits to act out different perspectives. In one skit, two students play the roles of businesswomen (one French, one American) having lunch at nearby tables at a Paris brasserie. The French woman wishes to smoke and the American asks her not to. The smoker is offended and a third (male) student, playing the role of the brasserie manager, approaches and attempts to resolve the conflict. He does this by cheerfully inviting the smoker to sit outside on the terrace, and the non-smoker to sit in an area where people are not smoking. Because the smoker is still angry, the manager offers her credit for three free cups of coffee, and makes the same offer to the non-smoker. A happy ending for all. In this case, even though the students have used French exclusively in their skit (i.e. situated practice), the manager's conflict-resolution strategies suggest a thoroughly American approach of 'making everyone happy', based on the cultural premise that 'the customer is always right'. This is an opportune moment for the teacher to ask students to reflect on the decisions and thinking processes they went through in developing the skit, why they improvised their actions as they did, why they represented the various roles as they did (i.e. introduce a critical framing component). In other words, the teacher could extrapolate beyond a discussion of the 'facts' of the smoking issue, to a discussion of the cultural and rhetorical underpinnings of the interaction. The discussion could then return to the newspaper editorials that they had read, looking at particular cultural assumptions and rhetorical decisions that the authors had made in writing for a particular audience (i.e. a French audience versus an American audience).

By acknowledging the importance of learners' agency in the meaning-making process and the cultural values inherent in language use, language teaching gains greater currency in an international framework. It not only promotes deeper understanding of the language being studied, but also equips learners to uncover the cultural frames within which language is used, even long past their formal language study.

Table 10.2 summarizes, in admittedly reductive fashion, shifts in teacher and learner roles corresponding to the goals set out in Table 10.1, situating the three Rs of responding, revising, and reflecting in relation to roles emphasized in structural and communicative approaches.

	Structural emphasis	Communicative emphasis	Literacy emphasis
Role models for teachers and learners	'philologists' or 'linguists'	'native speakers'	'discourse analysts' and 'intercultural explorers'
Primary instructional role of teacher	Organizing overt instruction and transformed practice	Organizing situated practice, overt instruction, and transformed practice	Organizing critical framing as well as situated practice, overt instruction, and transformed practice
Primary mode of teacher response	Correcting (enforcing a prescriptive norm)	Responding (to communicative intent)	Responding (to language as used), focusing attention for reflection and revision
Predominant learner roles	Deference to authority: focus on absorption and analysis of material presented	Active participation: focus on using language in face-to-face interaction	Active engagement: focus on using language, reflecting on language use, and revising

Table 10.2:   Summary of teacher/learner roles in structural, communicative, and literacy-based curricula

Potential obstacles to implementing a literacy-based curriculum

There are many individual teachers throughout the world who successfully engage their students in the kinds of learning experiences I have proposed in this book. But they tend to be the exceptions, rather than the rule. Cultivating a literacy-based approach on a widespread, curricular basis is not an easy task, and it can be impeded by practical, pedagogical, and political obstacles.

On a practical level it might be objected that a literacy-based approach demands too much time. Especially at the introductory level, the amount of material that needs to be covered in a language curriculum is substantial, and adding critical reflection about texts may seem unreasonable. It is true that literacy-based teaching takes more time than teaching focused strictly on acquiring language skills or content knowledge. Consequently, in some cases, the breadth of 'coverage' in a given course may have to be reduced. But this is not necessarily a bad thing. Racing through a densely packed syllabus may give teachers a sense of accomplishment, but it does not necessarily lead to high quality learning. Essentially, the question comes down to the way that one conceives of teaching and learning. Curricula that emphasize breadth over depth imply a model that sees teaching and learning as the dissemination and absorption of facts. What language learners need is not sheer facts, however, but an understanding of how the facts of a language connect to social, historical, and cultural realities. This mapping takes time. Ultimately, administrators, teachers, and students may have to make changes in the way that time is used inside and outside of language classrooms. In settings where computer technology is available, multimedia applications might allow students to do some of their structure-based learning outside of class. Certain class meetings might need to be scheduled back to back, in order to afford time for more in-depth discussion of a particular topic, or to permit continued work on a collaborative project.

On a pedagogical level, many teachers observe that their students have sufficient difficulty learning and using the basic structures of the language (i.e. at the level of situated practice and overt instruction), they fear that any greater challenge (i.e. critical framing and transformed practice) would overwhelm their students. It is, of course, essential to be realistic in designing instructional tasks, ensuring that the requisite knowledge, resources, and assistance are available to students. At the same time, it is important to recognize that incorporating tasks involving critical framing and transformed practice can boost learners' interest and motivation in ways that situated practice and overt instruction alone may not. Students tend to rise to whatever realistic challenges are set for them, as long as they are motivated.

A related pedagogical concern has to do with students' learning styles. Many respond well to visual and audiovisual media, but consider reading and writing to be 'dry' activities. At the beginning, in working with these students, the same principles of leading from situated practice to critical framing and transformed practice can be applied to non-verbal, or partially-verbal, texts such as photographs, paintings, films, and advertisements. The skills they develop in interpreting texts in these media can then be called upon in their analyses of written texts, can bolster their confidence and motivation, and can ultimately make their reading more rewarding. Again, some students think of reading and writing as 'difficult' because reading and writing have traditionally been treated as solitary activities. Brought into the mainstream of classroom activity, they can become a more collaborative (and motivating) enterprise.

It must be kept in mind, however, that differences in cultures of learning and teaching can make it difficult to implement a literacy-based approach. As we saw in Chapters 5 and 7, conceptions of reading, writing, and appropriate pedagogy can vary considerably across teaching settings. Learners who do not understand the beliefs and values their teachers hold may not benefit optimally from their instruction. Because underlying beliefs and values influence learning styles, teaching styles, and learners' and teachers' expectations about the dynamics of classroom interaction and assessment, the teacher's task is to help bring differences into explicit awareness—not necessarily to socialize learners into a new set of beliefs and values, but to sensitize them to where cultural differences lie, how they manifest themselves, and to discuss differences with some degree of critical distance.

Another pedagogical concern of many foreign language teachers is that they do not consider themselves sufficiently 'expert' in their own cultural knowledge to help their students understand all the relevant aspects of the context and cultural presuppositions of texts they read. Here, it is important to bear in mind that no one can exhaust all the possible contextual information that could potentially enrich students' reading of a given text. The point is to make students aware of how important background knowledge is in the reading process through example, and then to show them how to find out more on their own. Again, the goal of reading foreign language texts is not to achieve a 'native-like', fully-informed, culturally-appropriate interpretation. What *is* important for learners to understand, however, is how the interpretations they do come up with are influenced by their beliefs, attitudes, values, and experiences—in other words, by their 'world' as constituted and constructed by cultural models. As we saw in the case of the foreign language students corresponding with native speakers in Chapter 8, cultural conflicts are real and cannot be simply swept aside. The teacher's crucial role is to focus learners' attention on those aspects of an experience or communicative exchange that are most revealing of cultural difference, and to explore opposing perspectives through critical discussion. The foreign language teacher's responsibility, then, is not to play the role of anthropologist or social scientist, but rather, as Kramsch (1998) characterizes it, to teach culture '*as it is mediated through language*' (p. 31). Kramsch points out that this approach draws learners and teachers into a collaborative process of exploration:

> . . . learners are likely to engage their teachers in a voyage of discovery that they had not always anticipated and for which they don't always feel

prepared. Allowing students to become intercultural speakers, therefore, means encouraging teachers to see themselves, too, as brokers between cultures of all kinds.
(Kramsch 1998: 30)

At the political level, there is the question of shared responsibility for curricular change. Without the support and co-operation of colleagues and the institution, curricular change is indeed unlikely to succeed. No one likes to have change imposed upon them. On the other hand, when colleagues see new things they like, they tend to follow. Therefore in working toward a literacy-based curriculum it may be best to think in terms of small steps: by concentrating on gradual change in one's own classes, and by sharing one's thoughts, experiences, accomplishments, and enthusiasm with colleagues, one can often begin to generate the interest and co-operation needed to make broader, programmatic changes possible. Byrnes (2000) describes the intense, collaborative effort of faculty members in the German Department at Georgetown University to design and implement a comprehensive four-year curriculum aimed at 'multi-voiced literacy' for learners at all levels.[2] Such extensive collegial co-operation is rare, but the rewards have been great at Georgetown. Through the many faculty meetings, development work-shops, and material creation sessions that involved graduate students as well as faculty, the departmental culture was transformed, as Byrnes put it, 'in ways that none of us would have thought possible . . . . I am unable to imagine how the intricate understandings about the relationship of meaning and language now available . . . could otherwise have entered our thinking actions in such a profoundly formative way' (p. 159).

Tied to the question of collegial support is the perception that a literacy-based curriculum, by including non-literary texts, seems to deprivilege literature. This perception is valid to the extent that the focus of instruction is broadened beyond an *exclusive* focus on literary texts, although certainly the value of literary study is not diminished. If anything it is enhanced, for textuality becomes a central focus of teaching at all levels. Explicit links can be made between literary writing and other forms of cultural expression, such as film, art, music, architecture, and news media, thus improving students' understanding of how literature fits into the 'big picture' of signifying practices in the foreign society. Time spent on the exploration of cultural narratives in various popular media might displace time spent on the next novel on the syllabus; but if such 'digressions' serve to illuminate students' understanding of certain cultural underpinnings of that novel and/or create a bridge to what students are learning in their culture/civilization courses, then it is time well spent. As students begin to understand the relationships and connections across different forms of cultural expression, their interest and motivation to study literature will be likely to increase significantly.

Implications for teacher education

The single most important factor in attaining the goals of a literacy-based curriculum is highly-qualified language teachers. In preparing teachers to deal with the demands of a literacy-based approach to language teaching, teacher educators must redefine the scope of teacher development. They must think of ways to prepare teachers not just as language experts but also as literacy experts. In terms of the design model in Figure 2.3, this means preparing them to teach not just Available Designs as stock items, but about relationships among Available Designs, communicative contexts, and larger sociocultural contexts.

Thus, one task of literacy-based teacher education is to broaden young teachers' perceptions of what language teaching is all about. Many begin a teacher education program with a notion that language teaching is a matter of transmitting language facts (perhaps this is what they remember from their own early language learning experiences). But their role is much more significant than they may expect. Language teachers do much more than instruct learners in the structural details of a language. They teach new ways of being in the world. As teachers of language and literacy, they are ultimately in the business of opening up to their students' new signifying systems and all the power that goes with the mastery of multiple levels of symbols. This often involves socializing learners into new ways of thinking about meaning and communication. Consequently, as Gee (1990) points out, language teaching is inevitably an ideological and political activity:

> The English teacher can cooperate in her own marginalization by seeing herself as 'a language teacher' with no connection to . . . social and political issues. Or she can accept the paradox of literacy as a form of interethnic communication which often involves conflicts of values and identities, and accept her role as one who socializes students into a world view that, given its power here and abroad, must be viewed critically, comparatively, and with a constant sense of the possibilities for change. Like it or not, the English teacher stands at the very heart of the most crucial educational, cultural and political issues of our time.
> (Gee 1990: 67–8)

As instigators of critical reflection about meaning design across cultural contexts, teachers need to realize that the true scope of their work is nothing short of *education* in the fullest sense.

In order to prepare for this important role, teachers certainly need a high level of competence in both spoken and written forms of the language, cultural knowledge, and a familiarity with literature. But they also need experience in mediating between multiple perspectives and meanings—those born of the learners' culture(s) and those arising from the culture(s) of the language being taught. Although this experience can be acquired by trial and error, it is probably most effectively gained through apprenticeship with a mentor teacher. One key feature of literacy-based teacher education, then, is provision for focused, critical observation of experienced teachers in a variety of classroom settings, combined with post-teaching analysis and discussion. As apprentices begin to take classes of their own, their mentors observe and discuss what happens in these classes with them, helping them analyze and interpret the 'texts' of their own interaction with students. In this way, both apprentices and mentors follow an ongoing rhythm of response, reflection, and revision.

Teachers in training also need academic coursework that brings to their attention the rich interplay between language use, context, and culture. Linguistics courses on the phonology, morphology, and syntax of the language may be of some use in helping teachers to understand the complexities of the language system, but they are not alone sufficient. Of particular relevance are courses that deal with pragmatics, discourse analysis, conversational analysis, sociolinguistics, and courses that deal specifically with language use in educational settings.[3] Literature courses are key in fostering an appreciation of the multiple levels at which texts signify, and in familiarizing teachers with some of the most important stories told in the culture. Study of the 'external' history of the language can complement literature courses, showing how social forces influence language use and language change over time. And finally, anthropology coursework focused on language and culture can provide cross-cultural scope.

In sum, just as the design metaphor leads toward a goal of thoughtful, appropriate communication, it also leads toward a goal of thoughtful, appropriate language teaching. That is, language teaching that is sensitive to relationships—configurations of Available Designs as well as relationships between teachers and students—within particular contexts of communication, and within larger sociocultural contexts of beliefs, values, and practices of communities.

Implications for research

Adopting literacy as an organizing principle for language teaching also establishes a broad agenda for research related to language acquisition. The design model described in Part One emphasizes the role of both the immediate situational context and the larger sociocultural context in the way language learners draw on Available Designs such as grammar, vocabulary, declarative and procedural knowledge, genres, styles, and stories in designing meaning. What this suggests is that many of the phenomena that have been explored under the rubric of the 'cognitive'—learning strategies, reading strategies, writing strategies, transfer, and the like—need to be simultaneously explored from the perspective of the 'social' (i.e. their functional significance within particular contexts of language use).

To illustrate, we will take the example of reading strategies. The tendency in research has been to abstract reading processes from functional contexts, to reify them as entities, and to list them in some sort of classification system that can then be used to inventory learners' self-reported or observed reading behavior. The problem with such an approach is that it separates the behavior from the social context that motivates the behavior, and that therefore makes the behavior *interpretable*. 'Scanning' a restaurant check for the name of the restaurant is not the same as 'scanning' a movie review to see if the reviewer liked the movie or not. The first involves simple word recognition, whereas the second involves interpretation (Lee and Musumeci 1988). The surface behavior may be the same, but the underlying motivations and processes are quite different. This problem of 'genericization' is compounded when notions of effectiveness are applied to reading strategies (i.e. when strategies are labeled 'good' or 'effective' because fluent readers report using them). Such labels break down, of course, when readers report using 'good' strategies but still do not understand what they are reading (or, conversely, when they report using 'ineffective' strategies and yet succeed in understanding). The effectiveness of a given reading strategy is not an inherent quality of that strategy, but is contingent on a variety of contextual factors, including the reader's purpose, language competence, L1 literacy background, and features of the particular text being read.

The design model suggests that researchers need to observe not just what *types* of strategies readers use, but also how particular readers use particular strategies in particular ways in particular contexts. In this way, they might better understand phenomena such as (1) shifts in attention between reader-based knowledge and text-based information, (2) shifts in attention between micro and macro elements of a text, and (3) shifts between bottom-up and top-down processing.

Moving to a broader level, the design model suggests a context-sensitive approach to literacy research, guided by the question: 'In what ways, and to what ends, do second language learners draw on the various linguistic and schematic resources available to them in particular contexts of reading and writing?'. This agenda highlights the need for a great deal more research on *variability* in reading and writing behavior, across language proficiency levels, across different text types, across familiar and unfamiliar topics, across different purposes and tasks, across different evaluation contexts, and across different cultures of learning and teaching.[4]

Methodologically, this agenda places key importance on ethnographic approaches, thick description, interviews, and think-aloud procedures, in order to allow both the immediate and larger sociocultural contexts of reading and writing to be taken into account. Also needed is closer analysis of the kinds of texts and tasks that are used in literacy research (for example, looking at researchers' assumptions in relation to research subjects' experience, cultural background, social milieu, reading history, and so forth).

Instructional research is also of crucial importance in validating the theoretical assumption made in this book that guided practice in a social context (i.e. apprenticeship) will eventually lead learners to internalize not only general strategies, but also principles of appropriateness that they will eventually be able to use on their own as they read and write outside of class. This agenda requires close analyses of learners and teachers in literacy-based classrooms, attentive to learners' and teachers' respective roles, classroom interaction dynamics, and the formulation and framing of instructional tasks—all in relation to school, community, and societal contexts. Exploration across different cultures of learning and teaching are particularly important in determining how literacy-based teaching might be adapted in different cultural settings.

Another important area of research under the instructional rubric is into the uses of computer technology in literacy education. How might interactive electronic environments affect social interaction? How might they affect meaning design processes? What affects the extent to which learners draw on well-established strategies from non-electronic literacy contexts? To what extent (and under what conditions) might they adopt new strategies? Again, such questions call for detailed ethnographic studies.

Finally, methods of evaluating literacy and preparing language/literacy teachers are two areas very much in need of research. Specifically, how are assessment techniques used? How are the results interpreted and used? How are these interpretations and uses related to teachers' understanding or philosophy of language learning and teaching? To what extent do assessment and evaluation contribute to language learning itself? In the area of teacher education: Which teacher qualities are most important to foster, and which lend themselves to fostering in a teacher education program? What kinds of apprenticeship experiences are most productive? What combinations of coursework offer optimal breadth and depth and yet maintain a suitable economy of time and resources? What balance of practice and reflection on practice is most appropriate (and in which contexts)?

Conclusion

The approach to language teaching I have described in this book is one focused on relationships—linguistic, cognitive, and social relationships between readers, writers, texts, and culture; relationships between form and meaning; relationships between reading and writing; relationships between spoken and written communication. The approach acknowledges the importance of textual analysis, but emphasizes the need to widen the scope of inquiry beyond the literary canon, to include a range of written and spoken texts that broadly represent the particular signifying practices of a society. The approach is also concerned with providing learners with structured guidance in the *thinking* that goes into reading, writing, and speaking appropriately in particular contexts. This emphasis on thinking blurs the traditional division between language skills and academic content because language use itself becomes an object of reflection, and therefore constitutes a source of intellectual content. For these reasons, it is hoped that an integrated focus on linguistic, cognitive, and social dimensions of literacy might ultimately enhance the coherence of language teaching and learning at all levels of language study.

Notes

1 See, for example, Valdman (1992) and Kramsch (1997).

2 A complete description of the Georgetown German Department's literacy-based curriculum can be found on the Department's web site at *http://www.georgetown.edu/departments/german/ curriculum/curriculum.html*

3 A scholar who has thought extensively about preparing teachers for their broadened role as linguistic and cultural mediators, van Lier (1996) proposes linguistics courses focused specifically on educational contexts and issues. He specifies three key criteria for such courses. First, they should adopt an experiential approach, requiring learners to observe and analyze language use. Second, they should reject a product-orientation to language. That is, they should

> focus not on language as a body of content matter which can be transmitted piecemeal to an audience, but rather as a living thing which shapes our existence and which we use to make sense of our world and our work

> (van Lier 1996: 89).

Third, such courses should emphasize critical approaches to language study, focusing on interrelationships between text (any piece of language produced in a specific context), sociocognitive processes (the relationships and thoughts expressed in language), and the sociohistorical context (the conventions, presupposed roles, and dominant views inherent in the setting)

> (van Lier 1996: 89).

4 One example of an important area of research in this regard, is differences in literacy practices and differences in teaching practices in language courses designed for 'heritage speakers' versus those designed for 'foreign language learners'.

Bibliography

ACTFL. 1986. *ACTFL Proficiency Guidelines.* Hastings-on-Hudson: American Council on the Teaching of Foreign Languages.

Alderson, J. C. 1984. 'Reading in a foreign language: a reading problem or a language problem?' in J. C. Alderson and A. H. Urquhart (eds.): *Reading in a foreign language.* London: Longman: 1–24.

Allaei, S. K. and **U. Connor.** 1991. 'Using Performative Assessment Instruments with ESL Student Writers' in L. Hamp-Lyons (ed.) *Assessing Second Language Writing in Academic Contexts.* Norwood, NJ: Ablex: 227–40.

Allen, E. D. and **R. M. Valette.** 1994. *Classroom Techniques: Foreign Languages and English as a Second Language.* Prospect Heights, IL: Waveland.

Allen, J. P. B. and **H. G. Widdowson.** 1974. *English in Physical Science.* Oxford: Oxford University Press.

Allen, J. P. B. and **H. G. Widdowson.** 1978a. *English in Social Studies.* Oxford: Oxford University Press.

Allen, J. P. B. and **H. G. Widdowson.** 1978b. 'Teaching the Communicative Use of English' in R. Mackay and A. J. Mountford (eds.): *English for Specific Purposes: A Case Study Approach.* London: Longman: 56–77.

Alvermann, D. and **S. A. Hague.** 1989. 'Comprehension of Counterintuitive Science: Effects of Prior Knowledge and Text Structure.' *Journal of Educational Research* 82/4: 197–202.

Anderson, J. R. 1980. *Cognitive Psychology and Its Implications.* San Francisco: Freeman.

Applebee, A. N., J. A. Langer, I. V. S. Mullis, and **L. B. Jenkins.** 1990. *The Writing Report Card, 1984–88.* Princeton: National Assessment of Educational Progress, Educational Testing Service.

Armbruster, B. B. and **T. H. Anderson.** 1982. *Idea mapping: The technique and its use in the classroom.* (Reading Education Report No. 36) Urbana: University of Illinois, Center for the Study of Reading.

Atkinson, D. and **V. Ramanathan.** 1995. 'Cultures of writing: An ethnographic comparison of L1 and L2 university writing/language programs.' *TESOL Quarterly* 29/3: 539–68.

Austin, J. L. 1962. *How to do things with words.* Cambridge, MA: Harvard University Press.

Avots, J. 1991. 'Linking the Foreign Language Classroom to the World' in J. K. Phillips (ed.) *Building Bridges and Making Connections.* Middlebury, VT: Northeast Conference on the Teaching of Foreign Languages: 122–53.

Bachman, L. F. 1990. *Fundamental Considerations in Language Testing*. Oxford: Oxford University Press.

Bailey, K. M. 1998. *Learning About Language Assessment: Dilemmas, Decisions, and Directions*. Boston: Heinle and Heinle.

Baker, C. D. and A. Luke (eds.). 1991. *Towards a Critical Sociology of Reading Pedagogy: Papers of the XII World Congress on Reading*. Pragmatics and Beyond. Amsterdam: John Benjamins.

Bakhtin, M. M. 1986. *Speech Genres and Other Late Essays*. Austin: University of Texas Press.

Ballard, B. and J. Clanchy. 1991. 'Assessment by misconception: Cultural influences and intellectual traditions' in L. Hamp-Lyons (ed.) *Assessing Second Language Writing in Academic Contexts*. Norwood, NJ: Ablex: 19–35.

Barnett, M. A. 1986. 'Syntactic and lexical/semantic skill in foreign language reading: Importance and interaction.' *Modern Language Journal* 70/4: 343–9.

Barnett, M. A. 1991. 'Language and literature: False dichotomies, real allies.' *ADFL Bulletin* 22/3: 7–11.

Barrera, R. 1981. 'Reading in Spanish: Insights from children's miscues' in S. Hudelson (ed.) *Learning to Read in Different Languages*. Arlington, VA: Center for Applied Linguistics.

Barrs, M. 1994. 'Genre Theory: What's It All About?' in B. Stierer and J. Maybin (eds.): *Language, Literacy and Learning in Educational Practice*. Clevedon, UK: Multilingual Matters: 248–57.

Barson, J. 1991. 'The Virtual Classroom is Born: What Now?' in B. F. Freed (ed.) *Foreign Language Acquisition Research and the Classroom*. Lexington, MA: D. C. Heath: 365–83.

Barthes, R. 1970. *S/Z*. Paris: Editions du Seuil.

Barton, D. 1994. *Literacy: An Introduction to the Ecology of Written Language*. Oxford: Blackwell.

Baudelaire, C. 1989. *The Parisian Prowler: Le Spleen de Paris, Petits poèmes en prose*. Athens, GA: University of Georgia Press.

Baynham, M. 1995. *Literacy Practices: Investigating Literacy in Social Contexts*. London, New York: Longman.

Beach, R. and D. Appleman. 1984. 'Reading Strategies for Expository and Literary Text Types' in A. C. Purves and O. Niles (eds.): *Becoming readers in a complex society: Eighty-third yearbook of the National Society for the Study of Education*. Chicago: University of Chicago Press: 115–43.

Beach, R. and D. Lundell. 1998. 'Early Adolescents' Use of Computer-Mediated Communication in Writing and Reading' in D. Reinking, M. C. McKenna, L. D. Labbo, and R. D. Kieffer (eds.): *Handbook of Literacy and Technology: Transformations in a Post-Typographic World*. Mahwah, NJ: Lawrence Erlbaum: 93–112.

Beaugrande, R. and W. Dressler. 1981. *Introduction to Text Linguistics*. London: Longman.

Beauvois, M. 1992. 'Computer-assisted classroom discussion in the foreign language classroom: Conversation in slow motion.' *Foreign Language Annals* 25/5: 455–64.

Beauvois, M. 1998. 'Write to Speak: The Effects of Electronic Communication on the Oral Achievement of Fourth Semester French Students' in J. Muyskens (ed.) *New Ways of Teaching and Learning: Focus on Technology and Foreign Language Education*. Boston: Heinle and Heinle: 93–115.

Becker, A. L. 1988. 'Language in Particular: A Lecture' in D. Tannen (ed.) *Linguistics in Context: Connecting Observation and Understanding (Lectures from the 1985 LSA/TESOL and NEH Institutes)*. Norwood, NJ: Ablex: 17–35.

Belanoff, P. and M. Dickson (eds.). 1991. *Portfolios: Process and Product*. Portsmouth, NH: Heinemann.

Belanoff, P., P. Elbow, and S. I. Fontaine (eds.). 1991. *Nothing Begins with 'N': New Investigations of Freewriting*. Carbondale, IL: Southern Illinois University Press.

Bell, J. S. 1995. 'The relationship between L1 and L2 literacy: Some complicating factors.' *TESOL Quarterly* 29/4: 687–704.

Bensoussan, M., D. Sim, and R. Weiss. 1984. 'The effect of dictionary usage on EFL test performance compared with student and teacher attitudes and expectations.' *Reading in a Foreign Language* 2: 262–76.

Berkenkotter, C. and T. N. Huckin. 1995. *Genre Knowledge in Disciplinary Communication: Cognition/Culture/Power*. Hillsdale, NJ: Lawrence Erlbaum.

Berman, R. 1975. 'Analytic syntax: A technique for advanced level reading.' *TESOL Quarterly* 9/3: 243–51.

Berman, R. A. 1984. 'Syntactic Components of the Foreign Language Reading Process' in J. C. Alderson and A. H. Urquhart (eds.): *Reading in a foreign language*. London: Longman: 139–59.

Berman, R. A. 1996. 'Reform and Continuity: Graduate Education toward a Foreign Cultural Literacy.' *ADFL Bulletin* 27/3: 40–6.

Bernhardt, E. 1986. 'Proficient texts or proficient readers?' *ADFL Bulletin* 18/1: 25–8.

Bernhardt, E. 1987. 'Cognitive Processes in L2: An Examination of Reading Behaviors' in J. P. Lantolf and A. Labarca (eds.): *Delaware Symposium on Language Studies: Research on Second Language Acquisition in Classroom Setting*. Norwood, NJ: Ablex: 35–50.

Bernhardt, E. 1991. *Reading Development in a Second Language: Theoretical, Empirical, and Classroom Perspectives*. Norwood, NJ: Ablex.

Bernhardt, E. and M. Kamil. 1995. 'Interpreting relationships between L1 and L2 reading: Consolidating the linguistic threshold and the linguistic interdependence hypotheses.' *Applied Linguistics* 16/1: 15–34.

Bernhardt, E. and M. Kamil. 1998. 'Enhancing Foreign Language Culture Learning through Electronic Discussion' in J. Muyskens (ed.) *New Ways of Teaching and Learning: Focus on Technology and Foreign Language Education*. Boston: Heinle and Heinle: 39–55.

Besse, H. 1984. 'De la communication didactique d'un document' in *Actas de las VIIas Jornadas Pedagógicas sobre la enseñanza del francés en España*. Barcelona: ICE de la Universidad Autónoma: 17–8.

Bhatia, V. K. 1991. 'A genre-based approach to ESP materials.' *World Englishes* 10/2: 153–66.

Bizzell, P. and B. Herzberg. 1991. 'A Brief History of Rhetoric and Composition' in P. Bizzell and B. Herzberg (eds.): *The Bedford Bibliography for Teachers of Writing, Third Edition*. New York: St. Martin's Press: 1–7.

Bland, S. K., J. S. Noblitt, S. Armington, and G. Gay. 1990. 'The naive lexical hypothesis: Evidence from computer-assisted language learning.' *Modern Language Journal* 74/4: 440–50.

Blanton, L. L. 1987. 'Reshaping ESL students' perceptions of writing.' *ELT Journal* 41/2: 112–8.
Block, E. 1986. 'The comprehension strategies of second language readers.' *TESOL Quarterly* 20/3: 463–94.
Bloomfield, L. 1933. *Language*. New York: Holt, Rinehart and Winston.
Bolter, J. D. 1991. *Writing Space: The Computer, Hypertext, and the History of Writing*. Hillsdale, NJ: Lawrence Erlbaum.
Booth Olson, C. 1984. 'Fostering critical thinking skills through writing.' *Educational Leadership* /November: 28–39.
Bourdieu, P. 1979/1984. *Distinction: A Social Critique of the Judgement of Taste*. Cambridge, MA: Harvard University Press.
Bourdieu, P. 1991. *Language and Symbolic Power*. Cambridge, MA: Harvard University Press.
Boyer, H., M. Butzbach, and M. Pendanx. 1990. *Nouvelle introduction à la didactique du français langue étrangère*. Paris: CLE International.
Braddock, R., R. Lloyd-Jones, and L. Schoer. 1963. *Research in Written Composition*. Urbana, Ill: National Council of Teachers of English.
Brandelius, M. 1983. 'Le déjeuner des canotiers.' *Le Français dans le monde* 23/179: 64–9.
Brandt, D. 1990. *Literacy as Involvement: The Acts of Writers, Readers, and Texts*. Carbondale, IL: Southern Illinois University Press.
Brannon, L. and C. H. Knoblauch. 1982. 'On students' rights to their own texts: A model of teacher response.' *College Composition and Communication* 33: 157–66.
Breen, M. P. and C. N. Candlin. 1980. 'The essentials of a communicative curriculum in language teaching.' *Applied Linguistics* 1/1: 89–112.
Brisbois, J. 1992. *Do first language writing and second language reading equal second language reading comprehension? An assessment dilemma*. Unpublished dissertation. Ohio State University.
Britton, J., T. Burgess, N. Martin, A. McLeod, and H. Rosen. 1975. *The Development of Writing Abilities: 11–18*. London: Macmillan.
Brotchie, A. 1993. *Surrealist Games*. Boston: Shambhala Redstone Editions.
Brown, R. G. 1991. *Schools of Thought: How the Politics of Literacy Shape Thinking in the Classroom*. San Francisco: Jossey-Bass.
Brumfit, C. J. and R. A. Carter (eds.). 1986. *Literature and Language Teaching*. Oxford: Oxford University Press.
Buck, K., H. Byrnes, and I. Thompson (eds.). 1990. *The ACTFL Oral Proficiency Interview Tester Training Manual*. Yonkers, NY: American Council on the Teaching of Foreign Languages.
Burtoff, M. 1983. *The Logical Organization of Written Expository Discourse in English: A Comparative Study of Japanese, Arabic, and Native Speaker Strategies*. Unpublished dissertation. Georgetown University.
Butler, R. O. 1992. *A Good Scent from a Strange Mountain*. New York: Penguin.
Butler, S. 1962. 'Thought and Language' in M. Black (ed.) *The Importance of Language*. Ithaca, NY: Cornell University Press: 13–35.
Byram, M. 1989. *Cultural Studies in Foreign Language Education*. Clevedon, UK: Multilingual Matters.

Byram, M. 1993. 'Language and Culture Learning for European Citizenship' in M. C. Beveridge and G. Reddiford (eds.): *Language, Culture and Education: Proceedings of the Colston Research Society, Bristol.* Clevedon, UK: Multilingual Matters: 84–95.

Byram, M. and V. Esarte-Sarries. 1991. *Investigating Cultural Studies in Foreign Language Teaching: A Book for Teachers.* Clevedon, UK: Multilingual Matters.

Byram, M., C. Morgan, and colleagues. 1994. *Teaching-and-Learning Language-and-Culture.* Clevedon, UK: Multilingual Matters.

Byrnes, H. 1998. 'Constructing Curricula in Collegiate Foreign Language Departments' in H. Byrnes (ed.) *Learning Foreign and Second Languages: Perspectives in Research and Scholarship.* New York: Modern Language Association: 262–95.

Byrnes, H. 2000. 'Meaning and form in classroom-based SLA research: Reflections from a college foreign language perspective' in J. F. Lee and A. Valdman (eds.): *Meaning and Form: Multiple Perspectives.* Boston: Heinle and Heinle: 125–79.

Calfee, R. and P. Perfumo (eds.). 1996. *Writing Portfolios in the Classroom: Policy and Practice, Promise and Peril.* Mahwah, NJ: Lawrence Erlbaum.

Cambourne, B. 1981. 'Oral and Written Relationships: A Reading Perspective' in B. M. Kroll and R. J. Vann (eds.): *Exploring Speaking-Writing Relationships: Connections and Contrasts.* Urbana, IL. National Council of Teachers of English: 82–9

Canale, M. 1983. 'From Communicative Competence to Communicative Language Pedagogy' in J. C. Richards and R. W. Schmidt (eds.): *Language and Communication.* London: Longman: 2–27.

Canale, M. and M. Swain. 1980. 'Theoretical bases of communicative approaches to second language teaching and testing.' *Applied Linguistics* 1/1: 1–47.

Candlin, C. N. 1978. 'Preface' in R. Mackay and A. J. Mountford (eds.): *English for Specific Purposes: A Case Study Approach.* London: Longman: vi–ix.

Caplan, R. and C. Keech. 1980. *Showing-Writing: A Training Program to Help Students Be Specific.* Berkeley, CA: Bay Area Writing Project.

Cardelle, M. and L. Corno. 1981. 'Effects on second language learning of variations in written feedback on homework assignments.' *TESOL Quarterly* 15: 251–62.

Carnicelli, T. 1980. 'The Writing Conference: A One-to-One Conversation' in T. Donovan and B. McClelland (eds.): *Eight Approaches to Teaching Composition.* Urbana, IL: National Council of Teachers of English: 101–31.

Carrell, P. L. 1984. 'The effects of rhetorical organization on ESL readers.' *TESOL Quarterly* 18/3: 441–169.

Carrell, P. L. 1985. 'Facilitating ESL reading by teaching text structure.' *TESOL Quarterly* 19/4: 727–52.

Carrell, P. L. 1991. 'Second language reading: Reading ability or language proficiency?' *Applied Linguistics* 12/2: 159–79.

Carrell, P. L. and J. Eisterhold. 1988. 'Schema Theory and ESL Reading Pedagogy' in P. L. Carrell, J. Devine, and D. E. Eskey (eds.): *Interactive Approaches to Second Language Reading.* Cambridge: Cambridge University Press: 73–92.

Carrell, P. L. and J. C. Eisterhold. 1983. 'Schema theory and ESL reading pedagogy.' *TESOL Quarterly* 17/4: 553–73.

Carson, J. G. 1992. 'Becoming biliterate: First language influences.' *Journal of Second Language Writing* 1/1: 37–60.

Carter, R. 1986. 'Linguistic Models, Language, and Literariness: Study strategies in the teaching of literature to foreign students' in C. J. Brumfit and R. A. Carter (eds.): *Literature and Language Teaching*. Oxford: Oxford University Press: 110–32.

Carter, R. and P. Simpson (eds.). 1995. *Language, Discourse and Literature: An Introductory Reader in Discourse Stylistics*. London: Routledge.

Carter, R. A. and D. Burton (eds.). 1982. *Literary Text and Language Study*. London: Edward Arnold.

Caudery, T. 1998. 'Increasing students' awareness of genre through text transformation exercises: An old classroom activity revisited.' *TESL-EJ* 3/3: A-2.

Cazden, C. and J. Lobdell. 1993. 'Writing-drama connections: A conversation.' *Quarterly of the National Writing Project and Center for the Study of Writing and Literacy* 15/3: 10–4.

Cazden, C. B. 1992. 'Performing Expository Texts in the Foreign Language Classroom' in C. Kramsch and S. McConnell-Ginet (eds.): *Text and Context: Cross-Disciplinary Perspectives on Language Study*. Lexington, MA: D. C. Heath: 67–78.

Chafe, W. L. 1985. 'Linguistic differences produced by differences between speaking and writing' in D. R. Olson, N. Torrance, and A. Hildyard (eds.): *Literacy, Language and Learning: The Nature and Consequences of Reading and Writing*. Cambridge: Cambridge University Press: 105–23.

Chapman, L. J. 1983. *Reading Development and Cohesion*. London: Heinemann.

Chatman, S. 1978. *Story and Discourse: Narrative Structure in Fiction and Film*. Ithaca: Cornell University Press.

Chen, H.-C. and M. F. Graves. 1995. 'Effects of previewing and providing background knowledge on Taiwanese college students' comprehension of American short stories.' *TESOL Quarterly* 29/4: 663–86.

Chen, J. and L. Hamp-Lyons. 1999. 'Nonnative students' reactions to teacher comments: What do Hong Kong tertiary students say?' Paper presented at the 1999 Meeting of the American Association of Applied Linguistics, Stamford, CT, March 1999.

Cheung, H. S. 1995. 'Poetics to Pedagogy: The Imagistic Power of Language' in C. Kramsch (ed.) *Redefining the Boundaries of Language Study*. Boston: Heinle and Heinle: 99–122.

Christensen, F. 1967. *Notes Toward a New Rhetoric: Six Essays for Teachers*. New York: Harper and Row.

Chun, D. M. 1994. 'Using computer networking to facilitate the acquisition of interactive competence.' *System* 22/1: 17–31.

Chun, D. M. and K. K. Brandl. 1992. 'Beyond form-based drill and practice: Meaning-enhancing CALL on the Macintosh.' *Foreign Language Annals* 25/3: 255–67.

Chun, D. M. and J. L. Plass. 1996. 'Facilitating reading comprehension with multimedia.' *System* 24/4: 503–19.

Church, E. and C. Bereiter. 1984. 'Reading for Style' in J. M. Jensen (ed.) *Composing and Comprehending*. Urbana, IL: ERIC Clearinghouse on Reading and Communication Skills: 85–91.

Cisneros, S. 1989. *The House on Mango Street*. New York: Vintage.

Clarke, M. A. 1979. 'Reading in Spanish and English: Evidence from adult ESL students.' *Language Learning* 29/1: 121–50.

Clarke, M. A. 1980. 'The short circuit hypothesis of ESL reading—or when language competence interferes with reading performance.' *Modern Language Journal* 64/2: 203–9.

Clifford, J. 1981. 'Composing in stages: The effects of a collaborative pedagogy.' *Research in the Teaching of English* 15: 37–53.

Cohen, A., H. Glasman, P. R. Rosenbaum-Cohen, J. Ferrara, and J. Fine. 1979. 'Reading English for specialized purposes: Discourse analysis and the use of student informants.' *TESOL Quarterly* 13/4: 551–64.

Cohen, A. D. 1990. *Language Learning: Insights for Learners, Teachers, and Researchers*. Boston: Heinle and Heinle.

Cohen, A. D. and M. C. Cavalcanti. 1990. 'Feedback on compositions: Teacher and student verbal reports' in B. Kroll (ed.) *Second Language Writing: Research Insights for the Classroom*. Cambridge: Cambridge University Press: 155–77.

Cohen, A. P. 1994. *Self Consciousness: An Alternative Anthropology of Identity*. London: Routledge.

Cole, M. 1996. *Cultural Psychology: A Once and Future Discipline*. Cambridge, MA: Belknap Press of Harvard University Press.

Connor, U. 1996. *Contrastive Rhetoric: Cross-cultural Aspects of Second-Language Writing*. Cambridge: Cambridge University Press.

Cononelos, T. and M. Oliva. 1993. 'Using computer networks to enhance foreign language/culture education.' *Foreign Language Annals* 26/4: 527–34.

Cook, G. 1994. *Discourse and Literature: The Interplay of Form and Mind*. Oxford: Oxford University Press.

Cook, V. 1996. *Second Language Learning and Language Teaching, Second Edition*. London: Arnold.

Cooper, M. 1984. 'Linguistic Competence of Practised and Unpractised Non-Native Readers of English' in J. C. Alderson and A. H. Urquhart (eds.): *Reading in a Foreign Language*. London: Longman: 122–35.

Cooper, T. and G. Morain. 1980. 'A study of sentence-combining techniques for developing written and oral fluency in French.' *French Review* 53/3: 411–23.

Cooper, T. C. 1981. 'Sentence combining: An experiment in teaching writing.' *Modern Language Journal* 65/2: 158–65.

Cooper, T. C., G. Morain, and T. Kalivoda. 1980. *Sentence Combining in Second Language Instruction*. Washington, D.C.: Center for Applied Linguistics.

Cope, B. and M. Kalantzis. 1993. *The Powers of Literacy: A Genre Approach to Teaching Writing*. Pittsburgh: University of Pittsburgh Press.

Corder, S. P. 1983. 'A Role for the Mother Tongue' in S. M. Gass and L. Selinker (eds.): *Language Transfer in Language Learning*. Rowley, MA: Newbury House: 85–97.

Cortese, G. 1985. 'From receptive to productive in post-intermediate EFL classes: A pedagogical experiment.' *TESOL Quarterly* 19/1: 7–23.

Coulmas, F. 1989. *The Writing Systems of the World*. Oxford: Blackwell.

Cowan, G. and E. Cowan. 1980. *Writing*. New York: Wiley.

Cowan, J. R. 1976. 'Reading, perceptual strategies and contrastive analysis.' *Language Learning* 26/1: 95–109.

Crookes, G. 1989. 'Planning and interlanguage variation.' *Studies in Second Language Acquisition* 11/4: 367–83.

Cummins, J. 1976. 'The influence of bilingualism on cognitive growth: A synthesis of research findings and explanatory hypotheses.' *Working Papers on Bilingualism 9*: 1–43.

Cummins, J. 1979. 'Cognitive/academic language proficiency, linguistic interdependence, the optimum age question and some other matters.' *Working Papers on Bilingualism 19*: 197–205.

Cummins, J. 1981. 'The Role of Primary Language Development in Promoting Educational Success for Language Minority Students' in *Schooling and Language Minority Students: A Theoretical Framework*. Los Angeles: Evaluation, Dissemination and Assessment Center, California State University, Los Angeles: 3–49.

Cummins, J. and D. Sayers. 1995. *Brave New Schools: Challenging Cultural Illiteracy through Global Learning Networks*. New York: St. Martin's Press.

Cziko, G. A. 1976. 'The effects of language sequencing on the development of bilingual reading skills.' *Canadian Modern Language Review* 32: 534–9.

Cziko, G. A. 1978. 'Differences in first- and second-language reading: The use of syntactic, semantic and discouse constraints.' *Canadian Modern Language Review* 34/3: 473–89.

D'Andrade, R. 1987. 'A Folk Model of the Mind' in D. Holland and N. Quinn (eds.): *Cultural Models in Language and Thought*. Cambridge: Cambridge University Press: 112–48.

D'Andrade, R. 1990. 'Some propositions about the relationship between culture and human cognition' in J. W. Stigler, R. A. Shweder, and G. Herdt (eds.): *Cultural Psychology: Essays on Comparative Human Development*. New York: Cambridge University Press.

de Groot, A. D. 1965. *Thought and Choice in Chess*. The Hague: Mouton.

de Vega, M. 1996. 'Spatial and Interpersonal Models in the Comprehension of Narratives' in M. Carreiras, J. E. Garcìa-Albea, and N. Sebastián-Gallés (eds.): *Language Processing in Spanish*. Mahwah, NJ: Lawrence Erlbaum: 275–303.

Delpit, L. D. 1988. 'The silenced dialogue: Power and pedagogy in educating other people's children.' *Harvard Educational Review* 58/3: 280–98.

Demel, M. C. 1990. 'The relationship between overall reading comprehension and comprehension of coreferential ties for second language readers of English.' *TESOL Quarterly* 24/2: 267–92.

Derrida, J. 1980. 'The law of genre.' *Critical Inquiry* 7/1: 55–81.

Devine, J. 1987. 'General Language Competence and Adult Second Language Reading' in J. Devine, P. L. Carrell, and D. E. Eskey (eds.): *Research in Reading in English as a Second Language*. Washington, D.C.: TESOL: 73–86.

Devine, J. 1988. 'A Case Study of Two Readers' in P. L. Carrell, J. Devine, and D. E. Eskey (eds.): *Interactive Approaches to Second Language Reading*. Cambridge: Cambridge University Press: 127–39.

Dillon, G. 1981. *Constructing Texts: Elements of a Theory of Composition and Style*. Bloomington: Indiana University Press.

Dixon, J. 1987. 'The Question of Genres' in I. Reid (ed.) *The Place of Genre in Learning: Current Debates*. Victoria (Australia): Deakin University Press: 58–82.

Dixon, J. and L. Stratta. 1992. 'New Demands on the Model for Writing in Education—What Does Genre Theory Offer?' in M. Hayhoe and S. Parker (eds.): *Reassessing Language and Literacy.* Buckingham, UK: Open University Press: 84–94.

Dvorak, T. R. 1986. 'Writing in the Foreign Language' in B. H. Wing (ed.) *Listening, Reading, Writing: Analysis and Application.* Middlebury VT: Northeast Conference: 145–67.

Dyson, A. H. 1990. *The Word and the World: Reconceptualizing Written Language Development or Do Rainbows Mean a Lot to Little Girls?* Technical Report no. 42. Berkeley, CA: National Center for the Study of Writing and Literacy.

Eagleton, T. 1983. *Literary Theory: An Introduction.* Oxford: Basil Blackwell.

Eco, U. 1979. *The Role of the Reader: Explorations in the Semiotics of Texts.* Bloomington: Indiana University Press.

Eisner, E. W. 1992. 'Rethinking Literacy' in P. H. Dreyer (ed.) *Reading the World: Multimedia and Multicultural Learning in Today's Classrooms* Fifty-Sixth Yearbook of the Claremont Reading Conference. Claremont, CA: Claremont Reading Conference: 1–16.

Elbow, P. 1973. *Writing Without Teachers.* London: Macmillan Education.

Ellis, R. 1993. 'The Structural Syllabus and Second Language Acquisition.' *TESOL Quarterly* 27/1: 91–113.

Ellis, R. 1994. *The Study of Second Language Acquisition.* Oxford: Oxford University Press.

Enkvist, N. E. 1990. 'Seven Problems in the Study of Coherence and Interpretability' in U. Connor and A. M. Johns (eds.): *Coherence in Writing: Research and Pedagogical Perspectives.* Alexandria, VA: TESOL: 11–28.

Ericsson, K. A. and H. A. Simon. 1984. *Protocol Analysis.* Cambridge, MA: MIT Press.

Faigley, L., R. D. Cherry, D. A. Jolliffe, and A. M. Skinner. 1985. *Assessing Writers' Knowledge and Processes of Composing.* Norwood, NJ: Ablex.

Farley, T. 1995. *An Ethnographic Study of Two College Teachers' Beliefs About Reading in the Introductory Foreign Language Literature Class.* Unpublished dissertation. Indiana University.

Fathman, A. and E. Whalley. 1990. 'Teacher Response to Student Writing: Focus on Form versus Content' in B. Kroll (ed.) *Second Language Writing: Research Insights for the Classroom.* Cambridge: Cambridge University Press: 178–90.

Favreau, M., M. K. Komoda, and N. Segalowitz. 1980. 'Second language reading: Implications of the word superiority effect in skilled bilinguals.' *Canadian Journal of Psychology* 34/4: 370–80.

Favreau, M. and N. S. Segalowitz. 1982. 'Second language reading in fluent bilinguals.' *Applied Psycholinguistics* 3: 329–41.

Ferris, D. 1995. 'Student reactions to teacher response in multiple-draft composition studies.' *TESOL Quarterly* 29: 33–53.

Ferris, D. and J. S. Hedgcock. 1998. *Teaching ESL Composition: Purpose, Process, and Practice.* Mahwah, NJ: Lawrence Erlbaum.

Finneman, M. D. and L. Carbón Gorell. 1991. *De lector a escritor: El desarollo de la comunicación escrita.* Boston: Heinle and Heinle.

Fish, S. 1980. *Is There A Text in This Class? The Authority of Interpretive Communities.* Cambridge: Harvard University Press.

Flower, L. 1990. 'Introduction: Studying Cognition in Context' in L. Flower, V. Stein, J. Ackerman, M. J. Kantz, K. McCormick, and W. C. Peck (eds.): *Reading-to-Write: Exploring a Cognitive and Social Process.* New York: Oxford University Press: 3–32.

Flower, L. 1994. *The Construction of Negotiated Meaning: A Social Cognitive Theory of Writing.* Carbondale, IL: Southern Illinois University Press.

Flowerdew, J. 1993. 'An educational, or process, approach to the teaching of professional genres.' *English Language Teaching Journal* 47/4: 305–16.

Floyd, P. and **P. L. Carrell.** 1987. 'Effect on ESL reading of teaching cultural content schemata.' *Language Learning* 37/1: 89–108.

Forman, E. A. and **C. B. Cazden.** 1985. 'Exploring Vygotskian perspectives in education: The cognitive value of peer interaction' in J. Wertsch (ed.) *Culture, Communication and Cognition: Vygotskian Perspectives.* New York: Cambridge University Press.

Foster, P. and **P. Skehan.** 1996. 'The influence of planning and task type on second language performance.' *Studies in Second Language Acquisition* 18/3: 299–323.

Foucault, M. 1966. *The Order of Things.* New York: Random House.

Foucault, M. 1985. *The Foucault Reader.* New York: Pantheon.

Fowler, R. 1986. *Linguistic Criticism.* Oxford: Oxford University Press.

Freedman, S. W. and **M. Sperling.** 1985. 'Written Language Acquistion: The Role of Response and the Writing Conference' in S. W. Freedman (ed.) *The Acquisition of Written Language: Response and Revision.* Norwood, NJ: Ablex.

Freinet, E. 1981. *Naissance d'une pédagogie populaire: Historique de l'école moderne (pédagogie Freinet).* Paris: François Maspero.

Freire, P. 1974. *Education for Critical Consciousness.* London: Sheed and Ward.

Freire, P. and **D. Macedo.** 1987. *Literacy: Reading the Word and the World.* South Hadley, MA: Bergin & Garvey Publishers.

Friedlander, A. 1990. 'Composing in English: Effects of a First Language on Writing in English as a Second Language' in B. Kroll (ed.) *Second Language Writing: Research Insights for the Classroom.* Cambridge: Cambridge University Press: 109–25.

Furry, N. M. 1990. *Explorations of Extratextual Space: Reading Comprehension in a Foreign Language.* Unpublished dissertation. University of Texas at Austin.

Furstenberg, G., J. H. Murray, S. Malone, and **A. Farman-Farmaian.** 1993. *A la rencontre de Philippe.* New Haven: Yale University Press.

Gaffney, J. 1993. 'Language and Style in Politics' in C. Sanders (ed.) *French Today: Language in its Social Context.* Cambridge: Cambridge University Press: 185–98.

Galisson, R. 1987. 'Accéder à la culture partagée par l'entremise des mots à C.C.P.' *Etudes de linguistique appliquée* 67: 119–40.

Garner, R. and **M. G. Gillingham.** 1998. 'The Internet in the classroom: Is it the end of tranmission-oriented pedagogy?' in D. Reinking, M. C. McKenna, L. D. Labbo, and R. D. Kieffer (eds.): *Handbook of Literacy and Technology: Transformations in a Post-Typographic World.* Mahwah, NJ: Lawrence Erlbaum: 221–31.

Gass, S. 1987. 'The resolution of conflicts among competing systems: A bidirectional perspective.' *Applied Psycholinguistics* 8: 329–50.

Gaudiani, C. 1981. *Teaching Writing in the Foreign Language Classroom.* Washington, D.C.: Center for Applied Linguistics.

Gee, J. 1986. 'Orality and literacy: From *The Savage Mind to Ways With Words.*' *TESOL Quarterly* 20/4: 719–46.

Gee, J. P. 1990. *Social Linguistics and Literacies: Ideology in Discourses.* London: Falmer Press.

Gee, J. P. 1996. *Social Linguistics and Literacies: Ideology in Discourses, Second Edition.* London: Taylor & Francis.

Genesee, F. 1979. 'Acquisition of reading skills in immersion programs.' *Foreign Language Annals* 12/1: 71–7.

Geva, E. 1992. 'The role of conjunctions in L2 text comprehension.' *TESOL Quarterly* 26/4: 731–47.

Goodlad, J. L. 1984. *A Place Called School: Prospects for the Future.* New York: McGraw-Hill.

Goodman, K. 1981. 'Miscue analysis and future research directions' in S. Hudelson (ed.) *Linguistics and literacy series 1: Learning to read in different languages.* Arlington, VA: Center for Applied Linguistics.

Goodman, K. S. 1970. 'Psycholinguistic universals in the reading process.' *Journal of Typographic Research* 1970/4: 103–10.

Goodman, K. S. 1985. 'Unity in reading' in H. Singer and R. B. Ruddell (eds.): *Theoretical models and processes of reading.* Newark, DE: International Reading Association.

Gouin, F. 1894. *The Art of Teaching and Studying Languages.* London: George Philip & Son.

Grabe, W. and R. B. Kaplan. 1996. *Theory and Practice of Writing: An Applied Linguistic Perspective.* London: Longman.

Graff, H. J. 1979. *The Literacy Myth: Literacy and Social Structure in the 19th Century City.* New York: Academic Press.

Gremmo, M.-J. 1985. 'Learning a language—or learning to read?' in P. Riley (ed.) *Discourse and Learning.* London: Longman: 74–90.

Grice, H. P. 1975. 'Logic and Conversation' in P. Cole and J. L. Morgan (eds.): *Syntax and Semantics, Vol. 3: Speech Acts.* New York: Academic Press: 225–42.

Haas, C. 1989. 'Seeing It on the Screen Isn't Really Seeing It: Computer Writers' Reading Problems' in G. E. Hawisher and C. L. Selfe (eds.): *Critical Perspectives on Computers and Composition Instruction.* New York: Teachers College Press: 16–29.

Haber, R. N. and M. Hershenson. 1980. *The Psychology of Visual Perception, Second Edition.* New York: Holt, Rinehart & Winston.

Halliday, M. A. K. 1978. *Language as Social Semiotic: The Social Interpretation of Language and Meaning.* Baltimore: University Park Press.

Halliday, M. A. K. 1989. *Spoken and Written Language.* Oxford: Oxford University Press.

Halliday, M. A. K. and R. Hasan. 1976. *Cohesion in English.* London: Longman.

Hamilton, M. 1994. 'Introduction: Signposts' in M. Hamilton, D. Barton, and R. Ivanic (eds.): *Worlds of Literacy.* Clevedon, UK: Multilingual Matters: 1–11.

Hammadou, J. 1991. 'Interrelationships among prior knowledge, inference, and language proficiency in foreign language reading.' *Modern Language Journal* 75/1: 27–38.

Hamp-Lyons, L. 1991a. 'Basic Concepts' in L. Hamp-Lyons (ed.) *Assessing Second Language Writing in Academic Contexts*. Norwood, NJ: Ablex: 5–15.

Hamp-Lyons, L. 1991b. 'Reconstructing 'Academic Writing Proficiency'' in L. Hamp-Lyons (ed.) *Assessing Second Language Writing in Academic Contexts*. Norwood, NJ: Ablex: 127–53.

Hamp-Lyons, L. 1991c. 'Scoring Procedures for ESL Contexts' in L. Hamp-Lyons (ed.) *Assessing Second Language Writing in Academic Contexts*. Norwood, NJ: Ablex: 241–76.

Hamp-Lyons, L. and W. Condon. 1993. 'Questioning assumptions about portfolio-based assessment.' *College Composition and Communication* 44/2: 176–90.

Hanf, M. B. 1971. 'Mapping: A technique for translating reading into thinking.' *Journal of Reading* 14: 225–30.

Harasim, L., S. R. Hiltz, L. Teles, and M. Turoff. 1995. *Learning Networks: A Field Guide to Teaching and Learning Online*. Cambridge, MA: MIT Press.

Harris, R. J., D. J. Lee, D. L. Hensley, and L. M. Schoen. 1988. 'The effect of cultural script knowledge on memory for stories over time.' *Discourse Processes* 11: 413–31.

Hart, R. 1987. 'Towards a third generation distributed conferring system.' *Canadian Journal of Educational Communication* 16/2: 137–52.

Hartman, G. H. 1996. 'The fate of reading once more.' *PMLA* 111/3: 383–9.

Hawisher, G. E. 1989. 'Research and Recommendations for Computers and Composition' in G. E. Hawisher and C. L. Selfe (eds.): *Critical Perspectives on Computers and Composition Instruction*. New York: Teachers College Press: 44–69.

Hawisher, G. E. and C. L. Selfe. 1991. 'The rhetoric of technology and the electronic writing class.' *College Composition and Communication* 42/1: 55–65.

Heath, S. B. 1980. 'Functions and uses of literacy.' *Journal of Communication* 30: 123–33.

Heath, S. B. 1982. 'What no bedtime story means: Narrative skills at home and school.' *Language in Society* 11: 49–76.

Heath, S. B. 1983. *Ways with Words: Ethnography of Communication in Communities and Classroom*. New York: Cambridge University Press.

Heath, S. B. 1986. 'Sociocultural Contexts of Language Development' in *Beyond Language: Social and Cultural Factors in Schooling Language Minority Students*. Los Angeles: Evaluation, Dissemination and Assessment Center, California State University, Los Angeles: 143–86.

Heath, S. B. 1987. 'The Literate Essay: Using Ethnography to Explode Myths' in J. A. Langer (ed.) *Language, literacy and culture: Issues of society and schooling*. Norwood, NJ: Ablex: 89–107.

Heath, S. B. 1991. 'The Sense of Being Literate: Historical and Cross-Cultural Features' in P. D. Pearson, R. Barr, M. L. Kamil, and P. B. Mosenthal (eds.): *Handbook of Reading Research Volume II*. New York: Longman: 3–25.

Hedge, T. 1988. *Writing*. Oxford: Oxford University Press.

Heimlich, J. E. and S. D. Pittelman. 1986. *Semantic Mapping: Classroom Applications*. Newark, DE: International Reading Association.

Henry, A. and R. L. Roseberry. 1998. 'An evaluation of a genre-based approach to the teaching of EAP/ESP writing.' *TESOL Quarterly* 32/1: 147–56.

Herman, G. 1986. 'How to make (French) composition more challenging and productive.' *French Review* 60/1: 56–64.

Herman, G. 1988. 'Developing logical thinking and sharpening writing skills in advanced composition classes.' *French Review* 62/1: 59–66.

Herman, J. L., M. Gerhart, and P. R. Aschbacher. 1996. 'Portfolios for classroom assessment: Design and Implementation Issues' in R. Calfee and P. Perfumo (eds.): *Writing Portfolios in the Classroom: Policy and Practice, Promise and Peril.* Mahwah, NJ: Lawrence Erlbaum: 27–59.

Hidi, S. and V. Anderson. 1986. 'Producing written summaries: Task demands, cognitive operations, and implications for instruction.' *Review of Educational Research* 56: 473–93.

Hillocks, G. 1986. *Research on Written Composition: New Directions for Teaching.* Urbana, IL: National Conference on Research in English/ERIC Clearinghouse on Reading and Communication Skills.

Hillocks, G. 1995. *Teaching Writing as Reflective Practice.* New York: Teachers College Press.

Hino, N. 1992. 'The Yakudoku Tradition of Foreign Language Literacy in Japan' in F. Dubin and N. A. Kuhlman (eds.): *Cross-Cultural Literacy: Global Perpspectives on Reading and Writing.* Englewood Cliffs, NJ: Regents/Prentice Hall: 99–111.

Hirsch, E. D., Jr. 1987. *Cultural Literacy: What Every American Needs to Know.* Boston: Houghton Mifflin.

Hoffman, E. 1989. *Lost in Translation: A Life in a New Language.* New York: Dutton.

Holland, N. N. 1975. *5 Readers Reading.* New Haven: Yale University Press.

Horowitz, D. 1986. 'Process, not product: Less than meets the eye.' *TESOL Quarterly* 20: 1.

Horowitz, D. 1991. 'ESL Writing Assessments: Contradictions and Resolutions' in L. Hamp-Lyons (ed.) *Assessing Second Language Writing in Academic Contexts.* Norwood, NJ: Ablex: 71–85.

Howard, D. R. 1976. *The Idea of the Canterbury Tales.* Berkeley: University of California Press.

Hudson, T. 1982. 'The effects of induced schemata on the 'short-circuit' in L2 reading: Nondecoding factors in L2 reading performance.' *Language Learning* 32/1: 1–31.

Hudson-Ross, S. and Y. R. Dong. 1990. 'Literacy learning as a reflection of language and culture: Chinese elementary school education.' *Reading Teacher* 44: 110–23.

Huey, E. B. 1908. *The Psychology and Pedagogy of Reading.* New York: Macmillan.

Hull, G. 1991. *Hearing Other Voices: A Critical Assessment of Popular Views on Literacy and Work.* Berkeley, CA: University of California National Center for Research in Vocational Education.

Hulstijn, J. H. 1993. 'When Do Foreign-Language Readers Look Up the Meaning of Unfamiliar Words? The Influence of Task and Learner Variables.' *Modern Language Journal* 77/2: 139–47.

Hymes, D. 1971. 'Competence and Performance in Linguistic Theory' in R. Huxley and E. Ingram (eds.): *Language Acquisition: Models and Methods.* London: Academic Press: 3–28.

Hynd, C. R. and D. E. Alverman. 1989. 'Overcoming misconceptions in science: An online study of prior knowledge activation.' *Reading Research and Instruction* 28/4: 12–26.

Inghilleri, M. 1989. 'Learning to mean as a symbolic and social process: The story of ESL writers.' *Discourse Processes* 12: 391–411.

Irvine, P. and N. Elsasser. 1988. 'The Ecology of Literacy: Negotiating Writing Standards in a Caribbean Setting' in B. A. Rafoth and D. L. Rubin (eds.): *The Social Construction of Written Communication*. Norwood, NJ: Ablex: 304–20.

Iser, W. 1974. *The Implied Reader: Patterns of Communication in Prose Fiction from Bunyan to Beckett*. Baltimore: Johns Hopkins University Press.

Iser, W. 1980. 'The Reading Process: A Phenomenological Approach' in J. P. Tomkins (ed.) *Reader-Response Criticism: From Formalism to Post-Structuralism*. Baltimore: Johns Hopkins University Press: 50–69.

Jackendoff, R. 1994. *Patterns in the Mind: Language and Human Nature*. New York: Basic Books.

Jin, L. and M. Cortazzi. 1998. 'The culture the learner brings: A bridge or a barrier?' in M. Byram and M. Fleming (eds.): *Language Learning in Intercultural Perspective: Approaches through drama and ethnography*. Cambridge: Cambridge University Press: 98–118.

John-Steiner, V., C. P. Panofsky, and L. W. Smith (eds.). 1994. *Sociocultural Approaches to Language and Literacy*. Cambridge: Cambridge University Press.

Johns, A. 1991. 'Faculty Assessment of ESL Student Literacy Skills: Implications for Writing Assessment' in L. Hamp-Lyons (ed.) *Assessing Second Language Writing in Academic Contexts*. Norwood, NJ: Ablex: 167–79.

Johns, A. M. 1997. *Text, Role, and Context*. Cambridge: Cambridge University Press.

Johnson, K. E. 1992. 'Cognitive strategies and second-language writers: A re-evaluation of sentence-combining.' *Journal of Second Language Writing* 1/1: 61–75.

Johnson, P. 1981. 'Effects on reading comprehension of language complexity and cultural background of a text.' *TESOL Quarterly* 15/2: 169–81.

Jones, S. and J. Tetroe. 1987. 'Composing in a Second Language' in A. Matsuhashi (ed.) *Writing in Real Time: Modelling Production Processes*. Norwood, NJ: Ablex.

Jurasek, R. 1993. 'Foreign Languages Across the Curriculum: A Case History from Earlham College and a Generic Rationale' in M. Krueger and F. Ryan (eds.): *Language and Content: Discipline- and Content-Based Approaches to Language Study*. Lexington, MA: D. C. Heath: 85–102.

Jurasek, R. 1996. 'Intermediate-level foreign language curricula: An assessment and a new agenda.' *ADFL Bulletin* 27/2: 18–27.

Kameen, P. T. 1979. 'Syntactic Skill and ESL Writing Quality' in C. Yorio, K. Perkins, and J. Schachter (eds.): *On TESOL '79: The Learner in Focus*. Washington, D.C.: TESOL: 343–50.

Kaplan, R. B. 1966. 'Cultural thought patterns in intercultural education' *Language Learning* 16: 1–20.

Kelm, O. R. 1992. 'The use of synchronous computer networks in second language instruction: A preliminary report.' *Foreign Language Annals* 25/5: 441–54.

Kepner, C. G. 1991. 'An experiment in the relationship of types of written feedback to the development of second-language writing skills.' *Modern Language Journal* 75/3: 305–13.

Kern, R. G. 1989. 'Second language reading strategy instruction: Its effects on comprehension and word Inference ability.' *Modern Language Journal* 73/2: 135–49.

Kern, R. G. 1994. 'The Role of Mental Translation in L2 Reading.' *Studies in Second Language Acquisition* 16/4: 441–61.

Kern, R. G. 1995a. 'L'Histoire, Mon Histoire: Comparing Family Histories via E-mail' in M. Warschauer (ed.) *Virtual Connections: Online Activities and Projects for Networking Language Learners*. Honolulu: University of Hawaii Second Language Teaching and Curriculum Center: 131–3.

Kern, R. G. 1995b. 'Restructuring Classroom Interaction with Networked Computers: Effects on Quantity and Quality of Language Production.' *Modern Language Journal* 79/4: 457–76.

Kern, R. G. 1996. 'Computer-Mediated Communication: Using E-Mail Exchanges to Explore Personal Histories in Two Cultures' in M. Warschauer (ed.) *Telecollaboration in Foreign Language Learning: Proceedings of the Hawaii Symposium*. Honolulu: University of Hawaii Second Language Teaching and Curriculum Center: 105–19.

Kern R. G. 1998. 'Technology, Social Interaction and FL Literacy' in J. Muyskens (ed.) *New Ways of Teaching and Learning: Focus on Technology and Foreign Language Education*. Boston. Heinle & Heinle: 57–92.

Kilborn, K. 1989. 'Sentence processing in a second language: The timing of transfer.' *Language and Speech* 32: 1–23.

Kintsch, W. and E. Greene. 1978. 'The role of culture-specific schemata in the comprehension and recall of stories.' *Discourse Processes* 1/1: 1–13.

Kirkland, M. R. and M. A. P. Saunders. 1991. 'Maxmizing student performance in summary writing: Managing cognitive load.' *TESOL Quarterly* 25/1: 105–21.

Knight, S. 1994. 'Dictionary: The tool of last resort in foreign language reading? A new perspective.' *Modern Language Journal* 78/3: 285–99.

Koda, K. 1987. 'Cognitive Strategy Transfer in Second Language Reading' in J. Devine, P. L. Carrell, and D. E. Eskey (eds.): *Research in Reading in English as a Second Language*. Washington, D.C.: TESOL: 125–44.

Koda, K. 1993. 'Transferred L1 strategies and L2 syntactic structure in L2 sentence comprehension.' *Modern Language Journal* 77/4: 490–500.

Koda, K. 1996. 'L2 Word Recognition Research: A Critical Review.' *Modern Language Journal* 80/4: 450–60.

Kohn, J. 1992. 'Literacy Strategies for Chinese University Learners' in F. Dubin and N. A. Kuhlman (eds.): *Cross-Cultural Literacy: Global Perspectives on Reading and Writing*. Englewood Cliffs, NJ: Regents/Prentice Hall: 113–25.

Kolers, P. A. 1966. 'Reading and talking bilingually.' *American Journal of Psychology* 79/3: 357–76.

Koretz, D., B. Stecher, S. Klein, and D. McCaffrey. 1994. 'The Vermont portfolio assessment program: Findings and implications.' *Educational Measurement: Issues and Practices* 13/3: 5–16.

Kramsch, C. 1984. *Interaction et discours dans la classe de langue*. Paris: Hatier-Crédif.

Kramsch, C. 1985. 'Literary texts in the classroom.' *Modern Language Journal* 69/4: 356–66.

Kramsch, C. 1989. 'Socialization and literacy in a foreign language: Learning through interaction.' *Theory into Practice* 26/4: 243–50.

Kramsch, C. 1993. *Context and Culture in Language Teaching*. Oxford: Oxford University Press.

Kramsch, C. 1995a. 'Embracing conflict versus achieving consensus in foreign language education.' *ADFL Bulletin* 26/3: 6–12.

Kramsch, C. 1995b. 'Rhetorical Models of Understanding' in T. Miller (ed.) *Functional Approaches to Written Texts: Classroom Application. The TESOL France Journal*. Paris: USIS: 61–78.

Kramsch, C. 1997. 'The privilege of the nonnative speaker.' *PMLA* 112/3: 359–69.

Kramsch, C. 1998. 'The privilege of the intercultural speaker' in M. Byram and M. Fleming (eds.): *Language Learning in Intercultural Perspective: Approaches through drama and ethnography*. Cambridge: Cambridge University Press: 16–31.

Kramsch, C. and T. Nolden. 1994. 'Redefining literacy in a foreign language.' *Die Unterrichtspraxis* 27/1: 28–35.

Krapels, A. R. 1990. 'An Overview of Second Language Writing Process Research' in B. Kroll (ed.) *Second Language Writing: Research Insights for the Classroom*. Cambridge: Cambridge University Press: 37–56.

Kress, G. 1989. *Linguistic Processes in Sociocultural Practice*. Oxford: Oxford University Press.

Kress, G. 1994. *Learning to Write, Second Edition*. London: Routledge.

Kress, G. and T. van Leeuwen. 1996. *Reading Images: The Grammar of Visual Design*. London: Routledge.

Kristof, N. D. 1995. Japan Expresses Regret of a Sort for the War. New York: *New York Times*, June 7, 1995, A1, A11.

Lado, R. 1957. *Linguistics Across Cultures*. Ann Arbor: University of Michigan Press.

Laing, D., A. van den Hoven, and V. Benessiano. 1991. 'L'emploi du traitement de texte dans un cours universitaire de première année portant sur la littérature française.' *Canadian Modern Language Review* 47/3: 477–85.

Landow, G. P. 1992. *Hypertext*. Baltimore: Johns Hopkins University Press.

Langer, J. A. (ed.) 1987a. *Language, Literacy, and Culture: Issues of Society and Schooling*. Norwood, NJ: Ablex.

Langer, J. A. 1987b. 'A sociocognitive perspective on literacy' in J. A. Langer (ed.) *Language, literacy and culture: Issues of society and schooling*. Norwood, NJ: Ablex: 1–20.

Lanham, R. A. 1993. *The Electronic Word: Democracy, Technology, and the Arts*. Chicago: University of Chicago Press.

Lay, N. D. S. 1982. 'Composing processes of adult ESL learners: A case study.' *TESOL Quarterly* 16: p. 406.

Lee, J.-W. and D. L. Schallert. 1997. 'The relative contribution of L2 language proficiency and L1 reading ability to L2 reading performance: A test of the threshold hypothesis in an EFL context.' *TESOL Quarterly* 31/4: 713–39.

Lee, J. F. 1986. 'Background knowledge and L2 reading.' *Modern Language Journal* 70/4: 350–4.

Lee, J. F. and D. Musumeci. 1988. 'On hierarchies of reading skills and text types.' *Modern Language Journal* 72/2: 173–87.

Lefevere, A. 1992. *Translation, Rewriting, and the Manipulation of Literary Fame.* London: Routledge.

Leki, I. 1990. 'Coaching from the Margins: Issues in Written Response' in B. Kroll (ed.) *Second Language Writing: Research Insights for the Classroom.* Cambridge: Cambridge University Press: 57–68.

Leki, I. 1995. 'Coping strategies of ESL students in writing tasks across the curriculum.' *TESOL Quarterly* 29/2: 235–60.

Levin, J., H. Kim, and **M. Riel.** 1990. 'Analyzing instructional interactions on electronic message networks' in L. Harasim (ed.) *Online Education: Perspectives on a New Environment.* New York: Praeger: 185–213.

Lewis, P. H. 1996. Judges Turn Back Law to Regulate Internet Decency. New York: *New York Times,* June 13, A1, A16.

Lodge, D. 1977. *The Modes of Modern Writing: Metaphor, Metonymy, and the Typology of Modern Literature.* Ithaca, NY: Cornell University Press.

Long, M. H. and **P. A. Porter.** 1985. 'Group work, interlanguage talk, and second language acquisition.' *TESOL Quarterly* 19/2: 207–28.

Lunde, K. R. 1990. 'Using electronic mail as a medium for foreign language study and instruction.' *CALICO Journal* 7/3: 68–78.

Lunsford, A. A., H. Moglen, and **J. Slevin** (eds.). 1990. *The Right to Literacy.* New York: Modern Language Association.

Mack, M. 1986. 'A study of semantic and syntactic processing in monolinguals and fluent bilinguals.' *Journal of Psycholinguistic Research* 15: 463–89.

Macnamara, J. 1967. 'The effects of instruction in a weaker language.' *Journal of Social Issues* 23/2: 121–35.

MacWhinney, B. and **E. Bates.** 1989. *The Cross-linguistic Study of Sentence Processing.* Cambridge: Cambridge University Press.

Madaus, G. F. 1988. 'The Influence of Testing on the Curriculum' in L. N. Tanner (ed.) *Critical Issues in Curriculum: Eighty-Seventh Yearbook of the National Society for the Study of Education.* Chicago: University of Chicago Press: 83–121.

Magnan, S. S. 1991. 'Just do it: Directing TA's toward task-based and process-oriented testing' in R. V. Teschner (ed.) *Assessing Foreign Language Proficiency of Undergraduates.* Boston: Heinle and Heinle.

Maley, A., A. Duff, and **F. Grellet.** 1980. *The Mind's Eye: Using Pictures Creatively in Language Learning.* Cambridge: Cambridge University Press.

Malmkjaer, K. 1997. 'Translation and language teaching.' *AILA Review* 12/1995/6: 56–61.

Mammeri, M. 1952. *La colline oubliée.* Paris: Plon.

Marriott, M. 1998. The Web Reflects a Wider World: As More Non-English Speakers Log On, Many Languages Thrive. New York: *New York Times,* June 18, 1998, D1, D7.

Marshall, J. D., P. Smagorinsky, and **M. W. Smith.** 1995. *The Language of Interpretation: Patterns of Discourse in Discussions of Literature.* Urbana, IL: NCTE.

Martin, J. R., F. Christie, and **J. Rothery.** 1994. 'Social Processes in Education: A Reply to Sawyer and Watson (and others)' in B. Stierer and J. Maybin (eds.): *Language, Literacy and Learning in Educational Practice.* Clevedon, UK: Multilingual Matters: 232–47.

McCarthy, M. and R. Carter. 1994. *Language as Discourse: Perspectives for Language Teaching*. London: Longman.

McKay, S. 1979. 'Communicative writing.' *TESOL Quarterly* 13/1: 73–80.

McPeck, J. E. 1981. *Critical Thinking and Education*. New York: St Martin's Press.

Mehan, H. 1985. 'The Structure of Classroom Discourse' in T. A. van Dijk (ed.) *Handbook of Discourse Analysis*. London: Academic Press: 120–31.

Messick, S. 1994. 'The interplay of evidence and consequence in the validation of performance assessment.' *Educational Researcher* 23/2: 13–23.

Mewhort, D. J. K., M. M. Merikle, and M. P. Bryden. 1969. 'On the transfer from iconic to short-term memory.' *Journal of Experimental Psychology: General* 81/1: 89–94.

Meyer, B. J. F. 1975. *The Organization of Prose and Its Effects on Memory*. Amsterdam: North Holland Publishing Company.

Miller, C. R. 1984. 'Genre as social action.' *Quarterly Journal of Speech* 70/2: 151–67.

Moffett, J. 1968. *Teaching the Universe of Discourse*. Boston: Houghton Mifflin.

Mohan, B. A. and W. A.-Y. Lo. 1985. 'Academic writing and Chinese students: Transfer and developmental factors.' *TESOL Quarterly* 19/3: 515–34.

Moirand, S. 1979. *Situations d'écrit: Compréhension, production en langue étrangère*. Paris: CLE International.

Monroe, J. H. 1975. 'Measuring and enhancing syntactic fluency in French.' *French Review* 48/6: 1023–31.

Mott, B. W. 1981. 'A miscue analysis of German speakers reading in German and English' in S. Hudelson (ed.) *Learning to Read in Different Languages*. Arlington, VA: Center for Applied Linguistics.

Motte, W. F. (ed.) 1986. *Oulipo: A Primer of Potential Literature*. Lincoln, Nebraska: University of Nebraska Press.

Mueller, M. 1991. 'Cultural literacy and foreign language pedagogy.' *ADFL Bulletin* 22/2: 19–24.

Murray, D. E. and P. C. Nichols. 1992. 'Literacy Practices and their Effect on Academic Writing: Vietnamese Case Studies' in F. Dubin and N. A. Kuhlman (eds.): *Cross-Cultural Literacy: Global Perspectives on Reading and Writing*. Englewood Cliffs, NJ: Regents/Prentice Hall: 175–87.

Murray, D. M. 1978. 'Internal Revision: A Process of Discovery' in C. R. Cooper and L. Odell (eds.): *Research on Composing: Points of Departure*. Urbana, IL: National Council of Teachers of English: 85–103.

Murray, J. H. 1997. *Hamlet on the Holodeck: The Future of Narrative in Cyberspace*. New York: Free Press.

Myers, J., R. Hammett, and A. M. McKillop. 1998. 'Opportunities for Critical Literacy and Pedagogy in Student-Authored Hypermedia' in D. Reinking, M. C. McKenna, L. D. Labbo, and R. D. Kieffer (eds.): *Handbook of Literacy and Technology: Transformations in a Post-Typographic World*. Mahwah, NJ: Lawrence Erlbaum: 63–78.

Nash, W. 1986. 'The Possibilities of Paraphrase in the Teaching of Literary Idiom' in C. J. Brumfit and R. A. Carter (eds.): *Literature and Language Teaching*. Oxford: Oxford University Press: 70–88.

National Standards in Foreign Language Education Project. 1996. *Standards for Foreign Language Learning: Preparing for the 21st Century*. Yonkers, NY: American Council for the Teaching of Foreign Languages.

Nelson, G. L. and J. M. Murphy. 1993. 'Peer response groups: Do L2 writers use peer comments in revising their drafts?' *TESOL Quarterly* 27/1: 135–41.

Nelson, T. H. 1981. *Literary Machines*. Swarthmore, PA: self-published.

Neufeld, J. K. and M. R. Webb. 1984. *25 Strategies: Reading skills for intermediate–advanced students of English as a second language*. New York: Holt, Rinehart, & Winston.

New London Group. 1996. 'A pedagogy of multiliteracies: Designing social futures.' *Harvard Educational Review* 66/1: 60–92.

Newman, D., P. Griffin, and M. Cole. 1989. *The Construction Zone: Working for Cognitive Change in School*. Cambridge: Cambridge University Press.

Nystrand, M. 1986. *The Structure of Written Communication: Studies in Reciprocity between Writers and Readers*. Orlando, FL: Academic Press.

Nystrand, M. 1987. 'The Role of Context in Written Communication' in R. Horowitz and S. J. Samuels (eds.): *Comprehending Oral and Written Language*. San Diego: Academic Press: 197–214.

Nystrand, M. and A. Gamoran. 1991. 'Instructional discourse, student engagement and literature achievement.' *Research in the Teaching of English* 25/3: 261–190.

Nystrand, M., S. Greene, and J. Wiemelt. 1993. 'Where did composition studies come from? An intellectual history.' *Written Communication* 10/3: 267–333.

O'Malley, J. M., A. U. Chamot, G. Stewner-Manzanares, L. Kupper, and R. P. Russo. 1985. 'Learning strategies used by beginning and intermediate ESL students.' *Language Learning* 35/1: 21–46.

Odlin, T. 1989. *Language Transfer: Cross-Linguistic Influence in Language Learning*. Cambridge: Cambridge University Press.

Ohmann, R. 1986. 'Reading and Writing, Work and Leisure' in T. Newkirk (ed.) *Only Connect: Uniting Reading and Writing*. Upper Montclair, NJ: Boynton/Cook: 11–26.

Oller, J. W. 1991. 'Foreign language testing, part 1: Its breadth.' *ADFL Bulletin* 22/3: 33–8.

Olson, D. R. 1977. 'From utterance to text: The bias of language in speech and writing.' *Harvard Educational Review* 47/3: 257–81.

Olson, D. R. 1994. *The World on Paper: The Conceptual and Cognitive Implications of Writing and Reading*. Cambridge: Cambridge University Press.

Ong, W. J. 1982. *Orality and Literacy : The Technologizing of the Word*. London: Methuen.

Osgood, C. E. 1971. 'Where do sentences come from?' in D. D. Steinberg and L. A. Jakobovits (eds.): *Semantics: An Interdisciplinary Reader in Philosophy, Linguistics and Psychology*. London: Cambridge University Press: 497–531.

Oulipo. 1973. *La littérature potentielle (Créations Re-créations Récréations)*. Paris: Gallimard.

Parry, K. 1996. 'Culture, literacy, and L2 reading.' *TESOL Quarterly* 30/4: 665–92.

Pascal, B. 1904. *Pensées*. Paris: Nelson.

Pearson, P. D. and R. J. Tierney. 1984. 'On becoming a thoughful reader: Learning to read like a writer' in A. C. Purves and O. Niles (eds.): *Becoming readers in a complex society: Eighty-third yearbook of the National Society for the Study of Education*. Chicago: University of Chicago Press: 144–73.

Pei, M. 1965. *The Story of Language*. New York: New American Library.

Pellettieri, J. 2000. 'Negotiation in cyberspace: The role of *chatting* in the development of grammatical competence' in M. Warschauer and R. Kern (eds.): *Network-Based Language Teaching: Concepts and Practice*. Cambridge: Cambridge University Press: 59–86.

Pennycook, A. 1996. 'Borrowing others' words: Text, ownership, memory, and plagiarism.' *TESOL Quarterly* 30/2: 201–30.

Peyton, J. K. and L. Reed. 1990. *Dialogue Journal Writing with Nonnative English Speakers: A Handbook for Teachers*. Alexandria, VA: TESOL.

Peyton, J. K. and J. Staton (eds.). 1993. *Dialogue Journals in the Multilingual Classroom: Building Language Fluency and Writing Skills through Written Interaction*. Norwood, NJ: Ablex.

Pica, T., R. Young, and C. Doughty. 1987. 'The impact of interaction on comprehension.' *TESOL Quarterly* 21: 737–58.

Pike, K. L. 1988. 'Bridging Language Learning, Language Analysis, and Poetry, via Experimental Syntax' in D. Tannen (ed.) *Linguistics in Context: Connecting Observation and Understanding*. Lectures from the 1985 LSA/TESOL and NEH Institutes. Norwood, NJ: Ablex: 221–45.

Piper, W. 1930. *The Little Engine That Could*. New York: Platt & Munk.

Pollack, A. 1996. Happy in the East (^_^) Or Smiling :–) in the West. New York: *New York Times*, August 12, 1996, C5.

Porter, P. A. 1983. *Variations in the conversations of adult learners of English as a function of the proficiency level of the participants*. Unpublished dissertation. Stanford University.

Pressley, M. and P. Afflerbach. 1995. *Verbal Protocols of Reading: The Nature of Constructively Responsive Reading*. Hillsdale, NJ: Lawrence Erlbaum.

Purves, A. C. (ed.) 1988. *Writing Across Languages and Cultures: Issues in Contrastive Rhetoric*. Newbury Park, CA: Sage.

Raimes, A. 1979. *Problems and Teaching Strategies in ESL Composition*. Arlington, VA: Center for Applied Linguistics.

Raimes, A. 1983. *Techniques in Teaching Writing*. New York: Oxford University Press.

Reddy, M. 1979. 'The Conduit Metaphor' in A. Ortony (ed.) *Metaphor and Thought*. Cambridge: Cambridge University Press: 284–324.

Reder, S. 1994. 'Practice-Engagement Theory: A Sociocultural Approach to Literacy Across Languages and Cultures' in B. M. Ferdman, R.-M. Weber, and A. G. Ramírez (eds.): *Literacy Across Languages and Cultures*. Albany: State University of New York Press: 33–74.

Régent, O. 1985. 'A Comparative Approach to the Learning of Specialized Written Discourse' in P. Riley (ed.) *Discourse and Learning*. London: Longman: 105–20.

Reid, J. M. 1993. *Teaching ESL Writing*. Englewood Cliffs, NJ: Regents/Prentice Hall.

Rice, C. D. 1996. 'Bring intercultural encounters in to classrooms: IECC electronic mailing lists.' *T. H. E. Journal* (Technical Horizons in Education) 23/6: 60–3.

Richards, I. A. 1935. *Practical Criticism: A Study of Literary Judgment.* New York: Harcourt, Brace and Company.

Rigg, P. 1977. 'The miscue ESL project' in H. D. Brown, C. A. Yorio, and R. H. Crymes (eds.): *Teaching and Learning ESL: Trends in Research and Practice (On TESOL '77).* Washington, D.C.: TESOL.

Riley, P. 1985. 'Reading and communicative competence' in P. Riley (ed.) *Discourse and Learning.* London: Longman: 67–73.

Rivers, W. M. 1983. *Speaking in Many Tongues: Essays in Foreign Language Teaching, Third Edition.* Cambridge: Cambridge University Press.

Robinson, P. J. 1993. 'Procedural and Declarative Knowledge in Vocabulary Learning: Communication and the Language Learner's Lexicon' in T. Huckin, M. Haynes, and J. Coady (eds.): *Second Language Reading and Vocabulary Learning.* Norwood, NJ: Ablex: 229–62.

Romeiser, J. and **M. Rice.** 1992. *French Reading Lab I.* Knoxville, TN: Hyperglot Software.

Rosen, H. 1985. *Stories and Meanings.* Sheffield, UK: National Association for the Teaching of English.

Rosenbusch, M. H. 1992. 'Is knowledge of cultural diversity enough? Global education in the elementary school foreign language program.' *Foreign Language Annals* 25/2: 129–36.

Ruddell, R. B. and **M. R. Ruddell.** 1995. *Teaching Children to Read and Write: Becoming an Influential Teacher.* Boston: Allyn and Bacon.

Ruddell, R. B., M. R. Ruddell, and **H. Singer** (eds.). 1994. *Theoretical Models and Processes of Reading, Fourth Edition.* Newark, DE: International Reading Association.

Rumelhart, D. E. 1977. 'Understanding and summarizing brief stories' in D. LaBerge and S. J. Samuels (eds.): *Basic Processes in Reading: Perception and Comprehension.* Hillsdale, NJ: Lawrence Erlbaum: 265–303.

Rumelhart, D. E. 1981. 'Schemata: the building blocks of cognition' in J. T. Guthrie (ed.) *Comprehension and teaching: Research reviews.* Newark, DE: International Reading Association: 3–26.

Ruth, L. and **S. Murphy.** 1988. *Designing Writing Tasks for the Assessment of Writing.* Norwood, NJ: Ablex.

Ryle, G. 1949. *The Concept of Mind.* London: Hutchinson.

Sachs, M. 1989. 'The foreign language curriculum and the orality-literacy question.' *ADFL Bulletin* 20/2: 70–5.

Saragi, P., I. S. P. Nation, and **G. F. Meister.** 1978. 'Vocabulary learning and reading.' *System* 6/2: 72–8.

Sarig, G. 1993. 'Composing a Study-Summary: A Reading/Writing Encounter' in J. G. Carson and I. Leki (eds.): *Reading in the Composition Classroom: Second Language Perspectives.* Boston: Heinle and Heinle: 161–82.

Sasaki, Y. 1991. 'English and Japanese interlanguage comprehension strategies: An analysis based on the Competition Model.' *Applied Psycholinguistics* 12: 47–73.

Savignon, S. J. 1983. *Communicative Competence: Theory and Classroom Practice.* Reading, MA: Addison-Wesley.

Saxena, M. 1994. 'Literacies Among the Panjabis in Southall' in M. Hamilton, D. Barton, and R. Ivanic (eds.): *Worlds of Literacy.* Clevedon, UK: Multilingual Matters: 195–214.

Schachter, J. 1983. 'Nutritional Needs of Language Learners' in M. A. Clarke and J. Handscombe (eds.): *On TESOL '82: Pacific Perspectives on Language Learning and Teaching*. Washington, D.C.: TESOL.

Schallert, D. L. 1987. 'Thought and Language, Content and Structure in Language Communication' in J. R. Squire (ed.) *The Dynamics of Language Learning*. Urbana, IL: ERIC Clearinghouse on Reading and Communication and the National Conference on Research in English: 65–79.

Schank, R. C. 1984. *The Cognitive Computer: On Language, Learning, and Artificial Intelligence*. Reading, MA: Addison-Wesley.

Schlesinger, I. M. 1977. *Production and Comprehension of Utterances*. Hillsdale, NJ: Lawrence Erlbaum.

Schmidt, R. 1990. 'The role of consciousness in second language learning.' *Applied Linguistics* 11/2: 129–58.

Schmidt, R. and S. Frota. 1986. 'Developing basic conversational ability in a second language: A case-study of an adult learner' in R. Day (ed.) *Talking to Learn: Conversation in Second Language Acquisition*. Rowley, MA: Newbury House: 237–326.

Schmolze, N. 1998. *American School of Guatemala Newsletter*. Web page. *http://www.geocities.com/~nschmolze/guat2.html*. Accessed on September 28, 1998.

Scholes, R. 1985. *Textual Power: Literary Theory and the Teaching of English*. New Haven: Yale University Press.

Schultz, J. M. 1991a. 'Mapping and cognitive development in the teaching of foreign language writing.' *French Review* 64/6: 978–88.

Schultz, J. M. 1991b. 'Writing mode in the articulation of language and literature classes: Theory and practice.' *Modern Language Journal* 75/4: 411–7.

Schultz, J. M. 1994. 'Stylistic reformulation: Theoretical premises and practical applications.' *Modern Language Journal* 78/2: 169–78.

Schultz, J. M. 1995. 'Making the Transition from Language to Literature' in M. A. Haggstrom, L. Z. Morgan, and J. A. Wieczorek (eds.): *The Foreign Language Classroom: Bridging Theory and Practice*. New York: Garland: 3–20.

Schultz, J. M. 2000. 'Computers and collaborative writing in the foreign language curriculum' in M. Warschauer and R. Kern (eds.): *Network-Based Language Teaching: Concepts and Practice*. Cambridge: Cambridge University Press: 121–50.

Scribner, S. 1984. 'Literacy in three metaphors.' *American Journal of Education* 93/1: 6–21.

Scribner, S. and M. Cole. 1981. *The Psychology of Literacy*. Cambridge: Harvard University Press.

Searle, J. 1969. *Speech Acts*. Cambridge: Cambridge University Press.

Selfe, C. L. 1989. 'Redefining Literacy: The Multilayered Grammars of Computers' in G. E. Hawisher and C. L. Selfe (eds.): *Critical Perspectives on Computers and Composition Instruction*. New York: Teachers College Press: 3–15.

Selinker, L., R. M. T. Trimble, and L. Trimble. 1976. 'Presuppositional rhetorical information in EST discourse.' *TESOL Quarterly* 10/3: 281–90.

Semke, H. 1984. 'The effects of the red pen.' *Foreign Language Annals* 17: 195–202.

Shaughnessy, M. P. 1977. *Errors and Expectations: A Guide for the Teacher of Basic Writing*. New York: Oxford University Press.

Shohamy, E. 1990. 'Language testing priorities: A different perspective.' *Foreign Language Annals* 23/5: 385–94.

Short, M. 1994. 'Understanding Texts: Point of View' in G. Brown, K. Malmkjær, A. Pollitt, and J. Williams (eds.): *Language and Understanding*. Oxford: Oxford University Press: 170–90.

Silberstein, S. 1994. *Techniques and Resources in Teaching Reading*. New York: Oxford University Press.

Silva, T. 1993. 'Toward an understanding of the distinct nature of L2 writing: The ESL research and its implications.' *TESOL Quarterly* 27/4: 657–77.

Simpson, P. 1993. *Language, Ideology and Point of View*. London: Routledge.

Smith, F. 1988a. *Joining the Literacy Club: Further Essays into Education*. Portsmouth, NH: Heinemann.

Smith, F. 1988b. *Understanding Reading: A Psycholinguistic Analysis of Reading and Learning to Read, Fourth Edition*. Hillsdale, NJ: Lawrence Erlbaum.

Smith, S. M. 1984. *The Theater Arts and the Teaching of Second Languages*. Reading, MA: Addison-Wesley.

Soh, B.-L. and **Y.-P. Soon.** 1991. 'English by e-mail: Creating a global classroom via the medium of computer technology.' *ELT Journal* 45/4: 287–92.

Spack, R. 1984. 'Invention strategies and the ESL college composition student.' *TESOL Quarterly* 18/4: 649–70.

Spack, R. 1997. 'The rhetorical construction of multilingual students.' *TESOL Quarterly* 31/4: 765–74.

Spack, R. and **C. Sadow.** 1983. 'Student–teacher working journals in ESL freshman composition.' *TESOL Quarterly* 17/4: 575–93.

Spolsky, B. 1994. 'Comprehension testing, or can understanding be measured?' in G. Brown, K. Malmkjær, A. Pollitt, and J. Williams (eds.): *Language and Understanding*. Oxford: Oxford University Press: 141–54.

Spolsky, B. 1995. *Measured Words: The Development of Objective Language Testing*. Oxford: Oxford University Press.

Staton, J. and **R. W. Shuy.** 1988. 'Talking Our Way in to Writing and Reading: Dialogue Journal Practice' in B. A. Rafoth and D. L. Rubin (eds.): *The Social Construction of Written Communication*. Norwood, NJ: Ablex: 195–217.

Stauffer, R. G. 1969. *Directing reading maturity as a cognitive process*. New York: Harper & Row.

Steffensen, M. S. and **E. T. Goetz.** 1997. 'Code, Imagery, and Affect in Reading Across Languages.' Paper presented at AAAL 1997 Annual Meeting, Orlando, FL.

Steffensen, M. S., C. Joag-Dev, and **R. C. Anderson.** 1979. 'A cross-cultural perspective on reading comprehension.' *Reading Research Quarterly* 15/1: 10–29.

Stowell, L. P. and **R. J. Tierney.** 1995. 'Portfolios in the Classroom: What Happens When Teachers and Students Negotiate Assessment?' in R. L. Allington and S. A. Walmsley (eds.): *No Quick Fix: Rethinking Literacy Programs in America's Elementary Schools*. New York: Teachers College Press: 78–94.

Street, B. V. 1984. *Literacy in Theory and Practice*. Cambridge: Cambridge University Press.

Street, B. V. (ed.) 1993. *Cross-Cultural Approaches to Literacy*. Cambridge: Cambridge University Press.

Street, B. V. 1994. 'Struggles Over the Meaning(s) of Literacy' in M. Hamilton, D. Barton, and R. Ivanic (eds.): *Worlds of Literacy*. Clevedon, UK: Multilingual Matters: 15–20.

Strickland, K. and J. Strickland. 1998. *Reflections on Assessment: Purposes, Methods and Effects on Learning*. Portsmouth, NH: Boynton/Cook.

Strong, W. 1973. *Sentence Combining: A Composing Book*. New York: Random House.

Suozzo, A. 1995. 'Dialogue and immediacy in cultural instruction: The e-mail option.' *French Review* 69/1: 78–87.

Sussex, R. 1996. 'The Production and Consumption of Text' in W. Grabe (ed.) *Technology and Language (Annual Review of Applied Linguistics, 16)*. New York: Cambridge University Press: 46–67.

Swaffar, J. K. 1991. 'Language Learning Is More than Learning Language: Rethinking Reading and Writing Tasks in Textbooks for Beginning Language Study' in B. F. Freed (ed.) *Foreign Language Acquisition Research and the Classroom*. Lexington, MA: D. C. Heath: 252–79.

Swaffar, J. K., K. M. Arens, and H. Byrnes. 1991. *Reading for Meaning: An Integrated Approach to Language Learning*. Englewood Cliffs, NJ: Prentice Hall.

Swain, M. 1985. 'Communicative Competence: Some Roles of Comprehensible Input and Comprehensible Output in Its Development' in S. M. Gass and C. G. Madden (eds.): *Input in Second Language Acquisition*. Cambridge, MA: Newbury House.

Swain, M., S. Lapkin, and H. C. Barik. 1976. 'The cloze test as a measure of second language proficiency for young children.' *Working Papers in Bilingualism* 11: 32–43.

Swales, J. 1971. *Writing Scientific English: A Textbook of English as a Foreign Language for Students of Physical and Engineering Sciences*. London: Nelson.

Swales, J. 1978. 'Writing "Writing Scientific English"' in R. Mackay and A. J. Mountford (eds.): *English for Specific Purposes: A Case Study Approach*. London: Longman: 43–55.

Swales, J. M. 1990. *Genre Analysis: English in Academic and Research Settings*. Cambridge: Cambridge University Press.

Taillefer, G. F. 1996. 'L2 Reading Ability: Further Insight into the Short-circuit Hypothesis.' *Modern Language Journal* 80/4: 461–77.

Tannen, D. (ed.) 1982. *Spoken and Written Language: Exploring Orality and Literacy*. Norwood, NJ: Ablex.

Tannen, D. 1983. 'Oral and Literate Strategies in Spoken and Written Discourse' in R. W. Bailey and R. M. Fosheim (eds.): *Literacy for Life: The Demand for Reading and Writing*. New York: Modern Language Association: 79–96.

Taylor, I. and M. Taylor. 1983. *The Psychology of Reading*. New York: Academic Press.

Tella, S. 1991. *Introducing International Communications Networks and Electronic Mail into Foreign Language Classrooms: A Case Study in Finnish Senior Secondary Schools*. University of Helsinki, Department of Teacher Education.

Tella, S. 1992a. *Boys, Girls, and E-Mail: A Case Study in Finnish Senior Secondary Schools*. University of Helsinki, Department of Teacher Education.

Tella, S. 1992b. *Talking Shop Via E-Mail: A Thematic and Linguistic Analysis of Electronic Mail Communication*. University of Helsinki, Department of Teacher Education.

Thomas, L. 1974. *The Lives of a Cell: Notes of a Biology Watcher*. New York: Bantam.

Thompson, S. 1978. 'Modern English from a typological point of view.' *Linguistische Berichte* 54: 19–35.

Thompson-Panos, K. and M. Thomas-Ruzic. 1983. 'The least you should know about Arabic: Implications for the ESL writing instructor.' *TESOL Quarterly* 17/4: 609–23.

Thorndike, E. L. 1917. 'Reading and reasoning: A study of mistakes in paragraph reading.' *Journal of Educational Psychology* 8/6: 323–32.

Tierney, R. J., M. A. Carter, and L. E. Desai. 1991. *Portfolio Assessment in the Reading–Writing Classroom*. Norwood, MA: Christopher Gordon.

Tierney, R. J. and J. LaZansky. 1980. 'The rights and responsibilities of readers and writers: A contractual agreement.' *Language Arts* 57/6: 606–13.

Tierney, R. J. and P. D. Pearson. 1984. 'Toward a Composing Model of Reading' in J. M. Jensen (ed.) *Composing and Comprehending*. Urbana, IL: ERIC Clearinghouse on Reading and Communication Skills: 33–45.

Tierney, R. J., J. E. Readence, and E. K. Dishner. 1985. *Reading strategies and practices: A compendium*. Boston: Allyn and Bacon.

Toqueville, A. de. 1988. *De la démocratie en Amérique*. Paris: Calman Levy.

Tribble, C. 1996. *Writing*. Oxford: Oxford University Press.

Tucker, A. 1995. *Decoding ESL: International Students in the American College Classroom*. Portsmouth, NH: Boynton/Cook.

Tucker, G. R. 1975. 'The development of reading skills within a bilingual program' in S. S. S. J. C. Towner (ed.) *Language and reading*. Bellingham, WA: Western Washington State College.

Tuman, M. C. 1992. *Word Perfect: Literacy in the Computer Age*. Pittsburgh: University of Pittsburgh Press.

Tuman, M. C. 1996. 'Literacy Online' in W. Grabe (ed.) *Technology and Language* (*Annual Review of Applied Linguistics, 16*). New York: Cambridge University Press: 26–45.

Tzeng, O. J. L. and D. L. Hung. 1981. 'Linguistic Determinism: A Written Language Perspective' in O. J. L. Tzeng and H. Singer (eds.): *Perception of Print: Reading Research in Experimental Psychology*. Hillsdale, NJ: Lawrence Erlbaum: 237–55.

Ullah, L., I. Sodrel, E. Maldonado, T. Callegaro, and E. Fredo. 1998. *Water Pollution in Brazil and California: A Collaborative, Interdisciplinary Study*. Web page. *http://www.garlic.com/~lullah/brazilus/water.html*. Accessed on September 28, 1998.

Uzawa, K. and A. Cumming. 1989. 'Writing strategies in Japanese as a foreign language: Lowering or keeping up the standards.' *Canadian Modern Language Review* 46/1: 178–94.

Valdés, G., P. Haro, and M. P. Echevarriarza. 1992. 'The development of writing abilities in a foreign language: Contributions toward a general theory of L2 writing.' *Modern Language Journal* 76/3: 333–52.

Valdman, A. 1992. 'Authenticity, Variation, and Communication in the Foreign Language Classroom' in C. Kramsch and S. McConnell-Ginet (eds.): *Text and Context: Cross-Disciplinary Perspectives on Language Study*. Lexington, MA: D. C. Heath: 79–97.

van Lier, L. 1996. *Interaction in the Language Curriculum: Awareness, Autonomy and Authenticity*. London: Longman.

Vygotsky, L. S. 1962. *Thought and Language*. Cambridge, MA: MIT Press.
Vygotsky, L. S. 1978. *Mind in Society: The Development of Higher Psychological Processes*. Cambridge: Harvard University Press.

Wagner, D. A., B. M. Messick, and **J. Spratt.** 1986. 'Studying Literacy in Morocco' in B. B. Schieffelin and P. Gilmore (eds.): *The Acquisition of Literacy: Ethnographic Perspectives*. Norwood, NJ: Ablex: 233–60.
Waller, R. 1987. 'Typography and Reading Strategy' in B. K. Britton and S. M. Glynn (eds.): *Executive Control Processes in Reading*. Hillsdale, NJ: Lawrence Erlbaum: 81–106.
Walworth, M. 1990. 'Interactive Teaching of Reading: A Model' in J. K. Peyton (ed.) *Students and Teachers Writing Together*. Alexandria, VA: TESOL: 36–47.
Warschauer, M. 1995a. *E-Mail for English Teaching: Bringing the Internet and Computer Learning Networks into the Language Classroom*. Alexandria, VA: TESOL Publications.
Warschauer, M. (ed.) 1995b. *Virtual Connections: Online Activities and Projects for Networking Language Learners*. Honolulu: Second Language Teaching and Curriculum Center, University of Hawaii.
Warschauer, M. 1996. 'Comparing face-to-face and electronic communication in the second language classroom.' *CALICO Journal* 13/2: 7–26.
Warschauer, M. 1999. *Electronic Literacies: Language, Culture, and Power in Online Education*. Mahwah, NJ: Lawrence Erlbaum.
Watson, C. 1982. 'The use and abuse of models in the ESL writing class.' *TESOL Quarterly* 16: 5–14.
Wells, G. 1981. 'Language, literacy and education' in G. Wells (ed.) *Learning Through Interaction: The Study of Language Development*. Cambridge: Cambridge University Press: 240–76.
Wesche, M. B. 1983. 'Communicative testing in a second language.' *Modern Language Journal* 67/1: 41–55.
Widdowson, H. G. 1975. *Stylistics and the Teaching of Literature*. London: Longman.
Widdowson, H. G. 1978. *Teaching Language as Communication*. Oxford: Oxford University Press.
Widdowson, H. G. 1983. 'New Starts and Different Kinds of Failure' in A. Freedman, I. Pringle, and J. Yalden (eds.): *Learning to Write: First Language/Second Language*. New York: Longman: 34–47.
Widdowson, H. G. 1984. 'Reading and communication' in J. C. Alderson and A. H. Urquhart (eds.): *Reading in a foreign language*. London: Longman: 213–26.
Widdowson, H. G. 1992. *Practical Stylistics*. Oxford: Oxford University Press.
Wigglesworth, G. 1997. 'An investigation of planning time and proficiency level on oral test discourse.' *Language Testing* 14/1: 85–106.
Wolf, D. F. 1993. 'A comparison of assessment tasks us ed to measure FL reading comprehension.' *Modern Language Journal* 77/4: 473–89.
Wolfe, T. 1987. 'Land of Wizards' in G. Talese (ed.) *The Best American Essays 1987*. New York: Ticknor & Fields: 298–314.
Wrigley, H. S. 1993. 'Ways of Using Technology in Language and Literacy Teaching.' *TESOL Quarterly* 27/2: 318–22.

WuDunn, S. 1995. Japanese Apology Is Met With Praise and Disagreement. New York: *New York Times*, August 16, A1, A14.

Yancey, K. B. and I. Weiser (eds.). 1997. *Situating Portfolios: Four Perspectives*. Logan, UT: Utah State University Press.

Zamel, V. 1976. 'Teaching composition in the ESL classroom: What we can learn from research in the teaching of English.' *TESOL Quarterly* 10: 67–76.

Zamel, V. 1980. 'Re-evaluating sentence-combining practice.' *TESOL Quarterly* 14/1: 81–90.

Zamel, V. 1982. 'Writing: The process of discovering meaning.' *TESOL Quarterly* 16/2: 195–209.

Zamel, V. 1983. 'Teaching those missing links in writing.' *English Language Teaching Journal* 37/1: 22–9.

Zamel, V. 1985. 'Responding to student writing.' *TESOL Quarterly* 19: 79–101.

Zamel, V. 1992. 'Writing one's way into reading.' *TESOL Quarterly* 26/3: 463–85.

Zarate, G. 1986. *Enseigner une culture étrangère*. Paris: Hachette.

Index

BICS (Basic Interpersonal
    Communication Skills) 133
bilingual education 118, 121, 127*n*
Bizzel, P. and B. Herzberg 181
Bland, S. *et al.* 74
Blanton, L. 193
Bleich, D. 112
Block, E. 299*n*
Bloomfield, L. 65*n*
Bolter, J. 44, 227
book reviews 261*n*
Booth Olsen, C. 214–16
bottom-up processing 169*n*
Bourdieu, P. 35
Boyer, H. *et al.* 219*n*
Braddock, R. *et al.* 181
brainstorming 243
Brandelius, M. 196
Brandt, D. 6, 22, 24, 43
Brannon, L. and C. Knoblauch 207, 286
Breen, M. and C. Candlin 19, 54–5
Brisbois, J. 121
British tradition 53
Britton, J. *et al.* 181
Brotchie, A. 211
Brown, R. 271
browsing 230
Brumfit, C. and R. Carter 53
Buck, K. *et al.* 267
Burtoff, M. 174
Butler, R. 92
Butler, S. 47, 50
Byram M. 22
    et al. 22
Byram, M. and V. Esarte-Sarries 22
Byrnes, H. 315

Calfee, R. and P. Perfumo 300*n*
CALP (Cognitive Academic Language
    Proficiency) 133
Camus, A. *L'Étranger* 145, 206
Canale, M. 19
Canale M. and M. Swain 19
Candlin, C. 19, 53, 54–5
Caplan, R. and C. Keech 166, 215
Capra, F. *It's a wonderful life* 234
Cardelle, M. and L. Corno 300*n*
Carnicelli, T. 284
Carrell, P. 83–4

Carrell, P. and J. Eisterhold 82, 103*n*
Carson. J. 176, 207
Carter, R. 158, 168*n*
Carter, R. and D. Burton 53
Carter, R. and P. Simpson 53
Caudery, T. 90, 210
Cazden, C. 54, 143, 169*n*
Cazden, C. and J. Lobdell 169*n*
Chafe, W. 26, 41*n*
Chapman, L. 150
chat forums 238–40, 242, 244, 261*n*
Chatman, S 114
Chen, H. and M. Graves 103*n*
Chen, J. and L. Hamp-Lyons, 176, 300*n*
Cheung, H. 169*n*
Chinese students 123–5, 189*n*
choices *see* language choices
Chomsky, N. 18
Christenson, F. 219*n*
Chun, D. 262*n*
Chun, D. and J. Plass 102*n*
Chun, D. and K. Brandl 261*n*
Church, E. and C. Bereiter 90–1
Cisneros, S. *The House on Mango Street*
    assessment 278–81
    cultural exploration 100–1
    integrated reading lesson 160–6
    mapping 151*fig*
    theater script 142
Clarke, M. 118
classical literacy approach 43
Clifford, J. 207
closed systems 236
code 47, 48
cognate languages 74
Cognitive Academic Language
    Proficiency (CALP) 133
cognitive psychology 32
cognitive-code learning theory 18
Cohen, A. D. 209, 220*n*
Cohen, A. D. and M. Cavalcanti 300*n*
Cohen, A. H. *et al.* 65*n* 76
Cohen, A. P. 155, 156, 218
coherence 78–82, 150
cohesion 78–82, 150
Cole, M. 4, 22, 24, 33, 34, 94
collaboration 38, 259
Common Underlying Proficiency (CUP)
    Model 118, 189*n*